THE FAMILY
MEDICI

THE FAMILY
MEDICI

THE HIDDEN HISTORY OF THE MEDICI DYNASTY

MARY HOLLINGSWORTH

PEGASUS BOOKS
NEW YORK LONDON

The Family Medici

Pegasus Books Ltd
148 West 37th Street, 13th Fl.
New York, NY 10018

First Pegasus Books hardcover edition March 2018

ISBN: 978-1-68177-648-4

10 9 8 7 6 5 4 3 2 1

Printed in the United States of America
Distributed by W. W. Norton & Company, Inc.

Previous page: Jacopo Pontormo,
Cosimo de' Medici, c.1518–19 (Florence, Uffizi),
an idealized portrait celebrating the founder of
the Medici dynasty. Cosimo was a man who
dishonestly amassed a fortune and used it to
subvert the Florentine republic, bribing his way
to power with the help of his private army.

For my mother
Elizabeth Hollingsworth
1922–2017

A NOTE TO THE READER

Names and Dates

The Medici, like other families in medieval and early modern Italy, often chose to name their children after their parents or grandparents, a habit that causes much confusion to modern historians. To help the reader identify the character correctly, I have followed the Italian convention of giving both Christian name and patronymic where necessary. Thus, Lippo di Chiarissimo, for example, refers to Lippo son of Chiarissimo.

Another source of confusion concerns the calendar and the dating of events. In Rome, New Year's Day was 1 January; but in Florence the year did not begin until 25 March, the Feast of the Annunciation. I have converted all relevant dates to conform to the modern style.

Money

In common with the other states that existed in Italy before the unification of the country, Florence had its own currency, the *lira* (1 *lira* = 20 *soldi* = 240 *denari*), a silver-based coinage that was used for everyday transactions, such as buying food or paying wages. For more weighty business – paying dowries, for instance, or assessing wealth for tax purposes, or international trade – the Florentines used their florin, a gold coin that was recognized across Europe. Over the years the value of the *lira* declined steadily in relation to the florin: when the florin was first minted in 1252 it was worth 1 *lira*; by 1500 its price had risen to 7 *lire*. Wherever possible, I have given the value of the sums involved in florins.

Other currencies are also mentioned in this book, notably the gold ducats of Venice and Rome, and the gold *scudo* (pl. *scudi*), which replaced the Roman ducat in 1530. These gold coins were broadly similar in value to the Florentine florin.

A CITY
UNDER SIEGE

'Florence in ashes
rather than under the Medici'

Midsummer's Day, 24 June: the Feast of St John the Baptist, patron saint of Florence, and the highlight of the Florentine year. 'San Giovanni', as the holiday was known, was traditionally a day for best clothes and parties, when dining-tables would be piled high with good food and the air would be filled with the sounds of music, chatter and laughter. Out on the streets, the people could inspect the eye-wateringly expensive goods on show at the stalls of the guilds, watch gaudy parades of floats and marvel at spectacular firework displays. Buskers and tumblers hoped to profit from the holiday mood, and there were bets to be placed on the annual horse race through the narrow cobbled thoroughfares, and tickets to be bought for the bull-fights, mock battles and football matches. Standing on their balconies or jostling on the pavements, the Florentines could witness the great procession of the city's churchmen making their way through the streets, singing and chanting, sprinkling holy water, shaking their thuribles to release clouds of incense and blessing the crowds, while the church bells rang out in a noisy, joyful clamour.

On the morning of the feast, the Florentines celebrated the power and wealth of their city in magnificent style, in the piazza in front of the Palazzo della Signoria – the seat of their republican government. Gathered there would be Florence's leading citizens and guild consuls, officials of the Mint with their bags of gold florins, foreign lords, knights and ambassadors riding superbly caparisoned horses, and, most thrilling of all, the delegations from Florence's subject towns and territories, who knelt in homage to the nine men of the republic's ruling council, the *Signoria*.

In 1530, however, things were very different. That year, San Giovanni was a funereal affair. There were no banquets nor bullfights, no laughter nor music, just one solemn procession. The sombre crowds who gathered on the streets that morning watched in silence as the *Signoria* and other government officials walked – barefoot – from the Palazzo della Signoria to the cathedral, dressed in brown, the colour of mourning. They carried lighted tapers behind a procession of treasured relics, their aim to implore God to aid their beleaguered city. Florence was under siege. Camped around the walls, in rows of tents that stretched as far as the eye could see, were 30,000 enemy soldiers – and their paymaster was one of Florence's own sons: Giulio de' Medici, now Pope Clement VII.

Three years earlier the Florentines had voted overwhelmingly to banish the Medici from the city, but Clement VII was determined to reverse this quite lawful decision, whatever the cost. He did not regard Florence as an independent republic but as the personal fiefdom of his own family; and his goal was to install his illegitimate son as its ruler. He had powerful allies. The troops outside the city gates were part of the mighty army of Holy Roman Emperor Charles V, who had agreed to help Clement VII in his naked bid for power. Pope and Emperor had also used their political muscle to ensure that Florence's allies – France, Venice and Ferrara – now deserted its cause. Florence's subject towns had been captured and its supply lines almost entirely cut off, depriving the city of food and munitions. Only the army remained to defend the city from the Medici, and it was a puny force of 12,000 men, only half of whom were professional soldiers, the rest being poorly trained militiamen.

Conditions inside the city were terrible. The population of 60,000 – plus another 30,000 refugees who had fled into Florence at the approach of Imperial troops – was shrinking fast. Weakened by a diet of coarse bread and water, 200 people a day were dying from hunger and disease. What wine, oil, grain and meat remained had been requisitioned for the troops. As the Venetian ambassador, who stayed in the city throughout the siege, reported in June, 'there is a little wheat but that is being given to the soldiers, and the rest are eating bread made from sorghum or semolina; there is no meat of any sort, no horsemeat or cats left, and mice are selling for 16 *soldi* each' – just below what had been the daily wage for a skilled craftsman before the siege.[1] 'They are all prepared to die for their liberty,' the ambassador concluded.

Alone, hopelessly outnumbered and starving, the Florentines had put their faith in God to save them from the impending catastrophe. The *Signoria* had ordered 'all persons not adapted and fitted for arms, such as priests, friars, monks, nuns, children and women of whatever age' to stop whatever they were doing when they heard the great bell of the Palazzo della Signoria – the signal that a battle had begun – and to 'kneel in churches and convents and in their houses, and to pray continuously to Almighty God while the aforementioned battle shall continue, to give strength and courage to the Florentine soldiers and give them victory against our enemies'.[2]

When the siege had started the previous autumn, the Florentines had been optimistic. Shops remained open and people went about their normal daily business, confident that a peaceful solution would be found. A picture of Clement VII appeared on one street wall, showing the hated pope on the steps of the scaffold, his eyes being bandaged in the moments before his execution. Some thought it sacrilegious to depict the Holy Father in this way, but the image encapsulated the general mood – a widespread hatred of the Medici and the patriotic belief that Florence would prevail. The *Signoria* sent ambassadors to negotiate with the Imperial commander, Philibert de Chalon, Prince of Orange. While the envoys were adamant that they would see, as one put it, 'Florence in ashes rather than under the Medici', they were hopeful that the Emperor could be persuaded to abandon his ally and make a separate peace in exchange for a large pot of cash.[3] The slogan 'Poor but Free' was daubed on houses throughout the city.

Orange and his men marched slowly north from Rome during the summer of 1529, giving the Florentines plenty of time to prepare their defences. On orders from the *Signoria*, all buildings within a one-mile radius of the city were destroyed – luxury villas, modest convents and mean hovels, all torched and obliterated. Inspired by patriotic fervour, shopkeepers, artisans and even rich merchants made no fuss when ordered to close their businesses and join the teams of labourers working day and night hauling carts of stone and rubble to reinforce the city walls. Most propitious of all, there was a bumper harvest that year, and Florentine larders were well stocked.

The Imperial army set up camp along the southern flank of the city in mid-October, but the roads north of the River Arno remained open. Wagons laden with saltpetre, organized by the Florentine ambassador in Ferrara, were able to cross the Apennines regularly, and plenty of food was coming in from the countryside. The Florentine troops were also seizing convoys of provisions intended for Orange's camp. But already meat and eggs were becoming too expensive for the limited resources of ordinary citizens, and the thrifty Florentines took precautions by planting vegetables on their roofs.

Wine and bread remained plentiful, and on 3 November the *Signoria* could inform the Florentine ambassador in Rome that 'we are in good heart and becoming more confident day by day'.[4] The heavy autumn rains that year were proving a bonus: 'the enemy camp is almost drowned in mud'. And there were rumours that the Imperial troops were in disarray, indeed on the verge of mutiny, because they had not received the cash owed to them by Clement VII, who had to find some 70,000 ducats a month for the purpose. The Florentines prided themselves on ensuring the loyalty of their own army by promptly paying the wages of the trained soldiers, who were mostly foreign mercenaries, despite the huge burden that this placed on the city's finances – the *Signoria* estimated that the war was costing 20,000 florins a month.[5] To add to the atmosphere of general optimism, the Florentines won a memorable victory on 10 November 1529, the eve of Martinmas, when they traditionally celebrated the end of the grape harvest by feasting on the new wine. In the expectation of finding the city in a drunken stupor that night, Orange's troops had launched a raid; but the city's soldiers and the militia were wide awake and sober, and had forced the enemy to retreat.

During the winter of 1529–30, however, the siege began to bite. The news on the diplomatic front was not promising. That Clement VII was as adamant as ever was no surprise, but it was discouraging that the Emperor continued to resist the efforts of the Florentine envoys to conclude a separate peace. The weather was cold, but it was too dangerous to forage for firewood as Orange had ordered that anyone coming out of the city was to be hanged without mercy. Wood was also needed to make charcoal for the gunpowder factories, so the *Signoria* appointed officials to commandeer beams and floorboards from houses and shops, even to strip churches of their treasured carved panels.

On 20 January 1530, Orange's guns scored a direct hit on the bastion at the church of San Miniato, causing enough damage to disable the Florentine cannons and allow him to move his troops closer to the walls. More worryingly for the city, that month several new companies of enemy troops had marched over the Apennines to set up their camp on the north bank of the Arno, building a bridge of boats to connect them with Orange's men across the river. The Medici pope was tightening his grip on the city, which was now virtually surrounded, though a trickle of supplies was still getting through the enemy lines from Pisa via the small fortified town of Empoli. But the lack of food was beginning to take its toll: in February 1530, as many as seventy people were dying each day from malnutrition; by March that figure had doubled. The Florentine army, too, was being steadily depleted – by bullet wounds, gangrene and disease – forcing the *Signoria* to raise the militia conscription age from fifty to sixty.

Hungry and cold, the Florentines were now living in daily terror for their lives as the besiegers relentlessly bombarded the city. The people packed into churches to be comforted by sermons from preachers who promised that their ordeal would soon be over, that God would grant them victory if they repented their sins. Despite the hardship, the government remained stoutly optimistic. 'We are in good heart,' the *Signoria* wrote to the Florentine ambassador in France on 12 March, 'and determined to endure while we still have life before submitting to the yoke of tyranny; our citizens deserve much praise for the way they endure such difficulties and no burden is too heavy in order to maintain our liberty.'[6] But the signs were not good. On 26 March, Orange's cannon damaged the Baptistery, and two days later there was an eclipse of the sun, which was interpreted by all as a bad omen. When the *Signoria* asked the preachers what more the city could do to earn God's favour, they recommended increasing the number of penitential processions. More controversially, they also suggested that the government should stop taxing the clergy to raise funds for the war effort and that the Florentines should pardon their enemies. The *Signoria* responded tersely, saying that priests should not poke their noses into political affairs.

On Good Friday 1530, 15 April, Florence's enemies seized a convoy of cattle on the road from Empoli, and the herdsmen were hanged by Orange. That day, the *Signoria* ordered all citizens to declare the contents of their storerooms: Michelangelo's larder, for example, contained just two barrels of beans, half a barrel of vinegar and eight barrels of wine.[7] There were no lambs for anyone for the traditional Easter banquet.

There was more bad news at the end of April when the Duke of Ferrara finally bowed to pressure from Clement VII and Charles V and expelled the Florentine ambassador from his court. The ambassador, with the connivance of the duke, had been responsible for ensuring the supplies of saltpetre for Florence's gunpowder factories, which now ceased. However, before his expulsion, the envoy had suggested to the *Signoria* a particularly gruesome scheme for achieving victory: 'given the stubbornness of your enemies and the ill-effects that the length of the siege is causing… I believe I could send two or three people into the camp carrying plague-infected goods, by which means it will be easy to set light to the said camp'.[8] He thought it a practicable and – at an estimated 100 ducats – a very cheap option. Whether the *Signoria* took his advice or not, in May 1530 plague did break out among the Imperial troops, bringing hope to the Florentines that this might be God's way of assuring their victory.

On 5 May there was another glimmer of hope, when the Florentines launched a successful attack on Orange's troops, and after four hours of fierce fighting managed to secure a large convoy of food and supplies from Empoli. Florence gave due thanks to God as a procession of the animals – sheep, cows and goats – made its way through the city, escorted by children dressed as Christ, St John the Baptist and angels. But it was soon evident that God had only granted the people a temporary respite from their ordeal. Disaster struck on 29 May when Empoli fell. Closing off this one gap in the blockade had been a priority for Orange, who brutally sacked the town and replenished his own stores with cartloads of goods intended for Florence.

Florence was, in turn, forced to adopt drastic new measures. After a week of anxious and divisive debate in the Palazzo della Signoria, the government finally voted to elect a team of sixteen magistrates with orders to search all private houses for hidden stocks of grain, wine, meat and other foodstuffs: these stores were to be requisitioned and the hoarders harshly punished. Other measures were taken to replenish the rapidly dwindling funds needed to pay the mercenaries. All church plate was confiscated – the gilded chalices and crucifixes, the silver lamps, and even the gold embroidery from copes and altar cloths were all melted down to make coins. Private citizens were ordered to deposit their gold and silver at the city's mint, where they handed over their jewels and other valuables with surprising willingness. The Venetian ambassador estimated that this had raised 120,000 ducats for the war effort. But there was nothing more of value left in the city.[9]

In desperation, the Florentines now seized at straws. One captured Imperial soldier attempted to buy his freedom by offering his services to the blockaded city. Claiming to know the man in charge of Clement VII's wine cellar, he said he could arrange for the pope to be poisoned. 'I would reward you with 1,000 ducats,' exclaimed one magistrate, in gratitude; '10,000 ducats,' countered another.[10] But the plot was leaked to Orange, and the soldier – apparently carrying two vials, the poison in one, the antidote in the other – was arrested when he returned to the Imperial camp.

Still defiant, Florentines prepared a surprise assault on the German troops camped by the convent of San Donato in Polverosa* in the hopes of opening the road north-west to Prato. Attacking before dawn on 21 June 1530, they killed many soldiers as well as nuns, still asleep in their beds. Unfortunately, the Imperial forces were able to regroup when reinforcements arrived from Orange's camp, and the Florentines were obliged to withdraw. They returned home with welcome supplies of food and weapons, but not the victory for which they had hoped. It was no wonder that the celebrations for San Giovanni, three days later, were so very sombre.

By the following month, Florence was sweltering in the high-summer heat. On 2 July, some 6,000 women, children and prostitutes – 'useless mouths' as the *Signoria* described them – assembled with their meagre belongings at the convent of Santa Caterina, from where they were to be evacuated to Pisa in order to preserve the shrinking stocks of food. It was a pitiful sight. Many of the refugees were crying hysterically, terrified of the violence they would encounter from the Imperial troops when they left the safety of the city. In the end, the *Signoria* relented, allowing those who wished to stay in Florence to remain and sending away just forty prostitutes.

In the middle of July, the Florentines, already weakened by malnutrition and disease, faced another nightmare when the plague broke out inside their city walls. News that the Prince of Orange himself had developed the dreaded pustules sent a brief thrill of hope through Florence, but it soon evaporated when the Imperial commander recovered. It was now evident that the end was approaching, as the stocks of food could not last much longer than a week or two. The Florentines

---

* Polverosa was near where Florence's airport stands today.

had few options: they could keep waiting for a miracle or surrender to the enemy; or they could make one final, last-ditch attempt to save their city.

The debates over the issue in the Palazzo della Signoria were heated. There was a small band of Florentine soldiers still holding out in Volterra, to the south-west, and some voices wanted to order them to march on Rome and sack the city. Surely, they argued, these troops would be joined by others, inspired by the Florentine example to rebel against the Medici pope? Perhaps fortunately, this foolhardy plan was rejected, and the *Signoria* voted instead to send the Volterra troops north to join soldiers guarding Pisa. This would, they hoped, create a relief force that could then march the 50 or so miles east to Florence where, with the trained mercenaries and the Florentine militia, it would break the enemy stranglehold. The commanders of the Florentine army were not confident – patriotic fervour was no match for cannon and muskets, nor for the superior number of troops at Clement VII's disposal.

In churches across Florence the friars preached sermons promising victory – 'God will not let us perish' – though more cynical Florentines worried about the 'mad brains who are ruling this country, who are expecting miracles from God to liberate us'.[11] According to the Venetian ambassador, in the event of the city's fall the men guarding the gates had been ordered 'to slay the women and children immediately and set fire to all the houses … so that with the destruction of the city there shall not remain anything but the memory of the greatness of the soul of its people and that they shall be an immortal example for those who are born, and desire to live, in freedom'.[12]

On 31 July, a Sunday, news arrived that 3,000 men and 300 cavalry were on the march from Pisa. Unfortunately, the news was also known to Orange, who had intercepted the correspondence, and on Monday he left at the head of a battalion of troops to intercept the Florentine relief force. In the Palazzo della Signoria the following morning, many urged an immediate attack on Orange's camp – now guarded by just 4,000 soldiers – but the army commanders prevaricated, insisting on any decision being approved by the Great Council, the assembly of all male Florentines eligible to hold political office. The delay was to prove fatal. Orange's troops, reinforced by some 10,000 men, attacked the men from Pisa on 3 August as they were encamped at the small town of Gavinana, north of Pistoia. The next morning, Florence was buzzing with rumours that their troops had overwhelmed the enemy and that Orange was dead. The joy was short-lived. Although Orange had indeed been killed – shot in the neck and chest by Florentine arquebuses – it was small recompense for a savage defeat in battle, fought out under the relentless heat of the August sun.

A week later, on 12 August 1530, Florence finally capitulated. According to the terms of surrender, the city was to pay 80,000 florins, the sum owed by the Medici pope to the Imperial troops in unpaid wages, to prevent them from sacking the city. And the Medici were to return as rulers of Florence. Clement VII guaranteed immunity from prosecution to all those who had opposed him, but, once the surrender was signed, vicious reprisals were inflicted on the leaders of the republic. The human cost of the pope's ambition was appalling. One-third of Florence's population was dead: 8,000 soldiers had been killed in battle or died later from their wounds, and 30,000 civilians had succumbed to starvation and disease. But the Medici had achieved their goal. With deceit and brute force, they had made Florence their own.

The family had come a long way since their obscure arrival in the city some 300 years earlier.

Overleaf: Workshop of Francesco Rosselli, 'Della Catena' view of Florence, *c.*1472, detail (Florence, Palazzo Vecchio). Medieval Florence was one of the largest cities in Europe, with a thriving economy, schools for its children and a unique republican government.

I

MIGRANTS

Bonagiunta, Chiarissimo and
their descendants
1216–1348

Giambono,
father of Bonagiunta *and* Chiarissimo

Bonagiunta (*1240*)

Galgano (*1240*) *and* Ugo (*1240*), *his sons*

Bonagiunta di Galgano (*1290*), *his grandson*

Ardingo di Bonagiunta (*1316*), *his great-grandson*

Chiarissimo (*1240*) ('Old Chiarissimo')

Filippo, *his son*

Chiarissimo *and* Averardo di Filippo (*1286*),
his grandsons

Imbono (d. 1302), Lippo di Chiarissimo (d. 1290),
and Averardo di Averardo (d. 1318),
his great-grandsons

Bernardino di Imbono (*1322*),
his great-great-grandson

Giovanni di Bernardino (d. 1363),
his great-great-great-grandson

Despite the heroic characters that the Medici family would later invent to embellish their past with military glory, their early history is irredeemably bourgeois.

They moved to Florence during the twelfth century as economic migrants from the Mugello, high in the inhospitable Apennine mountains north of the city, having been lured by the prospect of riches and security within its walls. The first document charting the history of the family dates from early in the next century, 1216, when a certain Bonagiunta de' Medici was given a seat on the civic council.[1] This appointment, and the fact that Bonagiunta even had a surname, suggests that the family had done well in the decades since their arrival and were now citizens of some standing. We also know that they were in the moneylending business, for in 1240 Bonagiunta, in partnership with his brother Chiarissimo, loaned funds to a monastery in Florence. Another document of the same year shows that his sons Ugo and Galgano were in the same profession.[2]

In truth, the Medici were just one family among many thousands of country-dwellers who streamed into Florence during the twelfth and thirteenth centuries, causing the city to grow at a dramatic rate. Once an insignificant settlement on the banks of the Arno in Ancient Roman times, its population had reached 25,000 by 1200, and 65,000 by 1250. A new circuit of walls was built in 1284, 5 miles in length and defended by massive gatehouses, to enclose an area seven times greater than that inside the old perimeter, built a century earlier. By 1250, Florence was not just the largest city in Tuscany, but the fourth-largest in Europe, after Milan, Venice and Paris. It was also spectacularly rich, its wealth based on a thriving cloth industry and the profits made by merchants dealing in luxury goods on the lucrative trade routes from the Middle East to the North Sea. The Florentines were very good at making money, and the city's top bankers – not yet the Medici – used their guile to establish Florence as the prime centre of credit in Europe. In London, these bankers were in the process of outmanoeuvring Flemish traders by using their capital to buy up England's wool production a year in advance, thus securing a steady supply of top-quality fleeces to be shipped to the cloth factories back home.

Italy more broadly was the commercial hub of thirteenth-century Europe, a hotbed of innovation and enterprise. Double-entry book-keeping – an Italian invention – dates from this period, as does Marco

Polo's epic journey into China, one of scores of Italian trading expeditions that travelled through the Byzantine and Muslim empires and to Persia and the Indies in the search for profits. Commerce provided the stimulus for important advances in science and technology, including the earliest maritime charts and compasses, the spinning wheel, spectacles, the weight-driven mechanical clock and a day logically divided into twenty-four equal hours. Many of these innovations came from the Muslim world, as did what was arguably the greatest advance of the period, the adoption of Arabic numerals – so much more practical for bankers like the Medici, wanting to calculate rates of interest and exchange, than the cumbersome Roman system which lacked a zero. And they could afford to record these transactions on another novelty from the region, paper, which cost half the price of parchment.

Money not only served to enrich; it had begun to talk loudly in politics. In the early 1200s, Florence's merchants and traders, the drivers of her booming economy, were largely excluded from the city's government, which was dominated by its old aristocracy – the magnates; but now the men of commerce took up arms to demand a greater share of political power. As this class conflict intensified, it merged with the older political rivalry that divided all of northern Italy, between those who aligned themselves with papal ambitions (the 'Guelfs') and those who supported the Holy Roman Empire (the 'Ghibellines'). The result, in Florence and elsewhere, was urban violence on a massive scale. For much of the thirteenth century, Florence was rocked by bloody street battles, riots, murders and more killings in revenge, as the magnates, who massed under the Ghibelline banner, attempted to crush their mercantile opponents, who were predominantly Guelfs.

The Medici were staunch Guelfs, and they must have been jubilant when their faction expelled the Ghibellines from Florence in 1250 to establish the city's first republic. The Guelfs marked this milestone in

The gold florin, first minted in 1252, prime symbol of Florence's commercial prowess.

Florentine history with a symbolic reversal of the colours of the city's flag – the white Ghibelline lily set in bloody red now became the red Guelf lily, shining on a pure white background. Two years later, in 1252, the Guelf republic issued its own currency, the florin, stamped with the image of the city's patron saint, St John the Baptist. The prime symbol of Florentine commercial prowess, this gold coin was soon an internationally recognized currency. The Guelfs also built the city's first town hall, celebrating their achievements with an inscription that was charged with an extraordinary degree of self-importance:*

> *Florence is filled with all imaginable wealth.*
> *She defeats her enemies in war and civic strife.*
> *She enjoys the favour of Fortune and has a powerful population.*
> *Successfully she fortifies and conquers castles.*
> *She reigns over the sea and the land and the whole of the world.*
> *All Tuscany enjoys happiness under her leadership.*
> *Like Rome she is always triumphant.*[3]

---

* The building is now the Palazzo del Bargello, home to Florence's Museo Nazionale.

The Florence Baptistery: begun in the eleventh century, built on the site of an earlier temple of Mars, and dedicated to Florence's patron saint, it was the most prestigious building in the city.

Despite these claims, the victory of the Guelfs was far from secure. Florence's fiercely competitive neighbouring city-states – Pisa, Lucca, Arezzo, Siena, San Gimignano, Pistoia, Prato and Volterra – viewed her remarkable growth with alarm. Pisa, with a maritime empire that included trading posts in North Africa and the Middle East (and, most impressively, its own wharf at Constantinople), must have been particularly scornful of landlocked Florence's claim to rule over the sea. For the next four decades, Tuscany was racked by war as these city-states manipulated the rivalry between the Guelfs and the Ghibellines in an attempt to curb Florence's increasing power in the region.

In 1260, Siena and her Ghibelline allies inflicted a heavy defeat over Guelf Florence at the Battle of Montaperti, and the fledgling republic collapsed. The Ghibellines celebrated their victory with an orgy of looting, setting fire to shops and homes of many prominent Guelfs. One of the targets of the rampaging mob was the Medici palace belonging to two of Bonagiunta's grandsons, where the damage inflicted by the rioters was estimated at almost 75 florins – a substantial sum, equivalent to the annual salary of a skilled craftsman and enough to support a family in comfortable, if modest, style.[4] The struggle between the factions continued to divide Tuscany, despite international efforts to stop the violence. In 1280, another of Bonagiunta's grandsons, Bonagiunta di Galgano, was a Guelf signatory to a treaty negotiated by Cardinal Latino, the nephew of Pope Nicholas II, though this peace too was short-lived.[5] In Florence the struggle finally came to an end in 1289 when the Guelfs won a decisive victory over the Ghibellines at Campaldino, near Arezzo. Riding out with the cavalry that day was the twenty-four-year-old poet Dante, and the battle remained etched in his memory. More than 1,700 Ghibellines were killed and 2,000 were taken prisoner, their leader, 'stabbed in the throat', dying after falling into a river, according to the poet.† The Guelfs were triumphant and declared the date of the battle (11 June, the Feast of St Barnabas) as henceforth a national holiday.

Four years later, the Guelf victory was completed in 1293 when the government passed the Ordinances of Justice. This momentous law excluded all magnates from political power 'in perpetuity', and it was

---

† Or so Dante claimed when he met the man among the unshriven in Purgatory. *The Divine Comedy*, Vol. 2, pp. 105–6.

to remain largely intact, in name at least, for the next 250 years. Nobility of birth no longer gave a Florentine the right to hold political office, which was now reserved exclusively for members of the city's trade guilds: wealthy silk merchants and cloth-factory owners, bankers such as the Medici, and lawyers. Also eligible were shopkeepers selling medicines, second-hand goods, bread, meat and wine; and artisans too – the makers of shoes, altarpieces, furniture and feather beds. Under the Ordinances, all guildsmen over the age of thirty were eligible for election, though bankrupts were excluded, as were those in arrears with their taxes: money, as ever, was king in this commercial republic. It is hard to overestimate the enormity of this revolution when elsewhere in Europe hereditary feudal power was the norm. It was to have a profound impact on the lives of the Florentines. The year 1293 was a defining moment in their history, its memory deeply embedded in the Florentines' psyche for centuries to come.

In the new republic, 'nobility' was a term of abuse. Anyone found guilty of crimes against the state was declared to be a magnate and so deprived of eligibility for public office. The sober burghers in charge of the government despised aristocratic idleness. They prided themselves on hard work and measured their success on the pages of their ledgers; they paraded in plain clothes and passed sumptuary laws that banned all hallmarks of aristocratic display (though the magistrates did turn a blind eye to the expensive fabrics and valuable jewels worn by many to celebrate the Feast of San Giovanni). Such attitudes infused education, too. The Florentines did not teach their children to hunt or joust but sent them to school, where they learned republican values along with reading, writing and arithmetic – the skills essential for trade. It is no coincidence that medieval Florence had one of the highest literacy rates in Europe, providing a ready audience for the historians and chroniclers who proudly charted their city's rise to greatness, and for the writers of verse and racy short stories, all penned in the Tuscan vernacular, and all evidence of the uniquely Florentine literary culture that emerged in the new republic.*

Pride in the Florentine achievement was soon visible on the streets

---

* One poem, for example, celebrated the Old Market, the city's commercial hub, and its heroes were not the valiant knights and virtuous gentlewomen of chivalric romance but the 'splendid butchers', whose 'stalls display the finest cuts of meat', and the buxom country girls with their baskets suggestively 'piled high with ripe round figs'. Acton & Cheney, pp. 112–14.

of the city. In 1294 the republic decided to replace the city's modest cathedral with a huge new church, the Duomo. Vast in scale and lavishly covered with inlaid panels of marble, imported at great cost from the quarries at Carrara, the Duomo provided solid proof of the religious devotion of the Florentines and also, perhaps more importantly, of their talent for making money. Four years later, in 1298, work began on the Palazzo della Signoria, the town hall with its great bell tower and crenellated upper gallery, intended to house the government and its bureaucracy. In contrast to the boastful cathedral, the Palazzo was built in local stone and unadorned, expressing the core values of the new regime – moderation and thrift.

To serve as propaganda for its cause, the republic also acquired some lions, the traditional symbols of authority in medieval Europe. They were kept in a cage beside the palace and were the objects of considerable curiosity to citizens and visitors alike. One Florentine chronicler was amazed when two cubs appeared, 'born alive, not dead like they say in the bestiaries, and I can confirm this because I myself saw them suckling milk from their mother soon after they were born'.[6] Unlike a pair that had been born in Venice and which soon died, the Florentine cubs thrived, which was 'seen by many as a sign of good and prosperous times for the city of Florence'.

In another calculated piece of propaganda, the Florentines demolished several palaces belonging to the deposed Ghibelline magnates in order to lay out a great piazza in front of the Palazzo della Signoria, creating a highly symbolic setting for republican ceremonial. It was here that the elections were held every two months for the *Signoria* – the council of eight priors with their chairman, the *gonfaloniere* (gonfalonier, 'standard bearer'), who ruled the republic. A few days before each new term began, the Florentines gathered on the piazza – not forgetting to check on the lions – to listen to a speech reminding them of the importance of the republican principles of liberty and civic virtue, and to watch as the names of the gonfalonier and priors were drawn from the sealed leather purses. No doubt there were some who grumbled as their names were read out, for they would have to leave their businesses in the hands of their partners and move into the Palazzo della Signoria for the duration of the two-month term – though there would be some compensation in the fine wines and lavish meals prepared specially for them in the palace kitchens. For the audience in

the great piazza, the elections gave a real sense of involvement in the business of government – a member of the new *Signoria* might be a family member, a next-door neighbour or even the local shopkeeper. It was not democracy as we know it; but it was a significant step along the road.

The Medici were active from the start in Florence's new republican government. The first member of the family to serve on the *Signoria* was Ardingo de' Medici, one of Old Bonagiunta's great-grandsons.[7] Over the next fifty years, Medici men served on this prestigious council on twenty-eight occasions, a boast bettered by only seven other families.[8] The story of the family emerges with more clarity following the foundation of the republic, because, as in the businesses they ran, Florentines knew the importance of keeping proper written records. And many of the ledgers detailing the day-to-day business of the city's government committees and law courts survived in the state archives.

We know that by the end of the thirteenth century there were three separate Medici palaces near the Old Market in the prestigious city centre, where the top Florentine families lived. We know, too, the names of more than sixty adult male descendants of Old Bonagiunta and his brother Chiarissimo, descendants who were active in Florence in the first half of the fourteenth century.[9] Many of them followed the family profession, trading as bankers and profiting from the economic boom that marked the first decades of the republic. Ardingo, the first of the Medici to serve on the *Signoria*, was listed as a member of the Bankers' Guild in 1300, and he ran his company in partnership with three of his brothers from an office in the Old Market near their palace.[10]

Although prosperous, the Medici at this time were significantly less wealthy than the great international banking houses like those of the Bardi and Peruzzi; when the Bankers' Guild levied a tax on its members in 1314, the Medici were assessed at a total of 3 florins while the Peruzzi clan, by contrast, contributed 18 florins.[11] But the Medici were on the rise. One of Chiarissimo's great-grandsons, Averardo, was a notably successful businessman and his sons owned a banking house that trad-

Left: Florence, Palazzo della Signoria, begun 1298.

Overleaf: Giotto, *St Francis Renounces His Worldly Goods*, c.1320 (Florence, Santa Croce, Bardi Chapel).

ed across Italy.[12] By 1322 the Medici were rich enough to appear on an official list of the 264 top companies that formed the elite of Florentine society.[13]

Despite the establishment of the republic, Florentine Society continued to be split by factional violence. These burghers, including the Medici, were a notoriously quarrelsome lot. Just a few years after extinguishing the Ghibelline threat, the Guelfs themselves split into the warring factions of the 'Whites' and the 'Blacks', alignments that responded to a bitter feud between the Cerchi and Donati families. The Medici were Blacks and made regular attacks on their White neighbours. In November 1301, the Blacks attempted to seize power by force: as the chronicler Dino Compagni recorded, 'they took up their arms and their horses and began to carry out the plan they had made and, after vespers, the Medici, who were influential men of the people, attacked and wounded another brave man... and left him for dead'.[14] Four years later, after even the papal legate failed to reconcile the factions, the Blacks launched another attack on the Whites – and again the Medici were in the midst of the fighting. 'The della Tosa and Medici gangs came into the Old Market armed with crossbows,' Compagni recorded, 'and attacked and destroyed a barricade in the Corso, which was manned by people more determined on vengeance than on peace.'[15] The situation spiralled out of control when a fire, lit by the Blacks to destroy a White barricade, turned into an inferno that consumed some 2,000 buildings and destroyed the centre of the city.

The banker Giovanni Villani claimed that this catastrophe had been predicted a month earlier when the May Day celebrations had ended in disaster. In his detailed history of Florence, which is a fascinating source for this period, Villani described how a pageant of Hell had been staged on a string of boats moored by a bridge over the Arno, 'with fires and pain and suffering and men dressed up as devils' who tortured screaming souls, 'dreadful to see'.[16] He went on to relate how large crowds gathered on the Ponte alla Carraia, to watch the spectacle, causing this old wooden bridge to collapse into the river, killing and injuring hundreds of people. 'This was a sign of forthcoming disaster,' he warned 'that will come to our city because of the wickedness of our citizens.'

Florentines watched anxiously for signs of God's intentions. Natural and man-made disasters, they believed, were punishments for their sins – their greed for money, too much eating and drinking, their wives and daughters dressing too richly, or something else entirely. For medieval businessmen the horrors of Hell were very real. Christ's command was explicit: 'it is easier for a camel to go through the eye of a needle, than for the rich man to enter the kingdom of God' (Matthew, 19: 24). Commercial profit might be the tangible sign of success in this world, but it could condemn a man to torments in the world to come. And bankers such as the Medici were especially tainted by the sin of usury – the charging of excessively high rates of interest on loans and other transactions. The Dominican Order argued that usury was the criminal seizure of another's possessions, in the same category as fraud, theft and rape. In his *Divine Comedy*, Dante gave a graphic description of what was in store for usurers: on his literary journey through the underworld, he encountered them scorched for eternity in burning sand, from which they could not escape because of the weight of the fat pouches, filled with gold florins, hanging round their necks.[17]

The Church urged the rich to expiate their sins by giving a percentage of these evil profits to charity – alms to beggars, for example, or clothes to the destitute, or dowries for poor girls to keep them off the streets, as well as the more visible (and permanent) option of spending money on religious institutions. The rich Bardi and Peruzzi bankers both financed family chapels in Florence's Franciscan church of Santa Croce, where, of course, it was not just their piety that was on display: the fact that they could afford to buy the rights to these chapels to house their tombs, and ornament them with altarpieces, frescoes and sculpture, was ostentatious proof of their immense wealth. The Bardi Chapel, significantly, was frescoed by Giotto with scenes from the life of St Francis, that son of a prosperous merchant from Assisi who had famously renounced his worldly goods for a life of evangelical poverty. While neither the Bardi nor the Peruzzi had any intention of following the example of this popular saint, their conspicuous expenditure in Santa Croce was designed to atone for their greed. And greedy they were. In 1337, they were anticipating massive profits from the huge loans they had made to Edward III of England, to finance his invasion of France in pursuit of his claim to the French throne – the event marking the start of the Hundred Years' War.

Despite Florence's endemic factional violence, its economy continued to prosper. 'At the end of June 1337', Giovanni Villani paid a visit to the lions by the Palazzo della Signoria and was thrilled to see that 'six lion cubs were born to the old lioness and to her daughters which, according to the ancient pagans, was a sign of great magnificence for our city'.[18] By 1338, the population of the city had reached 90,000, almost four times larger than it had been in 1200, and, as Villani boasted, the annual output of the woollen cloth industry – comprising 200 factories employing 30,000 people – was worth around 1.2 million florins.[19] With an eye for financial detail, this banker's analysis of the city's massive wealth ran to four chapters in his chronicle, the last of which was entitled 'More on the Greatness and Prestige and Magnificence of the Republic of Florence'.[20] His statistics were impressive, for this was a city that contained, among other things, 80 banking houses, 100 apothecary shops and 146 bakeries; there were 680 judges and notaries to guarantee the rule of law, and 80 monks, 500 nuns and 300 priests to attend to the religious life of the Florentines in 110 churches, monasteries and convents; and the sick could be treated by 60 doctors in 30 hospitals with a total of 1,000 beds.

Within a year, though, Villani's pride had turned to shame. By the end of the 1330s it was evident that the great economic boom, which had heralded the birth of the republic, had ended and Florence was in the grip of a disastrous recession. In August 1339, the city was hit by terrible thunderstorms, which ruined the harvest and caused the price of grain to rocket: 'If it had not been for the foresight of the government which brought grain in by sea, the people would have died of hunger,' Villani recorded, 'and every business in Florence went into recession.'[21] There were more bad omens the following year, when 'a great comet appeared in the sky', soon to be followed by an outbreak of plague, 'and there was not a single family who did not lose someone', for 'more than fifteen thousand bodies, men women and children had to be buried, and the city was full of weeping and pain'.[22]

The Bardi and Peruzzi banks faced impending disaster. Having loaned over a million florins to the English Crown – a highly leveraged sum, far in excess of their capital – they had made up the shortfall by dipping their fingers into the deposit accounts of their clients.[23] While the extent of their gamble was not yet public knowledge in Florence, there was considerable nervousness in the city. Many rich merchants now pulled their funds out of risky commercial ventures, and several members of the Medici family did the same, buying land and property in their ancestral heartland of the Mugello.[24] It was a less profitable investment but a much safer one in the difficult economic times.

By July 1341, the Florentine republic was faced with economic meltdown, and the city turned to its bankers for help. The Medici were among the financiers elected to the committee set up by the *Signoria* to deal with the crisis, and this committee concluded that strong government was needed to introduce the unpopular measures required.[25] Accordingly, in June 1342 Walter of Brienne, Duke of Athens, was invited to take over power in the city for a term of one year. Despite his ducal title, he was a French nobleman with close links to the papacy and the ruling Anjou dynasty of Naples.* Scornful of the city's republican tradition, Brienne promptly announced that he was taking the title 'Lord of Florence' for life, and he moved into the Palazzo della Signoria together with his court. Worse, his punitive fiscal policies rapidly alienated the wealthy elite, including those bankers such as the Medici who had been responsible for inviting him to the city. The Medici were also among the early victims of his repressive regime. As Villani recorded, 'at the beginning of August [1342] the duke arrested Giovanni di Bernardino de' Medici, who had been our governor in Lucca, accusing him of treason and forcing him to confess and had him beheaded'.[26]

Brienne's lordship over Florence proved short-lived. On 26 July 1343, after just over a year in power, he was expelled, and the date – the Feast of St Anne – was declared a national holiday, adding another saint to the Florentine pantheon. According to Villani, the Medici played a prominent role in the coup:

> On 26 July, the Feast of St Anne, when the bell sounded in the afternoon and the workers left the factories, the Adimari, the Medici and the Donati had arranged that some ruffians, pretending to be soldiers, were to start fighting together in the Old Market and at Porta San Piero, shouting 'To Arms! To Arms!' Everyone was frightened and immediately... they all armed themselves, some on horseback, others on foot... shouting 'Death to the duke, long live the people, the

---

* Brienne was Duke of Athens in name only, his ancestors having lost most of the duchy as well as their claim to be kings of Jerusalem.

republic and liberty'… the duke's men, hearing the noise, armed themselves and mounted their horses making about three hundred cavalry riding around the Piazza della Signoria… and the Medici, Altoviti, Ricci and Rucellai… seized the exits from the *piazza*, of which there were more than twelve, and erected barriers and reinforced them so that nobody could enter or leave, and all day and night they fought with the duke's men in the Palazzo della Signoria and in the piazza, where many of them died.[27]

In the chaotic days that followed, the magnates, with the support of the Bardi and several other wealthy banking families – though not the Medici – took the opportunity to seize power. Their first act was to abolish the Ordinances of Justice, the foundation stone of the republic. When news of this dramatic move leaked onto the streets, Florence erupted into violence. The Medici clan shrewdly joined the mobs of petty tradesmen who were rioting across the city, leading a

*Expulsion of the Duke of Athens, c.*1343 (Florence, Palazzo Vecchio). Commemorating the restoration of the republic on the feast of St Anne, this fresco shows how the Florentines cultivated the memory of their past with annual celebrations of the events that shaped their history.

band of a thousand men 'including butchers and other artisans' from their quarter of San Giovanni in an orgy of violence that saw destroyed twenty-two Bardi palaces and ensured the end of this short-lived, unpopular regime.[28] Thanks to their role in this coup, the Medici acquired a reputation as champions of the ordinary people – a reputation that would play an important role in the decades to come.

The government crisis had been resolved and the Ordinances of Justice reinstated; but the economic recession continued to worsen. The situation deteriorated dramatically during the autumn of 1343 when the Peruzzi bank crashed, followed by the Bardi company in January 1345. Villani's chronicle blamed both Edward III, for failing to repay the vast sums he had borrowed, but also the bankers themselves, whose greed for profits had, in Villani's view, encouraged them to ignore the high risks involved. The crash left many of their customers destitute and 'brought greater ruin and defeat than has ever happened before in our republic', judged Villani.[29] The impact on the Florentine economy was terrible: between 1333 and 1346, more than 350 Florentine firms went bankrupt, not just great trading houses but also small businesses.[30] The Medici, however, managed to survive the disaster, thanks to their foresight in moving their money out of commercial ventures.

For their city more generally, though, worse was to come. Heavy storms in October and November 1345 were followed by an unusually wet spring in 1346, resulting in 'the worst harvest of grain and animal fodder and wine and oil and everything in over a hundred years'.[31] The price of wheat 'rose to 30 *soldi*... and it kept on climbing and by the following May, just before the next harvest, the price had reached 61 *soldi*'. The 1347 harvest was poor too, the crops flattened by massive hailstones. 'Please God,' Villani prayed, 'these signs will make us correct our defects and sins so that God will not condemn us to harsher punishments.'[32] But the catalogue of disasters continued, culminating in the following year, 1348. That summer, bubonic plague – the Black Death – swept through Italy. For Florence it was three months of horror – of watching loved ones die in agony, while the air filled with the stench of putrefaction as 50,000 corpses were stacked in mass graves. By September, more than half the population of Florence was dead. Among the victims were Giovanni Villani himself and four-fifths of the Dominican friars at Santa Maria Novella. And the ranks of the Medici had been reduced, too.

Overleaf: Domenico di Michelino, memorial to Dante, 1465 (Florence, Duomo). Heaven and Hell were familiar places to medieval Florentines. They could see images of the saved and the damned in churches across the city and, with a literacy rate amongst the highest in Europe, could read their own hero-poet's account in Tuscan prose.

2

SURVIVORS
Salvestro, Foligno, Bicci
and Vieri
1348–1400

Chiarissimo di Filippo, *Old Chiarissimo's grandson*

> Lippo (d. 1290), *his son*

> Cambio di Lippo (*1367*) *and* Alamanno di Lippo (d. 1355),
> *his grandsons*

> **Vieri di Cambio** (1323–95), Giovanni di Cambio (*1383*), *and*
> **Salvestro di Alamanno** (d. 1388), Africhello (*1378*), Bartolomeo (*1375*),
> Andrea (*1400*), Giovanni (d. 1353) *and* Michele di Alamanno (*1350*),
> *his great-grandsons*

Averardo di Filippo (*1286*), *Old Chiarissimo's grandson*

> Averardo (d. 1318), *his son*

> Conte di Averardo *and* Chiarissimo di Averardo (*1346*),
> *his grandsons*

> **Foligno di Conte** (*1378*), Jacopo di Conte (d. 1348),
> Giovanni di Conte (d. 1372), *and*
> **Bicci di Chiarissimo** (d. 1363), *his great-grandsons*

The chaos in Florence in the wake of the Black Death was vividly described by the late Giovanni Villani's brother, Matteo, who continued the chronicler's work:

> Those few who were still alive expected many things… they believed that those who had been saved by God's grace… would become better people, humble and virtuous… but as soon as the plague stopped we saw the opposite. Because there were so few men and because they had inherited so much material wealth, they forgot what had happened and behaved in a more scandalous and disorderly fashion… abandoning themselves to gluttony, feasts, taverns and expensive food, to gambling and immoderate lust… while the women dressed themselves in the beautiful and costly garments of those who had died… [and then] everything became scarce… and most goods became more expensive, often double the price they had been before the plague.[1]

As the suffocating summer heat gave way to autumn, life in Florence returned slowly to its old routine. The members of the *Signoria* moved back into the palace to hold their daily meetings, and the law courts re-opened to begin work on the flood of disputes that had arisen over legacies and inheritance, the legal aftermath of so much death. Shopkeepers raised their shutters, and the scaffolding around the half-finished Duomo was once again filled with bricklayers and stonemasons, even if their numbers were much depleted, a bleak reminder of the carnage that had rocked the city.

Overall, the Medici had been lucky. Four cousins, who would play pivotal roles in the history of the family, had survived – Vieri di Cambio, Salvestro di Alamanno, Foligno di Conte and Bicci di Chiarissimo. So had many of their close relatives, though Salvestro's wife had died and so had Foligno's brother. Out of twenty-nine males of their generation, twenty-three were still alive. Other families were not so fortunate – the lawyer Donato Velluti recorded in his diary that nearly two-thirds of the men in his own family had died.[2]

The offices of the Bankers' Guild were open on 13 October, and that day its ledgers recorded the name of a new Medici member: Vieri di Cambio, aged twenty-five and the youngest of the four cousins.[3] A modest financier, he would go on to earn the respect of his fellow bankers and be elected to the prestigious position of consul of the guild on many occasions, taking his seat on this committee responsible for regulating the banking industry in Florence.[4] His decision to go into

Francesco Traini, *Triumph of Death*, early 1350s, detail (Pisa, Camposanto).

commerce at this time of severe economic recession was an adventurous step. Indeed, Vieri and his brother Giovanni, who owned a factory producing woollen cloth, were the only members of the Medici family of their generation to remain in the world of business.[5] The rest of the family, like the majority of wealthy Florentines, had begun to withdraw their capital from speculative ventures after the crash of the late 1330s and were keeping it in the safer havens of land and property.

Salvestro and his brothers were just such wealthy landowners, inheriting a substantial estate of farmland, vineyards, woods and buildings in the Mugello when their father, Alamanno, died in 1355.[6] They were not apprenticed to any trade, nor were they known for their strict observance of the republican values of hard work, moderation and duty, though Salvestro had taken the first steps in what would prove a colourful political career. In the anarchic years following the Black Death, two of his brothers, Michele and Andrea, and their friends became burglars, breaking into shops and houses.[7] More in need of excitement than cash, the youths were arrested – Michele was accused of pawning stolen goods worth 25 florins – and the judges imposed the death penalty on them all, an unusually harsh punishment designed to curb the wave of petty crime sweeping through the city. Although the sentences were commuted, the leader of Andrea's gang was executed, much to the shock of his respectable family. Salvestro and his brothers were a wild bunch, in contrast to the sober and law-abiding Vieri and Foligno.

Foligno was also a wealthy landowner, but by temperament a cautious, conscientious man with a strong sense of familial duty, as we know from his memoir. Its opening words convey the sense of despair and mortality felt by many Florentines at the time: 'I Foligno di Conte de' Medici, seeing the recent misfortunes of civil and foreign wars and the terrible deaths from the plague sent by Lord God, which we fear he may send again as our neighbours have it, will write down the things I see which may be needful for you who remain or will come after me.'[8] Much of his text is devoted to details of the family estate in the Mugello, which his father, Conte di Averardo, had begun to acquire in the 1330s. Over the next few decades, they spent more than 10,000 florins on some 180 buildings and pieces of land, including arable fields, woods and a mill and cottages around their house at Cafaggiolo.[9] They also owned shops and houses in Florence, where, in 1349, Conte bought a palace left empty after the plague. It was a substantial building, large enough to accommodate his two surviving sons and their families: Foligno described it as 'a palace with a courtyard, an orchard and a well, in the parish of San Lorenzo'.[10]

This palace, known as the Casa Vecchia, on the Via Larga (literally Broad Street, now Via Cavour), was to remain in the family for centuries. It was situated in the quarter of San Giovanni, where the Medici traditionally lived. Florentines, rich and poor, owed their primary loyalty to their families but they defined their status in society through membership of various institutions, including trade guilds and religious confraternities, and also through the areas in which they lived: the quarters, parishes and wards. San Giovanni and the other three quarters of Florence – Santa Maria Novella, Santa Croce and Santo Spirito – were each divided into four wards, and it was these sixteen wards in total, rather than the parishes, that formed the basic administrative and social units of the city. The Casa Vecchia lay in the San Giovanni ward of the Golden Lion, while Vieri and Salvestro lived nearby in the quarter's Green Dragon ward. All the city wards had striking names – among the others were Unicorn, Keys, Viper, Whip and Ladder. Their symbols were painted on the banners behind which the Florentines marched in civic processions (and, less enthusiastically, paid their contributions to the forced loans that the *Signoria* levied to cover unexpected shortfalls in government income, especially in time of war).

The poorest of the four Medici cousins was Bicci. Like Salvestro and Foligno, he had inherited property from his father, though on a much smaller scale.[11] He owned some small shops in Florence and a few fields in the Mugello, from which he received annual rents ranging from 5 to 25 florins, and he supplemented this modest income with moneylending.

Despite the disparities in their wealth, the Medici had achieved enough status in society for the cousins to contract prestigious marriages. Typically, Florentine men married at about the age of thirty, once they were established in business, unlike aristocrats who were often wed before they were twenty years old. Around the time of the Black Death, Salvestro, Foligno and Bicci all chose brides from prominent Guelf clans. The identity of Vieri's first wife, whom he married in 1364, is unknown.

For the cousins, as for all Florentines, marriage was a weighty matter. It was not a personal choice but a family decision, one that would create new sets of kinship ties designed to be of social, commercial and political advantage to both sides. Above all, marriage involved large sums of money. First there was the hard bargaining over the dowry, which was negotiated by the senior males of each family in the presence of a marriage broker. We know that Bicci's bride, Jacopa Spini, who gave birth to their first son in 1350, brought him a dowry of 800 florins, a decent sum at a time when well-to-do Florentines could expect to pay between 400 and 1,000 florins for the marriage of their daughters.[12] (For comparison, at the time the annual wages of a master craftsman came to around 60 florins.) Foligno received the same sum in 1348 when he married a girl from the Alfieri family, and Salvestro acquired a dowry of 1,000 florins when he married his second wife, Bartolomea Altoviti, the following year.[13]

A formal marriage betrothal was usually celebrated with a party, for men only, at which the bride's father or guardian promised to give her away and the groom formally promised to marry her. This contract was recorded by a notary and sealed with a kiss on the mouth between the groom and his future father-in-law. The next event was the day when the groom gave his bride a ring – this ceremony took place in the presence of both families, females as well as males this time, and the notary drew up another contract (it is hardly surprising that Florentine lawyers were among the city's rich elite.) Finally, the couple were able to celebrate the wedding itself, often several months after the ring day. Many chose to wait for the Feast of San Giovanni, a popular date for weddings. The wedding was not a church service – few Florentines of this period received the blessing of a priest to sanctify their marriage – but the procession of the bride to the groom's house, where she was welcomed to her new home with feasts that could last for days. It was not until the last feast was over that the bride and groom were finally allowed to share a bed.

Thanks to the survival of so many of their men, the Medici were regularly elected to government office in the decades following the Black Death, serving nineteen times on the *Signoria* between 1343 and 1378, a total only exceeded by the Strozzi clan.[14] Among those playing a more prominent role in Florentine politics was Salvestro. But the old social and political order had been irrevocably changed by the plague, above all by the many thousands of country-dwellers who migrated to the city in its aftermath. Many of these 'new men' became successful entrepreneurs – as ambitious for wealth and status as the Medici had been two centuries earlier. Having monopolized the guilds, they now threatened the old ruling elite's hold on power.

That elite was divided on how to respond. The Medici belonged to the majority conservative faction, led by the powerful Albizzi family, which openly despised the 'new men' and wanted to restrict their eligibility for public office by giving political rights to the current generation of magnate families, the wealthy property-owners like themselves. Salvestro spoke heatedly in support of this view in the lively

Left: Andrea Orcagna, tabernacle, 1359 (Florence, Orsanmichele). This sumptuous marble tabernacle housing a miracle-working image of the Virgin has a tragic history. As the Black Death swept through Florence in 1348, a staggering 350,000 florins poured into the coffers of the confraternity in charge of the image, thanks to a government ruling that the fortunes of all those dying intestate were to go to the confraternity, who used the funds to pay for this magnificent work.

debates that took place in the autumn of 1354 in the Palazzo della Signoria: 'let the magnates be honoured with offices and let the Ordinances [of Justice] be relaxed,' he insisted.[15]

The conservatives won the vote, though only in part: the strength of the populist opposition ensured that the magnates were only allowed to serve on minor committees, not on the prestigious *Signoria* itself. Support for the populists continued to grow, and in 1360 they hatched a plot to topple the governing regime. And one of the conspirators was a Medici, none other than Salvestro's brother, Bartolomeo, who, at the last moment he decided to betray his new friends. Whether motivated by a belated sense of family loyalty, or by doubts as to the success of the scheme, he revealed the plot to Salvestro, who – having received assurances from the *Signoria* that his brother would escape punishment – passed the information on to the priors. The conspirators were arrested and found guilty of treason. Two were executed, while the others were exiled and their property confiscated.

Salvestro's prompt action saved Bartolomeo's life and livelihood – and the family honour. But four years later, Bartolomeo repaid his brother by murdering his own nephew – Salvestro's son, Niccolò – and was sentenced to death.[16] The judgement was annulled, though the court documents do not reveal the reason. Astonishingly, it seems likely that Salvestro had, once again, used his influence with the conservatives to save his brother's life.

In the spring of 1363, the dreaded plague returned to Florence, and, though less ferocious than the previous outbreak, it left many thousands dead. One of its victims was Bicci, the least successful of the Medici cousins. In his will, dated 21 May of that year, he named Foligno as his executor and restored to his widow, Jacopa, her dowry of 800 florins.[17] He also left money to be used for the marriages of his four daughters and bequests of 1 *lira* (0.3 florins) to the building funds of the cathedral and the city walls. The remainder, which was very little, was divided among his five sons. Foligno now took the widowed Jacopa and the nine children under his wing, moving them into a small house attached to his palace on the Via Larga.

Thanks to surviving records of a forced loan levied in 1364, to raise 94,000 florins to fund a war against Pisa, we know that Foligno was the richest of the cousins.[18] He contributed 58 florins to the fund, with Salvestro (32½ florins) and his brothers Africhello (33 florins) and

Bartolomeo (26½ florins) not far behind. The records also reveal the sad reality of Bicci's business ventures: the sum levied on Bicci's capital, now divided between his five sons, was assessed at just 6 florins.

Cousin Vieri's status is more difficult to evaluate because he was part of his father's household; moreover, contributions were assessed on the basis of capital investments and property, not commercial profits. But other evidence shows him doing well: that year he served as consul for the Bankers' Guild and used his influence to extract a debt of 166 florins from the heirs of the Bishop of Florence, who had borrowed the sum from his bank.[19] Five years later, the firm 'Vieri di Cambio de' Medici & Co.' was included among the Florentine businesses engaged in international trade, exporting goods through the port of Pisa.[20] Vieri's company – the only Medici company on the list – was now one of the largest in Florence.

Nevertheless, the records of the forced loan reveal that the Medici family as a whole was, at this time, still only *modestly* wealthy and far below the ranks of the super-rich. The total of 304 florins contributed by all the Medici households was substantially less than the sums paid by the Albizzi (566 florins), for example, or the Strozzi (2,063 florins). However, Salvestro and his brothers, along with Foligno and probably Vieri, were all considerably better off than the rest of the family. Of the twenty Medici households recorded in 1364, more than half contributed less than 10 florins, the sum typically paid by shopkeepers and artisans – one of the butchers in their quarter of San Giovanni was assessed at 9 florins. And two of the Medici households were assessed at the minimum rate of 2 florins, as poor as labourers.

Foligno's story continues with a modest walk-on part in a landmark architectural event: the design of the dome of Florence's new cathedral. Like most important medieval structures, the cathedral had been planned in a piecemeal fashion. In the summer of 1367, with the nave nearing completion, a decision had to be made about the form of the east end, in particular the dome. The committee in charge announced a competition for the project, and in a move that epitomized the republican mentality of the Florentines it was decided that the winner should be chosen by the city itself. The entire electorate was invited to

Andrea da Firenze, *The Church Triumphant*, c.1368 (Florence, Santa Maria Novella, Spanish Chapel).

vote in a referendum held on 26–27 October. Foligno was the only one of the Medici cousins to do his civic duty on this occasion. His name is inscribed in the committee's ledgers together with those of a large cross-section of Florentine society: the Albizzi and other members of the wealthy landowning elite, successful company bosses and scores of shopkeepers and artisans – innkeepers, dyers, blacksmiths, copper-smiths, goldsmiths, grocers, bakers, haberdashers, farriers and sad-dlers.[21] Their choice in this vote produced a lasting visual expression of the power of the Florentine republic.

Foligno opted, along with the overwhelming majority of his fellow citizens, for the majestic ribbed octagonal cupola, which had been designed by a group of stonemasons and painters. A year or so later, one of these painters recorded their vision of the future cathedral in the fresco titled *The Church Triumphant* in Santa Maria Novella. The dome's design tells us much about the self-belief of the Florentines: it was strikingly innovative, bearing little resemblance to any other Italian cathedral, and it would make the Duomo the largest church in Christendom. No thought was given at this stage as to how this extraordinary structure should be built – it was only thanks to the technical expertise of Filippo Brunelleschi, the master in charge, that work on its construction finally got underway some fifty years later (giving rise to the erroneous belief that Brunelleschi was the originator of the design).

Despite Foligno's own relative prosperity, his memoirs show that he was worried about the state of the Medici family: 'today, thanks be to God, we number fifty men but about a hundred of our men have died since I was born, there are only a few households left and we lack children.'[22] Uppermost in his mind was the fear that the prestige of the family was under threat. He urged his relations 'to preserve not only the possessions of our ancestors but also the position they achieved, which is considerable but was once much greater', and which, he wrote regretfully, 'has declined on account of the lack of capable men of whom we once had many'. Foligno might have had in mind his unfortunate cousin Bicci; but he must also have deplored Salvestro's recent political manoeuvres.

In the mid-1360s, Salvestro had decided to ignore the loyalty he owed to his family and to switch sides in the political debate – just as his brother, Bartolomeo, had done some years earlier. In March 1367, when the conservatives again attempted to restrict the access of the 'new men' to political office, Salvestro joined the populist opposition, unleashing his anger on his old friends, and his cousins, calling them 'evil men who want to control the government of Florence and to crush the less powerful citizens'.[23] He argued forcefully that 'the merchants and craftsmen must join together to avoid being divided by those who wish to seize power in Florence'. Thanks in part to Salvestro's demagoguery, the conservatives failed to get their measures passed.

Salvestro's political ambitions took a further step in 1369, when

Piero degli Albizzi, the head of the conservatives, successfully bribed the leaders of the populist opposition to change sides.[24] Albizzi must have been disappointed when, far from collapsing, the populists regrouped under the leadership of Salvestro; moreover, they were growing in strength, especially among Florence's business community and the 'new men'. The rivalry between the factions came to a head in the summer of 1372, when Pope Gregory XI asked Florence to support his campaign to restore his authority in his Italian territories, the Papal States. In a heated debate in the Palazzo della Signoria, the conservatives argued in favour of giving aid to the pope. Salvestro vociferously opposed the motion with characteristic bluntness: 'Under no circumstances,' he thundered, 'should the government commit itself to any military action, nor should it become involved in this war.'[25] He and his supporters won the vote. They had ended Florence's long Guelf tradition of support for papal policy, and they now challenged the conservative faction's hold on power.

On 27 June 1375, Salvestro was appointed as one of the envoys sent by the *Signoria* to Siena, Lucca and Pisa to persuade these city-states to join an alliance *against* Pope Gregory, who, it was feared, was now making plans to conquer Tuscany.[26] That autumn, once the alliance was in place, Salvestro's faction took Florence to war against the pope – the so-called War of the Eight Saints (1375–8), named after the eight members of the committee in charge of the campaign, who raised funds for the war by taxing the city's clergy and confiscating Church possessions. But Gregory XI proved a tough opponent: the following spring, he excommunicated the entire city of Florence and banned all Christendom from doing business with any of its citizens. In another noisy exchange in the Palazzo della Signoria, Salvestro argued that Florence should send her churchmen to the pope to ask him to make peace. 'If he still refuses,' he threatened, 'then all the property belonging to the clergy should be seized by the government so that we can fight this war at their expense.'[27] However, support for Salvestro and his populists had begun to wane, especially among those owners of international companies suffering from the embargo on trade. With the economy at risk of collapse, they urged the government to sue for peace. In June 1377, the *Signoria* sent envoys to Rome to negotiate with Gregory XI.

During that summer, while Salvestro was making himself heard in the Palazzo della Signoria, the Medici family was also making headlines in the law courts, where a particularly colourful case had come up before the judges. Africhello, perhaps the wildest of Salvestro's brothers, was accused of murdering a widow and stealing her property.[28] According to the petition presented by the widow's son, she had inherited an estate in the Mugello from her father, 'a farm with houses, threshing floor, arable land and vineyards... worth 200 florins or more', as well as other properties in the area. Africhello, described by the son as 'a man who has always led a dishonest life by robbing and preying on the poor', wanted the property in order that 'he could live like a magnate off the possessions of the poor'. The son continued: 'so he planned to do to her what he had done to others in the area whom he has driven out of their properties' and that 'by these means he has been able to double the estate which he inherited from his father, so that he neither has to pursue a career in business nor in any trade and he has never earned a penny honestly'. When the widow refused to give up her estate, Africhello forced his way into her house and 'seized her by the hair and beat her unmercifully with the spurs he had with him' such that the widow later 'died from her wounds and her grief'. Not surprisingly, given the damning evidence against him, Africhello was found guilty. He was declared a magnate and deprived of his political rights, but, thanks to Salvestro's influence, he managed to escape the death penalty.

The envoys returned from their mission to Gregory XI at the beginning of October, bringing such excessive demands from the pope that both factions in the Palazzo della Signoria united to reject them. For once, the conservative Foligno agreed with his populist cousin: 'As we cannot have peace, then let us wage war vigorously,' argued Foligno in a general meeting to discuss the issue, 'and let us find the necessary funds.'[29] But the united front did not last long. By the end of the year, Salvestro and his populists were again under attack from the conservatives. On 27 March 1378, just as the debate over the war threatened to descend into violence on the streets of Florence, Gregory XI suddenly died. The *Signoria* made peace with his successor, Urban VI, that summer, but not before the factional rivalry had indeed erupted into riots across the city.

At the end of April, when the elections were held in the great piazza for the new *Signoria* that would start its term on 1 May, Salvestro

Ambrogio Lorenzetti, *Allegory of Good Government*, 1338–9 (Siena, Palazzo Pubblico).
The Tuscan city states were immensely proud of their independence. Here, the female
personification of Siena is guided by the Christian virtues of Faith, Hope and Charity;
and she ensures proper republican government by consulting Peace, Justice and
Magnanimity.

himself was chosen as gonfalonier. Albizzi and the conservatives were horrified and tried, unsuccessfully, to have him deselected; but the fact that four of the eight priors were their men promised a turbulent two months of argument. The rows came to a head in the middle of June, when news leaked out that the conservatives were plotting to seize power in an armed rebellion. Gonfalonier Salvestro took swift action: in the words of a chronicler, he 'sent for those he trusted and talked to some of them in person and to others via messengers, and they made their plans'.[30] On 18 June, he announced his intention to reverse the 1354 law that had relaxed the Ordinances of Justice to allow magnates to hold government office – a law, of course, that he himself had helped to pass. He was acting, he said, 'on behalf of the ordinary people, the merchants and craftsmen of Florence, and also the poor and those without power… so that they can live peacefully on the fruits of their labour and possessions'.[31]

On 22 June, four days after Salvestro's faction had failed to muster sufficient votes to pass the measure, which was blocked by conservatives, the 'ordinary people' gave vent to their fury by staging a mass riot and setting fire to the palaces of many of Albizzi's supporters. There were rumours that the order for the riot had come directly from the *Signoria* – from Gonfalonier Salvestro himself – and it was soon to escalate into something far worse. Prominent among the looters were the impoverished labourers in the cloth industry, known as the Ciompi, who were insisting on the right to form their own guild and thus be eligible to participate in government. Salvestro's term as gonfalonier came to an end a week later with the issue still unresolved. The new *Signoria* took office on 1 July, and continued to vacillate over the Ciompi's demands. On 22 July, these infuriated and unenfranchized labourers stormed the Palazzo della Signoria, forced the priors to resign and took over the government themselves.

Although short-lived, the Ciompi Revolt was a dramatic event in the history of Florence. The radical policies of the new regime appalled tradesmen, entrepreneurs and landowners alike, and generated a horror of mob rule that was to have a lasting impact on Florentine politics. The regime fell after just six weeks, crushed by Salvestro and his populist supporters who set up their own government in the name of all the city's guildsmen. Salvestro himself had shrewdly joined the Silk Merchants' Guild in July to give credibility to his position as their leader.[32] Not a businessman himself, Salvestro played only a modest role in the new administration; but he was widely respected as its figurehead, 'the author of the present new regime' as one of its leaders described him.[33] And moreover, the dramatic events of that summer did much to enhance the Medici family's reputation for championing the ordinary people, a reputation that was to prove of enduring significance to their story.

Salvestro's prestige in Florentine politics was not destined to last. The guild government attempted to destroy the conservatives by barring them from political office and executing their leader, Piero degli Albizzi; but his supporters regrouped behind the leadership of Piero's son Maso, and in January 1382 they overthrew the guild regime to re-establish the conservatives in power with the backing of many wealthy businessmen, landowners and magnates. Salvestro was exiled to Modena for ten years. His banishment was lifted early, though, enabling him to die at home, in 1388.

Although the conservatives' coup spelled the end of Salvestro's influence, it now brought other members of the Medici clan to power. One of the key figures in Maso degli Albizzi's inner circle was Salvestro's cousin, Vieri. Aged fifty-nine in 1382, he had made a substantial fortune in recent years and now ranked among the wealthiest men in Florence. In a forced loan of 1378, he was No. 16 in the city's rich-list, contributing the sum of 73 florins to the tax.[34] (We can assume that Vieri had invested the profits of his highly successful bank in real estate.) Foligno, the next wealthiest member of the family, paid only 22 florins; in fact, this is the last record we have of him. Meanwhile, Vieri, whose wife was childless, had used his wealth to help his poorer relatives, especially Foligno's wards – the sons of the unfortunate Bicci who had inherited little from their father apart from the Medici name. Vieri offered apprenticeships at his bank to Francesco di Bicci and his younger brother Giovanni, promoting Francesco as junior partner in 1382 and Giovanni to the same rank four years later. Giovanni had recently married and now invested his bride's substantial dowry of 1,500 florins in Vieri's business. In return, Vieri appointed this promising twenty-six-year-old cousin to take charge of managing the Rome branch of the bank, which proudly bore the new name 'Vieri & Giovanni de' Medici in Rome'.[35]

At the end of 1391, Vieri decided to sell the bank. He had married again after the death of his first wife and his young bride Bice Strozzi, the daughter of a political ally, gave birth to several children including two sons: Nicola (born 1385) and Cambio (born early in 1391). Vieri was sixty-eight years old when Cambio was born and eager to secure his fortune for his sons, who would probably still be too young to inherit the business when he died. So he divided the bank into three separate units, selling one to Francesco, another to Giovanni, and the third to another relative, which soon closed.[36] Thanks to Vieri's generosity and sense of familial duty, Bicci's sons Francesco and Giovanni were now independent businessmen.

It was after his retirement from banking that Vieri redirected his energies to politics, playing an active role in the Palazzo della Signoria as a key ally of Maso degli Albizzi and serving as gonfalonier in 1392 for the May–June term.[37] Fuelled by the vivid memories of the mob rule in 1378, the conservative regime was steadily tightening its grip on power, much to the dismay of ordinary Florentines, many of whom hoped that Vieri could be persuaded to take up Salvestro's mantle as their champion. One chronicler claimed that Vieri was approached in 1393 by leaders of the minor guildsmen, who 'implored him to take over the government and liberate them from this tyranny of those citizens who were destroying the republic'.[38] 'If Messer Vieri had been more ambitious,' the chronicle continued, 'he could have made himself prince of the city.' Vieri remained loyal to Maso degli Albizzi, but it is evident that the rest of the Medici had joined the populist opposition, and several of them were implicated in this abortive coup.

Vieri died on 14 September 1395, at the age of 'seventy-two years, seven months and twenty days', according to his tombstone in Florence's Cathedral where he was buried with all the honours of a state funeral.[39] In his will, written a month before his death, he named several of the leading conservative elite as his executors and left the handsome sum of 1,200 florins to each of his daughters for their dowries.[40] Aware that his huge fortune had not been entirely honestly earned, he was also anxious about the future of his soul and left donations totalling more than 200 florins to churches for prayers to be said for his salvation. He also endowed a Florentine convent with the substantial sum of 3,000 florins, on condition that a Medici nun be nominated as abbess. Despite the money spent on these handsome bequests, enough remained to ensure that Vieri's young sons Nicola and Cambio were now immensely rich. In a forced loan of 1396, they paid 220 florins, while Giovanni di Bicci, still at the beginning of his banking career, contributed just 14 florins.[41]

Vieri's death marked the end of an era in the history of the Medici. The family had survived the financial disasters of the mid-fourteenth century and still ranked among the city's wealthy elite but they were about to squander the political capital they had inherited after the Black Death. In 1397, Francesco di Bicci, a conservative like Vieri, was elected to the *Signoria*. That same year, one of his cousins was arrested on a charge of attempting to assassinate Maso degli Albizzi and was executed for the crime.[42] Three years later, several more Medici were implicated in another plot to overthrow the Albizzi regime – and this time the government reacted decisively: the *entire* Medici family was prohibited from taking public office for twenty years. It was a sorry end to two centuries of political service.

There was, however, a gleam of hope. Out of respect for Vieri and his unswerving loyalty to Albizzi, exceptions to these prohibitions were made for Vieri's sons Nicola and Cambio when they came of age, and for his cousins Francesco and Giovanni di Bicci. The financial and political future of the family now rested in their hands.

3

THE FORTUNE

Giovanni di Bicci

1400–1425

Giovanni di Bicci (age 40)
Nannina (32), *his wife*

> Cosimo (11) *and* Lorenzo (6), *his sons*

Francesco di Bicci (44), *Giovanni's brother*

> Averardo di Francesco (27), *his son*

Nicola (15) *and* **Cambio** (9), *sons of Vieri di Cambio,*
Giovanni's distant cousin and the founder of the first Medici bank

Francesco and Giovanni di Bicci had been very fortunate. Vieri's political reputation had secured their status within the ruling conservative elite under the leadership of the Albizzi family. Unlike the rest of the Medici clan, who were cast into the political wilderness in 1400, the two brothers were able to play an active role in the Palazzo della Signoria, where Francesco served as a prior for the first time in 1397, and where Giovanni achieved the same honour five years later. And, thanks to Vieri's decision to sell his profitable company, they were both independent businessmen. Francesco's bank, based in Florence, was an international operation with branches in cities across Italy and agents in Avignon, Barcelona, Bruges, Paris and London.[1] Giovanni's operation was the old Rome branch of Vieri's bank, which made its profits in the lucrative market of the papal court. The two banks were separate companies, but they co-operated closely, with Giovanni acting as Francesco's agent in Rome.

Francesco di Bicci fades from the family history at this point. He died in 1402, the year Giovanni was first elected to the *Signoria*, and left his bank to his son Averardo, who continued to work closely with Giovanni in business and political matters. Giovanni was a quiet man by all accounts, with a shrewd mind and a dry sense of humour. He had been married since 1385 to Piccarda Bueri (affectionately known to all the family as 'Nannina'), who, on 27 September 1389, gave birth to twin boys. They were named Cosimo and Damiano after the saints on whose feast day they had been born – a rather witty choice, as Cosmas and Damian were famous miracle-working 'doctors', in Italian, *medici*. Little Damiano did not survive long, dying the following year, but in 1395 Piccarda gave birth to another son, Lorenzo.

In 1397, Giovanni moved the headquarters of his company from Rome to Florence, where the new bank had been registered in the ledgers of the Bankers' Guild on 7 April. It had a modest capital of 8,000 florins, three-quarters of which was put up by Giovanni himself, with the remaining quarter supplied by Benedetto de' Bardi.[2] Bardi, who had been Giovanni's junior partner in Rome before the move, stayed behind as general manager of what now became the branch office at the papal court. When Giovanni drew up the balance sheet for his company after the first eighteen months of trading, he found that he had made a net profit of 1,200 florins, which was divided, in the same proportion as the capital, between himself and Benedetto. [3]

It was an acceptable performance but not outstanding. Over the next few years, however, the Medici bank was to become one of the richest in Italy and the foundation of the family fortune.

The story of how Giovanni di Bicci transformed the fortunes of his small company is one of luck and opportunism as well as talent. As Vieri's general manager in Rome, he had learned how to survive and prosper in this notoriously corrupt city. Everything in Rome, from posts in the curia (the papal administration), could be bought for a price, making it a highly lucrative market for bankers. There was money to be made in loans to finance the extravagant lifestyles of popes and cardinals, and, even more profitably, from the charges banks could levy on the endless transactions of Church business. There was also the potential for substantial loss too, as Giovanni well knew, for when he acquired the assets of Vieri's Rome branch he also took on its bad debts of 860 florins.[4]

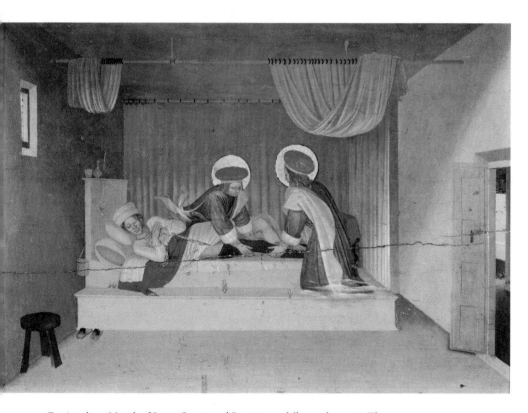

Fra Angelico, *Miracle of Saints Cosmas and Damian*, predella panel, *c.*1438 (Florence, Museo di San Marco). Famous for their miraculous grafting of a new leg onto their patient, the saints would have been immediately recognizable as doctors by their red hats.

Success depended on recognizing the stars rising through the ranks of the Church; a close financial relationship with a future pope could bring the ultimate prize of becoming the papal banker. In the Rome of the 1390s, one of these rising stars was Baldassare Cossa, a Neapolitan aristocrat, whose early career as a pirate made him an unlikely cleric. But he had ambition and, moreover, the favour of Pope Boniface IX, who had succeeded Urban VI in 1389 and appointed his protégé as papal treasurer. It is not clear precisely when Giovanni di Bicci met Cossa, nor do we know much about the early business dealings between banker and treasurer; but the friendship between them almost certainly dates from this period. It was to have important implications for the future of the bank.

In February 1402, news arrived from Rome that Boniface IX had made Cossa a cardinal. It was widely rumoured that the ex-pirate had paid 10,000 florins for this honour, and that the money had been loaned to him by Giovanni's bank.[5] And thus, a decade after he had bought his share of Vieri's bank, Giovanni's business acumen had started to bear fruit. While we do not know for certain that Giovanni was acting as Cossa's financial agent at this stage, it is unlikely to be mere coincidence that 1402 was also the year in which he began cautiously to expand his operations.

So far, Giovanni's bank was still a modest affair, with branches in Florence, Rome and Naples employing just thirteen men; but in March 1402, he opened a fourth branch in Venice, adding another manager and three more clerks to the payroll.[6] The following month, he started to diversify his investments, buying a small factory to produce woollen cloth, which, following the tradition of Florentine businessmen, he put in the name of his son, Cosimo. A few years later he acquired a second cloth factory, in the name of Cosimo's younger brother Lorenzo.

There were teething problems with the new Venice office. The first manager, Neri Tornaquinci, proved a disastrous choice, a rare mistake by Giovanni, who was usually a good judge of character. In direct contravention of the contract he had signed with Giovanni, Tornaquinci had made a loan to some Germans, who defaulted on their debt. He then borrowed funds to conceal the loss and compounded the mess by massaging the figures in the accounts ledger to report a non-existent profit. Inevitably, he had to be sacked – however, several years later, when Giovanni learned that Tornaquinci was destitute, he sent him 36 florins.[7]

Giovanni di Bicci's personal wealth started to increase. In the Florentine forced loan of 1403, to pay for war against Milan – which would last several decades – he was listed as the forty-eighth richest man in Florence.[8] His contribution of 37 florins was slightly higher than that paid by his brother's household (33 florins), and both assessments would have been larger if their banking fortunes had been included. They were still a long way behind their young cousins Nicola and Cambio (187 florins), who, with Vieri's vast fortune, were now the fifth-richest household in the city. The records also reveal a contrasting picture – showing how the wealth of the rest of the Medici family had declined as spectacularly as their political status. Only two other Medici households made it into the top 600 contributors: Alamanno (11 florins), the son of Salvestro, who had played such a key role in the political battles of the late fourteenth century; and Antonio (15 florins), the son of Salvestro's homicidal brother Africhello.

Meanwhile, Giovanni di Bicci's links with Cardinal Cossa were paying political as well as financial dividends. In 1403, the *Signoria* chose Giovanni for the prestigious post of ambassador to Bologna, where Cossa had just been appointed as papal governor – and where he was reputed to be taking his pleasures in the company of the ladies of the city. Cossa's new position made him a powerful figure on the Italian political stage, and it is at this point that the nature of the relationship between him and Giovanni begins to emerge. Our first piece of concrete evidence dates from 1404, when an entry in Giovanni's private account book recorded a hefty loan of 8,937 florins to Cossa.[9] There are also letters from Cossa to 'my most dear friend' Giovanni, suggesting a well-established friendship. Over the following seven years, the flamboyant cardinal and the cautious banker were to do a lot of business together.

Cardinal Cossa's move from Rome to Bologna occurred during a difficult time for the Church. For the previous three decades, while some rulers of Christian Europe had maintained allegiance to the pope in Rome, others had pledged allegiance to a rival pope, based in Avignon.

With both pontiffs claiming to be the rightful successor to the throne of St Peter, the credibility of the Church itself was at stake. Calls for a council to end this Great (or Western) Schism were becoming increasingly urgent. For the ambitious Cossa, this was the ideal opportunity to advance his own career. After the death of his benefactor Boniface IX, in 1404, he expediently changed sides, abandoning his allegiance to Rome to join a group of independent cardinals who, with the support of many princes, were planning to inaugurate a council to address the issue of the Schism. The Council of Pisa, which opened in March 1409. It voted to depose both of the current popes, and on 26 June, thanks to Cossa's shrewd manoeuvring, one of the cardinal's allies was elected as Pope Alexander V. The election of a third pope did not, of itself, end the Schism – indeed, for a time there were three popes, as neither of Alexander V's two rivals would agree to resign – but it did enhance Cossa's reputation. When Alexander V died suddenly, less than twelve months later, the cardinals who had attended the Council of Pisa gathered in Bologna to choose his successor. Their choice, not entirely unexpectedly, was Cardinal Cossa himself, who took the name John XXIII.*

For Giovanni di Bicci this was a golden opportunity, quite literally. Cossa's first priority as pope was to establish his authority in Rome, where the Roman claimant to the throne of St Peter, Gregory XII, held power, aided by the King of Naples. He needed to raise money for what would be an expensive campaign. Inevitably, he turned to Giovanni, who initiated an immensely lucrative business venture for the Medici bank. The scale of the proposed operation was too large for Giovanni to handle alone – John XXIII needed 10,000 florins immediately – so he shared the capital investment with his nephew Averardo and with two Florentine merchants based in Bologna.[10] The new company was fronted by managers: in name at least it did not appear to be a Medici project, but it was funded largely by Medici money, and it was the Medici who were to profit on the deal.

In April 1411, John XXIII left Bologna at the head of a large army and successfully conquered Rome. Unfortunately – for him, not for the Medici – he was unable to defeat the powerful armies of King Ladislas of Naples, who had opposed his election. On 17 June 1412,

---

* Not to be confused with the modern Pope John XXIII (1958–63), Angelo Giuseppe Roncalli. The Catholic church classifies Cossa as an 'antipope'.

John XXIII was obliged to sign an expensive peace treaty with Naples requiring him to pay the huge sum of 95,000 florins to the king within one year.[11] As before, the pope turned to Giovanni di Bicci, lodging valuable papal mitres and plate with the Medici bank in Rome as pledges for the loan. In Florence the following year, when the *Signoria* levied another forced loan for the war against Milan, Giovanni's assessment of 260 florins surpassed that of Vieri's sons for the first time.[12] Evidently, the papal account was proving highly profitable for the Medici bank, though Giovanni di Bicci was unable to persuade John XXIII to extend his favour to the Florentines themselves – the Pisan pope turned down an offer of 50,000 florins from the *Signoria* for the venerated relic of the head of St John the Baptist, and Florence had to be satisfied with the finger of their patron saint instead.[13]

With three popes still vying for the throne of St Peter's, serious efforts were now under way in the wider European political arena to end the Schism. Another council opened in 1414 at Constance (Konstanz). John XXIII arrived in the German city in October, together with his cardinals and his court. Representing Giovanni's bank in Constance was the partner-manager of the Rome branch, Ilarione de' Bardi, who had taken over the position from his brother Benedetto. (In reality the title 'Rome' was something of a misnomer – the branch was in fact as peripatetic as the pope himself, and it would be six years before it would return to Rome.) Travelling with Ilarione was Giovanni's eldest son, Cosimo, now twenty-five years old. He was learning his trade as a banker, but his journey to Constance would also give him invaluable lessons in the art of politics and the chance to form close friendships with several of the learned 'humanists' who were employed at the papal court – those intellectuals who studied the literary culture of the ancient world and earned their living working in the papal administration.†

On 15 February 1415, the Council of Constance voted to depose all

---

† Humanism, which would become a trusty prop of the Medici myth, involved the revival of the rules of classical Latin, which had degenerated since the fall of the Roman Empire, as the basis for a new body of literature, history and ethics in imitation of the Roman and Greek authors. Florentines made significant contributions to humanist culture, but humanist scholars found employment at courts across Italy, where they worked as secretaries and provided propaganda for their masters' ambitions. The literature of classical antiquity offered plenty of useful models for promoting dukes and kings as the heirs of Imperial Rome, as well as examples to champion the cause of republican liberty in Florence.

three contending popes; a month later, with his enemies calling for his arrest on charges of corruption, the now ex-Pope John XXIII fled from the city disguised as a groom. He was recaptured and put on trial at the end of May, charged with (among other crimes) making huge profits in collaboration with the curial bankers – 'wicked usurers' as one of his accusers described them – and buying his cardinal's hat with Medici money.[14] He was found guilty of simony, perjury and gross misconduct. The serious-minded churchmen at Constance were appalled by the gossip claiming he had seduced more than 200 women during his seven years as Governor of Bologna – and the council ordered him to be imprisoned in Germany. But Giovanni did not forget his disgraced friend. He sent Bartolomeo de' Bardi, a cousin of Benedetto and Ilarione, to Germany to negotiate Cossa's release and pay the ransom of 3,500 florins.[15] When Cossa died on 22 November 1419, having named Giovanni di Bicci as executor of his will, Giovanni commissioned a lavishly gilded tomb for the former pope, which can still be seen in the Baptistery in Florence.

Finally, the Council of Constance brought an end to the Schism, which had split the Church for half a century, with the election of Martin V on 11 November 1417. It also meant the end of Giovanni di Bicci's brief spell as papal banker, for Pope Martin appointed a rival Florentine firm, the Spini, in his place. But the hefty profits earned by Giovanni and his nephew Averardo through their financial dealings with John XXIII had established them among the top banking houses in Florence. When, in 1419, the Bankers' Guild decided to commission a bronze statue of St Matthew, the patron saint of moneylenders, for the Florentine church of Orsanmichele, Giovanni and Averardo were prominent contributors.[16] This expensive project, which cost 945 florins, was financed by levies on members of the guild: the Medici contributed 104 florins, the largest share, while the second-largest came from the Strozzi family (68 florins).

Giovanni di Bicci also had more domestic reasons for celebration. He had arranged the marriage of his eldest son Cosimo to Contessina de' Bardi, a cousin of his Bardi banking partners, and Contessina gave birth to her first child, Piero, on 19 September 1416. Earlier that year,

Lorenzo Ghiberti, *St Matthew*, 1419 (Florence, Orsanmichele).

Giovanni had arranged the marriage of his younger son Lorenzo to Ginevra Cavalcanti, the daughter of one of his political allies in the conservative elite. To mark this event, the Venetian humanist Francesco Barbaro, a friend of Cosimo and Lorenzo, dedicated a treatise on wifely duties to the groom. The text of *De re uxoria*, inspired by Plutarch and other classical authors, gave advice about the proper behaviour of a wife – as partner, hostess and, above all, as mother – recommending moderation in demeanour, speech, love-making, food and dress ('if a particular dress is offensive to a husband, then we advise her not to wear it').[17]

Giovanni, Nannina and their two sons all lived in the Casa Vecchia, the comfortable palace in the ward of the Golden Lion, which had once belonged to Foligno di Conte. Drawn up in March 1418, an inventory of this spacious home provides a fascinating glimpse into the domestic life of the banker and his family.[18] The entrance hall, flanked with kitchens, storage rooms and stables, led through the palace from the street to a loggia that opened onto a courtyard with a well and garden beyond. The main reception room was on the first floor, looking out over the street and ornamented with a painting of the doctor-saints Cosmas and Damian. Next door, also overlooking the street, was the apartment belonging to Giovanni and Nannina, a suite of four rooms consisting of a drawing room, bedroom, study and lavatory. Cosimo and Contessina had a similar suite at the back of the palace, with a view over the garden, while Lorenzo and Ginevra had a smaller apartment – without a drawing room – also at the back. Baby Piero and his nurse lived on the top floor, where there were more reception rooms, and the servants slept in the cramped space under the eaves above. The rooms were sparsely furnished by our cluttered standards, and the inventory lists only those contents of value. Giovanni and Nannina's rooms, for example, contained a painting of the Virgin, several boxes of rosary beads and a birth tray, the traditional present given to a pregnant wife. Cosimo and Lorenzo also both had pictures of the Virgin on their walls, and there was the birth tray given to Contessina for the birth of Piero.

The real surprise of the inventory is the quantity of books owned by Cosimo. They offer proof of his humanist interests, for he had collected some seventy manuscripts, including works in Latin by classical authors such as Cicero, Julius Caesar, Virgil, Martial, Ovid and Tacitus

The interior courtyard of the Palazzo Davanzati in Florence, built in the mid-fourteenth century.

(a rare copy), along with a Bible and plenty of lighter Italian literature by Dante, Boccaccio and other Florentines.[19] This was a sizeable library for the period by any standards; but it was a very unusual collection for a twenty-nine-year-old, especially one pursuing a career in commerce rather than scholarship. Cosimo's father and brother were far more typical – Giovanni di Bicci owned just three books, all of which were devotional works, while Lorenzo had none.[20]

In 1420, Giovanni di Bicci reached his sixtieth birthday and decided it was time to hand over the bank to his sons. His old business partner, Benedetto de' Bardi, had died that April, dissolving all their partnership agreements, and Giovanni took this opportunity to reorganize the business. According to documentary evidence, it is clear that the bank was going from strength to strength, with Giovanni's share of profits amounting to more than 113,865 florins in 1397–1420.[21] While he had reinvested much of this in the business, he had also begun to acquire land and properties in the ancestral Medici heartland in the Mugello, to create an estate that he could pass on to his sons, something his father had been unable to do. Moreover, the fact that over 50 per cent of the profits came from the Rome branch affirms just how lucrative Giovanni's friendship with Baldassare Cossa had been.[22]

A new partnership was formally established on 16 September 1420.[23] Ilarione de' Bardi, younger brother of Benedetto, was appointed as the new general manager – he had proved his worth by his judicious management of the Rome branch over the past nine years. His cousin Bartolomeo de' Bardi, who had successfully handled the negotiations in Germany for the release of Cossa, now took over as manager in Rome. There were three partners: Cosimo and his brother Lorenzo owned two-thirds of the company (16,000 florins), while Ilarione de' Bardi contributed the other third (8,000 florins). Despite the changes at the top, the bank continued to operate much as it had done previously, suggesting that the old man's hand was still firmly on the tiller. But within just two months the circumstances in which it operated were about to change in a very providential manner. In November, the Spini bank went bust; and Martin V appointed the Medici as papal bankers in their place. It was the beginning of a long and profitable association that would bring considerable benefit to Cosimo and his family.

In his retirement, Giovanni di Bicci now began to think about his mortality. He had a private conversation with Martin V about his ill-gotten gains, and in June 1421 he noted that the pope was allowing him to atone for his sins with a donation of 350 florins for the upkeep of churches in Rome.[24] As a favour to his banker, Martin V gave Giovanni permission to install an altar in the Casa Vecchia and to appoint a personal priest to celebrate mass in the palace for the entire household.[25]

Giovanni also began to spend large sums on religious projects in Florence – a policy that served to advertise his wealth as well as compensate for his sins – and he played a conspicuous role in the rebuilding of his parish church of San Lorenzo. In 1416, he was one of the six prominent parish residents elected to serve a three-year term on the committee in charge of building the new church, which, it was hoped, would smarten up this area so close to the city centre. Accordingly, the committee petitioned the *Signoria* for permission to demolish the houses of 'women of the vilest condition' – in the previous year, the government had set up two public brothels on the outskirts of Florence, supposedly 'in places where the exercise of such scandalous trade can best be hidden'.[26] The new San Lorenzo was financed by selling patronage rights to chapels inside it, giving wealthy parishioners a prestigious site for their family tombs. Giovanni ensured that his own contribution eclipsed those of his neighbours: not only did he buy the largest chapel, which he dedicated to saints Cosmas and Damian, but he also took over responsibility for building and endowing a new sacristy attached to the church. The design of the sacristy, attributed to Brunelleschi, was to be a landmark in the development of Renaissance architecture. Instead of the familiar pointed Gothic arches preferred by his contemporaries, Giovanni opted for a distinctively Florentine design, exhibiting the round arches and fluted Corinthian pilasters that could also be seen in the city's ancient Romanesque churches, notably the Baptistery.

The stellar success of Giovanni di Bicci's bank had made him a powerful financial force in Florence, and in his later years he began to play an increasingly prominent role in the political life of the city. In 1419, shortly before retiring, he had been elected to the council of the

The Old Sacristy, San Lorenzo, Florence, begun in 1421. The tombs of Giovanni di Bicci and his wife, Nannina, are in the centre.

Dieci di Guerra ('Ten of War'), in charge of conducting the war against Filippo Maria Visconti, Duke of Milan, whose ambition to extend his rule over the city-states of northern Italy was becoming a serious threat to Florentine independence. In 1421, he was elected as gonfalonier of the *Signoria* for the September–October term, and later that year he was appointed as ambassador to Martin V in Rome. Over the years 1424–6, Giovanni was regularly listed among those leading citizens summoned to the Palazzo della Signoria to advise the government – his presence there recorded on twenty occasions.[27] And it was not just Giovanni di Bicci who was becoming a familiar Medici face in the palace. His nephew Averardo, who had been active in politics since 1409, was also a prominent member of the conservative regime; so too was their cousin Nicola di Vieri. Averardo was invited to advise the *Signoria* on thirty-two occasions over these two years, while Nicola attended fifteen sessions.[28]

The Medici, who had been on the verge of political oblivion in 1400, were now in the process of re-establishing themselves at the heart of government.

4

POLITICS

Giovanni di Bicci,
Averardo and Cosimo
1426–1433

Giovanni di Bicci (66)
Nannina (58), *his wife*

Cosimo (37), *Giovanni's eldest son*
   Contessina de' Bardi (30), *his wife*

    Piero (10) *and* Giovanni (5), *their sons*

Lorenzo (31), *Giovanni's younger son*

    Ginevra Cavalcanti, *his wife*

Averardo (53), *son of Giovanni's brother, Francesco*

    Giuliano (30), *his son*

Nicola (41) *and* **Cambio** (35), *the sons of Vieri di Cambio, Giovanni's distant cousin and founder of the first Medici bank*

There was one problem with Giovanni di Bicci's loyalty to Florence's conservative elite in the early fifteenth century – it was just show. The Medici were not as respectable as they outwardly seemed. Behind the scenes, the family were conspiring against the regime, and doing so in a manner calculated to deceive. With Giovanni's tacit approval, his son Cosimo and nephew Averardo were building up their own network in the Palazzo della Signoria. Using the substantial financial resources at their disposal, they offered tempting favours – loans at preferential rates, jobs in the Medici banks, posts in the state administration – in return for the promise of votes. They were fully aware that they were acting illegally: manipulating the voting in government committees by calling in these favours went very much against the spirit of the republic, which expected each man to vote according to conscience rather than follow a party line. Indeed, the Medici party was necessarily a secretive affair. Cosimo and Averardo were careful to avoid naming members in their correspondence, instead preferring veiled references to *amici* or 'friends'. 'Our friend is not what I thought him; enough said,' Cosimo succinctly informed his cousin, warning him of one supporter's unreliability.[1]

The *amici* came from all strata of Florentine society – magnates and businessmen, shopkeepers and artisans, the rich and the poor. The party provided a magnet both for those within the political elite who disliked the Albizzi regime and for those who were excluded from power. Significantly, more than half of the *amici* were from families that had migrated to Florence in the decades following the Black Death (1348) – the 'new men' who had been championed by Old Salvestro in the 1360s and 1370s, and who were so despised by the conservatives.[2] Indeed, it would seem that Cosimo and Averardo had learned a lesson or two from Old Salvestro's mistakes. They, too, were in the process of shunning the political establishment in pursuit of power; but, unlike Salvestro, they understood just how important family unity would be to achieving their goal, and they needed to avoid the rifts that had split the Medici during the previous century.

The Medici 'party' was all about family. As heir to the widely respected Giovanni di Bicci, Cosimo was the nominal head of the party and probably the brains behind the venture. But we know, thanks to the quantities of letters that have survived in the Florentine archives, that it was Averardo who was largely responsible for its organization.

THE FAMILY MEDICI

Masolino, *Healing of the Cripple and Raising of Tabitha*, begun *c.*1427 (Florence, Santa Maria del Carmine, Brancacci Chapel), set against a backdrop of fifteenth-century Florentine streets and houses.

Other family members were also prominent in the party hierarchy, notably Cosimo's brother Lorenzo and Averardo's son Giuliano, and their cousins Nicola and Cambio di Vieri.

Averardo and Cosimo also went out of their way to cultivate the support of their poorer kinsmen. Many of the employees in their banks, and all the senior staff, were relations, either Medici cousins or Bardi in-laws.[3] They cemented the loyalty of important *amici* through marriage: Averardo's sons-in-law, for example, were all top party deputies, while his daughter-in-law, Giuliano's wife, was the niece of another party loyalist.[4] The complicated web of familial bonds created by these unions was to prove an important factor in the party's success.

The contest between the conservatives and the Medici party came out into the open during the summer of 1426, when Rinaldo degli Albizzi addressed a public meeting of his supporters. In a rousing speech, recorded by Giovanni Cavalcanti in his chronicle, Albizzi urged them to unite against the evidently growing influence of the Medici or they would lose their hold on power.[5] 'How glad I am to see you, my lords and gentlemen, and what a comfort it is to me to see such a large gathering,' he began, 'all of you with such long experience of politics which you have inherited from your ancestors.' He deplored the way the government was being taken over by ordinary people and outsiders: the 'new men have no idea how things are done here' and 'if you let them take over the government, it will be your ruin'. It was his belief that the conservative elite had the moral right to rule: 'we are well-born,' he harangued, 'and now we find ourselves companions in the government with men from Empoli or the Mugello' – a thinly veiled reference to the Medici – 'even with those who were once our household servants... and now they treat us as servants while they themselves behave like lords'. He asked the audience: 'is it not more appropriate that men from good families should have authority over those from artisan backgrounds and not the other way round?' In conclusion, he begged them 'to arrange things so that the important offices of government are given to men of the right background, and that these upstarts return to their paltry trades and focus on providing food for their family tables'.

One immediate result of this speech was to increase the popularity of the Medici party on the streets of Florence. Cosimo and Averardo also celebrated a major coup later that year when Albizzi's brother Luca changed sides in the debate. Luca's reward for joining the *amici* was a Medici bride, one of the daughters of Nicola di Vieri.[6]

Meanwhile, in the Palazzo della Signoria the two factions were now involved in heated debates over the reform of the tax system. The cost of financing the ongoing wars with Milan was escalating, and the old system of forced loans was creaking under the strain. The government faced a fiscal crisis of unprecedented proportions when it became clear that many members of the conservative elite, whose fortunes were invested in real estate, were unable to find the cash to pay their share. The system itself was also open to abuse as it relied heavily on the probity of the heads of the city's wards, who were responsible for assessing what each household could pay, and they routinely exploited their positions to favour their friends. Both sides agreed that the tax system had to be reformed – but there was little agreement as to how this should be done.

The conservatives championed a new method of taxation, the *catasto*, which would factor into the assessments the capital value of financial investments, along with the usual real estate, and thus spread the tax burden more evenly among the rich. Property-owners had nothing to lose, and the proposal was popular with poorer sections of

Florentine society; but the city's wealthy businessmen were understandably reluctant to see their commercial profits diminish, and they opposed the motion. Giovanni di Bicci argued vociferously that the *catasto* would damage trade, the backbone of Florence's wealth. However, aware that his opposition would damage the Medici party's populist image, he changed his mind just days before the council was to vote on the issue.[7] The legislation scraped through on 22 May 1427, by just a single vote, thanks to the support of Giovanni and his allies.

The *catasto* required the head of every household in Florence to submit a tax return, detailing all financial and real-estate investments. Family homes were exempt from the tax, as were tools of trade; but rented properties, farmland and even slaves were all subject to assessment, though deductions were made for dependants such as wives, children and grandparents. Many people resented this intrusion into their personal lives, along with the drudgery of filing the tax returns and, particularly, the officiousness of the clerks and notaries, who meticulously double-checked the tax returns in order to compile their registers in the back rooms of the Palazzo della Signoria. Modern historians, on the other hand, have inherited a veritable mine of social data on every person living in the city. So we know that there were thirty-two Medici households registered in Florence for the first *catasto* in 1427, their returns revealing much about the scale of the family's wealth. With financial investments included for the first time, Giovanni di Bicci was assessed as the richest man in his quarter of San Giovanni, with a net capital estimated at 79,472 florins.[8] Moreover, he was listed as the second-richest man in the city, eclipsed only by Palla Strozzi (101,422 florins), one of Albizzi's most loyal supporters; and Rinaldo degli Albizzi himself came in at No. 67. Giovanni's wealth was even more exceptional when compared to the rest of the family. Of the other Medici households, only three made it into the top six hundred: Averardo (15,097 florins) at No. 43, the brothers Nicola and Cambio di Vieri (6,245 florins) at No. 161 and their distant cousin Orlando di Guccio, who worked in Giovanni's bank, at No. 435 (2,236 florins).

On 20 February 1429, after almost a decade of retirement from his bank, Giovanni di Bicci died at the age of sixty-nine. In his chronicle,

The nave of the church of San Lorenzo in Florence, begun in 1418.

Giovanni Cavalcanti recorded the patriarch's last words of advice to his sons Cosimo and Lorenzo:*

> 'Beloved sons... I know I am approaching the last days of my life... and I leave to you the great wealth that fortune has bestowed upon me... I leave you with a greater business than any other merchant in Tuscany. You have the respect of every good citizen, and the majority of the populace who have chosen our family as their guiding star. If you do not stray from the traditions of our ancestors, the people will be generous in honouring you. To do this you must be merciful to the poor, and gracious and kind to the miserable, and do all in your power to help them. Never go against the will of the people, unless they choose to do something of little worth, and then do not tell them what to do but discuss the matter with them in a gentle and kindly manner. Also do not make the Palazzo della Signoria your workplace, indeed you should wait to be called there, and then be obedient and not become too conceited... Receive my blessing, my sons. You Cosimo, be kind to your brother Lorenzo; and you Lorenzo, honour Cosimo as your elder.' And having said all this, he passed away from this life.[9]

Giovanni's advice to 'to wait to be called to the Palazzo della Signoria' was not a warning to his sons to stay out of politics, as is often thought, but rather a caution that they should respect Florence's republican traditions. As Giovanni well knew, the Medici party was about to challenge Rinaldo degli Albizzi and his conservatives for control of the government, hoping to oust the faction that had dominated the palace for the past four decades. By now, the rift between the conservatives and the Medici party had hardened into open hostility, exacerbated by the defection of several more of Albizzi's key allies to the *amici*. As Cosimo reported to Averardo, 'the Knight' – his nickname for Rinaldo, mocking the man's aristocratic pretensions – was losing support: 'let us hope that all will end well,' he wrote with quiet confidence.[10] One of the *amici* told Averardo that he thought Albizzi's supporters, having been 'used to behaving like horses without bridles', now had 'a stubborn bit in their mouths'; fearing that he had said too much, he finished the letter: 'that is enough for now, I will tell you more in person'.[11] Tension began to mount in the city.

---

* Cavalcanti might well have had privileged access to what the dying Giovanni di Bicci said, as he was the nephew of Lorenzo's wife, Ginevra.

In November 1429, Niccolò Soderini, an *amico*, was arrested and charged with attempting to assassinate a leading conservative, Niccolò da Uzzano. The Medici insisted on Soderini's innocence and accused the conservatives of inventing the story for their own ends. The trial was headline news, but the *Signoria*, which was evenly split between the Medici and conservative factions, decided to drop the charges, fearful that the political animosity was about to erupt into larger violence.

The priors were diverted by more pressing matters that month – above all, whether or not to go to war against Lucca. In the rowdy debates in the Palazzo della Signoria, Rinaldo degli Albizzi argued that a short, sharp military strike was all that was required to add this prosperous city to the Florentine dominion. Cosimo and Averardo, by contrast, strongly opposed the war, advocating a more cautious, diplomatic approach; but they were defeated when the motion was put to the vote. On 10 December 1429, the names were announced of those men chosen to serve on the Ten of War council, and, although the result slightly favoured the Medici party, both sides decided to co-operate in the Florentine interest. As Cosimo informed Averardo, 'it is my opinion that whether we approve of this undertaking or not, it has come to the point where the honour of the commune is involved so that we must give it all the support we can'.[12]

The war did not go according to plan. Differences soon emerged between the Ten of War and the commissioners at the army camp outside Lucca, one of whom was Rinaldo degli Albizzi, who had his own ideas about how to proceed and who was reluctant to carry out the orders sent from the Palazzo della Signoria. Worse, Florence's chances of an easy victory were ruined when Filippo Maria Visconti, Duke of Milan, came to the aid of Lucca because he was eager to add Florence to his dominion. Far from being the quick affair promised by Rinaldo, the conflict turned into a long and massively expensive military campaign. Cosimo wrote to Averardo on 21 October 1430 that 'it seems to me that the Lucca affair is not going to turn out as successfully as expected, which I regret'.[13] He also informed his cousin that he had decided not to serve on the Ten of War and advised Averardo to do the same: 'It does not seem a good idea at present, partly to let others serve their term but also because I do not think our city can prosper on account of the party divisions.' The truce between the factions, which had been agreed at the beginning of the campaign, had begun to break down. Evidently, Cosimo was making plans to ensure he would not be associated with the party that had advocated the war and which was responsible for its mismanagement.

On 2 December 1430, news arrived from Lucca that the Florentine army had been heavily defeated by the Milanese. The city was in shock. 'It is no longer a matter of obtaining Lucca,' wrote one citizen, 'but of preserving our own state.'[14] Cosimo and Averardo, however, shrewdly guessed that this disaster could be used to give the Medici party the chance of victory over the conservatives – though they kept their glee at this prospect to themselves. According to one of the *amici*, the cousins believed that 'the way to become great in the city was in times of war, when there was the new business of military supplies and that of helping the government with loans, which were secure and brought

Luca della Robbia, *Cantoria*, *c.*1432, detail (Florence, Museo dell'Opera del Duomo). This elaborate singing gallery was commissioned by the Wool Guild after a ban on public sculptural projects was lifted in the aftermath of the war with Lucca.

huge profits as well as the esteem of the people'.[15] Cosimo and Averardo now expediently threw themselves into the war effort. When the new Ten of War was elected a week later, the names included Cosimo himself and several of the *amici*. And Averardo served as one of the commissioners in charge of supplies for the army, working so hard that his health began to suffer.[16]

The huge costs of the Lucca campaign soon started to escalate beyond what the city could raise through taxation. Over the years 1424–32, the government raised 3,847,461 florins in taxes, and even the very rich were hurting (Palla Strozzi, the wealthiest citizen in the 1427 *catasto*, claimed he was unable to pay his creditors.)[17] The *Signoria* now turned to the city's financiers and set up a committee of bankers to arrange the loans needed to see Florence through the crisis. Many conservatives, disappointed that the short, sharp strike had failed, were now playing the blame game and refused to part with their cash. But the astute Averardo advised Cosimo to co-operate: 'We must not be sparing with our wealth as this might threaten the success of our cause.'[18]

In September 1431, Cosimo began the first of several terms on this committee of bankers, where he served alongside several other prominent *amici*. He was to play a pivotal role in raising short-term loans to tide Florence over the crisis. The extent of his involvement is meticulously recorded in the committee's ledgers.[19] More than 60 per cent of the loans came from wealthy supporters of the Medici party, while Cosimo himself, who had evidently taken Averardo's advice, was the largest contributor. Charging short-term interest rates equivalent to 33 per cent a year, the loans would prove a heavy burden on the Florentine economy but very profitable investments for the Medici bank. Nevertheless, by the end of 1431 even Cosimo was beginning to run out of funds. With his Florence branch in the red, he took the gamble of borrowing money in Venice, at an even higher rate of interest, and using the profits from the Rome branch to cover the shortfall.

Despite his financial problems – indeed, perhaps to prove they did not exist – Cosimo and brother Lorenzo decided to invite the builders into their palace on the Via Larga in January 1432. Along with the original house they had inherited from their father, there were three adjacent properties, which had been rented out, and the brothers now decided to join them all together to create a residence that would accommodate their growing families. Cosimo and Contessina had two sons – Piero, aged fourteen in 1432, and Giovanni aged eleven; Cosimo also had an illegitimate son by his Armenian slave-girl, the two-year-old Carlo, who was being brought up in the palace under Contessina's care. Slaves were common in wealthy Florentine households, and it was not unusual for illegitimate children to be brought up with their legitimate siblings. Lorenzo and his wife Ginevra also had a two-year-old toddler, Pierfrancesco. The refurbished palace provided spacious apartments for the two families, and it was considerably embellished at the rear, where Cosimo and Lorenzo laid out a new garden, ornamented with fountains, fruit trees and roses, along with a well, a terrace and a herb garden.[20]

As for the war, there was welcome news from the camp at Lucca. In June 1432, the Florentine army won a resounding victory at the Battle of San Romano, its first after almost three years of fighting. That summer too, it was evident that Cosimo's shrewd financial gamble was bringing handsome monetary dividends: to date he had loaned the huge sum of 155,887 florins, which accounted for almost a third of Florence's state debt.[21]

The war finally came to an end the following year, with Florence gaining some small territories from Lucca; but the peace treaty, signed on 26 April 1433, marked the beginning of six months of political turmoil in Florence itself. The conflict had been a disaster for Rinaldo degli Albizzi and the conservatives, who were blamed for starting this unpopular campaign, for its mismanagement and for signally failing to contribute their wealth to the cause. The Medici, by contrast, were seen to have opposed the war but then to have risked their personal wealth for the benefit of the republic.

Cosimo judged that a confrontation between the two factions was not far away, and he took careful precautions. On 30 May 1433, just a month after the treaty was signed, he began to transfer large sums of money out of the city.[22] He placed some of the cash (8,877 florins) in the safekeeping of religious orders at San Miniato al Monte and San

Medal of Cosimo de' Medici, late fifteenth century
(London, Victoria & Albert Museum).

Paolo Uccello, *Battle of San Romano*, late 1430s (London, National Gallery), one of a set of three scenes of this landmark battle in the war with Lucca commissioned to decorate the Palazzo Medici.

Marco, sending the rest to his branches in Venice (15,000 florins) and Rome (10,000 florins). In early summer, he took his family out of Florence, moving them to Cafaggiolo, the family estate in the Mugello. On 1 September 1433, a new *Signoria* took office. Four days later, the priors summoned Cosimo to Florence, on the pretext of inviting him to join an advisory council of prominent citizens. But when he arrived at the Palazzo della Signoria on 7 September, instead of being summoned into the *Signoria* chambers as he had expected, he was locked up in a small cell in the palace tower and charged with treason. More specifically, he was charged with causing the war with Lucca for his own profit. Averardo, fortunately for him, was in Pisa, where he managed to evade arrest, while Lorenzo hastily left Florence for the Mugello as soon as he heard of Cosimo's imprisonment: 'had they

A view of the Villa Medici at Cafaggiolo by Justus Utens, late sixteenth century (Florence, Museo di Firenze com'era).

taken all three of us,' Cosimo recorded in his diary, 'it would have been disastrous'.[23]

Cosimo's trial opened later that month. It was soon clear that the prosecuting counsel had a powerful case against him, based on the evidence of lawyer Ser Niccolò Tinucci, an *amico* who had changed sides.[24] Tinucci's statement included accusations that the Medici had been involved in fixing the voting in the Palazzo della Signoria, citing specific examples that implicated not only Cosimo, Lorenzo and Averardo, but also Giovanni di Bicci. Tinucci's most damning evidence concerned the way the Medici had manipulated the war with Lucca to

their financial advantage. He claimed that Averardo and Cosimo had worked behind the scenes to ensure that the campaign had continued as long as possible, and that the taxes imposed to finance the campaign had been designed to beggar their domestic enemies while filling their own coffers. As modern historians have shown, much of Tinucci's evidence against Cosimo was true; however, there is no evidence to support his most outrageous claim: that the Medici used the war to cloak their plans for armed regime change to topple the conservatives in Florence.

Inevitably, Cosimo was found guilty; but there were heated debates in the Palazzo della Signoria as to how he should be punished. Rinaldo degli Albizzi had used vociferous arguments, and large bribes, to try and get his rival condemned for treason, for which the penalty was death. The plan failed, but he did manage to push through sentences of exile on all the male members of the Medici family. Cosimo protested his innocence, with crocodile tears. 'I have not led the life of a villain but that of an honest merchant,' he insisted, proclaiming his loyalty to the republic: 'As I go into exile I leave my heart and my soul with you [and] every trouble will be easy to bear as long as I know that my adversity will bring peace and happiness to the city.'[25] Cosimo and Averardo were banished for ten years, Lorenzo for five, and the entire Medici clan was barred from political office for ten years. An exception was made for Nicola di Vieri, who was currently serving as gonfalonier of the *Signoria*. He had agreed to take the post reluctantly, asking for 'one favour, for God's sake,' that de did 'not have to be present when my relatives are sentenced, so that in the future no one will be able to say that I added my vote to the ruin of my house'.[26]

On 5 October 1433, Cosimo bid farewell to the soldiers of the armed guard that escorted him to the border of the Florentine state. His journey to exile in Venice had more in common with a triumphal progress than an enforced deportation. 'I reached Modena where the governor met me and presented me with gifts on behalf of his lord [the Marquis of Ferrara],' he recorded in his diary.[27] He arrived in Venice on 11 October, to be 'received like an ambassador not like an exile'. Averardo's seventeen-year-old grandson Francesco described how on the next morning Cosimo visited the Doge of Venice, 'who embraced him warmly, and greatly lamented his misfortune,' adding with boyish enthusiasm: 'I am hardly able to describe the friendly affection which all these citizens have extended to him, and to all our house.'[28] Later that month, the Venetian republic offered concrete proof of its good-will by sending an envoy to ask the *Signoria* to lift the sentences of exile. The ambassador was received politely, but his request was turned down, as was an appeal in November from Averardo, now sixty years old and too ill to travel, who was asking for more time to reach his own place of exile, Naples. Averardo was coldly refused.

Cosimo intended to use the period of exile well. In fact, it would soon be evident that this shrewd politician had engineered his exile for his own advantage. Thanks to his foresight, most of his wealth was safe, he had the goodwill of the Venetian republic, and, above all, back home the *amici* remained loyal. He judiciously kept out of Florentine politics and refused to be drawn into any of the conspiracies to secure his return. In public, he was vigilant in maintaining a strict show of loyalty to the *Signoria*; in private he cautioned both family and friends to be patient.

5

FOR HONOUR
AND PROFIT
Cosimo the banker
1434–1450

Cosimo di Giovanni (45)
Contessina de' Bardi (38), *his wife*

> Piero (18) *and* Giovanni (13), *their sons*

Lorenzo di Giovanni (39), *Cosimo's brother*
Ginevra Cavalcanti, *his wife*

> Pierfrancesco (4), *their son*

Averardo di Francesco (61), *Cosimo's first cousin*

> Giuliano (38), *his son*

> Francesco (19), *his grandson*

Cosimo di Giovanni had the gift of patience. After he, and his relatives, had headed into exile, the conservatives in Florence were jubilant, and in the Palazzo della Signoria the victors discussed how to cripple the Medici party. There were wild schemes for mass assassinations, and more practical ones for mass banishment. In the end, however, little was done to dismantle the Medici network, a decision that would prove to be a serious miscalculation.[1] Just one of the *amici*, Agnolo Acciaiuoli, was exiled in February 1434, on the trumped-up charge of communicating prohibited information to Cosimo – though, as Cosimo pointed out, Acciaiuoli's letters were 'in truth not of any importance, certainly not important enough for exile'.[2] And the celebrations soon flagged when realization dawned that banishing some of the Medici had done little to weaken their power-base in the city. That spring, rumours began to circulate that the *amici* were planning a coup, and the *Signoria* announced a night-time curfew across the city to stop clandestine meetings. Rinaldo degli Albizzi and his ally, Palla Strozzi, secretly approached foreign mercenaries with a view to securing their aid in the event of such an attack.[3] In public, at least, Rinaldo and his allies were still in power, but in private they were worried; the *amici*, by contrast, were growing in confidence.

In late August 1434, the moment came for which Cosimo and his supporters had all been waiting – the election of a *Signoria* with a majority of Medici partisans. When one of Rinaldo's key allies died a few days later, the manager of the Florence branch of the Medici bank informed Cosimo that 'people are now saying that God has paid [Rinaldo] back for how he behaved to you and the rest of your family'.[4] For three weeks, the new *Signoria* kept the city in suspense. Finally, on 20 September, the priors summoned Rinaldo to the palace and informed him that the government intended 'to restore those who had been banished' and 'to rectify many other injuries which have been committed'.[5] Somewhat rashly, Albizzi decided to force the issue.

On the afternoon of Sunday 26 September 1434, a large mob of conservative supporters attempted to storm the Palazzo della Signoria; but the *amici* had been forewarned and had surrounded the building with their own guards. The tension on the streets was palpable. With Florence on the verge of civil war, Palla Strozzi decided to put his loyalty to the republic before the factional interests of Rinaldo's regime. He instructed his men to lay down their arms. The coup collapsed after

Rinaldo fled to the sanctuary of Santa Maria Novella. There, Eugenius IV, who had succeeded Martin V in 1431, was temporarily in residence, and he persuaded Rinaldo to withdraw. The pope's decision to back the Medici at this crucial stage was no coincidence. Having been forced to flee from a hostile Rome that summer, he needed the resources of the Medici bank to restore his authority on the papal throne; and he knew that Cosimo's gold would not be forthcoming if he missed this chance to do a favour for his bankers.

On the following morning, 27 September, the *Signoria* declared Rinaldo degli Albizzi and his supporters to be rebels and exiled them for attempting to overthrow the legally elected government. By an odd coincidence that day was the feast of the miracle-working doctors Cosmas and Damian, and Cosimo's forty-fifth birthday. The news of Albizzi's downfall travelled fast to Venice, where Cosimo was just as swift in his reaction. He ordered his private army – 'more than 3,000 men from the Mugello, the Alps and the Romagna' as he noted in his diary – under the command of a distant cousin, Papi de' Medici, to march on Florence.[6] Two days later, on 29 September, the *Signoria* summoned a *parlamento*, a general meeting of the Florentine electorate, to ratify its decision to banish Rinaldo degli Albizzi and recall the Medici. By the time the vote took place on the Piazza della Signoria, the city was swarming with Medici soldiers. Cosimo evidently was taking no risks as to its outcome, and he was able to return home in triumph on 6 October.

Cosimo was to prove brutal in the way he enforced his authority in Florence. Over the next few months, the Albizzi regime was totally dismantled with a ruthlessness that the conservatives had failed to show the previous autumn when they decided against breaking up the Medici party. Among those punished with the Albizzi family were many of the oldest Florentine clans, including the Peruzzi and the Strozzi, though the decision to banish Palla Strozzi, whose selfless action had stopped civil war, was very unpopular. Some ninety men and their families were exiled; another eighty were fined and stripped of their political rights.

In addition to this decisive action against his opponents, Cosimo secured his hold on power by openly subverting the ideals of the republic. Henceforth, Cosimo himself would take charge of choosing the names that went into the leather purses for election to the *Signoria* and other important offices of state – he justified this draconian manipulation of the electoral process on the grounds of the threat to state security posed by the war between Milan and Florence's ally, Venice. It came as no surprise in late December 1434 when Cosimo himself was elected as gonfalonier of the *Signoria*, for the second term of the new regime.

Cosimo and his inner circle now dominated all decisions made in the Palazzo della Signoria. However, during the course of 1434 – an eventful year in Medici history – he had also lost two of his closest advisers. Averardo, who had done so much to establish the party in the 1420s, had been too ill to travel to Florence when the amnesty was announced in October, and he died in Venice on 5 December. Averardo's son Giuliano had predeceased him by a few months, dying in Rome during the summer. Of Cosimo's remaining allies, most of the closest had proved their loyalty in the years before exile – men like Alamanno Salviati, who was Averardo's son-in-law, Agnolo Acciaiuoli, and Luca Pitti, who had been one of the priors in the *Signoria* to vote for Cosimo's return in September.

The coup brought many new faces to political prominence, too. Andrea de' Pazzi, for example, was one of several pro-Medici magnates to be given the right to hold political office; he underlined his loyalty to the Medici by building a chapter house at Santa Croce that bore a striking resemblance to the sacristy at San Lorenzo built by Cosimo's father, Giovanni di Bicci. Another was the builder Puccio Pucci, who put away his tools and took up business, moving dramatically up the social scale when he joined the prestigious Bankers' Guild in the autumn of 1434. Pucci was an example of a trend. The historian Francesco Guicciardini, whose own great-grandfather was one of the *amici*, recorded how Cosimo established his regime by promoting 'many men of low status to replace [the exiles]', and that 'when he was warned that it was unwise to get rid of so many patricians because Florence would suffer by lacking these well-born men, he replied that a few lengths of expensive cloth would fill the city with patricians again, by which he meant that it only took honours and riches to make lowly men into nobles'.[7]

Cosimo was to become one of the pillars of the Medici myth, a man whose image as a benevolent patriarchal leader has been deftly crafted down the centuries. His humanist contemporaries, in the rhetorical style of the time, praised him as a Roman republican statesman whose greatest virtues were prudence and patriotism – and the parallels with Cicero, who also endured exile before a triumphant return, did not go unnoticed. But what do we really know about him? He was a shrewd banker and a devious politician, who could be ruthless when necessary. By all accounts he was also a devoted family man, fond of Contessina and their children, even tolerant of the way his wife fussed over him during his frequent attacks of gout. He enjoyed parties, celebrating the feast day of his patron saints, Cosmas and Damian, with

The Chapter House of the Basilica of Santa Croce, Florence, begun after 1442.

THE FAMILY MEDICI

a dinner for family and friends, to which he also invited his servants and bank employees. He pruned his own vines every February, played chess after supper and evidently read the books that he had started to amass in his youth. He marked passages that caught his eye – on the analogies between managing a family and a state, for example, or on the evils of envy – with the same mark, three dots arranged in a fancy triangle, which the managers of his bank used to authenticate financial documents.[8] 'He was more cultured than merchants usually are,' conceded a later pope, Pius II.[9]

The exile of Cosimo and Lorenzo had done little to dent the success of their bank, which reported profits of 186,382 florins over the fifteen years from 1420 to 1435.[10] Still holding the papal account, it was the Rome branch that continued to prove the most lucrative area of the business, securing 62 per cent of the total profits. The years following Cosimo's exile saw the bank expand its operations north of the Alps. He opened a branch in Basel to take advantage of the Church council that was meeting in that city, and another in Bruges, with a sub-office in London.[11] The manager of the Bruges operation had a broad portfolio: in addition to his financial responsibilities, he was instructed to buy tapestries and horses for the Italian market, to find boy sopranos for the papal choir at San Giovanni in Laterano in Rome, and to search for manuscripts of classical texts in the monastic libraries of northern Europe to furnish Cosimo's own book collection.[12] Most importantly, though, the international branches of the Medici bank functioned as centres of intelligence-gathering, sending political news and gossip back to Cosimo in Florence.

In 1436, Cosimo opened a branch of the bank at Ancona, a small but prosperous port on the Adriatic with trading links to the eastern Mediterranean. Unlike the other new branches, this one did not have a commercial basis; rather, it was a deliberate and high-risk investment in the notoriously fickle world of international politics. It was set up with the unusually large capital of 20,000 ducats. The Venetian branch of the bank; commercially far more important than that of Ancona had been set up with capital of just 8,000 ducats - and; moreover; its manager was authorized to lend directly to Ancona's ruler, Count Francesco Sforza, who was given a very generous overdraft limit of 3,000 ducats.[13] Sforza, the holder of several papal fiefs in northern Italy, was a formidably talented mercenary soldier and ambitious for power. With

Bonifacio Bembo, *Francesco Sforza*, c.1460 (Milan, Pinacoteca di Brera).

Cosimo as his financier, he now had access to the money necessary to achieve his goals. The count and the banker formed what would prove to be one of the most audacious partnerships of the century. For the present, however, it was essential that their alliance remained a secret affair.

The politics behind the plan were complex. Milan and Venice were currently at war in northern Italy, and both Florence and Rome had been drawn into the conflict on the Venetian side to protect their borders from the advance of the armies of Milan's Duke Filippo Maria Visconti. From Cosimo's point of view, the situation was complicated by the fact that Rinaldo degli Albizzi and other exiles were fighting alongside the Milanese in the hope of securing military aid to challenge the Medici party's dominance in Florence. However, the success of Cosimo's partnership with Sforza depended on the count maintaining good relations with Duke Filippo Maria, who had bought Sforza's loyalty by betrothing him to his illegitimate daughter, Bianca Maria. The formal marriage contract had been signed in 1432 – Sforza had been thirty-one years old, his bride just a month short of her seventh birthday – and, as the duke had no sons, the unspoken subtext of the match was that Sforza would become his heir. Provided, of course, that the marriage took place. The duke was adept at using the threat of preventing the marriage to keep the count's allegiance: as Sforza explained to Cosimo in 1438, affectionately addressing the banker as 'my dearest father', he was unable to agree to a particular course of action against the duke, who 'has sent me instructions in duplicate saying he will never give me Madonna Bianca nor anything else I desire from him'.[14] It was to be another three years before Duke Filippo Maria finally gave his permission for the marriage to take place, enabling Cosimo and Sforza to make plans for the next stage of their campaign.

In the meantime, Cosimo was also polishing his relationship with Pope Eugenius IV, whose authority had been challenged by the Council of Basel. In response, the pope opened the Council of Ferrara in 1438, to begin negotiations for union between the Western and Orthodox churches. This was an international conference on a grand scale. Among the guests were the Patriarch of Constantinople and the Greek emperor, John Palaeologus, as well as many Greek churchmen. As the pope's banker, Cosimo was also present, with his two sons Piero and Giovanni, who were currently both employed in their father's company. But the seventeen-year-old Giovanni was unhappy in Ferrara, where the summers were notoriously humid. On 6 June his mother, Contessina, chided him: 'you should be glad to be there, not least to be working in the bank and learning the business' and advised him to 'be careful to keep cool'.[15] She went on to worry about her husband: 'I do not know why Cosimo has not asked me to send his summer clothes, but I think he is hoping to return any day now; do your best to please him in all things, and see that he has all he needs.' A month or so later, plague broke out in Ferrara, and Cosimo sent his sons home. By the middle of October they were staying with their uncle and aunt, Lorenzo and Ginevra, at one of the Medici properties in the Mugello, where Piero asked his mother to send his cloak lined with lynx fur, for cold weather was the problem now. Contessina warned Piero, now twenty-two years old, to be on his best behaviour: 'I am sure you are all very busy there, particularly Ginevra, so make sure you help her in any way you can, and keep your own things tidy and don't leave one thing here and another there, and tell my other son to do the same.' Evidently, a mother's preoccupations do not change much across the centuries.[16]

The plague, and the threat posed by marauding Milanese troops in the area, gave Cosimo the excuse he needed to persuade Eugenius IV to move the council from Ferrara to Florence.* He offered the impoverished pope tempting financial inducements too, promising to arrange for the Florentine government to cover the cost of accommodation for the Greek delegates. Hosting the council was a prestigious coup for Florence; but the shrewd banker also knew that he would personally make a handsome profit on the loans the republic would need to cover its expenses. In December 1438, the *Signoria* sent Cosimo's brother Lorenzo to Ferrara to negotiate the details: 'should His Holiness ask for anything particular for the Greeks, you are to answer that we will willingly provide houses for them without demanding any rent,' ran Lorenzo's official orders, but 'if money for the maintenance of the Greeks is mentioned,' he was cautioned, 'you are to say that the republic is very short of funds because of the war' and only 'if absolutely necessary that we are ready to lend His Holiness the said amount of 1,500 florins a month'.[17]

---

* It is therefore often referred to by historians as the Council of Ferrara–Florence.

On 27 January 1439, Eugenius IV arrived at the gates of Florence to be met by Cosimo who, as gonfalonier, had the honour of welcoming him. Cosimo, of course, had deliberately arranged for his election to this post for the January–February term in order to perform this role, with all the appearance of a head of state. He also welcomed the Patriarch of Constantinople and Emperor John Palaeologus when they arrived in early February. The council lasted for more than four months, coming to an end on 6 July when Eugenius IV issued the bull *Laetentur coeli* ('Let the Heavens Rejoice') announcing the union between the Western and Orthodox churches. It was an impressive achievement, though one of very brief duration. Cosimo's own achievement was more substantial. Thanks to his shrewd commercial manoeuvring, the papal branch of his bank made almost 14,400 florins in profit that year, twice its usual amount and largely the result of the extra business of the council. He marked the occasion by commissioning a new a fresco in the sacristy built by his father at San Lorenzo; painted in the vault over the altar, it showed an astronomical configuration of the date of the papal bull.[18]

Like Giovanni di Bicci before him, Cosimo spent liberally at San Lorenzo, where renovation work had begun in 1416. When the project faltered a few years later, through lack of funds, Cosimo offered to take over responsibility for the nave, choir and main chapel: 'he pledged himself to complete that section of the building within six years out of the fortunes God had granted him, at his own expense'.[19] Cosimo also donated 900 florins to provide a service every Monday for the soul of his father, and he completed the tomb in the centre of the sacristy where his parents were buried.[20] But Cosimo's account with God required expenditure beyond the confines of his parish church. The Medici family emblem was balls, *palle* in Italian, and the word carried the same anatomical overtones as it does today. Now, sharp-eyed Florentines were quick to notice it proliferating in churches across the city – in the new dormitories at Santa Croce, for example, or on the costly reliquary Cosimo donated to Santa Maria degli Angeli. Nor did they miss the chapels dedicated to the Medici saints, Cosmas and Damian, in Santa Croce, San Marco and the Baptistery.[21]

Cosimo was one of the most prolific patrons of art in fifteenth-century Italy, and it is true that he commissioned many seminal works of the Italian Renaissance. However, the claim that Florence was the cradle of the Renaissance is a fiction; part of the Medici myth created in the sixteenth century to enhance the family name – a myth that has overshadowed the significant contributions made to this important cultural movement by the churches and other religious institutions; rulers of Milan, Mantua, Ferrara, Venice, Urbino, Rome and Naples. Moreover, Cosimo's motives for artistic patronage were not primarily aesthetic. Far more compelling for him were his Christian beliefs and his very real fear of Hell. Most of his projects were commissioned for church buildings, and he meticulously recorded this expenditure in a ledger entitled 'God's Account'.[22] Eugenius IV explicitly gave him permission to atone for his sins by taking over patronage of the Dominican convent of San Marco in Florence – and the words of the papal bull granting the banker absolution were carved on the convent door.[23] Cosimo provided the convent with a new church, cells for the friars, cloisters, a refectory and a splendid library, to which he donated many valuable manuscripts. He also paid for a lavishly gilded altarpiece for the high altar, painted by one of the convent's friars, Fra Angelico, in which the Medici saints Cosmas and Damian were prominently on display.

Elsewhere in Florence, Cosimo used his political influence to initiate the renovation of Santissima Annunziata, encouraging many of his supporters to buy chapels in the new church. It housed a miracle-working image of the Annunciation, the fame of which had spread far beyond the walls of Florence to become a popular cult that did much to enhance the reputation of the city. The interior of the church must have been an awesome sight. Hanging from the ceiling and lying all over the floor were pieces of broken armour, statuettes of horses, wax models of limbs and eyes, all ex-voto images sent to the Virgin in gratitude for answering the prayers of thousands in their hour of need – in battle, in storms at sea, in childbirth, and on sick beds. Most spectacular of all were the quantities of life-size statues, modelled in wax and made even more realistic by the addition of human hair (the craftsmen who made these images had their own workshop in the convent). The miracle-working image itself was set in an ostentatiously expensive tabernacle, commissioned by Cosimo's son Piero: 'the

Fra Angelico, *San Marco altarpiece*, *c.*1438 (Florence, Museo di San Marco).
Commissioned by Cosimo shortly after his return from exile, the copious amount of gold
was visible evidence of his immense wealth. Kneeling prominently in the foreground are
the Medici patron saints, Cosmas and Damian, the former looking out of the painting to
remind us who paid for the work.

marble alone cost 4,000 florins,' ran its boastful inscription.

The enormous cost of settling Cosimo's account with God was a direct reflection of the profits that continued to pour into the coffers of the Medici bank under his leadership. By 1450, the company had branches in Rome, Venice, Geneva, Bruges, London, Avignon, Basel and Ancona, as well as investments in silk and wool factories in Florence. The bank reported profits of 104,370 florins for the six years 1435–41, rising to 186,420 florins in the ten years 1442–51, with the Rome and Venice branches accounting for over half the total.[24] But ownership of the company changed after the unexpected death in September 1440 of Cosimo's brother Lorenzo, at the age of just forty-five. Cosimo buried his much-loved sibling in San Lorenzo and took over guardianship of Lorenzo's only son, Pierfrancesco. The ten-year-old boy was now assigned his father's half-share in the Medici bank. However, until his twenty-first birthday, he could receive only the interest on the capital, which he loaned to Cosimo at 5 per cent, and Pierfrancesco was not allowed to take a share in its burgeoning profits, something that was to cause problems in years to come.[25] The immense wealth of the family increased three years later, when Averardo's grandson, Francesco, died at the age of just twenty-seven. With no sons to follow him, the line descending from Giovanni di Bicci's brother was now extinct – and all its property, which included extensive estates in the Mugello, passed to Cosimo and Pierfrancesco.[26]

Meanwhile, Cosimo had the future of his own family to consider. He was bringing up his two legitimate sons to follow him into politics and commerce, Piero as the future head of the Medici party and Giovanni as the head of the Medici bank. His illegitimate son Carlo was earmarked for a career in the Church, and, thanks to Cosimo's influence at the papal court, he was appointed as canon of Florence cathedral. In 1444, Cosimo arranged for Piero, now aged twenty-eight, to marry the seventeen-year-old Lucrezia, daughter of Francesco Tornabuoni, one of Cosimo's closest friends and political allies, bringing a dowry of 1,200 florins.[27] Lucrezia was a delightful addition to the family. Clever, well-educated, lively and affectionate, she would prove an excellent wife for the rather dour Piero and a loving mother to their children – seven in all, of whom only four survived into adulthood.[28] Cosimo reinforced this kinship tie by giving a job in the Rome branch of the bank to Lucrezia's brother Giovanni Tornabuoni, and by arranging the marriage of her sister Dianora to another member of his inner circle, the recently widowed Tommaso Soderini.

It was also time to rethink the family home and Cosimo decided to build a new residence next door to the Casa Vecchia, which now became the property of Pierfrancesco. Cosimo began acquiring properties from his neighbours and then, to the surprise of many, cleared the site before building afresh. Even wealthy citizens usually took the cheaper option of renovating their collection of houses to suit their needs and fronting them with a new facade. But Cosimo decided on a grander statement.

The building work started in 1445, and under the watchful eyes of neighbours the new palace slowly started to take shape. It was slightly larger than other palaces in the city, but not markedly so, as befitted Cosimo's position as first citizen of the republic rather than its ruler. 'One must be careful not to go beyond the proper bounds in expense and display,' as Cosimo's favourite author, Cicero, advised.[29] There was no doubt about the ownership though – the facade was plastered with family emblems, notably the Medici *palle*, carved on every window and even on the metal torch-holders set into the stone facade. This new Palazzo Medici standing next door to the Casa Vecchia created, together, a massive Medici block along Via Larga, providing visual proof of the family's pre-eminence in Florentine society.

Among the many priorities demanding Cosimo's attentions, domestic and international, was the situation of Count Francesco Sforza. His expectation of being named the Duke of Milan's heir was strengthened in 1444, when his young wife Bianca Maria Visconti gave birth to a healthy son, Galeazzo Maria. Two years later, with the duke's health visibly deteriorating, Piero underlined his father's alliance with the count by naming his own first child 'Bianca' after Sforza's wife. A succession crisis was now looming. In April 1446, Piero's wife Lucrezia was at the baths of Petriolo, south of Siena, regaining her strength in the warm sulphur springs when her husband sent news that Sforza and Bianca Maria had had a second child, a daughter named Ippolita. Lucrezia reassured her husband of her own convalescence ('do not give way to melancholy, for I shall return cured');[30] but she worried about

Bianca Maria, for childbirth was a dangerous affair, in particular the post-partum threat of puerperal fever, which was often fatal. The death of Sforza's wife at this point would jeopardize the Medicis' long-term plans regarding the duchy of Milan: 'I leave you to imagine how much I pray to God that she may continue to improve,' Lucrezia told Piero, 'as you, I and her husband all wish.'

Duke Filippo Maria finally died on 13 August 1447, having named Francesco Sforza as his heir. But, as the count and Cosimo had anticipated, Sforza's succession was far from guaranteed. On the day after the duke's death, the Milanese themselves took power, establishing the 'Ambrosian Republic' – named after St Ambrose, patron saint of Milan. Moreover, the Venetians now made plans to take advantage of Milan's vulnerability to expand their authority on the north Italian mainland. The new republic, although suspicious of Sforza's motives, agreed to appoint him as captain-general of the Milanese army, which was soon in action against the Venetians. The following spring, Sforza inflicted a heavy defeat on the Venetians at Caravaggio, before moving on to attack the city of Brescia.

As Niccolò Machiavelli later explained, in his history of Florence, the Venetians now made Sforza a devious offer, worthy of Machiavelli himself: 'The Venetians knew that the Milanese did not trust the count, and that the count did not want to be Captain-General of Milan but Lord of Milan'; so they 'decided to make peace with the count and offered him aid to conquer Milan, knowing that when the Milanese saw how the count had deceived them, they would be so enraged that they would prefer anyone rather than him' and would 'be forced to fall into the lap of the Venetians'.[31]

Sforza accepted the Venetian offer, only to discover that his new masters were also secretly negotiating peace with the Milanese. It was now that his partnership with Cosimo began to pay real dividends. As Machiavelli related, Sforza:

> … immediately requested help from Florence, both from the public purse and private friends, notably from Cosimo de' Medici, who had always been his close ally and had given him trustworthy advice and support in all his enterprises; and Cosimo did not abandon him in his hour of need but helped him generously from his own pocket and inspired him to continue the fight.[32]

In late 1449, reinforced by generous sums from the Medici bank, Sforza and his troops laid siege to Milan.

In February 1450, with the campaign in the balance, Cosimo fell ill with gout. Piero and Lucrezia had taken their three children – Bianca, her two-year-old sister Nannina (named after Cosimo's mother) and their one-year-old brother Lorenzo (named in memory of Cosimo's brother) to one of the family castles in the Mugello. On 6 February, Contessina brought reassuring news for son Piero, along with some domestic details: 'I am sending you a haunch of venison, a hare and a kid… and the capers… tell Lucrezia that the child's frock will be relined and that she will have it on Monday and that she must encourage the baby [Lorenzo] to suck… Cosimo is well though his knee was a little painful this morning, a touch of the gout but it will get better soon as the pain is so slight.'[33]

But Cosimo's gout did not improve as quickly as Contessina had hoped. A week or so later, she wrote to her other son, Giovanni, who was in Rome, to say that 'Cosimo has continual fever as he had when you left' and that 'one can never be sure what may happen from one day to the next'.[34] She worried about the plague in Rome too, for 'had Cosimo known that the plague was there he would never have let you leave'. Cosimo himself wrote to Giovanni on 28 February with news of Sforza's campaign. 'Milan is surrounded so that no supplies can enter,' he reported, 'and any attempt to send food into Milan must be made from the hills through places that he is guarding so there would be fighting; they say Milan is in dire straits.'[35] The Milanese were indeed suffering – starving and dying – but Sforza was about to crush the city. On 11 March he was installed as ruler.

On 25 March, the Feast of the Annunciation, Duke Francesco Sforza made his formal entry into Milan, the capital of his new duchy. He was now one of the most powerful ruling princes on the Italian peninsula. He commissioned a wax statue of himself for Santissima Annunziata in Florence, in gratitude to the Virgin for his conquest of Milan and in acknowledgement of his debt to Cosimo. Later that year, Piero was chosen by the *Signoria* as one of the ambassadors sent to Milan to congratulate the new duke. The Florentine embassy 'proceeded in triumph through Milanese territory and all their expenses were paid,' wrote an eye-witness, 'and the duke in person advanced to meet them, and embraced and kissed them; never was greater honour paid to Florentine ambassadors'.[36] In the business-speak of the day, Cosimo had used his wealth for *honore e utile* ('honour and profit'), though the two goals were not always easy to distinguish.[37] With Cosimo's gold and influence, the Florentine republic had gained the kudos of an international summit with the Council of Florence, and it had acquired a powerful new ally when Cosimo financed the coup to install Sforza in Milan. But the real winners, of course, were the Medici themselves.

6

THE
REPUBLICAN
TOGA

Cosimo the politician

1450–1464

THE MEDICI IN 1451

Cosimo di Giovanni (62)
Contessina de' Bardi (55), *his wife*

Piero (35), *Cosimo's eldest son*
Lucrezia Tornabuoni (24), *his wife*

    Bianca (6) *and* Nannina (3), *their daughters*

    Lorenzo (2), *their son*

    Giovanni (30), *Cosimo's younger son*

    Pierfrancesco di Lorenzo (21), *Cosimo's nephew*

When asked in around 1460 by Pope Pius II what he thought of Florence, the Bishop of Orte replied that 'it was a pity such a beautiful woman did not have a husband.'[1] 'Yes,' retorted the pope, 'but she has a lover.'

He meant Cosimo de' Medici, and his choice of metaphor wittily demonstrated the ambiguities of Cosimo's position. For Pius II, Cosimo was 'not so much a private citizen as lord of his city' and 'king in all but name'. Dealing with the republic was no easy task for men accustomed to the absolute power of princes. 'Popular governments are alien and different,' explained Duke Francesco Sforza's ambassador in Florence, so 'if you would have one thing done rather than another, write privately to Cosimo and he will arrange it for you.'[2] In the eyes of foreigners, and in his own eyes too, Cosimo was the *ruler* of Florence. But this reality was unacceptable to his supporters, so he had to be careful to wear the republican toga in public and to ensure that they believed the lie that they were equal partners in the regime.

Art provided Cosimo with a useful tool to promote this fiction of shared power. In the great hall of the Palazzo Medici there was a cycle of paintings depicting the labours of Hercules – 'the giant who destroyed tyrants and evil lords', as one fifteenth-century historian explained. Hercules was one of the heroes of the republic, and it was his image, carrying his knotted club and the skin of the Nemean lion, that was embossed on the city's official seal.[3] Also prominently on display at the palace were two bronze statues by Donatello, both depicting popular biblical images of liberation from the yoke of tyranny. One was the young David standing over the severed head of the giant Goliath, a choice that consciously imitated a marble David by the same artist in the audience chamber of the Palazzo della Signoria. The other bronze showed Judith, who rescued the Hebrews from oppression by seducing Holofernes before cutting off his head. Each was ornamented with an inscription proclaiming Cosimo's loyalty to the republic; the one on Judith read: 'Kingdoms fall through luxury, cities rise by virtues, behold the neck of pride severed by the hand of humility.'[4] The fact that both statues were of bronze had its own significance, for bronze-casting was an extremely expensive process, affordable only by the very rich.

Cosimo was very rich indeed. The *catasto* returns of 1457 assessed his wealth at 122,669 florins, making him the wealthiest man in the city by some considerable margin.[5] And it would have been greater still had he not indulged in some creative accounting by asking the manager of the Venice branch of the bank to draw up an entirely fraudulent balance sheet that halved the capital invested.[6] Even so, his tax assessment of 576 florins was more than four times the amount paid by the second-largest contributor (132 florins). This second sum, too, was testimony to the success of the Medici bank: it was paid by the heirs of Giovanni de' Benci, the general manager of the company.

Cosimo and Contessina moved into the Palazzo Medici around 1457 with their two sons Piero and Giovanni and the illegitimate Carlo. Their nephew Pierfrancesco remained in the Casa Vecchia next door, though the two households continued to operate as a single unit for tax purposes. Cosimo actively encouraged Piero and Giovanni to play a prominent role in Florentine public life by serving on the civic committees responsible for various state, guild and parish projects, and he secured Carlo's future with the position of Dean of Prato. Piero, who was destined to inherit his father's political mantle, played an active role in Cosimo's inner circle. He was elected to the *Signoria* for the first time in 1448 just two years after his thirtieth birthday, the age at which he became eligible for political office. When Pope Eugenius IV was succeeded by Nicholas V in 1447, Piero was one of the ambassadors sent to Rome by the *Signoria* to congratulate the new pope on his election; and Giovanni, who was destined for the bank, fulfilled the same role eleven years later, when Nicholas V was succeeded in turn by Calixtus III.

Piero and Giovanni were highly cultured, keen musicians and involved in the commissioning of artworks that decorated the Palazzo Medici. Like Cosimo, they were patrons of humanism and collected ancient manuscripts. They also commissioned, from Mino da Fiesole, *all'antica* portrait busts, early examples of this distinctive genre inspired by the art of Ancient Rome. As Cosimo himself liked to say, Florence was 'a city of commerce, literature and leisure', and it became more so after 1453, when Constantinople fell to the Turkish armies of Sultan Mehmet II, causing many Greek scholars to seek refuge in Florence, where they enhanced the city's growing reputation as a centre of learning.[7]

The Palazzo Medici was a lively family home. With Piero and his wife Lucrezia Tornabuoni were their two daughters, Bianca and

Nannina, and two younger sons, Lorenzo and Giuliano, the latter born in 1453. Piero also had an illegitimate daughter, Maria, whose birth date is not known, but she was brought up with her half-siblings. Also in the palace was Piero's younger brother Giovanni, with his wife, Ginevra degli Alessandri (daughter of another Medici partisan) and their baby son, named Cosimino.

Contessina was a hands-on grandmother, who took charge of Cosimino when Ginevra went to the baths at Petriolo to recover her health, a year after his birth. 'Dearest daughter,' she wrote to her, 'your boy is well, he has cut two teeth and is getting used to the nurses,' and 'we look after him night and day.'[8] Piero's boys soon started their humanist education, and in 1458 Lucrezia could report to her husband that 'Lorenzo is learning the verses his tutor has given him and then he teaches them to Giuliano,' adding affectionately that 'it seems a thousand years since we saw you'.[9] A few years later, Lorenzo's tutor reported to Piero on the thirteen-year-old's progress: 'we are well advanced in Ovid and also in Justinian, four books of history and stories, and you need not ask how much he delights in these studies,' noting indulgently that the boy's 'behaviour is excellent and he is very obedient'.[10]

The Medici parents and children alike lived in considerable comfort. Cosimo recorded that he had some fifty servants, including four slaves as well as the nursemaids and tutors needed for the children.[11] There were expensive gold and silver plates and fine linen napkins on their dining-table, and costly Flemish tapestries, supplied by the manager of the Bruges branch of the bank, on the walls. The family attended mass in their own private chapel, which was lavishly decorated with gilded frescoes by Benozzo Gozzoli depicting the Journey of the Magi – in which the family's own portraits mingled with those of many political supporters among the riders in this superb cavalcade. They slept in luxurious beds decorated with their coat of arms and hung with silk. The expensive brocaded coats lined with fur, velvet dresses embroidered with pearls, gilded belts and purses belonging to Piero and Giovanni and their wives suggest that this younger generation of Medici were fashion icons of the time.[12] They may not have been noble; but the resources of the bank enabled the Medici to adopt the trappings of aristocracy.

Donatello, *David*, 1430s (Florence, Bargello).

The Medici bank witnessed several changes during the 1450s. In 1452, Cosimo opened a branch in Milan, to the mutual benefit of himself and Duke Francesco Sforza. The loans made to Sforza helped to stabilize his new regime, while the sales of luxury goods to his court brought handsome returns – almost half of the profits of the Milan branch came from silks, velvets, damasks, jewellery and tapestries purchased by other branches of the bank that were sold in Milan with a hefty mark-up.[13]

The biggest change at the bank, though, took place the year before, in 1451, when Cosimo's nephew Pierfrancesco came of age and took control of his father's half-share of the company. On 25 March of that year, Cosimo formed a new partnership, passing his own holding to his two sons. This was not exactly retirement, since, despite his increasingly frequent attacks of gout, Cosimo remained very much in charge. When Giovanni de' Benci died in July 1455, Cosimo appointed his son Giovanni, now thirty-four years old, as the bank's new general manager. Giovanni was in Milan at the time with Alfonso of Calabria, heir to the King of Naples, but his father ordered him back to Florence in peremptory style: 'As I have already told you… I do not want you to continue to accompany the Duke of Calabria; we will lose more than we can gain by this and you have already done quite enough by accompanying him this far and you must come home.'[14]

The division of the bank between these three grandsons of Giovanni di Bicci was legal and proper; but it had ramifications for the Medici family. Pierfrancesco, an only son, now owned 50 per cent of the business, while Piero and Giovanni had to be content with just 25 per cent each. The family property also had to be divided between the two branches by a panel of independent arbitrators.[15] Cosimo and his sons were assigned the Palazzo Medici as well as the estates of Cafaggiolo in the Mugello and Careggi near Florence, while Pierfrancesco received the Casa Vecchia and the Mugello estate at Trebbio. With his extensive landholdings and his half-share of the bank, the twenty-one-year-old Pierfrancesco was a very wealthy young man.

Pierfrancesco married in May 1456, and the bride chosen for him by Cosimo was Laudomia Acciaiuoli, the daughter of Cosimo's close friend and ally Angelo Acciaiuoli. Pierfrancesco's preference for a life of idle pleasure at Trebbio and lack of interest in a more productive career exasperated his new father-in-law. 'You have reached the age

Mino da Fiesole, *Giovanni de' Medici*, late 1450s (Florence, Bargello).

when you should be learning some skills and you should not waste time,' Acciaiuoli wrote four months after the wedding, counselling Pierfrancesco that 'adopting the habits of your family will bring you honour and profit, and take you away from this way of life.'[16] The following spring, Acciaiuoli wrote again to his son-in-law, urging him to keep in close contact with Cosimo: 'you don't make as much effort with him as I would like, nor do you try to learn from him as you need to do,' adding that Pierfrancesco needed 'to spend as much time as you can with him while he is still alive'.[17]

Although Cosimo was still widely respected for his commercial prowess, his political activities were less highly regarded. There was growing uneasiness about the way his lieutenants manipulated the electoral process in Florence and even evidence of a split emerging over the issue within the Medici party itself. The chronicler Giovanni Cavalcanti described the system with venom: these 'ten tyrants' with 'such loathsome power,' he raged, 'decide who is to be chosen for high offices even before the names are drawn in public'.[18] It was fraud in his opinion, and unworthy of the republic. He was also scathing about the size of the Palazzo Medici, 'which will make the Colosseum in Rome look futile', and about the fortune that Cosimo was making from government loans, which had to be repaid through taxes on ordinary citizens. 'Who wouldn't build so grandly if they could spend money that did not belong to them?', he asked sarcastically.[19] Others made more colourful protests: one night Cosimo's doorstep was covered with blood, so much of it that Cavalcanti believed it had to be the work of a member of the Butchers' Guild.[20]

Characteristically, Cosimo took decisive action to silence his enemies. When Luca Pitti, one of his most loyal supporters, was elected gonfalonier for the July–August term in 1458, Cosimo seized the opportunity to stage a coup that was to change the mould of Florentine politics, in much the same way as his expenditure on art and architecture had transformed the fabric of the city. In late July, Pitti's *Signoria* put forward a radical plan to set up a permanent council to regulate access to high office; but the proposal was soundly rejected by the committees required to vote through legislation. Cosimo now took the risky step of bypassing the committees altogether by summoning a *parlamento*, a general meeting of the electorate, to decide the issue. And he ensured that this devious scheme became law in very unrepublican fashion. When the vote was forced through on 11 August 1458, the city was teeming with armed mercenaries supplied by his old friend, Duke Francesco Sforza.

Cosimo now had legal control of the electoral process. It was a major coup. As Francesco Guicciardini explained, the Medici had 'restricted the authority and power in the city to themselves, exiling or punishing a great many citizens, so that Cosimo and his supporters were in total and secure control of the government'.[21] The new committee, the Cento (Council of One Hundred), manned by Cosimo's closest allies, now had legal control of access to political office, and its influence was soon manifest when some 1,500 Florentines were removed from the lists of those eligible for election. One of the new faces in the Palazzo della Signoria was Pierfrancesco, who had finally taken the advice of his father-in-law and embarked on a political career. Cosimo also arranged for Acciaiuoli and Pierfrancesco to be among the ambassadors sent to Rome that autumn to congratulate Pius II on his election as pope. The following year, Pierfrancesco was elected to the *Signoria* despite being six months short of his thirtieth birthday.[22]

Cosimo largely retired from politics after the coup, his health weakened by frequent attacks of gout. Nevertheless, although he was not among the *Signoria* that greeted Pius II's state visit at the gates of Florence, on 25 April 1459, his authority was much in evidence when the papal procession made an unprecedented detour to include the Palazzo Medici during its noisy parade past the city's major monuments. Also in Florence for the occasion was Francesco Sforza's fifteen-year-old son, Galeazzo Maria, who had been sent by his father to escort the pope to Mantua, where he was to host a congress to organize a crusade against the Turks (after their capture of Constantinople six years earlier). While Pius II was accommodated in the official guest apartments at Santa Maria Novella, Galeazzo Maria and his entourage stayed at the Palazzo Medici, and Pierfrancesco had the honour of providing lodging for the senior member of the papal court, Cardinal d'Estouteville, at the Casa Vecchia next door.[23]

Benozzo Gozzoli, *Journey of the Magi*, 1459, detail (Florence, Palazzo Medici-Riccardi). Among the portraits of Medici family and friends in this section of the fresco are Galeazzo Maria Sforza (front right) and the young Lorenzo de' Medici standing beside his brother Giuliano (second row).

The *Signoria* had taken enormous care to arrange appropriately magnificent entertainments for Pius II and Galeazzo Maria, spending 22,532 florins on the visit.[24] On Sunday 29 April, there was a joust in the piazza at Santa Croce in front of a large audience who had bought tickets for the event. This was not entertainment for the masses, though; the notary Ser Giusto d'Anghiari spent 12 *soldi* on tickets for his three sons, more than a day's wage for a manual labourer.[25] The following day, there was a ball attended by many young Florentines. The Florentine herald praised the genteel behaviour of the girls, dressed 'with such a quantity of pearls and most noble jewels' – the sumptuary laws had been suspended for the duration of the visit.[26] The waspish pope was rather less impressed, though it should be remembered that, as a citizen of Florence's great rival Siena, he was not the most reliable of witnesses. 'The ladies were richly clad and there was a marvellous variety of costumes,' he recorded, 'but their whitened faces clearly betrayed the use of cosmetics.'[27]

In honour of the distinguished visitors, the May Day celebrations that year were particularly splendid, though the hunt in the Piazza della Signoria was not the success that had been anticipated. Ser Giusto described how 'bulls, cows, buffaloes, horses and wild boar were enclosed in the piazza and then about twelve lions were brought in but they made no attempt to catch the said animals, indeed they tried to flee away and were terrified'.[28] The republic's lions, it seems, had been tamed by their long captivity. However, the crowds, who paid 5 *soldi* for their tickets, roared their approval at an ingenious wooden ball in which a man rolled himself 'wherever he wanted all over the piazza chasing the lions and other animals and it was a wonderful device,' as the notary concluded.

On the evening of 1 May, Cosimo himself hosted an entertainment on the Via Larga outside his palace. A group of young men paraded in their splendid costumes, all 'very well-behaved and handsome', according to Ser Giusto, and put on a choreographed performance of their riding skills, standing up on shortened stirrups and performing synchronized dressage. The finale was a triumph of Cupid, 'with many lights and torches, it was a very beautiful and splendid thing,' he recorded; it was led by Cosimo's ten-year-old grandson Lorenzo, who closed the proceedings with an invitation to the participants to dine at the Palazzo Medici.

The young prince, Galeazzo Maria Sforza, was very impressed with the palace and its gardens, where the Sforza viper was on display in the planting alongside the Medici *palle*. It was 'the most beautiful house I have ever seen,' he informed his father.[29] 'I went to visit Cosimo, whom I found in his chapel which was as well decorated as the rest of the house, and he embraced me most tenderly,' continued the fifteen-year-old prince, who then listened to speeches in praise of the Duke of Milan made by young Lorenzo and his brother Giuliano. Cosimo also entertained Galeazzo Maria for a few days at his villa at Careggi, where the atmosphere was less formal. When dinner was over there was musical entertainment, 'a delightful show given by the ladies' – Lucrezia, Ginevra, Bianca, Laudomia and several others – 'and all did dances in the Florentine fashion, skipping and moving in refined fashion'.[30] The Medici were keen musicians. Giovanni and his sister-in-law Lucrezia both sang and played instruments, and Lucrezia passed on her love of music to her children: Bianca played the organ and sang French chansons with her younger sister Nannina to entertain their guests.[31]

Bianca was now fourteen years old, and it was time for her to be wed. Cosimo and Piero chose Guglielmo de' Pazzi, grandson of Cosimo's old friend and ally Andrea de' Pazzi. Two years later, Cosimo asked Pierfrancesco's opinion on a possible match for Nannina: 'there are few options, for one reason or another and, as it is necessary to do as well as possible, we are thinking of one of Giovanni Rucellai's sons'.[32] This was an unexpected choice. Rucellai was a wealthy banker but not part of the Medici inner circle; indeed, he was politically suspect: the son-in-law of Palla Strozzi, who had been exiled in 1434, he had spent many years lobbying to join the elite. However, just two weeks after the betrothal was signed, Cosimo arranged for Rucellai's name to be put on the Council of One Hundred's shortlist and he was elected to the *Signoria* for the first time, at the age of sixty.

Illness was beginning to plague the Medici, and not just the older members of the family. Little Cosimino, five years old, died suddenly in 1459, and his father Giovanni's own health was declining. Giovanni and Piero had both inherited their father's gout. One visitor to the Palazzo Medici recounted how he had found the old banker 'sitting in

his room with his two sons, all three afflicted with gout; he only a little, and Piero his elder son was not suffering at the time, but they were all seated as if they were unable to move from that position, nor could they ride and had to be carried everywhere'.[33] In 1458, worried that his son was finding the job of running the Medici bank too onerous, Cosimo had decided to appoint Francesco Sassetti, the manager of the Geneva branch, to act as Giovanni's assistant.[34] Two years later, in August 1460, Giovanni was at the spa at Morba with wife Ginevra, trying out a new cure, when Contessina sent them a letter. 'Dearest children,' she wrote, 'I understand you have heard that Cosimo and Piero have been ill, which annoys me because I did not want anything to upset you, so that the baths might be efficacious.'[35] She tried to be reassuring: 'Cosimo had a cold, which was soon cured and he is now well and Piero had some pain, which is not yet gone, but you both know what always happens, so he too will soon be well.'

Attacks of gout usually did clear up after a time, but the complications, in particular the impact on the kidneys, were invariably fatal. Giovanni died of kidney failure in October 1463, at the age of only forty-two. Pius II wrote a personal letter to Cosimo commiserating on his loss: 'the news has grieved us deeply,' the pope wrote sympathetically, 'not only because it is in itself premature, but also because we fear it is likely to prove harmful to a man of your age and state of health'.[36] The grief-stricken father replied: 'I am striving to the best of my ability, and so far as my weak spirit will permit, to bear this great calamity with calmness… and I trust that God in the abundance of his mercy will pity us that are left behind.'[37]

The autumn of 1463 was an anxious time for all the family. Piero's younger son, Giuliano, was now ill in Pisa, from where Lucrezia wrote several letters each day to keep her husband updated on the ten-year-old's condition: 'I want you to know every little change,' she informed him on 24 November.[38] 'His pulse is good and all his functions are normal but the fever has returned almost as strong as it was ten days ago,' she wrote, and 'he is not so lively during the day as I could wish,' though she counselled Piero 'not to be worried as Giuliano is strong and, although he is pale, his complexion is good'. After joining his wife and son in Pisa, Piero received regular letters from his father. There was plague in Florence that winter, but 'the recent cold weather with snow and ice has put an end to it,' Cosimo told him on 23 January 1464,

The Palazzo Medici, Florence, begun in 1445.

adding encouragingly that 'Contessina and I are very well, and so are Bianca and Guglielmo and the little Contessina', referring to the couple's first child, named for her great-grandmother; 'they come to us often to keep us company'.[39]

Cosimo's own health was about to deteriorate rapidly as the gout began to affect his kidneys, and that summer he left Florence for his villa at Careggi. When Contessina asked him why he was so quiet, he drily reminded her that it had taken her as long as a fortnight to plan their move out of the city and 'as I have to move on from this life to another, don't you think that I have much to think about?'[40] On 26 July, Piero wrote sadly to his sons Lorenzo and Giuliano, at Cafaggiolo, that 'it appears to me that he is gradually sinking, and he thinks so himself'.[41]

Cosimo died on 1 August 1464. He was buried the following day in San Lorenzo after a simple ceremony, 'without the customary pomp of the funerals of great citizens and with little display, as he had wished, accompanied only by the priests of San Lorenzo and the friars of San Marco and the Badia of Fiesole, churches he had built, and with his relatives and friends walking behind the bier', as one observer recalled.[42] It was a mark of Cosimo's international reputation that Piero received letters of condolence from courts across Europe: from Pius II, himself on his deathbed in Ancona, and from King Louis XI of France, who, as a mark of respect to Cosimo, gave the Medici the right to quarter the French lily in their coat-of-arms. A few days after the funeral, the *Signoria* set up a committee to decide how best to honour this eminent citizen of the republic. They bestowed on him the title of *Pater patriae*, 'Father of the Nation', the title once accorded to Cicero, that hero of the Roman Republic. It was the first brick in what was to become the enduring edifice of the Medici myth, confirming the image that Cosimo had so assiduously promoted for himself.

Cosimo's death marked a significant moment in the history of the Medici. Even his enemies were gracious in their praise of this statesman who had steered Florence through the crises of the previous three decades. But, as one of them explained, there was also a strong feeling of release, as Cosimo's death changed everything:

Not for many years had Florence been so prosperous… and she remained in this happy state during the life of Cosimo de' Medici until the first day of August 1464. And although this prosperity was due to the goodness of the times, due to the league* and the peace that held throughout Italy, nevertheless Cosimo made every effort to maintain this, arranging it for the well-being of Florence and using his authority in the city to bring it into effect. On his death, however, everyone rejoiced, such is the love and desire for liberty. It appeared to the Florentines that his method of government had brought them to subjection and servitude, from which they believed his death would liberate them. This they desired.[43]

---

*   A reference to the peace treaty signed by Florence, Venice and Milan in 1454.

7

THE SUCCESSION CRISIS

Piero the Gouty

1464–1469

THE MEDICI IN 1464

Piero di Cosimo (48)
Lucrezia Tornabuoni (37), *his wife*

      Bianca (18), *his daughter,* m. Guglielmo de' Pazzi

      Nannina (16), *his daughter*

      Lorenzo (15), *his son*

      Giuliano (11), *his son*

Contessina (68), *Piero's mother*

Carlo di Cosimo (34), *Piero's illegitimate brother*

Pierfrancesco di Lorenzo (34), *Piero's first cousin*
Laudomia Acciaiuoli, *Pierfrancesco's wife*

      Lorenzo (1), *their son*

On 7 August 1464, six days after Cosimo's death, Piero had a visit from Nicodemo Tranchedini, the Milanese ambassador to Florence. The diplomat reported back to Duke Francesco Sforza on an anxious Piero who was begging for help in the succession: 'your lordship alone can save and confirm the position, reputation and authority left to him by his father'.[1] The plea had been echoed by Contessina and Lucrezia, 'on their bended knees'.

Reserved and aloof, Piero did not appear well fitted to the task of leadership. He had inherited neither his father's charisma nor the respect that Cosimo had earned as a businessman. In the event though, the Medici need not have worried; Florence remained calm during those long hot summer days as Piero took up the reins of power. Unfortunately, his gout made him rather short-tempered and confined him to the Palazzo Medici, where now much of the business of the bank and the government had to take place.

The bank was one of Piero's priorities that autumn. He asked the general manager, Francesco Sassetti, to report on the state of the company, and the audit of the ledgers revealed the unwelcome news that the business was not doing as well as expected.[2] Cautious by nature, Piero took the decision to retrench. In October 1464, the Bruges branch refused to extend any more credit to the Duke of Burgundy, and the Milan branch pursued the same policy with Sforza. Also, in what would prove a disastrous move, Piero called in many of the loans that Cosimo had made to his Florentine customers, causing several companies to go bankrupt. 'Many of our businessmen are being hit hard,' Angelo Acciaiuoli wrote to his friend Filippo Strozzi in Naples that December, adding that 'this is the worst crash that has happened in this city since 1339, and the poor lack bread, the rich their brains and the learned their senses; we are in need of God's help but keep these words to yourself.'[3] Acciaiuoli evidently had his doubts about the new head of the Medici regime.

There were also problems at the Rome branch of the bank, where Giovanni Tornabuoni, Lucrezia's brother, was one of the staff. The senior partner, who had been with the bank for years, had a low opinion of Tornabuoni's abilities and complained to Piero when he was promoted: 'this company used only to promote those who deserved it and paid no attention to family connections'.[4] Tornabuoni, for his part, accused his boss of being unfairly prejudiced against him, and in

Mino da Fiesole, *Piero de' Medici*, 1453 (Florence, Bargello).

March 1465 he threatened to resign unless he was given the top job. Piero, inevitably, bowed to family pressure and sacked the senior partner, appointing his brother-in-law his place. Luckily, Tornabuoni proved his worth the following year when the bank secured the lucrative papal monopoly over the recently discovered alum mines at Tolfa, near Viterbo. (Alum, essential in the cloth industry, had previously been imported from the Levant at considerable expense.)

Despite Piero's smooth assumption of power, behind closed doors in Florence there was much talk of how to throw off the Medici yoke. Acciaiuoli was not the only member of the Medici party to have his doubts about Cosimo's son. Nobody challenged Piero's right to inherit his father's position at the head of the family, but many questioned whether the same dynastic principle should be applied to Cosimo's political role as leader of the republic. The Medici themselves certainly thought it should – and so did the canons of San Lorenzo, who, in an unprecedented move, gave Piero the right to allocate chapels in the church to families of his own choice, thus transforming what had been a parish project into a Medici institution.[5] But there were many in the city who blamed Piero for their economic woes and who challenged the legitimacy of his position. As Palla Strozzi, who had been in exile since 1434, had predicted, 'while Cosimo is alive it is impossible to obstruct him but once he is dead things will soon change'.[6]

Just how much was changing in Florence became evident in February 1465, when Lorenzo Strozzi, one of Palla's cousins, arrived at the city gates. He was hoping to persuade the *Signoria* to lift the sentences of exile that Cosimo had imposed on their family back in 1434. Although the gamble failed, and Strozzi was forbidden from entering the city, he learned much about the true state of Piero's regime from private discussions with his friends, many of whom were opponents of the Medici. He informed his brother that the anti-Medici voices were growing in confidence and that, significantly, two men who had been prominent members of Cosimo's inner circle, Dietisalvi Neroni and Angelo Acciaiuoli, had defected to join them. That two of his father's closest allies had withdrawn their support for him was bad news for Piero: Acciaiuoli, father-in-law of his cousin Pierfrancesco, now spitefully described the Medici as 'the worms devouring the rose, the devils in Paradise'.[7] There were even rumours that Luca Pitti, who had helped Cosimo engineer the 1458 coup, was planning to change sides, though Strozzi judged that he 'plays the whore with them but is tight with Piero' and 'anything else you hear is just hot air'.[8]

Lorenzo Strozzi and his elder brother Filippo had been small boys when their family was exiled by Cosimo in 1434; but they had prospered over the years to become rich bankers in the Kingdom of Naples and close friends with its monarch, Ferrante I. Moreover, in their bid to lift the sentence of banishment, the brothers knew they had a trump card: as Lorenzo informed Filippo, 'what is certain is that Piero desires the friendship of the king'. Piero did indeed want to improve his standing with Ferrante I, who had recently put aside the long-standing rivalry between Milan and Naples by agreeing to the betrothal of his heir Alfonso, Duke of Calabria, and Ippolita Sforza, the daughter of Duke Francesco. Thanks to Cosimo, Piero already had close ties with Milan; but he was ambitious for a more central role in this new diplomatic alignment, not least to improve his prestige at home. However, he was not prepared to go quite so far as to allow the Strozzi brothers back home, where their wealth and influence would bolster the camp of his enemies. When he received a letter from Ferrante I asking, as a personal favour, if the Strozzi brothers could return to Florence, Piero declined politely, replying that 'it grieves me that it is not in my power to do what you ask'; but he did make overtures to the Strozzi.[9] With their eyes on the longer term, the brothers agreed to act on Piero's behalf. They arranged for several lavish presents, including a galley, to be given to the king – and they sent several gifts of their own to Florence, including a roll of expensive linen for Lucrezia.[10]

Ferrante I responded by agreeing to the offer made by the *Signoria* to host the Neapolitan wedding party on its journey north to Milan, and on its return south with Alfonso's bride. On 17 April 1465, Federigo of Aragon, Ferrante's younger son who was to act as proxy at his brother's marriage, arrived in Florence. With the gouty Piero confined to his rooms, it was his sixteen-year-old son Lorenzo who did the duties as host – and the two teenagers became firm friends. They shared an interest in literature, and Lorenzo later sent Federigo a manuscript containing the works of Dante, Boccaccio and other Tuscan poets. In the long letter that accompanied the volume, he reminded Federigo of the time they had spent together and 'we spoke of those who had written poetry in the Tuscan language, and your lordship expressed a desire that I should collect their works in one book for you'.[11]

Lorenzo also stood in for his father at the wedding ceremonies in Milan, riding north in the company of his brother-in-law Guglielmo de' Pazzi, via Ferrara and Venice, ostensibly on an inspection tour of bank branches. But Piero had an ulterior motive – to introduce his son to the rulers of northern Italy, and he knew how much appearances mattered. As he wrote anxiously to Lorenzo on 11 May 1465, 'you will have had my letter of the 4th telling you how to behave, all of which you must remember.'[12] He repeated his earlier instructions, almost verbatim: 'In a word, it is necessary now for you to be a man and not a boy, and to be so in words, deeds and manners, so if you give dinner parties or other entertainments do not stint on expenditure or whatever else is necessary to do yourself honour.'

Federigo of Aragon returned to Florence with his new sister-in-law, Ippolita Sforza, in mid-June in time to celebrate the city's San Giovanni holiday. Both stayed at the Palazzo Medici, though Piero, gout-ridden and tetchy, was not looking forward to the prospect. 'As the *Signoria* has commanded me to do, and I obey willingly,' he informed Lorenzo, 'we are preparing great festivities to entertain these princes for San Giovanni and we will try to honour them in other ways.'[13] He added that Giuliano was going to 'arrange a tournament in a more magnificent fashion than usual; the *Signoria* wishes it but I am against it as I do not want to have so many bothers at the same time'.

During that summer of 1465, Piero was preoccupied with more worrying political matters. In September, Marco Parenti, the brother-in-law of Filippo and Lorenzo Strozzi, had important news: Luca Pitti had finally moved beyond flirting with the opposition and had now defected to the campaign to unseat Piero. Worse, as the economic crisis fuelled disaffection with his leadership, Piero was unable to stop the supporters of Pitti, Neroni and Acciaiuoli from overturning Cosimo's system, established in 1458, of controlling elections to the *Signoria*. 'This was done to reduce the authority of Piero,' the anti-Medicean Parenti wrote in his memoirs, 'in order that he would not be able to choose the priors according to his own wishes.'[14] So, just a year after Cosimo's death, the opponents of Medici rule had finally broken cover. Parenti made a telling contrast between the Palazzo Pitti

Luca della Robbia, *Labours of the Months*, c.1455 (London, Victoria & Albert Museum). These twelve glazed terracotta roundels originally decorated Piero's private study in the Palazzo Medici.

and the Palazzo Medici, 'where everyone used to go to discuss private and political matters' but where Piero's 'reputation has fallen much recently and Luca Pitti holds court at his own house where the majority of citizens now go to talk about government affairs'.[15]

The next year, 1466, began with ill omens. The Arno burst its banks on 12 January, 'without a drop of rain having fallen', killing horses in their stables and ruining the wines stored in cellars.[16] The economic crisis deepened as Piero's policy of calling in the Medici bank's loans caused many more Florentine companies to go bankrupt: eight of these businesses lost more than 300,000 florins.[17] Then came dreadful news from Milan. Duke Francesco Sforza died suddenly on 8 March after being ill for just two days, leaving his son Galeazzo Maria, now aged twenty-two, as the new ruler. 'I am in such distress at the sad and untimely death of the Illustrious Duke of Milan that I do not know where I am, and you can imagine what this means to us in both our private and public affairs,' a very worried Piero wrote to Lorenzo.[18] 'We must do all we can to preserve the stability of the duchy, for you know what our debts and duties are to the blessed memory of the late lord.' But Piero no longer had the power to act decisively. When his supporters on the *Signoria* voted to loan 40,000 florins to Milan, his opponents blocked the legislation. According to historian Francesco Guicciardini, whose grandfather witnessed the debate, 'when they started to discuss the particulars, Luca Pitti, Angelo Acciaiuoli and Dietisalvi Neroni obstructed the offer, in the hopes that Piero would lose the great reputation he had with the Duchy of Milan and the money was never paid'.[19]

Tension was rising on the streets of Florence. Piero escaped an assassination attempt in late May, but a few days later more than 400 prominent citizens swore an oath to uphold the original constitution of the republic and to prune the embellishments by which the Medici had held on to power: 'the city is to be governed in the traditional way by a just and populist government and that in future the *Signoria* is to be elected by lot, as it is at present, and not in any other way, and that citizens should not be threatened with violence but be able freely to advise and judge public affairs'.[20] Among the signatories were, as expected, the three leaders of the opposition – Pitti, Neroni and Acciaiuoli – but also, more worryingly, Piero's own cousin Pierfrancesco, who had chosen to vote with his father-in-law rather than with his own family.

On 8 June 1466, in a show of confidence to mask the severity of the crisis, Piero went ahead with the celebrations planned for the marriage of his daughter Nannina and Bernardo Rucellai. He attended the great banquet hosted by the groom's father, Giovanni Rucellai, outside his palace on the Via della Vigna Nuova, where the cost of the food alone came to the enormous sum of 1,185 florins.[21] The event gave the Medici a very public opportunity to display their international prestige: Lorenzo wore a cloak richly decorated with Sforza emblems, a present from Duke Galeazzo Maria, which had been rushed to Florence specially for the event.[22]

By August, the factions were preparing for the showdown. Piero's men emptied the city's shops to fill the larder and armoury at the Palazzo Medici – and to deprive the opposition of supplies. With the anti-Mediceans gathering at the Palazzo Pitti across the river, Piero prepared his defences at his own palace. Marco Parenti described how Ambassador Nicodemo 'built scaffolding above the windows of Piero's house, like fortress defences, amassed quantities of stones and other missiles, and he guarded the streets around the house with armed soldiers'.[23] Thanks to Nicodemo, Piero was able to arrange for Milanese troops to be ready at the border. To finance the high cost of this venture, Piero even asked Pierfrancesco for a loan of 10,000 florins, which, rather surprisingly – given his cousin's support for the opposition – he supplied.[24]

On 27 August, Piero gave orders for the Milanese soldiers to cross into Florentine territory. On the next day, tension mounted as the names were chosen for the September–October term of the *Signoria*. Piero had been unable to interfere with the selection of these men, so the news that several of the new priors were Medici partisans came as a great relief to him, and he now made his plans, shrewdly advised by Nicodemo and by his brother-in-law Tommaso Soderini, one of Cosimo's allies who had remained loyal. With Florence on the verge of civil war, the *Signoria* summoned both Piero and Luca Pitti to the palace to ask them to disarm their men.

However, it soon became clear that something had changed. Piero had, in fact, been engaged in secret talks with Pitti, who had agreed to betray his friends in return for political favours. Pitti's price included a Medici husband for his daughter, though he must have been disappointed that his new son-in-law was not to be Piero's son Lorenzo, as he had hoped, but rather Piero's brother-in-law, the banker Giovanni Tornabuoni.

With Milanese troops massing at the frontier, Piero ordered his own private army of some 8,000 men into the city on 1 September – and the show of armed force soon crushed the rebellion. Within weeks, the Medici had regained control of the electoral process and strengthened their hold on power. One of Piero's first acts was to curry favour with King Ferrante I by allowing Filippo and Lorenzo Strozzi to return to Florence, a gesture of good will that would prove invaluable in years to come. But he followed this by banishing both Dietisalvi Neroni and Angelo Acciaiuoli. The latter wrote witheringly to Piero from Siena on 17 September: 'I laugh at what I see; God has put it in your power to cancel all the debts you owe me... I was exiled and lost my estates for your father, and you are in a position to restore all to me.'[25] Piero replied that 'your laughter is the cause of my not weeping... your guilt, as I said in my earlier letter, is clear and so great that neither my intercession, nor that of anyone else, would be of any help'.

Despite Pierfrancesco's disloyalty to the family, Piero did not exile his cousin – perhaps in gratitude for the financial help he had received during the crisis – but he did ensure that Pierfrancesco was excluded from political office. The two branches of the family continued to observe social niceties. Lucrezia was at the baths at Morba, near Volterra, in October 1467 when Pierfrancesco's wife Laudomia gave birth to a second son (named Giovanni after his great-grandfather), and Contessina reassured her that 'the visits to Laudomia have been made in your name'. [26] But relations between Piero and Pierfrancesco were becoming increasingly strained. In August 1469, Piero decided that the time had come for the two cousins to file separate returns for the *catasto* and was disappointed by Pierfrancesco's response, writing: 'I thought it would have been a good idea for us to have a long talk together to discuss our affairs which are, in my opinion, a matter of some importance; you do not think so, and I am willing to accept this.'[27] As the *catasto* records show, they did indeed file separate returns that year. Piero's wealth (66,452 florins) was substantially greater than that of his cousin (45,065 florins), though the Medici fortune had slipped some-

Antonio Pollaiuolo, *Portrait of a Young Woman* (Milan, Museo Poldi-Pezzoli), thought to be a portrait of the young Lucrezia Tornabuoni

what since 1457 when Cosimo had declared a total of 122,669 florins.

Meanwhile, Piero was grooming Lorenzo for power both at home and on the international stage. In December 1466, in the aftermath of the succession crisis, Lorenzo had been elected to the Council of One Hundred, even though he was several years short of the required age. He began to play a public role in state patronage elected to the committee of citizens and craftsmen advising on the completion of the great cupola of the Duomo, and served a four-year term as an official in charge of the shrine of Santissima Annunziata.[28] More importantly, in early 1467 Piero and Lucrezia started to look for a wife for their eighteen-year-old son. By Florentine standards this was very young to marry – businessmen preferred to make their fortunes first – but, in a telling sign of Medici ambitions, this was the normal marital age at the aristocratic courts of Italy. The Medici were beginning to detach themselves from their commercial roots. And their choice of bride was another break with tradition: at the suggestion of Giovanni Tornabuoni, they opted for Clarice Orsini, who was not only a foreigner – a Roman – but one of noble blood and the niece of Cardinal Latino Orsini.

Before making a final decision, Lucrezia travelled to Rome to meet Clarice and her mother at mass in St Peter's. On 27 March 1467, she wrote to Piero giving details of Clarice's good complexion and modest manners, her round face 'which does not displease me', a rather thin throat, well-proportioned bosom, 'long delicate hands' and 'reddish and abundant hair', and also much information about the prestige of the baronial Orsini clan. A few days later, she reported, more succinctly, that Clarice 'has two good qualities, she is tall and not unattractive; her face is not pretty but it is not common, and her figure is good; Lorenzo has seen her, so find out if she pleases him; there are so many advantages that if he likes her we may be content'.[29]

Lucrezia fell ill on the journey back from Rome, and that September she went to the baths at Morba, in the hope that the hot sulphur springs would improve her delicate health. Lorenzo planned to join her there, but on 19 September he wrote to say that the doctor 'does not think it would be good for my eczema, so I have decided not to come,' adding that 'we are all well here, particularly Piero, whose only wish is to hear from you more often' – it was not unusual for children to call their parents by their Christian names.[30] Lucrezia did get better, much to Piero's relief. On 1 October he wrote: 'I hope for your complete recovery, which is certain, indeed it cannot be otherwise given all the prayers and supplications which have been and are being made, some by those of whom you know, others by those of whom you know nothing'.[31] The following month he wrote again: 'Lucrezia mine,' he began, 'I shall not write at length because your return is imminent and I await it with infinite longing'.[32]

Meanwhile, negotiations were under way in Rome for the betrothal of Lorenzo and Clarice, a lengthy process conducted by the couple's uncles, Giovanni Tornabuoni and Cardinal Orsini. The contract was finally signed in November 1468 – more than eighteen months after Lucrezia had inspected the girl in St Peter's. For the cardinal, writing to Piero, 'it is with great joy that we have signed the contract Giovanni Tornabuoni brought from you', and he hoped that the union between their two families would 'lead to the happiness of your house and ours, for it pleases us old people and also the boy and the girl, and indeed everyone'.[33]

Giovanni Tornabuoni's brother, Francesco, who was also working in the Medici bank in Rome, spent much time with Clarice on Lorenzo's behalf, educating her for her new life in Florence. On 4 January 1469, he wrote to his nephew. 'Not a day passes when I do not see your Madonna Clarice and she has bewitched me,' he rhapsodized, 'she is beautiful, has the sweetest of manners and an admirable intelligence' and 'she has begun to learn to dance, and each day she learns a new one.'[34] He also advised Lorenzo: 'as you cannot visit her in person, at least write to her often as it would give her great pleasure'.

Lorenzo himself was busy in Florence with preparations for a magnificent joust he was to hold on 7 February 1469, as part of the annual celebrations for Carnival. As he proudly recorded in his memoirs, 'it was done at great cost and with great extravagance, and I spent around 10,000 florins… I was judged the winner and received a silver helmet'.[35] Clarice was thrilled by the news of her fiancé's success. Francesco Tornabuoni informed Lorenzo on 16 February that 'for four days she has been sad because she feared for you in the tournament, she also had a slight headache but as soon as she heard the news the headache disappeared and she was merry again'.[36] A week or so later, Clarice herself wrote to Lorenzo thanking him for his letter 'telling me of the tournament' and 'I am most glad that you have been satisfied in something which gives you pleasure'.[37]

Overleaf: Filippo Lippi, *The Feast of Herod*, begun 1452 (Prato, Cathedral). A fifteenth-century banquet was designed to delight all the senses, with dining-tables laden with good food and wines as well as music and dancing to entertain the guests.

The marriage was celebrated in Florence with due pomp. On 2 June 1469, a Saturday, presents of food started arriving at the Palazzo Medici from the towns of the Florentine state – 150 calves, 2,000 pairs of capons, geese and chickens, sugar plums, wine, and more. On the Sunday, the bride herself arrived at the Palazzo Medici, 'riding the big horse given to Lorenzo by the king [Ferrante I of Naples], preceded by many trumpeters and pipers', to attend the first of five banquets hosted at the palace. There was dancing each afternoon, on the stage that had been erected outside the palace and ornamented with hangings displaying the Medici and Orsini coats-of-arms. There were also parties at the house of Cosimo's illegitimate son, now canon of the cathedral: 'at Messer Carlo's one hundred barrels of wine were drunk each day'.[38] Unfortunately, it rained on the day of the wedding, 'so sudden and so heavy that many could not reach shelter in time and it enveloped everything and soaked the beautiful dresses', as one observer recorded; but he did not think that 'anywhere among so many people could there be such a splendid and fine spectacle'.

In early July 1469, Lorenzo left his new wife behind in Florence while he travelled to Milan, where he was to act as proxy for his father, who had been made godfather to Giangaleazzo Sforza, the baby son of Duke Galeazzo Maria and his wife, Bona of Savoy. On Piero's behalf, Lorenzo presented the duchess with a lavish gold necklace containing a large diamond worth 2,000 florins.[39] Piero must have had some worries about his son's developing taste for extravagance, because he asked Lucrezia to 'tell Lorenzo that he is not to exceed his orders or to make a great show'.[40] Travelling with Lorenzo were his brother-in-law Bernardo Rucellai and his old tutor, Gentile Becchi, who sent Clarice regular bulletins on her husband's progress: 'He will be at Milan on Saturday and, after fulfilling the orders of his magnificent father, will return at once to you, who are the only one from whom he regrets being absent; he is very well and happy and so is Bernardo.'[41] Lorenzo also wrote to his bride to inform her of his safe arrival in Milan, urging her to 'make much of Piero, Mona Contessina and Mona Lucrezia' and explaining that 'I will hasten to finish here and return to you, for it already seems like a thousand years since I saw you'.[42]

In the autumn of 1469, Piero's health went into a steep decline. He died of the complications of gout on 2 December, at his villa at Careggi, much mourned by his wife and close family but less so by the Florentines. Despite leading the Medici party for just five years, he had played a pivotal rule in the family story. He had managed to survive a succession crisis, developing the ruthless political skills necessary to stabilize the Medici regime, and he had set the Medici family on its road to international power. The Medici were now close associates of both Duke Galeazzo Maria of Milan and King Ferrante I of Naples, and related by marriage to the powerful Orsini clan in Rome.

Above all, Piero's actions had underlined the extent to which the Medici had begun to see themselves as rulers of Florence by right.

8

YOUTH
AT THE HELM

Lorenzo and Giuliano

1469–1479

THE MEDICI IN 1469

Lorenzo di Piero (20) (Lorenzo)
Clarice Orsini (19), *his wife*

Lucrezia Tornabuoni (42), *Lorenzo's mother*

Bianca (24), *Lorenzo's sister*
Guglielmo de' Pazzi, *her husband*

Nannina (21), *Lorenzo's sister*
Bernardo Rucellai, *her husband*

Giuliano (16), *Lorenzo's brother*

Pierfrancesco (39), *Lorenzo's cousin*
Laudomia Acciaiuoli, *his wife*

    Lorenzo (6) *and* Giovanni (2), *their sons*

The males of the Medici family lined up in order of precedence to follow Piero's coffin to San Lorenzo for his funeral on 3 December 1469. Canon Carlo and Pierfrancesco, as the senior members of the family, led the procession, accompanied by the ambassadors of Naples and Milan, followed by the sons Lorenzo and then Giuliano. However, it was neither Carlo nor Pierfrancesco who had been appointed as Piero's successor.

The previous evening, within hours of Piero's death, some 700 Medici partisans held a meeting at which the elderly Tommaso Soderini, loyal ally of both Cosimo and Piero, persuaded them to accept Lorenzo as leader and agree to waive the age limit on holding office, so that both Lorenzo and Giuliano could play their part in government. The majority present evidently preferred youth and inexperience to the questionable loyalty that Pierfrancesco had exhibited towards the Medici party over the past four years. Lorenzo was a month short of his twenty-first birthday when he found himself at the apex of political power. He recalled a few years later, somewhat disingenuously, that he had been reluctant to accept the position 'on account of my age' but that he had agreed for the sake of his friends and family, adding, more convincingly, that 'the rich do not prosper in Florence unless they rule'.[1] But the story of his early years at the helm was to prove a depressing tale of greed and inexperience, and his lack of political nous would nearly cost him his life.

Smooth relations with Pierfrancesco were an immediate priority. After Piero's funeral, as Marco Parenti saw Lorenzo 'crying as they walked home', he also noticed that Lorenzo and Pierfrancesco 'made grand gestures to each other, and their friends are trying to keep them united; we shall see what happens'.[2] The day after the funeral, Lorenzo asked his cousin for the substantial loan of 8,166 florins (at a time when a skilled craftsman earned less than 40 florins a year), and, far from showing resentment at the way Lorenzo had been given precedence, Pierfrancesco seized his chance to exploit the request for immediate gain.[3] His reward was to be allowed back into politics, and on 17 December 1469 he took over Piero's position on the committee in charge of the public debt (the Monte). The following year, he was sent

as ambassador to King Ferrante I; Lorenzo also gave him a place on the committee that nominated those suitable for 'election' to the *Signoria*.

At a more general level, the new regime brought a new generation to the fore, a significant change from the middle-aged men who had dominated the political, social and cultural life of Florence since the foundation of the republic in 1293. With youth and wealth at the helm, Florence partied – rather to the disapproval of those who would have preferred a more mature leader. The celebrations for San Giovanni in 1470 were the grandest the city had ever seen, lasting seven days, with jousts and mock battles as well as the traditional parades and processions. This military play-acting had a particular resonance for the Florentines. As Benedetto Dei proudly boasted in his chronicle, written in the 1470s, the city had no need itself for real fortresses, drawbridges and guards, though there were plenty in Florence's subject towns and territories. Much of Dei's text consisted of lists charting the city's wealth: the richest men in Florence, the city's grandest buildings (the paved streets were fifth in this list), the quantity of feasts, the numbers of shops in various trades, and so on. More frivolously, he also included a list of his favourite Florentine proverbs: 'don't give

Above: Andrea del Verrocchio, *Lorenzo de' Medici*, late fifteenth century? (Washington D.C., National Gallery of Art). *Overleaf*: Sandro Botticelli, *Adoration of the Magi*, 1472–5 (Florence, Uffizi). A piece of undisguised flattery, this altarpiece was commissioned by a money lender, who had one of the kings portrayed as Lorenzo de' Medici, and there are other Medici portraits in the royal retinues.

bread to the dog every time he barks'; 'guard against the man who eats lentils with a pin'; 'he who wants to be rich in a year will be poor in six months'; and, colourfully, 'shit well and piss clear and jeer at the doctor'.[4]

Dei's rich-list of Florence, headed inevitably by Lorenzo and Giuliano, was a roster of Medici allies whose loyalty to the family had enabled them to prosper over the previous four decades.[5] As one on the list (Giovanni Rucellai) boasted, 'since I became connected to the Medici, I have been honoured, esteemed and valued'.[6] Once suspect because of his links with Palla Strozzi, but now Lorenzo's uncle by marriage, he had made a very public statement of his wealth in 1470 by financing a spectacularly expensive inlaid marble facade for the church of Santa Maria Novella, which was emblazoned with his name and his emblem, the sails of fortune. Among the others named by Dei was Tommaso Soderini, who had been too poor to own a house in 1427 but could now count himself among the ruling elite, as could Lorenzo's uncle, Giovanni Tornabuoni, the senior partner of the Rome branch of the Medici bank, and Francesco Sassetti, the bank's general manager

Below: Florence, Santa Maria Novella, façade dated 1470.
Opposite: Domenico Ghirlandaio, *Confirmation of the Franciscan Rule*, 1483–6 (Florence, Santa Trinita, Sassetti chapel). Commissioned by the elderly Francesco Sassetti, general manager of the Medici bank, the donor had himself portrayed on the right of this fresco standing next to Lorenzo.

THE FAMILY MEDICI

who had recently doubled his fortune by investing in the company.[7] Also on the list were the descendants of Cosimo's old ally Andrea de' Pazzi, whose son Jacopo now ran a commercial empire rivalling that of the Medici, with companies in Rome, Florence, Lyons, Avignon, Marseilles, Bruges and Valencia.

Lorenzo himself was intelligent and talented but surprisingly ill-equipped for his new position. His father and grandfather had been middle-aged when they had taken over the reins of power; both were cautious characters with experience of negotiating the treacherous mire of Italian politics. Lorenzo knew little about diplomacy. His pampered upbringing in the Palazzo Medici had left him spoilt and arrogant, while his trips abroad had given him a taste for aristocratic extravagance and prepared him for courtly society rather than republican debate. His schooling, which had enabled him to read Latin with ease by the age of twelve, to write classical poetry and to play music, had not included a commercial apprenticeship. He had no interest in the

Medici bank, except as a source of funds. Accordingly, he left the entire responsibility for the company in the hands of Sassetti.

Lorenzo could not, however, delegate political responsibilities, and his initiation into their international complexities was abrupt. Within days of his father's death, he was appointed by the *Signoria* to take Piero's place on the committee attending the summit under way in Florence to negotiate a peace treaty between the republic, Milan and Naples: the so-called Triple Alliance. Given the traditional rivalry between Milan and Naples, this was an ambitious project, but one that held the promise of substantial rewards by putting Florence, and the Medici, on a par with two of Italy's major powers. In January, Lorenzo recorded that the talks were 'some of the most vexatious and laborious the city has had to face'; at least he was aware of his own ignorance, for 'never having had experience of such things, they are new to me and therefore more daunting'.[8] When the discussions were finally completed in July, he sighed with relief: 'I think this is the best news I have ever received'.

Lorenzo's relief, though, was to be short-lived. By the end of 1470, the old rivalry between Milan and Naples had begun to re-emerge, with a twist that would affect the Medici. His hasty decision to allow his cousin back into politics proved a mistake. Instead of supporting Lorenzo and the Triple Alliance, Pierfrancesco decided to side openly with Naples, where his father-in-law, Angelo Acciaiuoli, was in exile. The Milanese ambassador scathingly described Pierfrancesco as 'that piece of meat who can see as little with his brain as with his eyes'.[9] Moreover, Lorenzo was very bitter about how much of the Medici fortune had passed to his cousin: 'the arbitration [of 1451] assigned half of all our wealth to Pierfrancesco,' he recorded in his memoirs, 'and all the best things, which gave him a huge advantage over us'; moreover, 'at the same time he took a third share in the bank, which has made him more profit than us as he has fewer expenses'.[10]

Milan and Naples competed for Lorenzo's favour – and Lorenzo assiduously curried favour with both courts. Ferrante I sent him 'two fine horses' and promised that if he 'wishes for more he is to say so because now that the king has discovered how much he likes them, the king intends to keep him supplied and nothing would give him greater pleasure than to be asked for others, or anything else'.[11] In 1471, Duke Galeazzo Maria Sforza and his new duchess, Bona of Savoy, made a state visit to Florence, ostensibly to fulfil a vow made to the miraculous Virgin of Santissima Annunziata – but in reality to confer privately with Lorenzo. The Florentine herald was awestruck by the ducal retinue: 'the number of his baggage trains, his household so nobly and richly attired in rich brocades,' he noted in his official diary, were such 'that it seemed to me more splendid than anything else in our city'.[12]

Not all the Florentines were so impressed. It was Lent and many were shocked that the ducal courtiers ignored church rules and 'all ate meat without respect to the Church or God'.[13] Because of the fast, it was not possible to lay on the balls, jousts and lion hunts usually staged to entertain important visitors, so Lorenzo ordered three confraternities to stage religious plays instead – the Annunciation (at San Felice), the Ascension (in Santa Maria del Carmine), and Pentecost (at Santo Spirito). According to the notary Ser Giusto, the duke 'went to the one in San Felice but not to the Carmine's or to ours'.[14] The Ascension play, which involved raising 'Christ' off the rood screen and up into the rafters of the church by means of elaborate mechanical devices, 'was done at serious risk to the lives of many people'. The play at Santo Spirito ended in disaster: 'ours was staged on 21 March, late in the evening because we were waiting for the duke' and 'when it was over the stage-hands went home without thinking about the risk of fire'. They had forgotten to extinguish the embers of the flames which had been lit on the crowns of the Apostles, and the church caught fire during the night.[15]

That August, Lorenzo's friendship with Duke Galeazzo Maria brought the opportunity for political gain when the duke's candidate, Cardinal Francesco della Rovere, was elected as Pope Sixtus IV. As a favour to the new pontiff, the duke agreed to the marriage of his illegitimate daughter Caterina Sforza to Sixtus IV's nephew Girolamo Riario, who had been a grocer in the Ligurian city of Savona before his uncle's election. One of the many favours the pope did for the duke was to confirm the Medici as papal bankers and as holders of the Tolfa alum monopoly. When Lorenzo went to Rome in September 1471, as part of the embassy dispatched by the *Signoria* to congratulate Sixtus IV on his election, the pope showered him with tokens of his goodwill – including the priceless Tazza Farnese, the largest cameo to survive from antiquity. As Lorenzo recorded, 'I was much honoured in Rome

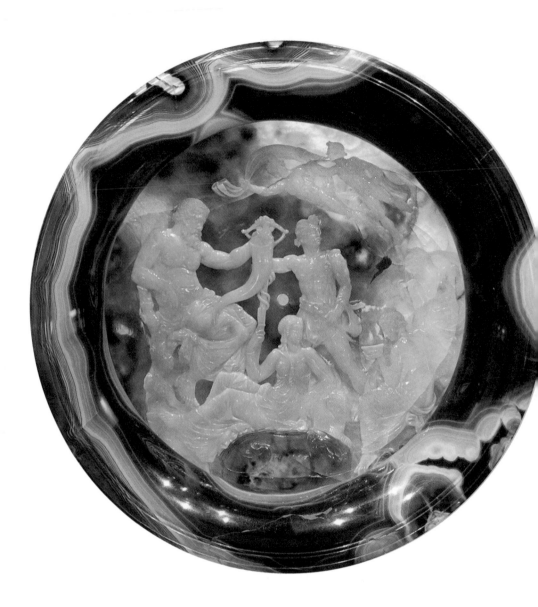

Tazza Farnese, Hellenistic sardonyx cameo, c.200 B.C. (Naples, Museo Archeologico Nazionale). This valuable cameo was valued at 10,000 florins in the inventory of Lorenzo's possessions compiled after his death.

from where I took the two antique marble busts of Augustus and Agrippa, which the Pope gave me, and also our engraved chalcedon cup'.[16] In February 1472, Sixtus provided further proof of his support for the Medici by granting plenary indulgences – the forgiveness of all sins – to Lorenzo and Giuliano, to their mother Lucrezia and grandmother Contessina, as well as to several Medici loyalists, notably Giovanni Tornabuoni and Bernardo Rucellai. A few months later, the pope allowed Lorenzo to buy jewels, cameos and precious gems from his predecessor's collection, worth 23,170 florins.[17]

Even more valuably, Lorenzo obtained a verbal promise from Sixtus IV that his brother Giuliano would be made a cardinal. This would be an unprecedented honour for the Medici bankers: cardinals had the social status of princes in Renaissance Europe and, moreover, enormous influence on the political stage, as well as the chance of being elected to the papal throne itself. In November 1472, Lorenzo sent a politely worded reminder to the pope: 'I have written to Giovanni Tornabuoni and asked him to talk with you about the long-standing desire to have a cardinal in our family,' he began; 'I am sure it is needless to ask again for what was promised so freely, but there are rumours that cardinals are soon to be created and I thought it best to remind you of our desire'.[18]

In the event, the pope did not create any cardinals that year; but Lorenzo continued his campaign with more circumspection, asking Cardinal Jacopo Ammanati for advice on how he should proceed. Ammanati replied the following April: 'It will not be long before the Holy Father will be obliged to make new cardinals, especially for those states which have none; you, for example, are without one, which is unseemly for several reasons.'[19] On Giuliano's prospects, Ammanati was less sanguine: 'There has been much talk here of your Giuliano and by fishing at the fountain-head I find he has been mentioned in the proper places... but I think he might be too unpolished at present to please here; it would be better for him to wear the surplice of the Church, or of a protonotary, then I think there would be no difficulty.' A few weeks later, Lorenzo received another letter from Cardinal Ammanati warning him of the pitfalls of obtaining a red hat for his only brother: if Lorenzo died 'and Giuliano were in the position we are striving for while your children were still young then it seems to me that your family would be in danger of losing the pre-eminence left by

Cosimo to Piero, and by Piero to you'.[20] He recommended nominating another Florentine candidate, preferably a churchman; but that, of course, was not Lorenzo's plan – he would only be satisfied with a cardinal from his own family.

Since their marriage in 1469, Lorenzo and Clarice had produced several children. In August 1470, Clarice gave birth to a daughter, named Lucrezia after Lorenzo's mother, and the following year she was delivered of 'twin boys, born prematurely at about five or six months old', who, as Lorenzo poignantly recorded, 'lived long enough to be baptized'.[21] In February 1472, a healthy son was born, named Piero after his grandfather. The following year, the family priest sent Lucrezia Tornabuoni news of her grandchildren. Little Lucrezia, now aged three, 'still has a little eczema but otherwise she is well', he reported, and 'is obedient like the wise little person she is'.[22] Piero, eighteen months old, 'has a fine colour and is happy and full of spirits', who 'often comes to the side door calling you all, saying Granny, Papa, Mamma, so that you would all laugh if you were here'. The Medici may have been part of the elite of wealthy families governing Florence since 1216 but little Piero was the first son who could boast noble blood – a fact that Lorenzo himself acknowledged.[23]

Lorenzo's own title, *Magnifico*, may be resonant of grandeur to us, but in the fifteenth century it was merely an honorific widely accorded to wealthy merchants who were unable to claim the prestige of an aristocratic name. He would have far preferred the princely tag – and he certainly spent on a princely scale. In 1472, he boasted in his memoirs: 'I find that from 1434 until now we have spent large sums of money on alms, buildings and taxes and other expenses amounting to 663,755 florins; I do not regret this, though many would prefer to have even a part of that total in their purse, and I consider that it gave great honour to our position; I think the money was well spent and I am well pleased.'[24] Without his father's influence, Lorenzo's taste for extravagance was developing fast. He was, for example, adding to his collection of antique gems; and in 1474 he allocated more than 6,000 florins for the purchase of Poggio a Caiano, a thriving rural estate just outside Florence, which Giovanni Rucellai had been obliged to sell after falling on hard times.[25] He also poured money into the racing stable he had established on his estates near Pisa: racing was an aristocratic sport – then, as now – and breeding winners was an expensive business. His grooms travelled to Sicily, Naples and Tunis to find suitable horses, Arabs for preference, which could cost as much as 100 florins each – two years' wages for a master craftsman.[26] Lorenzo may not have been able to acquire a princely title for himself, but he could at least buy the trappings of princely prestige.

Unfortunately, Lorenzo's spending far exceeded the resources of the Medici bank, and so he began to borrow money on a substantial scale, using the company's great reputation as surety. He obtained 10,000 florins from Galeazzo Maria Sforza. When the duke asked him to repay it the following year, Lorenzo refused.[27] The Milanese ambassador reported that Lorenzo did not believe the duke could be in need of such a small sum; in addition, as 'his last and most powerful reason, the division of the bank with Pierfrancesco, to whom he owes dozens and dozens of thousands of ducats' had to be refunded 'before anything else'. Indeed, the accounts of the Medici bank drawn up in March 1474 revealed that Lorenzo then owed the huge sum of 61,000 florins to his cousin.

Like the prince he desired to be, Lorenzo failed to make the distinction between his own private interests and those of the state. The two collided when a rich deposit of alum was discovered near Volterra, one of Florence's subject cities. The Volterrans developed the mine with capital from several Florentine companies, including the Medici bank, and undercut the price of alum charged by the papal mine at Tolfa, which had been, until now, the sole Italian source of this valuable chemical. As the holder of the Tolfa monopoly, Lorenzo needed to keep the price as high as possible to protect the profits of his bank. To ensure that the Volterrans complied, he used his political clout to solve what was essentially a private commercial argument by persuading the *Signoria* to send troops to quell what he argued was a revolt against Florentine rule. On 18 June 1472, Volterra was brutally sacked by 12,000 soldiers under the leadership of the battle-scarred Federigo da Montefeltro, Count of Urbino. He let his men ransack the town for a full twelve hours, looting shops, and raping and murdering many of the inhabitants. Tommaso Soderini had warned Lorenzo to be careful: 'better a lean truce than a fat victory,' he had counselled, and when

Lorenzo asked him what he thought of the conquest, he replied, with some sadness, that he thought Volterra had been lost, not won.[28]

Soderini had a point. It was Lorenzo himself who was blamed for the violent suppression of the uprising. His action alienated many Florentines, who now began to gather around the Medici's main rivals, the influential Pazzi banking clan and their leader, Jacopo de' Pazzi.

Lorenzo was soon to make another mistake. In 1473, he was offered the opportunity to do a substantial favour for Sixtus IV, who wanted the title 'Lord of Imola' for his nephew Girolamo Riario. However, when the pope asked Lorenzo for a loan of 40,000 ducats to buy this small state, on the Florentine borders, from Duke Galeazzo Maria, Lorenzo refused on the grounds of state security. Sixtus IV was furious and instead obtained the money from Jacopo de' Pazzi, who had ignored Lorenzo's order to decline the loan – and who seized his chance of gaining papal favour.

For a few months, Lorenzo's influence in Rome remained intact. When Cardinal Pietro Riario, another of Sixtus IV's nephews, died early in 1474 leaving the see of Florence vacant, Lorenzo managed to obtain the benefice for his brother-in-law, Rinaldo Orsini. During the summer of 1474, however, the pope took his revenge for Lorenzo's earlier recalcitrance by removing the highly profitable papal account from the Medici and then by appointing the Pazzi in their place. That October, he further humiliated Lorenzo by appointing Francesco Salviati, a cousin of Jacopo de' Pazzi, to the vacant Archbishopric of Pisa. Lorenzo asked the Duke of Milan to intervene in what he saw as an 'outright injustice', expressing his great fear that 'certain citizens here', by whom he meant the Pazzi, were intruding on his rights as ruler of Florence.[29] And Lorenzo's financial affairs deteriorated further in June 1476, when Sixtus IV transferred the Tolfa alum monopoly to the Pazzi bank as well. Worse was to follow that December, when news arrived from Milan that Duke Galeazzo Maria – Lorenzo's closest ally – had been assassinated, leaving his widow, Bona of Savoy, acting as regent for their seven-year-old son Giangaleazzo.

The only glimmer of hope came when cousin Pierfrancesco, to whom Lorenzo owed so much money, suddenly died. Lorenzo was appointed guardian to his two sons: Lorenzo, aged fourteen, and the nine-year-old Giovanni.

In Rome, buoyed by his new prestige, Jacopo de' Pazzi was making plans to crush both the Medici regime and their bank. He had found ready support among his own family, including his nephews Francesco and Guglielmo (the latter married to Lorenzo's sister Bianca) and among those Florentines disaffected with Lorenzo's administration. Pazzi also had the support of Sixtus IV's nephews and, more covertly, the approval of King Ferrante I of Naples and of the pope himself.

On the morning of 26 April 1478, the conspirators gathered in Florence's Duomo for mass, where Lorenzo and his brother Giuliano were present. Just as the Host was raised, Francesco de' Pazzi viciously stabbed Giuliano, while two priests fell upon Lorenzo. He managed to escape with just a scratch, thanks to Francesco Nori, a partner in the bank, who received a fatal knife wound to his stomach while shielding his boss. But Giuliano died at the scene.

Largely thanks to Nori, the coup failed. Jacopo de' Pazzi and his supporters rode into the Piazza della Signoria that afternoon shouting 'The People! Liberty!'; but his attempt to incite a popular revolt against the Medici was soon drowned out by cries of 'Kill the traitors!' and '*Palle! Palle!*' from loyal Medici partisans. As one of them recorded, 'I was in the cathedral and when I saw that Giuliano was dead, I rushed to Lorenzo's house' where 'I armed myself with a breast-plate, shield and a sword' and stood guard 'on an empty stomach' all afternoon.[30]

The plotters were arrested and summarily executed. Their fate was witnessed by the apothecary, Luca Landucci, who recorded in his diary how 'the conspirators were hung alive out of the windows of the Palazzo della Signoria'.[31] By evening, the palace had become a hideous gibbet, its walls festooned with dangling corpses – among them Francesco de' Pazzi and his cousin Francesco Salviati, Archbishop of Pisa. Francesco's brother, Guglielmo, was lucky just to be exiled. Jacopo de' Pazzi himself fled into the mountains, only to be captured by local peasants a few days later and returned to Florence to join his fellow conspirators, dangling from a rope on the wall of shame. The two priests who had tried to assassinate Lorenzo were found hiding in a monastery by rioters, who cut off their ears and noses before handing them over to the authorities: one was hanged, the other beheaded.

The murdered Giuliano was buried in the family church of San Lorenzo on 30 April. Less than a month later, on 26 May, his mistress gave birth to their son, who was named Giulio. Lorenzo arranged for him to be brought up in the Palazzo Medici with his cousins – and his illegitimate nephew was to play an important role in the Medici story.

The Pazzi Conspiracy sent shockwaves across Europe. 'We have just been informed of the great and inhuman outrage, dishonour and injury which has been committed against you,' wrote Louis XI of France, 'and we cannot allow this deed to go unpunished.'[32] Lorenzo replied to the king's letter of condolence, expressing his outrage at the behaviour of Sixtus IV, who 'has imposed an iniquitous sentence of excommunication on me, my children, successors and my close friends'.[33] 'Not satisfied with that,' he continued, the pope 'is raising an army to fight against this republic, has persuaded King Ferrante to join him and has urged the king's eldest son [Alfonso, Duke of Calabria] to march against us with a formidable army.'

Sixtus IV was just as angry. On 1 June 1478, he issued his papal bull excommunicating Lorenzo as punishment for the execution of the churchmen. When the bull was debated by the *Signoria* on 12 June, Lorenzo volunteered to go into exile in order to save the city from war, but his offer was refused: 'the house of Medici must be defended in the same way as the republic,' insisted one citizen; 'it is not possible to separate Lorenzo's safety from that of the state,' proclaimed another.[34] Evidently, the Medici supporters had closed ranks to protect their leader. On 13 June, Lorenzo was elected to the Ten of War. A week later, Sixtus IV pronounced an interdict on Florence and declared war on the city. The real target was Lorenzo himself, for, as the pope told the Duke of Urbino, 'we make war on no one save that ungrateful, excommunicated and heretical Lorenzo de' Medici, and we pray God will punish him for his wicked deeds'.[35]

Giovanni Tornabuoni and his staff were now expelled from Rome, and the assets of the Medici bank were seized; Ferrante I did the same in Naples. Lorenzo could not even count on the support of his old ally, Milan, which remained neutral under the regency of Bona of Savoy. In early July 1478, troops commanded by Alfonso of Calabria and the Duke of Urbino marched across Florence's southern border. On 13 July, the apothecary Landucci reported the arrival of ambassadors from Ferrante I, 'who were sent to say that [the King] and the Holy Father would make peace if Florence expelled Lorenzo de' Medici'; but, as Landucci continued, 'the citizens did not agree to that, so the war went ahead'. By 'citizens', he meant not the people but rather the Medici majority in the Palazzo della Signoria.[36]

By the middle of July, Lorenzo was raising troops and negotiating terms with several mercenary leaders, furious with one of them who was hoping to profit by Florence's dire need: 'we were willing to pay him 25,000 ducats,' he wrote to an agent, 'but now he wants double in time of war, and is also making other dishonest demands'.[37] He was in desperate need of funds. On 25 July, he told the Florentine ambassador in Milan to see the ducal secretary in private, 'without either you or he conferring with others,' he warned, to 'find out whether I can count upon 30,000 or 40,000 ducats for six or seven months in case of need'.[38] He also investigated his own resources, which, conveniently for him, contained an unexpected windfall from the guardianship of the late Pierfrancesco's two sons: since they were not yet of age, that summer, without asking their permission, Lorenzo was able to siphon off 53,643 florins from their fortune.[39]

It was necessary to ensure the family were safe, so Clarice and the children were sent to friends in Pistoia. Six-year-old Piero was accompanied by his tutor, the poet Angelo Poliziano, who sent Lorenzo regular updates on the family's welfare, recording how Giovanni, aged two years and nine months, was 'on his pony all day', while Clarice was 'very well but takes little pleasure in anything except for any good news we hear from Florence'.[40] Piero was doing well in the schoolroom. 'I am encouraging him to write, and soon I think he will send you a letter in a fashion that will astonish you,' the tutor reported on 26 August; 'we have a master here who teaches writing in fifteen days and he is excellent at his trade.'[41] On 21 September, Piero did indeed write to his father, 'to tell you we are well, and although I do not as yet know how to write well, I will do what I can.'[42] That autumn, plague broke out in Florence and Lorenzo sent his family on to Cafaggiolo, where it was tiresome and very wet in the mountains: Poliziano informed Lucrezia Tornabuoni that 'the rain is so heavy and so continuous that we cannot

Bertoldo di Giovanni, medal commemorating the Pazzi Conspiracy, 1478 (London, Victoria & Albert Museum).

leave the house and have swapped hunting for ball games to give the children some exercise'. 'I am bored to death,' he concluded.[43]

Meanwhile, Alfonso of Calabria and his armies were threatening Florence. On 19 August 1478, Landucci reported that the soldiers had attacked the castles at Radda and Panzano, just 20 miles south of the city walls.[44] In November, with most of Florence's subject territories under enemy control, the troops took their customary winter break – the fighting season would start again in March – but the Christmas celebrations were muted. 'The citizens are living under the threat of war, of plague and of the papal excommunication, and they are very frightened,' lamented Landucci, 'God help them.'[45] Support for Lorenzo, which had been so solid in the immediate aftermath of the Pazzi plot, now began to waver as the war drained the economy. Anonymous anti-Lorenzo placards appeared overnight on street corners; according to Machiavelli, one friend warned Lorenzo that 'this city is exhausted and wants the war to end'.[46]

Clarice and the children remained at Cafaggiolo for much of the year. On 12 March 1479, she gave birth to another son, named Giuliano in memory of Lorenzo's murdered brother. That May, the seven-year-old Piero sent his father news of his other siblings – Lucrezia (aged eight), Maddalena (six), Giovanni (three), Luisa (two) and Contessina (one). 'We are all well and studying and Giovanni is beginning to spell' while 'Lucrezia sews, sings and reads; Maddalena knocks her head against the wall but without doing herself any harm; Luisa has begun to speak a few words, and Contessina fills the house with her noise.'[47] He also begged his father for the pony he had been promised, and which Lorenzo duly sent: 'I cannot tell you how glad I am to have the pony,' the boy enthused, 'he is so handsome and so perfect' and 'I send you many thanks for such a fine gift; I shall try to repay you by becoming what you wish.'[48]

Lorenzo was preoccupied with more weighty matters. The skirmishes during that second summer of fighting were indecisive, but on 17 September Alfonso of Calabria's troops took the important stronghold of Poggio Imperiale. Moreover, the cost of the war was causing serious problems for the Florentine economy, and for Lorenzo's authority, while the damage done by the soldiers to farmland in the war zone augured a poor harvest. But, just when everything seemed to be going against him, Lorenzo received encouraging news from Milan. Earlier that year, Galeazzo Maria's brother, Ludovico Sforza, had seized power from the regency council, and he now ruled the duchy in the name of his young nephew, Duke Giangaleazzo. Sforza now asked Lorenzo's agent in Milan to inform his master that Ferrante I was ready to negotiate peace, and that Lorenzo should act as quickly as possible before the king changed his mind.

Lorenzo entrusted the delicate task of negotiations to Filippo Strozzi, a close friend of Ferrante I. Strozzi left Florence on 24 November, recording in his diary that 'I was to tell the king that Lorenzo placed himself in the king's hands and would willingly do all the king wished in order to make peace'.[49] However, within days of Strozzi's departure Lorenzo realized that more drastic action was necessary; he took the decision to go to Naples himself, to negotiate in person. He left on 6 December, informing the *Signoria* of his decision only the following day, but reassuring them: 'it is not from presumption that I did not notify you of my departure but because it seemed to me that the agitated and disturbed condition of our city demands deeds not words'.[50] 'Being the one person most hated and persecuted by our enemies,' he thought that 'by placing myself in their hands I might be the means of restoring peace to our city.' If the king's intentions were 'good, there is no better way of testing them than by putting myself voluntarily in his power'. Lorenzo's offer to sacrifice himself for the sake of Florence was a generous one, and it was welcomed by the *Signoria*, who gave him permission to negotiate on their behalf: 'only to you would such large powers be granted in such an important matter,' they informed him, and 'this is the first time such unlimited authority has been granted'.[51]

Lorenzo had learned much during his first decade as leader. Though he had not shown any great grasp of commercial matters, he was proving adept at finding other, more devious ways of raising the funds he needed to finance his extravagant ambitions. He had managed to survive the Pazzi Conspiracy, which had been a very real threat to the Medici; and he was now beginning to develop a talent for diplomatic cunning. Would his gamble with the King of Naples pay dividends?

9

PRIDE
Lorenzo the Magnificent
1480–1492

Lorenzo di Piero (31)
Clarice Orsini (30), *his wife*

> *Their seven children:*
> Lucrezia (10)
> Piero (8)
> Maddalena (7)
> Giovanni (5)
> Luisa (3)
> Contessina (2)
> Giuliano (1)

Lucrezia Tornabuoni (53), *Lorenzo's mother*

Bianca (35), *Lorenzo's sister*
Guglielmo de' Pazzi, *her husband*

Nannina (32), *Lorenzo's sister*
Bernardo Rucellai, *her husband*

Giulio di Giuliano (2), *Lorenzo's illegitimate nephew*

Lorenzo (17) *and* **Giovanni** (13),
Lorenzo's wards, the sons of his cousin, Pierfrancesco

Lorenzo was far too arrogant to have worried about throwing himself into the Neapolitan lion's den. As it was, he spent the winter of 1479–80 as Ferrante I's guest, enjoying splendid hunts in the royal parks, theatrical entertainments, and the company of his cultured friends Federigo of Aragon and Ippolita Sforza, Duchess of Calabria. The pleasures of court life must have been a welcome diversion to the more serious political agenda. Lorenzo was not just negotiating peace between Naples and Florence; it was his own political future that was at stake. He was 'received by the king with the greatest honour,' wrote Francesco Guicciardini later, whose father was a loyal Medici partisan, and 'he tried his hardest to convince the king of the advantages of a peace which would keep him in power'.[1] One of Lorenzo's more persuasive arguments was the threat that if the Medici lost control of the government, 'it could fall into the hands of men with whom the king might find it more difficult to do business'. Ferrante I, who was under pressure from Sixtus IV *not* to do a deal with Lorenzo, 'waited to see what happened in Florence during Lorenzo's absence; in the end, as nothing changed in Florence, he decided to preserve Lorenzo's position'.

On 15 March 1480, a jubilant Lorenzo returned to Florence waving the signed peace treaty. 'There was astonishment that he returned,' apothecary Landucci noted, 'because everyone expected that the king would not let him come home'.[2] The next day, the treaty was made public 'and it was celebrated with lots of fireworks and the ringing of the bells'. There were more noisy celebrations in December, when, after several months of negotiations, Sixtus IV finally lifted the interdict on Florence – and Giovanni Tornabuoni was able to reopen the Medici bank in Rome.

Lorenzo was quick to take advantage of his diplomatic triumph. In April 1480, just weeks after his return, he tightened his control of the government by setting up the Council of Seventy. Like his grandfather's Council of One Hundred, it was composed of handpicked Medici partisans who regulated access to the *Signoria*; but its influence extended much further into the heart of the republican constitution. There were no elections for Lorenzo's senators, who were appointed for life; nor was there any open debate, as they were all sworn to secrecy to ensure loyal backing for his policies. Most significantly, the new council had the power to veto all decisions made by the *Signoria*. And

Lorenzo himself personally took control of foreign policy, ordering Florentine diplomats to keep two sets of correspondence: brief, official letters for the *Signoria*, and private, more informative ones for himself.

Just how far Lorenzo's regime had evolved from the original ideals of the republic was evident in the decoration of the new council's meeting hall (the Sala dei Gigli) in the Palazzo della Signoria. The portraits of famous heroes of republican Rome testified that Florence was still nominally free, but their accompanying inscriptions celebrated the virtues of patriotism rather than of liberty. Cicero, for example, was commended not for his eloquent defence of republican values, but rather for his part in quelling the Catiline conspiracy, a deliberate allusion to the Pazzi plot. More telling were the profile portraits of Roman emperors in the roundels above, whose presence in the palace would have been unthinkable a century earlier.[3]

Lorenzo's public position within the ruling elite had also subtly changed. He no longer presented himself as 'first among equals' as his father and grandfather had done, but unequivocally as Florence's 'first citizen'. He alone was exempt from the law banning all Florentines from carrying arms, and he went out onto the streets with a personal bodyguard of ruffians armed with swords, crossbows, and names to match – Black Martin, Morgante the Giant, Mutant and so on.[4] The Milanese ambassador was impressed at how Lorenzo 'so clearly wields the baton of command without actually holding it'.[5] In a fitting tribute to his new status, it was his own horse Lucciola (meaning 'Firefly', also slang for lady of the night) that won the San Giovanni *palio* in June 1481, a prize usually carried off by a foreign aristocrat.

Many people were appalled at the way Lorenzo and his allies had seized power 'with snares, traps and deceit', as one critic recorded, in order 'to create their own government which is more tyrannical than republican'.[6] Others likened Lorenzo to Julius Caesar, who had overridden the Roman constitution to install himself as the first emperor. But they kept their thoughts to themselves, for Lorenzo was ruthless in silencing opposition. In 1481, three men accused of plotting his assassination were hanged, much to the shock of one foreign ambassador: 'According to the law they should not have been killed,' he wrote, 'however the *Signoria* and the Council of Seventy decided the men had committed the crime of *lèse-majesté*.'[7] As the diplomat rightly concluded, the verdict was one 'which certainly gives honour and respect to

Lorenzo'. A few years later, another plot to kill Lorenzo was uncovered, and this time the accused was interrogated by men who were 'all leading citizens, friends and relatives of the Magnificent Lorenzo… and they conducted this examination very secretly and would not admit that it had taken place'.[8] Lorenzo even had one of his mother's cousins, Alessandro Tornabuoni, exiled for libel: under torture he had 'confessed to wicked things like robbery and other bad deeds but, however, he did not confess to have done anything against the state, though he did admit to writing defamatory works'.[9]

With his position in Florence secured, Lorenzo's next goal was to obtain a cardinal's hat for his second son, Giovanni. When the boy celebrated his seventh birthday in December 1482, the proud father recorded in his memoirs that Sixtus IV 'has declared him capable of holding benefices and made him an apostolic protonotary'.[10] The following month, Lorenzo instructed the staff at the Lyons branch of the Medici bank to identify suitable French benefices for the boy. He also applied directly to King Louis XI, who promised that 'I will gladly do whatever I can when a benefice falls vacant'.[11]

After Louis XI died in August 1483, Lorenzo was quick to ingratiate himself with the new French monarch, Louis's thirteen-year-old son Charles VIII. He sent him a valuable racehorse from his stud, which was taken to France by his cousin Lorenzo di Pierfrancesco.[12] Charles VIII reciprocated: 'On 19 September,' Lorenzo recorded in his memoirs, 'came the news that the King of France, by his own free will, has given the abbey of Font-Douce to our Giovanni.'[13] The appointment, however, still required confirmation in Rome, where Sixtus IV prevaricated. While the support of France could do much for his son's career, Lorenzo needed papal favour to secure the red hat for his boy; yet there was little chance of this favour from the current pope.

It was not until Sixtus IV's long pontificate finally came to an end in August 1484 that Lorenzo had the opportunity to establish closer ties with Rome, not least for the immediate goal of confirming Giovanni's possession of Font-Douce. Within hours of Innocent VIII's election, the Florentine ambassador informed Lorenzo that the key figure in the new regime would be Cardinal Giuliano della Rovere, one of Sixtus IV's nephews, who had played a key role in the conclave. 'He is the pope, and even more than pope,' the ambassador judged, and he advised Lorenzo to 'send him a proper letter for he is the only one I have any fear of in the business of Font-Douce'.[14] The envoy was reassuring, however, for 'His Holiness is well disposed towards you and has always been very friendly to me'.

Lorenzo arranged for his eldest son Piero, now twelve years old, to travel to Rome with the ambassadors appointed to congratulate Innocent VIII on his election. He instructed Piero to explain to the pope 'that I have sent you in my place as the strongest proof that I could give of my wish to be there in person', and he was to 'add that I have experienced how hurtful it has been to be out of favour with the late pope, although as it seems to me I was treated unjustly'.[15] Piero was also to beg Innocent VIII 'to add to the other obligations our house has towards the Holy See by favouring this affair of Giovanni'. Innocent VIII duly complied, confirming Giovanni's benefice of Font-Douce. Lorenzo, though, had worries about Piero, who was becoming a celebrity in Florence: 'the poor lad cannot go outside the door without all Florence running after him,' observed one friend, who testified as to 'how much charm he has, so that all who talk to him are captivated'.[16] In Rome, Piero was 'to obey Giovanni Tornabuoni in all things and not to do anything without him' and, above all, he was to respect the other ambassadors: 'Be careful not to take precedence over those who are your seniors,' Lorenzo ordered, 'for although you are my son, you are still a citizen of Florence.'

Despite dispensing initial favours to the Medici, Innocent VIII's first foray into Italian politics did not bode well for Lorenzo. During the summer of 1485, the Neapolitan barons staged an uprising against the Spanish-born Ferrante I and appealed to the pope for aid. Innocent VIII took their side and declared war on Ferrante I, while Florence and Milan came to the aid of the beleaguered king. But Lorenzo's luck was about to turn. With the troops of Alfonso of Calabria camped outside the gates of Rome, Innocent VIII was forced to make peace – and he let it be known that he favoured an alliance with Florence, or, more particularly, with the resources of the Medici bank. This time, Lorenzo proceeded with care into the minefield of papal politics. 'This ecclesiastical regime is always the ruin of Italy because they are ignorant and do not know how to govern and thus they place the whole world in danger,' he told the Ferrarese ambassador.[17]

With a supplicant pope and a grateful king, Lorenzo used his skills to exploit the situation to his advantage. And just how successful he had become at the diplomatic game was evident early in February 1487, when he betrothed his fourteen-year-old daughter Maddalena to Innocent VIII's son Franceschetto Cibò, a dissolute gambler in his thirties. In March, the news was made public in Florence, and to counter the unpopularity of this foreign match Lorenzo announced Florentine husbands for his two younger daughters: Piero Ridolfi for the nine-year-old Contessina, and his ward Giovanni di Pierfrancesco for Luisa, aged ten.

Lorenzo had to pay handsomely for his papal son-in-law. According to the terms of the contract signed in person by the pope and the Archbishop of Florence, Rinaldo Orsini, Maddalena's dowry was fixed at 4,000 florins. By June 1487, before the marriage had taken place, the ledgers of the Rome branch of the Medici bank recorded that 7,000 florins had been spent on Cibò.[18] Among other expenses, Lorenzo had settled his prospective son-in-law's large gambling debts and paid the price of making him Lord of Cerveteri, a papal fief bought from Lorenzo's Orsini in-laws.

The marriage took place in November 1487 in the Vatican, where Innocent VIII hosted a banquet for the bridal couple. Rather touchingly, Maddalena fell madly in love with her dissolute husband: 'she thinks and dreams of nought else, so great is her love for him,' wrote her priest to a friend.[19] But Lorenzo must have been uneasy about his son-in-law's gambling habits. When Innocent VIII fell ill the following year, he wrote to his ambassador in Rome, unsurprisingly using code in parts: 'in case [the pope] gets any worse, I think it would be a good idea to keep an eye on two things; one to secure somehow what the bank holds on Signor Franceschetto's account... so that it does not pass to the next pope; and the other, to test if it would be possible for him [italics in code] *to get his hands on some of the cash that is in the papal coffers* so that he and Maddalena do not die of hunger'.[20]

Most importantly, Lorenzo himself was now a papal in-law, a position that promised the potential of massive rewards. When Innocent VIII restored the Tolfa alum monopoly to the Medici bank, Lorenzo asked his ambassador in Rome to thank the pope for the contract, 'which I greatly appreciate, not just for the profits it will bring' but

Filippino Lippi, Carafa chapel, 1488–93 (Rome, Santa Maria sopra Minerva).

also, as the astute politician explained, 'because everyone now knows that I am in favour with His Holiness and that will gain me much more'.[21] Lorenzo's prime objective remained a cardinal's hat for his son Giovanni, an issue that had been brought up during the negotiations for Maddalena's marriage. He had written to his ambassador in Rome in the summer of 1487 asking him to do whatever was necessary to gain favour with the College of Cardinals, whose support would be necessary. 'You can offer them everything you can in my name,' he urged, 'and whether they want one thing rather than another... I will ensure that it is done.'[22]

As a power-broker at the papal court, Lorenzo was now an influential figure in Italian politics, and he milked his position to great advantage. He was able to increase his popularity in Florence by doing favours for his fellow citizens, who also benefited from the restoration of economic ties with Rome after twelve years of hostilities. Likewise, the favours he did for Ferrante I and Ludovico Sforza considerably enhanced his status within the Triple Alliance with Milan and Naples, in which, as leader of the small republic of Florence, Lorenzo had been very much the junior partner. His ambitions did not stop there. He urged his ambassador in Rome to advise him of any favours that he could do for Charles VIII of France, 'which will bring me honour, opportunity and great advantage with the king'; as his agent in France remarked, 'the one hand washes the other'.[23]

Lorenzo did not restrict himself to financial and political favours to woo allies. Culture, too, provided an invaluable diplomatic tool in his quest for prestige, and he assiduously cultivated Florence's reputation as a centre of artistic excellence – as well as his own reputation as a connoisseur – by doing favours for those he needed to impress. He sent Alfonso of Calabria a design for the villa the prince was building at Poggioreale, along with a craftsman, Giuliano da Maiano, to take charge of its construction.[24] As part of his campaign to curry favour with the College of Cardinals for Giovanni's red hat, he arranged for the painter Filippino Lippi to stop work on a project in Florence in order to take up the commission to decorate Cardinal Carafa's chapel in Santa Maria sopra Minerva in Rome – and asked one of the employees at the bank to make sure Carafa was satisfied with the result, ensuring that the cardinal would owe him a favour in return.[25]

Lorenzo's networking skills were soon paying handsome dividends for the Medici family. Ludovico Sforza appointed Giovanni as Abbot of Miramondo, near Milan, while Ferrante I gave the boy the lucrative Benedictine abbey of Montecassino, the first of several benefices that the king would bestow on Giovanni as a favour to Lorenzo. As Ferrante I explained, 'it was unnecessary for you to thank us for the benefice we have given your son' because 'we desire to do everything possible to show our gratitude for what you have done for us and this kingdom'.[26]

Ferrante I also gave his approval to a prestigious marriage for Lorenzo's eldest son Piero, now aged sixteen, who was betrothed to Alfonsina Orsini, the daughter of the Count of Tagliacozzo, a close ally of the king. A year younger than her fiancé, she brought him an immense dowry of 12,000 ducats, and the couple were married by proxy in Naples in February 1488.[27] It was April before the married couple finally met one another, in Rome, where the groom's mother Clarice had been staying since daughter Maddalena's marriage the previous November. Poor Clarice had developed tuberculosis and had been too ill to travel home in the winter cold; but she regained enough strength to join the bridal party on its way back to Florence in early May. On the journey, though, she received the tragic news that her daughter Luisa, aged just eleven, had died. Not only was this a family loss, it also brought to an end Lorenzo's plans to unite the two branches of the family through the marriage with Giovanni di Pierfrancesco.

The celebrations for the arrival of Piero and his bride were postponed until June to coincide with the San Giovanni festivities, which were particularly grand that year in honour of both this couple and Franceschetto Cibò and Maddalena, who were in Florence for the feast. Unfortunately, not all went to plan. Landucci recorded in his diary that a Bolognese cutpurse had been arrested during the celebrations, and 'an hour later, without any regard for the solemnity of such a day, they hung him'.[28] The weather also provided some drama, for 'in the evening, at the hour when the horse race was run, a great wind blew with a storm of rain and hail such as has never been seen before and the awnings in Piazza San Giovanni were ripped into thousands of pieces'.

Clarice lasted just a few weeks after these festivities, dying of consumption on 30 July 1488, aged just thirty-eight. The envoy from Ferrara reported that 'Lorenzo's grief for the loss of Clarice, to whom he was sincerely but not passionately attached, was mitigated by the information that his heart's desire, the nomination of his second son, Giovanni, a boy of fourteen, to the cardinalate, would not be long delayed'.[29]

Lorenzo was at a spa near Lucca when his wife died, and he did not attend her funeral. He was battling his own health problems, for his gout was increasingly troublesome, and he sought relief at spas across Tuscany. From Spedaletto he assured his youngest daughter, Contessina, that 'these continued baths suit me excellently so that I hope, if it pleases God, to return as full of health as ever I was; I shall leave very soon and come back to you'.[30] Behind this cheerful facade, however, he knew he was very ill, and he scoured Italy in search of a cure. Various were suggested. One doctor sent a recipe for an ointment, and promised that summer to find 'a red stone that grows in the stomach of a swallow', which should be 'tied in a piece of linen and sewn into your shirt at the nipple of the left breast'.[31]

Illness, though, could not dampen Lorenzo's joy when his 'heart's desire' was granted on 9 March 1489: Giovanni was made a cardinal by Innocent VIII. He was given the titular church of Santa Maria in Domnica, and his red hat and ring were sent to him in Florence, with orders that he was not to wear them for three years on account of his youth. 'This is the greatest thing that has ever happened to our house,' Lorenzo wrote ecstatically to his ambassador in Rome a few days later.[32] He crowed with good reason. Giovanni now had the social status of a prince, and, while it was normal to hand out red hats for political reasons to the ruling aristocratic elite (Ludovico Sforza's brother and Ferrante I's son, for example, were both cardinals), it was an unprecedented honour for a mercantile 'ruler'. On 25 April 1489 Lorenzo gained even more leverage in Rome, when the Medici bank lent 100,000 ducats to Innocent VIII; for surety, Lorenzo received 'two-tenths on the stipends of all newly-appointed priests, 70,000 ducats, and he will hold Città di Castello until it is repaid'.[33]

Lorenzo had carefully crafted his image as the magnificent and wealthy ruler of an equally grand state; and his status with foreign rulers had done much to shore up his popularity in Florence: 'without their esteem, he would not be so highly regarded at home,' judged the Ferrarese ambassador.[34] The international respect he acquired convinced Florentines that their city had real power on the world stage. Apothecary Landucci was very impressed when a menagerie of exotic animals – 'a very tall giraffe, beautiful and graceful' and 'a large lion and very unusual goats' – arrived from Constantinople in 1487 as a present to the city from the sultan, for 'it was understood from such a fine gift that he was certainly friends with Florence'.[35]

Humanist scholars in Lorenzo's Florence contributed to this sense of self-esteem by fabricating propaganda to prove the superiority of the city's rich artistic traditions. Having learnt from Pliny and other classical authors that great art was the hallmark of a great civilization, they exploited this idea to show that Florence's cultural achievement equalled, and even surpassed, the glories of antiquity. Lorenzo himself organized a monument in the Duomo to the fourteenth-century painter Giotto, an honour previously reserved for military and literary heroes (including the poet Dante and several mercenary soldiers, including the Essex-born John Hawkwood). Above all, Lorenzo's propagandists took the first steps in crafting the Medici myth. Writing in the 1480s, Antonio Manetti claimed that Filippo Brunelleschi had revived the language of classical architecture and that it had been Lorenzo's great-grandfather, Giovanni di Bicci, 'a man of great taste who had seen Filippo's new and beautiful creations' and, recognizing the architect's genius, had commissioned him to design the church of San Lorenzo.[36] Vespasiano da Bisticci, who was writing his biographies of the famous at the same time, made no mention of an architect but more correctly attributed the rebuilding of San Lorenzo to Cosimo. A bookseller by trade, Vespasiano had known Cosimo and he now detailed the huge sums that the banker had spent on religious projects: he even included an account, almost certainly apocryphal, of how Cosimo, when warned by one of his bank employees that the builders at San Lorenzo were overspending, had reproved the man and insisted that, on the contrary, the builders were not spending enough.[37]

The crafting of the image of Lorenzo as a great patron of the arts was also under way. 'First Citizen' Lorenzo was compared by his contemporaries with Lucullus and Maecenas, the two most extravagant patrician patrons of Ancient Rome. The comparison did not bear scrutiny, but it would be considerably embellished in the sixteenth century. In truth, Lorenzo was far from being a patron on the scale of his

Sandro Botticelli, *Primavera*, 1480s (Florence, Uffizi).

father or grandfather, and many of the Renaissance masterpieces traditionally associated with the Medici at this period actually belonged to Lorenzo di Pierfrancesco and his brother Giovanni – works such as Botticelli's *Primavera* (*Spring*) as well as a statue of St John the Baptist, an early work by Michelangelo: in 1499, these were valued at just 15 florins each, for paintings did not have the same princely cachet as gems or cameos.[38]

Lorenzo used art as a political tool; but what he was really interested in was amassing a truly princely collection of valuable objects: antique sculpture, vases of semi-precious stones, gems, medals, coins, cameos and rare manuscripts, together worth many thousands of florins. His expenditure on these trappings of aristocratic prestige impressed Duke Ercole I d'Este, who was shown 'medals, cameos and other noble things of great value' when he stayed at the Palazzo Medici on his way to Rome in May 1487.[39] 'Rare and lordly' was another verdict. Unusually for the period, Lorenzo boasted his ownership by conspicuously engraving his initials, 'LAV.R.MED', on many of the items – though modern scholars are divided over whether the enigmatic 'R' represents *Rex* ('King') or something else.[40] More telling of his princely ambitions was the grandiose family palace he planned near to the church of Santissima Annunziata (and its famous miracle-working image of the Virgin), though it was never built. His major project was the conversion of the farmhouse at Poggio a Caiano into a magnificent villa, which, with a pedimented facade inspired by Ancient Roman temples, would prove a landmark in the history of architecture, influencing the design of country houses across Europe for centuries to come.

Lorenzo's interest in classical antiquity was also evident in his financing of public entertainments in Florence. In 1491, the pageant floats for the Feast of San Giovanni were rather disappointing, 'to our great shame,' as one observer recorded, 'because there were many visitors present'; but what followed certainly made up for any embarrassment.[41] Lorenzo 'had the Company of the Star do fifteen triumphs of his own invention relating how Paulus Aemilius made his triumphant

Above: Antique sardonyx vase incised with LAV.R.MED (Florence, Museo degli Argenti).
Opposite: Poggio a Caiano, Villa Medici, mid-1480s. The innovative idea of decorating this rural farmhouse with an entrance loggia based on the temples of Ancient Rome was almost certainly Lorenzo's – he had books on classical architecture read to him while in his bath.

entry into Rome after he returned from a foreign city with so much treasure that the Romans did not have to pay taxes for forty or fifty years' and 'everyone thought that nothing more beautiful had ever been done in Florence'. Fans and critics alike would have understood this very explicit piece of propaganda, designed by Lorenzo to display his image not only as their city's political and cultural leader but also as its most generous benefactor.

The truth was, though, that the image of wealth that Lorenzo strove so successfully to create was a hollow illusion. The cost of everything – his lavish entertainments, his princely collection, his racing stables, the favours he promised and the backhanders needed to secure Giovanni's red hat – far outstripped the dwindling resources of the Medici bank. Although the company still retained its reputation, a fiction Lorenzo worked hard to maintain, behind the scenes it was in serious trouble. Giovanni Tornabuoni may have been able to reopen the Rome branch after Sixtus IV had lifted the interdict, but Lorenzo was forced to liquidate the Bruges and London branches of the company because of heavy losses. When the London manager returned home, Lorenzo had him arrested for a debt of 3,549 ducats he owed the bank for a cargo of currants: the unfortunate man spent a year in the Stinche, Florence's grim debtors' prison.[42] There were problems too at the branch in Lyons, which were serious enough for Lorenzo to send Francesco Sassetti to France. Sassetti identified issues with the personnel and

wrote to Lorenzo, warning him that 'your staff need to be managed with more discipline and firmness... because any relaxation of authority is a tempting bait leading to immorality and disobedience'.[43] One of the problems, unfortunately, was Sassetti himself, who was not really up to the job of general manager.

Lorenzo's personal finances took a serious hit in 1485, when Lorenzo di Pierfrancesco came of age and demanded the repayment of the 53,643 florins that the senior Lorenzo had taken illegally from him and brother Giovanni in 1478.[44] The two brothers also demanded the enormous sum of 158,766 florins, which they claimed was due on unpaid interest and other loans, and more besides. As they explained, Lorenzo had 'forced us to lend this money, and if we had not done so, as he once told me in his study, as guardians of our inheritance he would take it'. Lorenzo had also tried to prevent his cousins from accessing their capital in the bank: 'we asked him every day and tried to take out as much money as possible from the bank, but he has prevented us from making withdrawals for the last four years,' declared a very unhappy Lorenzo di Pierfrancesco.

The arbitrators appointed to settle the dispute found in favour of the young brothers. Lorenzo was forced to transfer the family villa at Cafaggiolo and other ancestral estates in the Mugello to pay off the debt to his relatives. The historian Francesco Guicciardini described Lorenzo's financial predicament: 'he did not neglect any manner of magnificence, however costly, with which he could keep the favour of powerful men and because of this, his expenditure on magnificence and presents at Lyons, Milan and Bruges, and other places where he did business, escalated while his profits dropped because his company was managed by men of insufficient ability'; moreover, 'his affairs were in such disorder that on several occasions he was on the verge of bankruptcy, and found it necessary to help himself to money belonging to his friends or to public funds'.[45]

Indeed, Lorenzo's corruption is a sorry tale of greed, and one that rarely makes its way into the annals of Medici history. In February 1482, for example, he withdrew 9,205 florins from a government fund in order – so he claimed – to build a hostel for one of the guilds; but it was soon evident that the money was intended for his own pocket. Later that year, he persuaded the government to grant him a special dispensation exempting him from paying his overdue taxes.[46] Ordinary

Florentines could expect to be imprisoned in the Stinche if they failed to pay up, and to be disqualified from holding public office. Thanks to the survival of the ledgers of one government committee, we know exactly how much money Lorenzo diverted from this fund for his own personal use: 2,197 florins over the two years 1483–5, and another 3,328 florins during 1486–8; but the following year his 'borrowing' sky-rocketed to 24,319 florins, and by 1491 the ledgers record that he had taken over 80,000 florins.[47] This was not the only government fund that he accessed: another set of ledgers reveals some 135,000 florins taken from the public purse. According to Piero Parenti, Lorenzo used fictitious accounts to raise money and persuaded the *Signoria* to make 100,000 florins available to him from the public purse to finance the campaign for Giovanni's red hat – though at least that would be to the advantage of Florence as well as the Medici.[48] Lorenzo also arranged for the government to devalue the Florentine currency in 1491, issuing a new coin, which, according to one of his critics, was designed to 'pay off the debts of Lorenzo'.[49]

Beyond the Medici bank's troubles, the reality was that Florence's economy itself was in decline. The only sizeable fortune made by a Florentine in the second half of the fifteenth century was that of Filippo Strozzi, whose successful career as a banker had started in Naples, after his exile there by the Medici. The cost of the Pazzi wars had been a terrible drain on the public purse and on the rich, who bore the burden of taxation. Bankruptcies were becoming increasingly common: Giovanni Rucellai, Lorenzo's uncle by marriage, lost his fortune, while Francesco Sassetti, who had invested his capital in the Medici bank, lost most of it, albeit through his own incompetence.

Fuelled by the economic slump, opposition began to grow to Lorenzo's princely ambitions. In his sermons, the charismatic Dominican friar Fra Girolamo Savonarola launched an attack, carefully cloaked in biblical precedent, on the materialistic culture of Florence's wealthy elite and, tellingly, on the secrecy of Lorenzo's regime and the corruption at the heart of his government. Although Lorenzo denied all accusations of sleaze, his fraudulent practices were common knowledge among the city's elite; indeed, many had been directly involved, such as Francesco Guicciardini's grandfather. Several chancery scribes, appalled by Lorenzo's lack of respect for the institutions of the republic, noted their protest in the margins of government documents (where they were found by a later historian trawling the Florentine archives). That Lorenzo made enemies among those he excluded from power is understandable; but what is significant is that by 1491 he had also made many enemies among his own allies.

At the same time, Lorenzo's gout continued to worsen and his health was becoming a matter of grave concern. In the middle of August 1491, he was warned by a doctor to 'beware of cold and damp feet, of moonlight and of the air at sunset, and do not eat pears or swallow grape pips'.[50] Early in the following year, the Ferrarese ambassador informed Ercole I d'Este that Lorenzo was in such severe pain that he was unable to receive the diplomats waiting to see him. On 11 February 1492, the same envoy sent news that Lorenzo was 'very ill and much tormented with pain all over', but reassured the duke with the report that 'the doctors do not think the illness is life-threatening'.[51] By 8 March, he reported that 'Lorenzo is better, though he still has painful attacks and it is thought that this unusually cold weather affects him'.[52]

On the following day, 9 March, Lorenzo must have been relieved to know that Giovanni was finally invested with his cardinal's robes in the monastery at Fiesole, before leaving for Rome to attend his first consistory. At sixteen years of age, he was the youngest member of the College of Cardinals – and indeed one of the youngest *ever* made. On 25 March 1492, he wrote to his father in some excitement: 'on Friday morning I was given a public reception and went from Santa Maria del Popolo to the Vatican, accompanied by all the cardinals, and by very heavy rain', adding that 'the news that you are so much better has been a great joy to me'.[53]

Cardinal Giovanni's new status was published officially on 26 March, and, despite his ill health, Lorenzo hosted a party in the Palazzo Medici to celebrate the event. He also wrote his son a long letter from his sick bed:

> Remember every hour that it is not by your own merits or regard that you have attained the cardinalate but by the grace of God and show your gratitude to Him by leading a saintly and honest life… you are now in Rome, that sink of all iniquities… and there will be no lack of inciters to vice… it is essential that you become a good churchman… and doing this, it will not be difficult for you to aid the city and our house… I would rather see a well-appointed stable and a well-ordered and cleanly household than magnificence and pomp. Let your life be

regular and reduce your expenses gradually in the future, for the
retinue and the master both being new, it will be difficult at first...
Ask people to your own house more often than you accept invitations
to theirs... Eat plain food and take exercise, for those who wear your
habit easily contract illnesses if they are not careful.[54]

Lorenzo would never know just how crucial Giovanni's red hat
would be for the family's survival: 'this was a ladder enabling his family to rise to heaven', as Machiavelli later put it.[55] Florence's leader died
on 8 April 1492, aged just forty-three, from the complications of gout,
just like his father and grandfather. The doctor who had been treating
Lorenzo – and who had been insisting that his patient would recover
– committed suicide the next day by throwing himself head-first into
a well.

Lorenzo's funeral took place in San Lorenzo on 10 April. Many
lamented his passing. In the view of the apothecary Landucci, 'he was
the most glorious man that ever existed, the richest and the greatest'.[56]
But there were others who rejoiced in his demise, 'thinking that the
republic would get its liberty back and they would be free of servitude'
as Piero Parenti noted, 'for under his rule, the city had been completely enslaved'.[57]

Lorenzo the Magnificent is a figure embalmed in myth, a myth
whose origins lie in the image that he himself promoted. He is celebrated by modern scholarship and tourist guidebooks alike as the epit-
ome of the universal Renaissance Man, an outstanding political leader
who guided Florence to prosperity, a wise diplomat, an enlightened
patron of Renaissance masterpieces, an intellectual giant and a talented poet. The reality was both less glorious and considerably more in-
teresting. By promoting himself as the magnificent and wealthy ruler
of an equally grand state, he achieved a position for himself and his
city far beyond what either merited. This self-assertion was to prove
the cornerstone of the myth of Lorenzo, one that would expand in the
sixteenth century – and is still widely believed today. Undoubtedly, the
determination with which he pursued his campaigns for personal prestige and the social advancement of his family showed him to be an
unscrupulous political operator; and his talents were honed by the
culture of his times.

Would his son Piero, still only twenty years old, be able to capital-
ize on his father's achievements?

10

NEMESIS

Piero and Cardinal Giovanni

1492–1503

Piero di Lorenzo (20)
Alfonsina Orsini (20), *his wife*

Piero's brothers:
Cardinal Giovanni (17) *and* Giuliano (13)

Piero's sisters:
Lucrezia (22) m. Jacopo Salviati
Maddalena (19) m. Franceschetto Cibò
Contessina (14) m. Piero Ridolfi

Piero's aunts:

Bianca (47) m. Guglielmo de' Pazzi
Nannina (44) m. Bernardo Rucellai

Piero's cousins:

Giulio (14), *illegitimate son of his dead uncle, Giuliano*
Lorenzo di Pierfrancesco (29)
Giovanni di Pierfrancesco (25)

The year 1492 marked more than just the end of an era in the Medici story: it was also a watershed in world affairs. That August, Christopher Columbus set sail from Palos, Spain, on the epic voyage across the Atlantic that would transform Europe's view of the world. Also in Spain, Ferdinand I's conquest of Granada set the scene for the Spanish kingdom to emerge as a major power to rival France on the European stage. In Rome, the worldly and corrupt Spaniard Rodrigo Borgia was elected as Pope Alexander VI. His dealings with France and Spain would radically alter the political map of Italy. A crisis was looming that would bring an abrupt end to peace and prosperity in Italy and take the Medici story into the pitiless world of international politics.

Thanks to Lorenzo's success at consolidating his hold on power in Florence, and despite the anti-Medici grumblings, Piero inherited his father's position with little fuss. On 20 May, six weeks after Lorenzo's death, Cardinal Giovanni returned home and was given the honour of a ceremonial entry, the first member of the Medici family – but by no means the last – to be accorded this distinction. It was his right as a papal legate, but the symbolism of the event would not have been lost on the observant Florentines. With Piero ruling the republic and his brother a prince of the Church, the Medici position may have appeared invincible. However, Piero's political skills were about to be severely tested.

His first mistake was the complacent decision to ignore the hostility towards the Medici regime that was growing in Florence. Arrogant and spoilt, Piero saw himself as a prince by right, and he soon fell out with his father's advisers. He disregarded the warnings voiced by Bernardo Rucellai, his uncle, and Paoloantonio Soderini, the son of Lorenzo's mentor Tommaso, who both urged him to moderate the more tyrannical aspects of his father's regime. In foreign affairs too, he was determined to be his own man. He abandoned the Triple Alliance, which had been the cornerstone of his father's prestige at home and abroad, and chose instead to side with Naples, a policy no doubt encouraged by his Neapolitan in-laws. His wife, Alfonsina Orsini, was the daughter of a close friend of Ferrante I, while Virginio Orsini, cousin to both Piero and Alfonsina, was the commander of Ferrante I's army. Inevitably, this policy earned Piero the enmity of Ludovico Sforza, who continued to rule Milan in the name of his nephew Duke

Giangaleazzo, and the change of alignment would bring about disastrous consequences.

It was bad luck for Piero that Pope Innocent VIII, who had done so much to enhance the status of the Medici, should die just months after his father, Lorenzo. Cardinal Giovanni entered the conclave with orders from Piero to vote with the pro-Naples faction, led by Cardinal Giuliano della Rovere. Unfortunately, it was della Rovere's great rival Rodrigo Borgia who was elected as Alexander VI on 11 August – and the Medici again lost favour at the papal court. The arrogant Piero then incurred the enmity of Ludovico Sforza by the grandiose show he put on as leader of the Florentine embassy in Rome to congratulate the new pope. Florence's tailors and jewellers had been hard at work for three months making the exceptionally costly outfits with which he intended to demonstrate his prestige by outshining the delegations from Naples and Milan. 'Ludovico Sforza was angry,' recorded Guicciardini, 'for it appeared to him that Piero wanted to compete with him and that not only did he want to be an equal of him and the other princes of Italy, but even to surpass them.'[1]

Despite his pretensions, Piero became increasingly marginalized on the political stage the following year, when Alexander VI made an alliance with Milan, marrying his daughter, Lucrezia Borgia, to Ludovico Sforza's cousin. Piero's alliance with Naples was looking even more frail by the end of 1493, when alarming news arrived from France. King Charles VIII, who was heir to the dukes of Anjou – the dynasty driven out of Naples by Ferrante I's father, Alfonso of Aragon – was making plans to reconquer the kingdom. Worryingly, the French campaign had the support of Ludovico Sforza and, more tentatively, of Alexander VI, though the pope was prevaricating, waiting to ensure he would end up on the winning side. And worse was to come when Ferrante I himself died very suddenly on 27 January 1494, to be succeeded by his son as Alfonso II. According to a Ferrarese chronicler, Ferrante 'died of a broken heart after hearing that King Charles of France was bringing an enormous army into Italy to seize his realm'.[2] 'These were the beginnings and origins of the ruin of Italy, and of Piero de' Medici in particular,' wrote Guicciardini later.[3] The historian, aged ten at the time, was a contemporary witness to the dramatic events that followed.

As war threatened, Piero seemed blindly unaware that his pro-

Naples policy was hugely unpopular in Florence. As Guicciardini recorded, 'seeing themselves being dragged needlessly into a terrible war they could not hope to win, and to support the Aragonese, who were widely detested, against the French, who were generally liked, the Florentines began to criticize Piero in public, as they knew the war was his idea and one he had decided upon against the wishes of the leading citizens'.[4] By April 1494, Piero's opponents had united behind his cousins Lorenzo and Giovanni di Pierfrancesco to form a pro-French party. Piero responded by having the brothers arrested on a charge of conspiracy, and 'although he wanted them dealt with in the harshest possible manner, the leading citizens did not wish for blood on their hands and so they were exiled'.[5]

In August 1494, ambassadors from Charles VIII arrived in Florence to request safe conduct for the French army on its way to Naples. Piero refused. The king retaliated by expelling Florentine merchants from France, and 'it was said all over the city that the king intended to attack Florence'.[6] The prospect of war had suddenly become very real. All summer, the French army had been massing on the borders of Savoy, and on 3 September 30,000 soldiers began their march across the Alps. Daily reports of Charles VIII's progress, of his warm reception by Ludovico Sforza and his approach to the Florentine border, brought panic to the city. In September, Lorenzo and Giovanni di Pierfrancesco broke the terms of their exile and rode north to join the French. That autumn, Savonarola preached a sermon to a packed cathedral, taking as his text the terrifying words with which God announced his intention to punish mankind: 'And behold, I, even I, do bring a flood of waters upon the earth' (Genesis 7:17).

In early October 1494, another embassy arrived from Charles VIII to request safe conduct for the French troops, but once again Piero arrogantly refused. With a large, hostile army now at the frontier, Piero took matters into his own hands, and, without consulting the *Signoria*, he left on 26 October to negotiate in person with Charles VIII. No doubt he was inspired by his father's dramatic journey to Naples in 1479, which had brought such a triumphant end to the wars following the Pazzi Conspiracy; but Piero patently lacked Lorenzo's diplomatic skills. He caved in to Charles VIII, surrendering Pisa and other Florentine territories to the French in exchange for peace. Despite the humiliation, on returning home on 8 November Piero behaved like the

Donatello, *Judith and Holofernes*, c.1460, detail (Florence, Palazzo Vecchio).

conquering hero: 'he threw sweetmeats to the crowd and gave wine to the people to appear benevolent and to show that he had reached a good agreement with the king'.[7] But much had changed in Florence over the past fortnight. Even loyal Medici partisans such as Bernardo Rucellai and Paoloantonio Soderini, as well as his own brother-in-law Jacopo Salviati, agreed that Piero had lost all credibility as leader.

When Piero went to the Palazzo della Signoria on the following day, 9 November, surrounded by his armed guards, he was refused entry. Crowds gathered quickly. 'Within an hour the piazza was full and everyone was shouting "The People! Liberty!"' wrote Landucci, and 'not many went to the Palazzo Medici.'[8] Outnumbered, Piero and his supporters fled. Later that day, the apothecary spied Cardinal Giovanni in the Palazzo Medici: 'I saw him through the windows on his knees praying to God,' and, judging him to be a 'good young man' he observed how Giovanni 'disguised himself as a friar and also left'. The *Signoria* voted to exile Piero, Cardinal Giovanni, their younger brother Giuliano and their cousin Giulio – and declared the date, the Feast of Christ the Saviour, to be henceforth a national holiday.

Many Medici supporters were then arrested, including those government officials who had connived at Lorenzo's fraudulent use of public funds. The dwindling assets of the Medici bank and all the family's possessions were confiscated. In a telling piece of propaganda, Donatello's bronze statues *David* and *Judith* were both removed from the Palazzo Medici and taken to the Palazzo della Signoria; just as the Medici had hijacked these republican heroes to boast their loyalty to the state, so the state now returned them to their proper home, the seat of power. The rest of the contents of the palace were later sold by auction. 'There were velvet bed hangings embroidered with gold and many other items, paintings, canvases and many fine things,' recorded Landucci, the sale demonstrating 'how transitory is Fortune… and that man should not grow proud.'[9]

Characteristically, Piero refused to admit defeat. He persuaded Charles VIII to ask the *Signoria* to rescind the sentence of exile – but he underestimated the extent of his unpopularity. The Florentines were adamantly opposed to his return. When the king made his formal entry into the city on 17 November, escorted by 11,000 troops, the *Signoria* decorated the gate with the royal arms and an inscription in French hailing Charles VIII as 'guardian and deliverer of our liberty', and lodged him in the Palazzo Medici.[10] Ten days later, Charles signed a treaty with the new regime, which, although it was vague about the return of Pisa and the other territories surrendered by Piero, did include a clause requiring Piero 'to remain 100 miles from Florence, and that there is a price of 2,000 florins on his head, and the same on his brothers, and all of this [Charles VIII] swore at the altar in the cathedral'.[11] The king left on 28 November. That day, the *Signoria* sent officials to evict Alfonsina Orsini and her mother from the Palazzo Medici: 'first they pulled off all their jewellery' and then sent the women 'sobbing to the monastery of Santa Lucia'.[12]

By Christmas 1494, Florence had a new republican constitution, shorn of all the committees through which the Medici had manipulated the electoral system. Leading this revolution was Fra Girolamo Savonarola, whose fiery sermons attacked the corruption and materialism of the old Medici regime. 'Give yourselves to the simple life, sons and daughters,' he instructed from the pulpit, 'and you women, I declare to you that if you do not let go of your pomp, your superfluities and your vanities, and do not devote yourselves to simplicity then you will die like dogs.'[13] The *Signoria* was reinstated as the prime organ of power, with a new body, the Great Council, to approve all legislation: with 25 per cent of all Florentine men aged over twenty-nine years old eligible for membership, this was a massive enlargement of the electorate, and the Great Council soon became the symbol of the city's freedom from Medici tyranny. Old Cosimo's burial plaque in San Lorenzo, inscribed with the words *Pater Patriae* ('Father of the Nation'), was removed by order of the *Signoria*. The Medici coats-of-arms were brutally hacked off buildings across the city, and the friars at Santissima Annunziata threw out Lorenzo's wax image, which had been placed in the church in 1478 in gratitude for his survival in the Pazzi Conspiracy.

In fewer than three years, Piero had squandered his father's legacy. Guicciardini's verdict was withering: 'With the city united behind him and the favour of foreign princes assured, Piero made an excellent start and if even a mediocre level of judgement had accompanied such good fortune,' he wrote, 'it would have been impossible for him to fail, but his lack of intelligence, and Florence's bad luck, made what initially seemed impossible become inevitable.'[14] The image that Lorenzo had so carefully crafted as the magnificent and wealthy ruler of an equally powerful state had shattered. The Medici family had lost its power and influence on the international stage – and so had Florence. Piero's Orsini in-laws in Rome were out of favour with Alexander VI, while those in Naples were busy with Alfonso II, preparing to defend the kingdom against the French. His alliance with Naples was worthless, and the French king had already shown himself unwilling to help. Nor could Piero expect any help from Milan, where Ludovico Sforza now ruled as Duke of Milan in his own right after the death of his nephew Giangaleazzo in October. All Piero could do was hope that the chaos engulfing Italy could be used to his advantage.

The events of the twelve months that followed redrew the political map of Italy. On 25 January 1495, Charles VIII and Pope Alexander VI signed a peace treaty abandoning Naples to its fate: Alfonso II abdicated the next day, giving his crown to his son Ferrante II, but the French captured Naples a month later. Piero must have been dismayed to hear that the Florentine embassy sent by the *Signoria* to congratulate Charles VIII on his victory included his cousin Lorenzo di Pierfrancesco and his uncle Bernardo Rucellai.

Then, in March 1495, Alexander VI tore up the treaty with France to make an alliance with Venice, Milan, Spain and the Holy Roman Empire. Ostensibly this was a Holy League against the Turks, but the pope's real aim was to expel the French from Italy. In May, a week after his Neapolitan coronation, Charles VIII began his journey back to France, leaving a garrison of troops in Naples. But many of the soldiers had caught a strange new disease, the *mal francese* as the Italians dubbed it, or syphilis. Its name was derived from a contemporary poem written by an Italian doctor, describing how Apollo punished the shepherd Sifilo for his sexual indiscretions. And that summer, Ferrante II started the reconquest of the kingdom, with the help of Ferdinand I of Spain and his able general Gonsalvo de Cordoba. The French were finally expelled from Naples in November 1495 – and the victory gave Spain a foothold in Italy.

Meanwhile, Alexander VI was also determined to enforce a change of government in Florence, where Savonarola had remained loyal to France and stubbornly refused to join the Holy League. In these tumultuous politics, Piero now found himself on the same side as the

Sandro Botticelli, *Portrait of a Woman*, *c*.1488 (Florence, Palazzo Pitti), thought to be
Piero's wife, Alfonsina Orsini.

Andrea del Sarto, *Punishment of the Gamblers*, c.1510; one of a series of five frescoes depicting scenes from the life of Filippo Benizzi that adorn the courtyard known as the Chiostrino dei Voti in the church of Santissima Annunziata, Florence.

pope; but he had little to offer Alexander VI, and the pope had little desire to aid this kinsman of Rome's Orsini clan. Piero's hopes rested on exploiting the growing unpopularity of Savonarola's theocratic regime. According to the Mantuan ambassador, the Florentines 'are so petrified by the Dominican friar that they have surrendered themselves to piety, fasting on bread and water three days a week, and on bread and wine for another two'.[15]

Life under Savonarola was indeed grim. A raft of new puritanical laws brought draconian penalties for swearing and gambling, and the friar urged the Florentines to stone homosexuals. He banned the bawdy games that were such a popular feature of Carnival and instead ordered children to set up altars on street corners to collect alms: 'they were so insistent that it was hard to pass along the streets unless one gave them a few coins,' reported the Milanese ambassador.[16] There were no colourful pageant wagons for the festivities of San Giovanni, and the *palio* too was banned. Worse, thanks to a very poor harvest, by the spring of 1497 the city was in the grip of famine.

That April, having raised 2,000 troops, Piero made his first attempt to take Florence by force. But when he reached the city, he was disappointed to find that there was no popular uprising. The gates remained closed and the streets quiet. As Guicciardini explained, 'he believed that the people would rise up and support him, but his designs were built on air, and founded on the hope, typical of exiles, that they have many friends and much loyalty in the city'.[17] Piero continued to plot, but his carelessness led to disaster in August when the *Signoria* arrested one of his agents, who revealed, under torture, the names of his co-conspirators in the city. Five of Piero's closest allies were executed, including his cousin Lorenzo Tornabuoni and his sister Contessina's father-in-law, Niccolò Ridolfi. Another sister, Lucrezia, was also implicated, but she was released from prison after the intervention of her husband, Jacopo Salviati.

There were, though, many among the wealthy elite who wanted an end to Savonarola's regime. Moreover, there was much support for a return to a Medici-led government – just not for one in which Piero played a leading role. 'It was their intention,' recorded Guicciardini, 'not to recall Piero de' Medici to Florence, but to concentrate power in the hands of a small group of well-born citizens, under the leadership of Lorenzo and Giovanni di Pierfrancesco.'[18] This plan to put

Piero's cousins in power had the support of Ludovico Sforza – no friend of Piero – and the duke confirmed the alliance by offering his niece, Caterina Sforza, as a bride for Giovanni di Pierfrancesco. The couple were married in secret in early September. Caterina, who was slightly older than her husband, was the widow of Sixtus IV's nephew, Girolamo Riario, Lord of Forlì, where she had continued to rule since his assassination in 1488. She gave birth to a son, and she would outlive her husband, who was dead within a year. The boy was named Giovanni in his memory. He would play his own part in a later chapter of the Medici story.

In Rome, Alexander VI continued his own campaign to force Florence to abandon its alliance with France. In May 1497, he excommunicated Savonarola, but the friar continued to preach his sermons in direct contravention of papal orders. The following spring, the pope warned the *Signoria* that he would place an interdict on the city unless Savonarola was stopped. On Palm Sunday, 8 April 1498, the *Signoria* finally bowed to papal pressure and arrested the friar – he was put on trial and hanged before being burnt at the stake in the Piazza della Signoria on 23 May. Alexander VI had succeeded in breaking Florence's alliance with France; but it was no help to the exiled Piero, who, much to his frustration, remained *persona non grata* with the new, more moderate regime that took over power in the city.

For a short spell, Piero's luck seemed about to change, thanks to an unfortunate accident in France. On 7 April 1498, Charles VIII died very suddenly, after knocking his head sharply against the lintel of a door. He was succeeded by his cousin Louis XII. The new king claimed not only the throne of Naples but also the Duchy of Milan: like the current duke, Ludovico Sforza, he was a great-grandson of Duke Giangaleazzo Visconti, but Louis was the old duke's legitimate heir, while Sforza had inherited through an illegitimate line. Thus, Louis XII the King announced his intention of enforcing his rights to both Naples and Milan.

That autumn, Alexander VI, never one to miss an opportunity, performed another of his political about-turns, this time to favour France, for their mutual benefit. Louis XII needed papal support for his imminent invasion of Italy, while the pope wanted military aid from the king to enable his son, Cesare Borgia, to carve out a state for himself in northern Italy. It was an alliance that would have a radical impact on the political map of Italy and on the fortunes of the Medici family.

On 1 September 1499, with Louis XII's armies on the borders of his duchy, Ludovico Sforza fled and French troops entered Milan five days later. With his first goal secure, the King honoured his promise to the pope and sent 6,000 troops to Cesare Borgia, who now began his conquest of the papal fiefs of the Romagna – funded by the papal coffers and by the sale of cardinals' hats. Once again, northern Italy was engulfed in war. Borgia proved a highly successful soldier: by the end of December 1499, he had taken Imola and Forlì, where the redoubtable Caterina Sforza had led a brave defence of the city. Guicciardini related how 'this lady, a woman of the greatest spirit and very courageous, sent her sons and all her valuable possessions to Florence' and 'bravely prepared to defend the city'; but she was taken prisoner when Borgia's soldiers stormed the citadel and sent to Rome.[19] (She was released the following year, and moved to Florence and the protection of her brother-in-law, Lorenzo di Pierfrancesco).

For Piero, the alliance between France and the papacy was a promising opportunity. Together with several of his Orsini relations, he joined Borgia's troops fighting alongside the French mercenaries. As a reward, Borgia agreed to help Piero once his own campaign was successfully completed, and in early May 1500 Borgia's soldiers crossed into Florentine territory – while Piero, prudently for once, remained

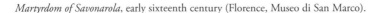

Martyrdom of Savonarola, early sixteenth century (Florence, Museo di San Marco).

behind the border. As troops laid waste to the countryside, Florence was forced to negotiate a deal. Unfortunately, Borgia was unable to persuade the *Signoria* to reinstate the Medici, and Louis XII refused to use his influence in Florence to intervene on Piero's behalf. Cesare Borgia left, satisfied by the large sum of 36,000 florins, and marched south to assist the French king in his conquest of Naples, which fell in early August.

With Louis XII now ruler of Milan and Naples, and the arbiter of power in Italy, Piero made strenuous efforts to ingratiate himself with the monarch, sending his brother, Giuliano, to France to negotiate on his behalf. The Florentines, too, desperate to ensure that the king did not come to an agreement with the Medici, sent their own embassy to Louis XII. At first, it seemed that Giuliano had met with some success. Guicciardini reported that the Florentine ambassadors 'wasted eight months in vain without ever having a good word from the king and, indeed, always being rebuffed by him… while he treated Giuliano de' Medici with favour and gave him long audiences'.[20] But by the end of 1501, it was evident that Piero would not be able to count on Louis. Fed up with the treatment their ambassadors had received in France, the Florentines had opened talks with Emperor Maximilian I and, in order to prevent this alliance, Louis XII promised that he would send military aid to Florence if the city were attacked – the Medici being the obvious enemy.

Piero may have failed with Louis XII; but he had regained the support of Cesare Borgia, whose troops took the Florentine city of Arezzo in early June 1502. With the Florentine army nearly 100 miles away at Pisa, this was Piero's great chance. In Guicciardini's words, Florence 'was unnerved at this sudden blow, and especially so because there was no money, no order, no proper government, no army, no agreement, no faith, so that if, immediately after taking Arezzo, they had moved to attack us in the name of the Medici, it is certain that our soldiers would not have been able to stop them, that there would have been a change of regime and Piero de' Medici would have returned'.[21] Over the next month, Cortona and several more Florentine towns 'were taken in the name of Piero and Cardinal de' Medici'; but Florence now called on Louis XII to honour the promise he had made the previous year, and the French soon restored the authority of the *Signoria*.

The Florentines had had a lucky escape. They viewed the narrowness of their escape with alarm, for although the Medici 'appeared weak with few friends and no faction in the city and could not hurt us on their own, they did have enough support… to be a useful instrument which our powerful enemies could use to flog us'.[22] Blaming the weakness of the committee system of government for the lack of decisive action that summer, they decided to appoint a permanent leader.

On 22 September 1502, Piero Soderini was elected as gonfalonier – for life. Soderini, the younger brother of Paoloantonio Soderini, had close Medici connections. His father, Tommaso Soderini, had been a key figure in Lorenzo's regime, while his mother was Dianora Tornabuoni, Piero's great-aunt. Despite these links, Piero Soderini had been one of the voices loudly in favour of ousting the Medici in 1494. In June 1503, the pre-eminence of a new first family in Florence was confirmed when – much to Piero de' Medici's fury – Alexander VI gave a red hat to Gonfalonier Soderini's brother, Francesco.

On 18 August 1503, Pope Alexander VI died very suddenly, probably of malaria. With Louis XII's authority in Naples under attack from the armies of Ferdinand I of Spain, the conclave, which opened on 16 September, was sharply divided between French and Spanish factions. Piero de' Medici, who was fighting with the French, ordered his brother Cardinal Giovanni to vote accordingly; but it soon became clear that neither faction could win. Giovanni proposed instead a compromise candidate, the elderly Cardinal Piccolomini, who was duly elected as Pope Pius III on 22 September – and who lasted a mere two months, dying after catching a cold during his coronation. This time, after one of the shortest conclaves in history, the cardinals voted almost unanimously for Giuliano della Rovere, who had the support of the Spanish faction. On 1 November, he became Pope Julius II.

The new pope would make little difference to the exiled Piero's fortunes. The French had launched a counter-attack against the Spanish in Naples, but were decisively beaten by Gonsalvo de Cordoba at the Battle of Garigliano in late December 1503, adding the Kingdom of Naples to a growing Spanish empire. On 27 December, while trying to escape the Spanish, Piero fell into the River Garigliano and drowned. He was just thirty-one years old. He left behind his widow, Alfonsina

Orsini, and their two children, a son born in September 1492 and named Lorenzo in memory of his grandfather Lorenzo, and a daughter, Clarice, born the following year and named after his mother.

Incompetent but also unlucky, Piero had wasted the legacy of his ancestors. In just a few years he had brought about the exile of his family and had failed completely in all his attempts to restore them to Florence. Guicciardini's judgement was unequivocal:

> … after the expulsion of the Medici from Florence, Piero's behaviour became arrogant and aggressive, according to his cruel nature… moreover, he should have known that the best method to restore his family would have been to establish some goodwill in the city but he was always plotting against Florence, with the Venetians, Milan, the King of France, the Pope and Cesare Borgia, and caused her endless expense, suspicions, wars and anxieties… all Florence detested him.[23]

Michelangelo, *David*, 1501–4 (Florence, Accademia). Commissioned originally by the Wool Guild for the cathedral, Michelangelo's statue was commandeered by the republic. A meeting of citizens was held to discuss the aesthetic, practical, ceremonial and political aspects of the 'giant' before it was decided to move it to the Palazzo della Signoria (now known as the Palazzo Vecchio).

I I

EXILE
Cardinal Giovanni, Giulio and Giuliano
1504–1512

THE MEDICI IN 1504

Giovanni di Lorenzo (29), Cardinal de' Medici

Giuliano (25), *his brother*

Giulio (26), *his illegitimate cousin*

Alfonsina Orsini (32), *his sister-in-law*

    Lorenzo (12), *his nephew*

    Clarice (11), *his niece*

His relations in Florence:

Lucrezia (34), *his sister,* m. Jacopo Salviati

Contessina (26), *his sister,* m. Piero Ridolfi

Cosimo de' Pazzi,
son of his aunt, Bianca, *and* Guglielmo de' Pazzi

Lucrezia Rucellai, *daughter of his aunt,* Nannina.
and Bernardo Rucellai

Pierfrancesco di Lorenzo (17), *his cousin*

Giovanni di Giovanni (6), *his cousin*

After the death of Piero di Lorenzo de' Medici, Cardinal Giovanni took over as head of the family. Fortunately for the Medici, this genial and shrewd prelate was a very different character to his arrogant brother. He recognized that diplomacy and patience would be far more effective tools than aggression and warfare in the campaign to enable the family to return to Florence. Inheriting both the political acumen and the extravagant tastes of his father Lorenzo, he lived in some style in the Palazzo Madama in Rome with his younger brother Giuliano and his illegitimate cousin Giulio. Also in Rome was Piero's widow Alfonsina Orsini, who was determined to safeguard her young son Lorenzo's rights as Piero's heir.

Within months of Piero's death, it was evident that the Medici had embarked on a different route to return to power. Cardinal Giovanni's first task was to gain influence at the papal court. While the death of the Borgia Pope Alexander VI had removed one major obstacle, the election of Julius II brought other problems. It was not an easy task dealing with new pope. This hawkish pontiff who, at the age of sixty-three and dressed in full armour, would be the last pope to lead an army into battle, was notoriously irascible. 'If the pope dislikes what you say, he either refuses to listen or insults you in the worst possible way,' noted Bernardo Dovizi da Bibbiena, Giovanni's secretary.[1] Luckily, Giovanni had an ally in the Vatican: Cardinal Galeotto della Rovere, one of Julius II's nephews who had been given a red hat within weeks of his uncle's election. In mid-February 1504, six weeks after Piero's death, the apothecary Landucci recorded Cardinal della Rovere in Florence, staying with Giovanni's uncle, Guglielmo de' Pazzi, and no doubt carrying messages from Giovanni to family members in the city. The following year, Julius II appointed his nephew to the key position of Vice-Chancellor of the Church, and thus also Cardinal Giovanni edged closer to the heart of power in Rome. Also in 1505, the pope made Giovanni legate to Perugia – and other favours would follow.

The Medici were able to use their new influence at the papal court to improve their standing in Florence, operating as power-brokers in much the same way as Cardinal Giovanni's father had done two decades earlier. Giovanni, Giuliano and Giulio 'endeavoured to arrange their return not with force or resentment but with love and goodwill, by helping the Florentines,' Guicciardini explained, and 'they never

Raphael, Pope Julius II in a detail from *Mass at Bolsena*, 1512
(Vatican Palace, Stanza della Segnatura).

omitted to do anything they could to please all those Florentines living in or visiting Rome, giving them aid and favours in all their affairs'.[2] The strategy proved highly successful. When Cardinal Giovanni hosted a banquet at his palace in Rome to celebrate the Feast of the Medici saints Cosmas and Damian on 27 September 1504, most of the bankers and merchants operating at the papal court were present – despite a law banning all contact with the Medici. 'Almost all Florentines who found themselves dealing with the papal court, whether for the expedition of benefices or other favours, would either visit Cardinal de' Medici in person, or write to him, even those who were his enemies,' Guicciardini confirmed, 'so that the name Medici, which had been so detested by almost everyone when Piero was alive, seemed to acquire approval and compassion now that he was dead.'

One Florentine in Rome who remained firmly opposed to the Medici was Cardinal Francesco Soderini, brother of the permanent gonfalonier. Giovanni and Soderini were rivals at the papal court, in Florentine politics and in their personal styles. The avaricious Soderini distrusted Giovanni's princely behaviour and, according to Guicciardini, 'never helped any Florentine, nor did any favours, and his behaviour made the largesse and generosity of the Medici seem even greater by comparison'.[3] Cardinal Giovanni, for his part, resented the fact that the Soderini had replaced the Medici as the 'first family' of Florence, and he refused to allow his cousin Pierfrancesco di Lorenzo to marry Gonfalonier Soderini's niece; according to Guicciardini, 'the Medici were so furious that they tore up the contract and the betrothal was cancelled'.[4]

However, Cardinal Giovanni had the upper hand at the papal court. In 1507, he persuaded his uncle, Rinaldo Orsini, to resign as Archbishop of Florence so that the see could be transferred to a Florentine. This was one of the streams of favours through which Giovanni was gradually improving relations between the Medici and their erstwhile enemies. But Gonfalonier Soderini, who wanted the post for his brother the cardinal, opposed the appointment. The issue remained unresolved for several months until, in a consistory at the Vatican the following July, Giovanni proposed a compromise candidate, suggesting his first cousin Cosimo de' Pazzi for the post. The appointment was confirmed, and Cardinal Soderini loudly reminded the other cardinals in the room that at least Pazzi came from a family that had always opposed tyrants – a rather offensive reference to the Pazzi Conspiracy.[5]

In Florence, the enthusiasm that had greeted the election of Piero Soderini as gonfalonier for life had, three years on, begun to wane as the city was hit by a series of natural disasters. In early 1505, the regime had to cope with a terrible famine affecting all of Italy. The copper-smith Bartolomeo Masi recorded in his diary that 'the government put much bread on sale every day... but the crowds were so great that it was impossible to get closer than ten feet, and not a day passed when someone wasn't crushed in the throng; and besides the crowds, there was the suffering of the famine so that every day some poor people died of hunger'.[6] The following year, the San Giovanni festivities were ruined by violent winds that tore down the hangings by the Baptistery; when a wheel fell off one of the carts carrying the tributes and a crucifix fell and broke, it was 'thought to be a very bad sign'.[7] In July 1507 came drought. Landucci noted that the Arno was almost dry and that the mills, which were normally powered by the water, were unable to operate: 'there have already been several months without rain and it is impossible to grind and there has been a poor harvest of grain and fodder'.[8]

Gonfalonier Soderini was also losing popularity through his failure to recapture Pisa. The city was determined to defend the liberty it had gained from Florence following the invasion of Charles VIII in 1492. Pisa called on Naples for help and was saved by the timely arrival of Gonsalvo de Cordoba and his Spanish troops. The war with Pisa underlined for Florentines the unreliability of the customary practice of hiring foreign mercenaries, since they could change sides at will and might be used by the Medici to force a change of regime. So, on the advice of his secretary, Niccolò Machiavelli, Soderini set up a militia manned by men from Florentine territories. Such a body of non-professional soldiers, who could be called on to take up arms when necessary, was a very novel idea in Italy at that time. On 15 February 1506, Landucci watched 400 of them parading in the Piazza della Signoria: 'the Gonfalonier gave each of them a white doublet, a pair of hose, striped red and white, a white cap, shoes, an iron breast-plate and lances' and 'a sergeant taught them how to use arms'.[9] In 1508 the militia, under the leadership of Machiavelli, managed to blockade Pisa, preventing supplies from entering the city by land or sea.

During the previous year, Piero's widow Alfonsina Orsini had travelled to Florence on the pretext of reclaiming her dowry, which had been seized along with the rest of the Medici possessions in 1494. In fact, Alfonsina was looking for a husband for her daughter, Clarice. Cardinal Giovanni had good political reasons for sanctioning a Florentine match for his fourteen-year-old niece. Ties between the Medici and a leading family would increase support for the Medici in the city and undermine the position of Gonfalonier Soderini. Alfonsina herself, scheming on behalf of her son, had more personal ambitions: she hoped that a prestigious match for Clarice would help to establish young Lorenzo's claim to be the rightful heir of his father as ruler of Florence.

Cardinal Giovanni and Alfonsina began highly secret negotiations with the Strozzi family, with the intention of betrothing Clarice to Filippo di Filippo Strozzi, the youngest son of the wealthy banker who had been an ally of Lorenzo. (Filippo's older brother was already a Medici in-law, after his recent marriage to Lucrezia Rucellai, the daughter of Giovanni's aunt, Nannina.) The betrothal was signed in Rome in July 1508, and when of it news leaked out in Florence that December, it rapidly became the talk of the town. The city was split on the issue, with detractors of the match maliciously claiming that Clarice had a 'beaked nose like an owl'.[10] Gonfalonier Soderini was firmly against it: he publicly accused those involved of plotting against him. He had a point, for, as Cardinal Giovanni had anticipated, many of Soderini's enemies supported the union in the hope of weakening the gonfalonier's hold on government. On 12 December, Filippo Strozzi, who was in Naples at the time, was charged with the crime of marrying an exile and summoned to attend the *Signoria* before 25 December or face a ten-year exile. Soderini must have hoped that the nineteen-year-old would be too scared to come to Florence, and he seized this opportunity to get rid of his most prominent opponents by charging twelve Florentines with engineering the match: on his list were Cardinal Giovanni's uncle Bernardo Rucellai, his sister Lucrezia and her husband Jacopo Salviati, and his nephew Cosimo de' Pazzi, the new Archbishop of Florence.

Donato Bramante's Tempietto, 1502, stands within the courtyard of the church of San Pietro in Montorio, Rome. At the beginning of the sixteenth century the papal court began to revive the architectural language of antiquity to promote the papacy as the heirs of the emperors of Ancient Rome.

Filippo Strozzi travelled to Rome for a private meeting with Cardinal Giovanni at the Palazzo Madama, before riding north to Florence in the company of Giulio – the friendship between Strozzi and Giulio would prove of vital importance to the future of the Medici family – to attend the *Signoria*. By the time Filippo arrived in Florence, on 25 December 1508, public opinion had swayed significantly in favour of the Strozzi. Moreover, Julius II, no fan of Soderini, had added his authority by favouring the match. At Strozzi's trial, the gonfalonier failed to persuade the *Signoria* to impose the sentence of exile and the case was adjourned. When the trial re-opened in early January 1509, Strozzi based his defence on the legal nicety that, as women could not be banished, Clarice was not legally an exile, and with it he won his case.

Back in Rome, on 3 February, Filippo attended mass with Clarice in the morning, signed all the relevant marriage contracts, and they were wed in the evening. The union had proved quite a coup for Cardinal Giovanni: not only was opposition to Gonfalonier Soderini growing apace in Florence, but so was support for the Medici.

Filippo and Clarice moved into the imposing Palazzo Strozzi in Florence, which had been built by Filippo's father and was the largest family residence in the city. In 1510, Clarice gave birth to a son, whom they named Piero after her father – and he, like his own father, would have a part to play in the Medici story. The Medici family was growing. That year, Giuliano's mistress also gave birth to a son, Ippolito, and a year or so later another illegitimate boy, Alessandro, was born to cousin Giulio's mistress. Alessandro, whose mother was an African slave in Alfonsina Orsini's household, was brought up in the Orsini palace, though Giulio chose not to recognize his son in public, promoting him instead as Lorenzo's child.

Cardinal Giovanni, meanwhile, had turned his attention to repairing relations with the other branch of the family, staying as a guest at Pierfrancesco's villa at Trebbio in the Mugello. He also arranged for Pierfrancesco's orphaned nephew (son of the late Caterina Sforza) – also named Giovanni and apparently a difficult and rebellious child – to be put into the care of his sister Lucrezia and her husband Jacopo Salviati.[11]

In Rome, papal policy was taking another U-turn. Julius II had decided it was time for action to curb the influence of Louis XII in northern Italy. In the summer of 1510, he signed a pact with Venice to drive the French out of the peninsula. Many people in Florence, which remained loyal to France, feared that the city would be one of the pope's targets and that if he were successful he would enforce the return of the Medici. Gonfalonier Soderini renewed the ban on contact between Florentines and Cardinal Giovanni and increased the penalties for offenders – they would now be declared rebels and have all their possessions seized. As it turned out, Julius II's first target was Louis XII's other Italian ally, Ferrara, which, after a successful campaign, was under siege by the end of January 1511. In May, Louis XII called for a Church council to meet in Pisa to depose the pope, before his troops routed a papal army and ended Julius II's siege.

To Cardinal Giovanni's alarm, Julius II appeared to have little time left. On 20 August 1511, he suffered a violent attack of fever, his third that month, and news spread through Rome that the pope was on his deathbed. Cardinal Giovanni informed the Venetian ambassador that 'the pope is… unlikely to last the night'.[12] The same envoy thought that 'Medici has hopes for the tiara but it is generally believed that one of the French party will be elected,' adding that 'the city is in chaos and everyone is carrying weapons'. On 24 August, Julius II received the last rites in his bedroom in the Vatican. But three days later, papal master-of-ceremonies Paride de Grassis recorded in his diary that the pope was clinging on, though only just: 'he has eaten nothing for four days and everyone, even his doctors, have given up hope'.[13] The patient apparently requested some fruits, even though they were banned by his doctors, and he was given 'peaches, nuts, plums and other fruits, which he chewed but did not swallow, and then some little onions and strawberries'. While plans were being put in place for the papal funeral at St Peter's, the forbidden fruits were giving nourishment to Julius II, who – to the surprise of everyone – recovered.

Less than a month later, the pope was back at work with renewed energy – and it was now that he turned his attention to Florence. On 23 September, furious at Gonfalonier Soderini's continued support for Louis XII, he placed the city under an interdict. Its impact was lucidly described by the coppersmith, Bartolomeo Masi: 'The clergy cannot say divine office for any reason to lay people… they cannot accept the

Michelangelo, Sistine Chapel ceiling, 1508–12 (Vatican Palace). Arguably Julius II's most famous commission, this is one of the iconic images of the High Renaissance.

dead bodies of lay people in any sacred place... they cannot hear anyone's confession... and they cannot give holy oil to any lay person... nor can they ring church bells... and it is said that Julius II has done this because the Florentine *Signoria* has agreed to the council in Pisa.'[14] By the end of September, Julius had negotiated a powerful coalition to expel the French from Italy – the treaty was signed by Emperor Maximilian I, Ferdinand I of Spain and Naples, and Henry VIII of England, as well as by the Venetians and the Swiss – and started to prepare for war against Louis XII. It was a mark of how successfully Cardinal Giovanni had cultivated relations with this notoriously difficult pope that he was now entrusted by Julius II with the task of running the campaign. The Medici cardinal was appointed as legate to the Romagna, to be the political counterpart to the military commander Ramón de Cardona, a Spanish general.

The first major encounter between the two armies was a disaster for the cardinal. On 11 April 1512, the Spanish and papal forces were defeated by the French at the Battle of Ravenna. It was one of the bloodiest conflicts of the period, leaving more than 10,000 dead, including the French commander Gaston de Foix. Cardinal Giovanni was one of the many prisoners taken by the French. Guicciardini's brother sent the historian a chilling account of the battle:

> ... it was truly dreadful to see how each cannonball drove a channel through the soldiers, throwing helmets, heads and limbs up into the air. The Spanish, who were being mown down before they could use their weapons, then rushed forwards and the hand-to-hand fighting began. It was terrible and lasted four hours. When the first wave had been repulsed... many fled... the Spanish infantry held their ground and resisted stubbornly but they were largely destroyed when the heavy cavalry charged.[15]

News of the defeat reached Rome on 14 April. But shortly before his capture, Cardinal Giovanni had managed to see his cousin Giulio and had despatched him with his own urgent message for the pope – one that would change the course of the war. Giulio reported that the situation was not as bad as it had at first appeared, that the French losses were heavy and their army badly demoralized by the death of its commander. There was no question of the French marching on Rome – as Julius II had feared – and moreover there were encouraging rumours of 20,000 Swiss troops on their way into Italy to aid the pope. Julius II instantly rallied, informing the Spanish and Venetian ambassadors that he intended to spend 100,000 ducats to get the French out of Italy. He issued orders for new ordnance that same day.

On 3 June 1512, Cardinal Giovanni escaped his French captors, and ten days later he reached Bologna. Meanwhile, the Swiss troops had retaken Brescia and other cities on the Lombard plain for Julius II, and the French were in flight. By 20 June, Milan had rebelled against Louis XII, who, with his own realm under threat (from Henry VIII's armies in the north and from Ferdinand I in the south), now recalled his troops to France.

In Florence, news of the French defeat was received with considerable apprehension. Julius II wanted revenge on the city that had remained stubbornly loyal to France; and the extent of Cardinal Giovanni's influence with the pope was revealed on 11 July 1512 when a letter arrived from Rome. As Landucci reported, 'the pope orders us to send the gonfalonier to his home and to close the *Signoria*, which seems a very malicious and strange thing and everyone thinks that he wants to change this regime and bring the Medici back to Florence'.[16] Increasingly, this was true. In Mantua that August, Julius II held a meeting of his allies to decide the future of the territories seized from Louis XII; and among those attending was Cardinal Giovanni, who had promised that he would reverse Florence's pro-French policy if the coalition helped to restore the Medici to their native city. One of the few points on which all the participants agreed was that Florence should be punished for its stubborn loyalty to France. And so, Ramón de Cardona was sent south with his Spanish troops to restore the Medici. After eighteen long years, the family finally had victory in their sights.

On 26 August 1512, Landucci reported the arrival in Florence of an envoy from de Cardona requesting 'three favours from the *Signoria*: that we must join the league; the second that the Medici be restored to Florence and the third, that the gonfalonier must leave office'.[17] And to show what would happen to the city if it failed to agree to the terms, Cardona brutally sacked the nearby town of Prato three days later. 'To take such a citadel in just one day was astonishing, because there were 4,000 troops there, as well as many men from the countryside who had fled there with their goods, wives and children,' commented Landucci;

'and once they were inside the city these cruel infidels killed everyone in their path… and it is said that 5,000 people are dead.'

It was a potent warning. The *Signoria* surrendered the following day, 30 August. On 1 September, the cardinal's brother Giuliano rode into Florence, wearing the clothes of a republican burgher, and went directly to the Palazzo della Signoria to request the repeal of the decree that had exiled his family. Four days later, the *Signoria*, without its gonfalonier, gave the Medici permission to move back to Florence as private citizens.

For the next fortnight, the Florentines remained cautiously optimistic that the return of the Medici would entail only minor changes to the 1494 constitution. But Giuliano and Cardinal Giovanni clearly had other ideas – they wanted a return to the old days of Medici supremacy. When he heard that a prominent anti-Medicean had been elected as gonfalonier on 8 September, Cardinal Giovanni left immediately for Florence, arriving at the city gates on 14 September with Ramón de Cardona and a contingent of Spanish troops. After two days of heated discussion, the great bell of the Palazzo della Signoria rang out summoning the Florentines to a *parlamento* in the piazza, which was bristling with Cardona's soldiers. The *Signoria* solemnly read out the terms of a new constitution to the gathered crowds, and many were appalled. The new government would be very much the same as the one they had triumphantly rejected in 1494 – technically republican, but manipulated and controlled by the Medici inner circle. The Great Council, which symbolized the victory of republican liberty over Medici tyranny, was disbanded and a new, pro-Medicean gonfalonier was elected. Many supporters of the old regime were deprived of their political rights, though only its most prominent members were exiled.

In early October 1512, the family coats-of-arms re-appeared on the Palazzo Medici and the *Signoria* issued 'a proclamation ordering anyone who had goods belonging to the family to return them, on pain of the gallows'.[18] The feast of the Medici patron saints, Cosmas and Damian, on 27 September, was made a national holiday, and the holiday marking the date of the family's expulsion in 1494 was cancelled. After eighteen long years of exile, the Medici had finally returned. And their fortunes were about to change, in a spectacular manner.

12

AGE OF GOLD
Pope Leo X
1513–1521

THE MEDICI FAMILY IN 1513

Giovanni (38), Cardinal de' Medici, Pope Leo X

Giuliano (35), *his brother*

    Ippolito (3), *Giuliano's illegitimate son*

Giulio (36), *his illegitimate cousin*

    Alessandro (2), *Giulio's illegitimate son*

Alfonsina Orsini (41), *his sister-in-law*

    Lorenzo (21), *his nephew*

    Clarice (20), *his niece,* m. Filippo Strozzi

Lucrezia (43), *his sister,* m. Jacopo Salviati

    Giovanni Salviati (23), *his nephew*

    Maria Salviati (14), *his niece*

Maddalena (40), *his sister,* m. Franceschetto Cibò

    Innocenzo Cibò, *his nephew*

    Caterina Cibò, *his niece*

Contessina (35), *his sister,* m. Piero Ridolfi

    Niccolò Ridolfi (12), *his nephew*

Pierfrancesco di Lorenzo di Pierfrancesco (26), *his cousin*

Giovanni di Giovanni di Pierfrancesco (15), *his cousin*

During the evening of 6 February 1513, the last Sunday of Carnival, a procession of floats illuminated by hundreds of torches wound its way through the streets of Florence. It was one of the highlights of the festivities. The torches were carried by the young men of the company of the Branch (*Broncone*), which had been founded by Lorenzo the Magnificent's grandson, Lorenzo, within months of the restoration of the Medici. Its emblem, a stump of dead *lauro* (laurel) putting forth new shoots, was an unambiguous symbol of the revival of the family fortunes. Certainly, the tableaux on the carts left little room for misinterpretation. Celebrating the classical theme of the return of the Age of Gold after the horrors of war, they glorified the myth of peace and prosperity that the Florentines had enjoyed under the Medici in the previous century. One cart, drawn by buffaloes disguised as elephants, represented Julius Caesar; another showed Emperor Augustus as lord of the world – no republican sentiment here. The last, a triumphal chariot, contained a 'dead' soldier dressed in rusty armour, from whose back erupted a naked, gilded child that symbolized the start of this new Golden Age. In a tragic postscript – and one that was to prove remarkably prophetic – the boy, a baker's son who had been completely smothered in gold leaf, died soon after the procession.

'To the people it appeared as though the time of Lorenzo the Magnificent had returned,' enthused a Medici supporter in the crowds.[1] Not all were so impressed. One former adherent of Savonarola was disgusted at how 'the people delighted in such nonsense' and criticized the cost of the display – some 3,500 florins, taken from the public purse – 'all this because Giuliano and Lorenzo have returned to their homeland as heads of the city'.[2] Indeed, there was widespread dismay at the way in which the Medici had resumed their former positions and had dismantled the hall of the Great Council in the Palazzo Signoria, turning it into barracks for their soldiers, complete with tavern, gaming tables and a brothel. On 18 February, ten days into Lent, several supporters of the deposed gonfalonier, Piero Soderini, were imprisoned on a charge of plotting to overthrow the Medici. Among them were two friends who would become famous Medici propagandists, Niccolò Machiavelli and Niccolò Valori. But the Medici regime was about to receive a boost from an unexpected quarter.

Three days after those arrests, news arrived from Rome that Julius II was finally dead, and so Cardinal Giovanni left Florence to attend the conclave, which opened on 4 March 1513. Suffering from a painful ulcer in his anus, he had to be carried into the Vatican on a litter, and he endured an operation inside the palace a few days later.[3] Initially, the cardinals were preoccupied with agreeing a list of measures that the future pope should observe, prominent among which was the reform of abuses in the curia and a crusade against the Turks; so it was not until 10 March that the first round of voting took place.

As Giovanni was the longest-serving cardinal-deacon present, it was his duty to read out the names on the voting papers.* He himself received just one vote. But he had made careful plans for this conclave, secretly securing the support of many cardinals; he even had Cardinal Francesco Soderini on board, after promising to lift the sentence of exile imposed on the Soderini family if he were to be elected.[4] That evening, Giovanni's supporters came out into the open. After the vote the following morning, 11 March, he read out the names, 'modestly and calmly' announcing that he had received the necessary two-thirds majority.[5] 'The election was greeted with pleasure by almost all Christendom,' wrote Guicciardini, 'thanks to the fame of his father and for his own widespread reputation for generosity and kindness.'[6] At last, a Medici was pope. It was an immense achievement. No longer merely successful bankers, the Medici now had power on the international stage and the resources of the Church to finance their ambitions.

Giovanni de' Medici chose the name 'Leo X'. At his coronation, which took place on 11 April 1513, he rode the horse he had used at the Battle of Ravenna to make his formal procession to San Giovanni in Laterano. Like many Christians of the period, he was superstitious and so chose the date for this important occasion in the belief that the eleventh of the month was his lucky day: he had been born on 11 December (1475), been taken prisoner on 11 April (1512) and was elected on 11 March (1513). All three events were visible on one of the triumphal arches that had been erected on the streets of Rome for the occasion – as were several others, which had been re-dated to occur on the eleventh of the

---

* There were three orders of cardinals: the highest-ranking were the cardinal-bishops, followed by the cardinal-priests. The cardinal-deacons included many who, like Giovanni, had not been ordained.

AGE OF GOLD   227

month, notably the exile of the Medici, which had actually occurred on 9 November (1494).

Genial, fun and rather plump, Leo X is rumoured to have crowed: 'God has given us the papacy, let us enjoy it.' He was also very short-sighted, needing to wear spectacles when indulging in his great passion, hunting. The Mantuan ambassador described how, in the woods near the papal villa at Magliana, 'a very large stag was caught in the nets in a very narrow place, which the pope entered on foot with his spear in one hand and his glasses in the other'.[7]

With the resources of the Church at his disposal, Leo X could live in sumptuous style in the Vatican, surrounded by tapestries, gold plate and chairs covered in crimson satin emblazoned with the Medici *palle*. His kitchen bills were huge – his successor was shocked at how much the cooks had spent on peacocks' tongues.[8] Within months of his election, he had to order the port authorities in Rome to double the monthly allowance they paid to his major-domo to cover the cost of food, drink and other supplies for the palace; and he had to increase the sum again four years later.[9]

The glittering court of the first Medici pope included all the leading intellectuals, artists and musicians of his day. The Venetian satirist Pietro Aretino judged that 'Leo X's character swung from one extreme to the other and it was anyone's guess which he enjoyed more: the virtues of men of letters or the tittle-tattle of buffoons'.[10] His official household roll contained 683 names, a large court by the standards of the time, including the master of the hunt, two doctors, an astrologer and fifty-four men involved in the cooking and serving of food for the papal dining-rooms. His buffoon, Fra Mariano, was famous for his coarse jokes and legendary appetite – he was said to have eaten forty eggs and twenty chickens at one sitting. Also on the list was the keeper of Leo X's pet Indian elephant, a present from King Manuel of Portugal: Hanno was a famous sight in Rome and even had his portrait painted by Leo X's court artist, Raphael.

Leo X was the first Florentine pope since the beginning of the republic, and his election was an immense boost to the city's prestige on the world stage, all the more welcome after two decades of ignominious decline. Florentines, even enemies of the Medici, hoped to profit with special privileges for businessmen at the papal court and coveted posts in the curia for clever legal minds. Moreover, as Leo X

Raphael, *Portrait of Pope Leo X with two Cardinals*, 1518 (Florence, Uffizi); the cardinals are believed to be Giulio de' Medici (Leo's cousin and later Pope Clement VII) and Luigi de' Rossi (Leo's eldest nephew).

After Raphael, *Giuliano de' Medici*, c.1515 (New York, Metropolitan Museum of Art).

was only thirty-seven years old – the youngest pope by far for at least a century – they could expect the benefits to last many years. For most Florentines, the prestige of having their own pope mitigated the less acceptable aspects of the Medici regime, and their noisy celebrations of Giovanni's triumph lasted three days. Machiavelli and Valori were released from jail as part of a general amnesty to mark his election, and Machiavelli spent that summer writing his most famous work, *Il principe* (*The Prince*), which he dedicated to the pope's nephew, Lorenzo. For his part, Leo X pope honoured his promise to Cardinal Soderini, and even went so far as to propose an alliance between the two families with the betrothal of Lorenzo to one of Soderini's nieces. But this project was rejected out of hand by Lorenzo's scheming mother, Alfonsina Orsini, who had far more ambitious plans for her son.

The real beneficiaries of the election were, of course, the Medici themselves. A year earlier they had despaired of ever returning to their home city; and they had now achieved power on the *world* stage. Leo X chose as his motto the opening words of Psalm 120, 'In my distress I cried unto the Lord, and he heard me'. Despite the promise he had sworn before his election not to promote more than two relatives to the College of Cardinals, he gave red hats to six of them: his sisters' three sons – Innocenzo Cibò, Giovanni Salviati and Niccolò Ridolfi – and three of his cousins, Luigi de' Rossi and Franciotto Orsini as well as Giulio, who had been with him throughout the long years of exile. Giulio, who was to be the senior figure in Leo X's administration, was appointed Archbishop of Florence on 9 May, to replace Cosimo de' Pazzi, who had died the previous week. It was not, though, until 23 September that he could be given his red hat, for, being a bastard, he had to wait for the paperwork that legitimised him to be completed.

There were also prestigious marriages for the papal nieces. Caterina Cibò, for example, was betrothed to Giovanni Maria da Varano, whom the pope ennobled with the title of Duke of Camerino. Leo X also took this opportunity to repair relations between the two branches of the Medici family, betrothing Giovanni, the son of Giovanni di Pierfrancesco and Caterina Sforza, to Maria Salviati, the daughter of his sister Lucrezia, who had taken the rebellious Giovanni into her home after his mother died. It was a union that was to have important repercussions in the family story.

Leo X gave his brother Giuliano and his nephew Lorenzo the responsibility for safeguarding the dynastic future of the Medici; but he needed the assistance of foreign rulers to establish their secular prestige. Initially, he hesitated over siding with either of the rival superpowers, France and the Empire, which competed in offering favours in return for his support. Emperor Maximilian I sold him the fief of Modena, while Louis XII gave Cardinal Giulio the lucrative see of Narbonne. When Louis died on 1 January 1515, he was succeeded by his cousin Francis I, who promptly renewed the French claims to Naples and Milan, to the anger of both the Emperor and Ferdinand I of Spain. To counter this powerful alliance, Leo X formed a coalition with the new French king, which brought immediate benefits for the Medici. Giuliano was appointed captain-general of the papal armies that January, and the following month he married Philiberta of Savoy, Francis I's aunt. The seventeen-year-old bride was 'large, pale, stick-thin, and hunch-backed, with a long nose', according to one observer, 'though apart from this, she is a good-looking woman'.[11] Giuliano was also made Duke of Nemours by Francis I – the first male in the Medici family to have his own aristocratic title.

Lorenzo would have to wait longer for his ennoblement, despite Alfonsina Orsini's frequent visits to the Vatican to lobby on behalf of her son. 'In truth, all I do here is to try to get His Holiness to give me an allowance for Lorenzo,' she wrote, but, according to one contemporary, she had 'begun to plague the pope to give her son a noble title'.[12] She was also lobbying on behalf of her son-in-law Filippo Strozzi, for whom she hoped to obtain the papal banking account.[13] Leo X's sister, Lucrezia, had hoped to obtain this lucrative post for her husband, Jacopo Salviati; but Alfonsina's persistence prevailed and Strozzi got the post. Either way, it was a family affair. The pope also gave Strozzi the government account in Florence, and the banker would soon become one of the richest men in Europe.

One of the major problems Leo X faced was the question of who was to govern Florence, which was now effectively a satellite of the papal court. While policy was to be decided by the pope and Cardinal Giulio in Rome, a figurehead was needed for the Medici regime. As one of his advisers warned the pope, though his forefathers 'maintained their rule by using skill not force, you must use force rather than skill'.[14] With the easy-going Giuliano unwilling to take on this role, Leo X decided, somewhat rashly, to entrust the task of running Florence to his arrogant young nephew Lorenzo, who took up residence at the Palazzo Medici on 10 August 1513.

Lorenzo, who had left Florence at the age of two and spent his childhood at the aristocratic Orsini court in Rome, was ill-suited to the subtleties of republican government. Leo X sent him a list of instructions and appointed eight members of the Medici inner circle as his advisers, among whom were his uncles Jacopo Salviati and Piero Ridolfi, and his banking brother-in-law Filippo Strozzi. But it was soon evident that all was not going as smoothly as the optimistic Leo X had hoped. In February 1514, Cardinal Giulio wrote to Lorenzo, offering two pieces of advice, 'which will cost you little and could be of much profit': 'the first is to make a show of affability and kindness with a liberal use of words', by which Giulio hoped Lorenzo might tone down his haughty manner; 'and the other is to choose with care sometimes one person and sometimes another and invite them to dine with you, not just in the city but also at the villa, because these are two ways of giving favour and every day you will acquire more approval'.[15]

Lorenzo, aided by his mother, continued to press Leo X for more power. Jealous of Giuliano's position at the head of the papal army, he demanded the post of Captain-General of Florence. In this instance, the pope bowed to pressure, joking that he had picked 'two greenhorns for jobs usually held by experts'.[16] The first Florentine to hold the post, Lorenzo now had, in effect, his own private army. His Aunt Lucrezia was appalled: 'Can you not see that this will be the ruin of the city; have you not thought how much power this will give him?'.[17] Alfonsina Orsini, however, was triumphant. She joined her son at the Palazzo Medici, from where she proceeded to exercise considerable control over the republic.

Like the prince he desired to be, Lorenzo put on lavish entertainments in Florence, and in 1514 introduced several novel features to the traditional San Giovanni festivities. On 23 June, the eve of the feast, after the usual procession of wagons carrying religious tableaux he staged a secular cavalcade representing the Triumph of Camillus, the general who had been exiled from ancient Rome but who had returned to help his country in its hour of need. And in case anyone missed the analogy with Lorenzo, there were musicians explaining the link in song. Lorenzo had wanted to include the elephant Hanno in the procession, but Leo X refused to loan his pet, telling his nephew that the

After Raphael, *Lorenzo de' Medici*, 1518 (New York, private collection).

animal's feet were too delicate for the long walk from Rome.[18] On 25 June, there was a hunt on the Piazza della Signoria, with a scandalous postscript that was witnessed by apothecary Landucci:

> They brought bears, leopards, bulls, buffaloes, stags and many other wild animals and horses and finally two lions… they had made a tortoise and a porcupine on wheels with men inside who made them move and they prodded the wild animals with lances... all the stands were crowded and people watched from windows and roofs… it was all was done very well except for a loathsome thing: someone put a mare among the stallions in the presence of 40,000 women and girls who could see the indecent acts, which shocked good and upright people and, I think, even shocked the less decent.[19]

In Rome a rapidly changing political system was forcing Leo X to alter his foreign policy.

Faced with Francis I's invasion of northern Italy in pursuit of his claims to Milan and Naples, the pope's relations with the king had started to deteriorate. In early August 1515, Leo X agreed reluctantly to join Emperor Maximilian I and the Swiss in an alliance against France. Unfortunately for him, his captain-general, Giuliano, was ill – he was suffering from tuberculosis – and unable to lead the papal army; and so, on 8 August, the pope promoted Lorenzo in his place. Later that month, this new Captain-General of the Church, with Cardinal Giulio acting as legate, left Florence to ride north to protect Parma and Piacenza from the French. Alfonsina, in charge of Florence during her son's absence, warned him of the diplomatic minefield ahead: 'Consider well that the king is in Italy with 80,000 men and that this city is most devoted to the French crown,' she wrote, 'also remember that it was because your father was so stubbornly set in his own views that we were nineteen years in exile.'[20]

Filippo Strozzi kept Lorenzo informed with news from Florence. Alfonsina, he reported, 'keeps herself busy, writing to Rome or to you, and giving audiences so the house is always full of people and such crowds give reputation to the regime'.[21] He added that 'she exercises a level of authority that would be impossible for another woman and only easy for a few men'. Alfonsina was certainly a redoubtable woman, but not popular, especially with her son-in-law. When she died in 1520, Strozzi joked to a friend – rather cruelly, given all she had done for him – that her Latin epitaph should read: 'Alfonsina Orsini, whose death no one and whose life everyone mourned and whose burial is most pleasing and beneficial to mankind'.[22]

On 13 September 1515, Francis I won a major victory at the Battle of Marignano, securing a French primacy in northern Italy that would last a decade. Leo X, against the advice of his cardinals and to the fury of the Emperor, decided to make peace with the king and invited him to a summit meeting in Bologna later in the year. The pope was planning a magnificent state visit to Florence on his way north from Rome, such that Alfonsina told Lorenzo: 'I now find myself in the greatest tangle here, arranging supplies of food for the court, as well as lodgings, furnishings and a thousand other things that would be difficult to tell you about in brief.'[23] But the optimism in Florence that had accompanied Leo X's papal elevation was fast evaporating. Alfonsina told her son that everything was being done 'to show that the city will receive him willingly', but 'I know that not everyone is happy about contributing funds'.[24] Landucci recorded that 70,000 florins was spent on decorations, 'on these temporary things that pass like shadows, which could have built a most beautiful church in honour of God and to glorify the city'.[25] But the apothecary added that at least it had given work to 'some 2,000 men from various guilds, carpenters, builders, painters, carters, porters, sawyers and others for more than a month'.

When Leo X made his entry into Florence on 30 November 1515, there was a fuss about precedence at the city gates: the *Signoria* demanded to be allowed to ride, like the cardinals, but the papal master-of-ceremonies refused and the priors had sulked, rather embarrassingly. The procession, led by eighty pack-mules bearing the papal coat-of-arms, was huge, consisting of some 3,000 people including mace-bearers, papal squires and valets, secretaries and lawyers, ambassadors, red-robed cardinals, archbishops and trumpeters. One of Leo X's dwarves, with a red hat and a jousting lance, rode a fine Arab horse, while Lorenzo was dressed in silver brocade lined with sable and mounted on a large grey. Finally came Leo X himself, not carried on his papal throne, as was the custom, but riding a mule. He tended to ignore the finer details of papal etiquette – he was heavily criticized by his master-of-ceremonies for going out hunting 'without his stole', and 'worse, he was not wearing his surplice and, most shocking of all, he had his boots on, which is entirely inappropriate, because nobody was able to kiss his feet'.[26]

The noisy, colourful cavalcade took seven hours to complete its journey into the city centre – a distance of less than 2 miles – because of the musical entertainments staged at each of the fourteen arches erected on the route. On the arch in Piazza San Felice was a portrait of Lorenzo the Magnificent with the inscription 'this is my beloved son' (Matthew, 3, 17), and Leo X apparently wept when he saw it. The procession was one of the most spectacular entries staged in sixteenth-century Italy, amply documented in the official records of the papal master-of-ceremonies and the Florentine herald, in reports of foreign ambassadors, and in the diaries and letters of men on the streets. Thanks to the new medium of print, descriptions of this Medici triumph were also widely disseminated in pamphlets published in both Rome and Florence.

On 3 December 1515, Leo X left Florence for Bologna with Cardinal Giulio, Lorenzo and Philiberta of Savoy. Giuliano, now in the late stages of tuberculosis, was too ill to travel. On meeting the French king, the pope presented Francis I with a valuable token of his goodwill, a relic of the True Cross set in a gold cross studded with precious gems, worth 15,000 ducats.[27] When the summit was over and the alliance between the two rulers became public, it was evident that Leo X's priorities were more personal than political: he had given Francis I Parma and Piacenza as well as unprecedented control over the Church in France, in return for a promise that the French army would protect the Medici regime. Leo X returned to Florence for Christmas, landing the city with the burden of playing host to the papal court over the holiday period. Landucci observed that it was the ordinary Florentines who suffered when supplies ran short: 'The poor were very miserable and they hoped that the pope would have grain brought in from abroad but he did nothing and everyone was dismayed to see the quantities of food consumed by the men who had come with the papal court.'[28]

Leo X left Florence on 19 February 1516, bidding a sad farewell to his brother Giuliano, who was now critically ill. He died less than a month later and was buried with full state honours in San Lorenzo. He had no children by his wife Philiberta of Savoy, though he did leave an illegitimate son, Ippolito, not quite five years old. With Giuliano dead, the hopes of the Medici family rested on the pope's young nephew Lorenzo. Leo X was finally forced to acquiesce to Alfonsina's incessant lobbying and agreed to oust Francesco Maria I della Rovere from his duchy of Urbino and install Lorenzo as duke in his place. And so, in March 1516 Leo X published a bull depriving Francesco Maria of his possessions; in early June, Lorenzo, at the head of the papal army, forced Urbino to surrender. Prominent among his cavalry commanders was his distant cousin Giovanni, whose company, known as the *Bande Nere* (black bands), established his nickname Giovanni delle Bande Nere. Although there were grounds for the usurpation – Francesco Maria had recently murdered a cardinal and had done his best to sour relations between Leo X and Francis I – this unashamedly nepotistic venture, designed to favour the private interests of the Medici, was a very unpopular move.

Meanwhile in Rome, a group of cardinals, angered by Leo X's pro-French policies and nepotism, were plotting to assassinate the Medici pope. Guicciardini, now Leo X's governor in Modena, explained that their leader Cardinal Alfonso Petrucci, who was 'burning with hatred' for Leo X, 'had childish thoughts of attacking him with weapons', but then 'turned all his thoughts to killing him with poison, using Battista da Vercelli, a famous surgeon he knew well, who advised – if such a word can be used for such a terrible anger – how it should be done'.[29] Cardinal Petrucci 'was to praise his skills to the skies so that the pope, who had long suffered from an ulcer on his buttocks and was always looking for doctors, would get the idea of asking him for a cure'.

Fortunately for Leo X, a letter detailing how the doctor was to gain access to the papal apartments was intercepted. The compromising evidence meant that Cardinal Petrucci, the doctor and the other conspirators were all arrested in May 1517. Battista da Vercelli was hung, drawn and quartered in public on 27 June, while Petrucci was executed in his cell in Castel Sant'Angelo a few days later. Among the others punished were Cardinal Soderini, who was fined 25,000 ducats, and Cardinal Riario, who was fined 150,000 ducats and deprived of the lucrative post of vice-chancellor, which Leo X now gave to Cardinal Giulio. To silence opposition in the College, Leo X flooded it that July with an unprecedented addition of thirty-one cardinals. The bold move enabled him to continue his alliance with Francis I and to continue to benefit from the steady stream of French favours for the Medici family.

The Medici and Francis I became further entwined in January 1518, when Lorenzo was betrothed to Madeleine de la Tour d'Auvergne, descended from French royalty. The groom travelled to France for the wedding, which took place at Francis I's château at Amboise in May; and the bride made her ceremonial entry into Florence on 7 September, followed by a lavish reception at the Palazzo Medici, organized by Lorenzo and his mother. Leo X himself was unable to attend, but Raphael's portrait of the pope was rushed to Florence in his place. The following day Alfonsina Orsini proudly wrote to a courtier that 'seventy-five damsels were invited to the nuptial banquet in the garden as well as many others: the duchess sat between Cardinal Innocenzo Cibò and Cardinal Luigi de' Rossi and the guests filled the garden... there were crowds at the windows, on the roofs, on the streets and on small stands that people had made everywhere so that they could see in'.[30]

The marriage, though, proved very short-lived. Madeleine gave birth to her first child the following April, a healthy daughter named Caterina; but the mother caught puerperal fever and died a fortnight later. And that was not all. Just a week after the death of his wife, Lorenzo himself died, from tuberculosis – and syphilis too, if the rumours are to be believed – at the age of twenty-seven.

Lorenzo's state funeral took place at San Lorenzo 'with the greatest magnificence but with very few tears'.[31] His death was a major blow to Leo X's plans for his family. To lose his two principal heirs in a matter of three years was more than unfortunate, and this tragedy left the future of his branch of the Medici family very insecurely in the hands of two small illegitimate children: Giuliano's son, the nine-year-old Ippolito, and Cardinal Giulio's boy, Alessandro, a year younger. In the other branch of the family, Giovanni della Bande Nere was proving an able soldier. That June, his wife, Maria Salviati, gave birth to a son, who was named Cosimo at the request of the pope. Leo X stood as godfather for the child.

The pope now appointed Cardinal Giulio to take Lorenzo's place at the head of the government in Florence. By now, the Medici regime

had become very unpopular, not least because of Lorenzo's arrogant behaviour and the taxes imposed on the city to raise the huge sum of 750,000 ducats to pay for the war over Urbino. Cardinal Giulio was careful to show that he was a very different sort of leader. Unlike Lorenzo, he maintained an exceptionally modest lifestyle and increased, a little, the number of families eligible for public office. In a move designed to be popular on the streets, Leo X announced his intention to canonize the Dominican Antonino Pierozzi, a popular fifteenth-century Archbishop of Florence.

The Medici also spent liberally on artistic projects in the city to enhance the standing of the family. In June 1519, Cardinal Giulio announced that he intended to spend 50,000 florins at San Lorenzo. What had once been the Medici's parish church was now effectively the religious expression of their power in the city; it was here that annual celebrations were held for the Feast of Cosmas and Damian and for the anniversary of Leo X's election. Giulio commissioned Michelangelo to design a splendid library, the Biblioteca Laurenziana, attached to the church, and added a second sacristy there as a counterpart to the one built by his great-great-grandfather, Giovanni di Bicci. The new sacristy was to house the tombs of Giulio's father, Giuliano, and his uncle, Lorenzo the Magnificent, as well as two grandiose sarcophagi, also designed by Michelangelo, for the recently deceased Giuliano, Duke of Nemours, and Lorenzo, Duke of Urbino. It was endowed with funds to pay for three masses a day and for continuous prayers for the souls of the dead. The priests were only released from night duty in 1629.

As part of this campaign to promote his family, Cardinal Giulio did much to develop the Medici myth. With the help of Alfonsina Orsini, the main reception hall at the villa of Poggio a Caiano was decorated with scenes of family history. This was a genre fashionable among the ruling dynasties of the sixteenth century, but it was an audacious choice for a house yet to achieve this rank. Significantly, the scenes were cloaked as episodes in Ancient Roman history, carefully chosen to represent key moments in the Medici story. *Cicero's Return from Exile*, for example, was the obvious choice to portray Old Cosimo's return from exile in 1434. But other scenes showed how the gulf between myth and reality had begun to grow. Lorenzo the Magnificent's diplomatic and political prowess was depicted as *The Tribute Presented to Julius Caesar*, which showed Lorenzo receiving the exotic animals

The staircase of the Biblioteca Laurenziana (designed by Michelangelo and begun in 1523), one of several projects commissioned by Cardinal Giulio de' Medici for the family's parish church of San Lorenzo.

sent to Florence by the sultan in 1487; but surely Cardinal Giulio, who was eight years old at the time and living in Florence, would have known that the famous giraffe had been a gift for the *Signoria*, not for Lorenzo himself.

Thanks to Cardinal Giulio, the myth was also developed in print by those previous supporters of the Soderini regime, Niccolò Valori and Niccolò Machiavelli, both now eager to ingratiate themselves with the Medici. Valori's biography of Lorenzo the Magnificent, written in 1519 and dedicated to Leo X, glorified Lorenzo's reign as a golden age; he eulogized Lorenzo's intellectual and diplomatic talents and his lavish patronage of the arts. For Valori, Lorenzo was 'miracle of nature', loved by all animals, whose favourite racehorse fell ill if not fed by Lorenzo's own hands.[32] He was the ideal ruler, chosen by God to lead his city to fame and fortune, and to preside over an era of peace in Italy. He was miraculously saved from the Pazzi Conspiracy through divine providence, and his death was heralded by a comet, howling wolves, a bolt of lightning and other supernatural portents.

Machiavelli contributed to the burgeoning myth with his *Florentine Histories*, commissioned by Cardinal Giulio in 1521 on the recommendation of Filippo Strozzi's brother, a close friend of Machiavelli. It was a challenging task for this confirmed republican, but one he seems to have relished. The book, described by one modern scholar as 'a deeply and intentionally ambiguous work', portrayed the fifteenth-century Medici as great leaders in a corrupt world, an image highly acceptable to Cardinal Giulio and Leo X.[33] On Lorenzo the Magnificent's fraudulent use of public funds, for example, Machiavelli explained that 'his unhappy lack of success in business matters' was the fault of his corrupt agents, 'so it was necessary for the state to help him with large amounts of money', a gloss that begged the question of whether the state had seen fit to rescue anyone else from financial embarrassment. Of Lorenzo's lavish expenditure, Machiavelli wrote that 'his aim was to keep the city in abundance' while his villas 'were not those of a private citizen but of a king'.[34] Much was open to interpretation. From the republican point of view, the text was a damning indictment of the Medici and their princely ambitions.

In addition to the expensive projects in Florence to glorify the Medici, Leo X also spent immense sums on buildings in Rome. He was one of the greatest patrons of the era, and his pontificate marked the

Andrea del Sarto, *Tribute to Caesar*, c.1519–20 (Poggio a Caiano, Villa Medici).

period later defined as the High Renaissance. Among his more famous projects were the Vatican rooms decorated by Raphael, including his private dining-room, the Stanza dell'Incendio, which was frescoed with scenes from the lives of popes Leo III (795–816) and Leo IV (847–55). Raphael also designed a set of tapestries for the Sistine Chapel depicting the Acts of the Apostles – with the eleventh-of-the-month events from the pope's own life woven ostentatiously into the frieze. The tapestries were made in Brussels at a cost of 15,000 ducats, while Raphael earned 1,000 ducats for the cartoons. Leo's grandest project, which was supervised by Cardinal Giulio, was the Villa Madama outside the Porta del Popolo. Built to Raphael's design, it was based on literary descriptions of the villas of Ancient Rome, with apartments for summer and winter decorated with *all'antica* stucco work, hot baths, fish pools and a theatre, all set in magnificent terraced gardens ornamented with fountains, flowerbeds and fruit trees.

Leo X funded his extravagant expenditure – on cultural projects, on military campaigns and on his lavish lifestyle – through an increasingly corrupt Church administration. A document drawn up in Rome in 1514 listed the prices of 1,231 venal offices for sale at the curia; the following year Leo X created another 200 venal posts, bringing 202,000 ducats into the papal coffers.[35] In 1520, he founded the Knights of St Peter, a chivalric order that would allow access to the Roman nobility for a price, by which means he raised 401,000 ducats.[36] By the end of his pontificate there were 2,228 posts for sale. In addition, many of the thirty-one cardinals he appointed in 1517 paid handsomely for the honour; one of the new intake, Ferdinando Ponzetti, was said to have paid 30,000 ducats for his red hat. In 1521 Leo X gave the post of

Raphael, *Coronation of Charlemagne*, c.1515–17 (Vatican Palace, Stanza dell'Incendio); part of a cycle of frescoes in Leo X's private dining-room depicting scenes from the lives of Popes Leo III (795–816) and Leo IV (847–55), both of whom were portrayed as the Medici pope.

CAROLVS
MAGNVS
RO.
ECCLESIAE

chamberlain to his nephew, Cardinal Innocenzo Cibò, in return for 40,000 ducats, and a few months later the job changed hands again when Cardinal Francesco Armellini offered 60,000 ducats for the lucrative job.[37]

It was not just the rampant corruption of the papal court that appalled visitors who travelled to Rome to see the sites of Christian legend; they were also disgusted at the luxury and immorality on show. Leo X's court was secular and princely, and often offensive to Christian sensitivities. During Carnival in February 1521, for example, the pope attended a theatrical performance that scathingly mocked religious piety.[38] The play opened with a woman praying to Venus for a lover, before eight grey-clad hermits entered the stage, dancing and driving Cupid away. Then Venus appeared with a potion, which the woman gave the hermits, who fell asleep – to be awoken by Cupid's arrows. Falling in love with the woman and shedding their grey habits, they turned into handsome youths. 'Many thought it was bad for the Church that its leader should prefer amusements, music, hunting and buffoonery rather than devoting himself to the needs of his flock,' commented a canon of Siena.[39]

Most damning for Leo X were the growing calls for Church reform, above all in Germany, where the sale of indulgences was proving very unpopular. This practice, begun by Julius II to finance the immense cost of rebuilding St Peter's, had massively increased under the Medici pope. On 31 October 1517, the Augustinian Martin Luther nailed his list of ninety-five objections on the door of Wittenberg Palace church, the act that was to mark the start of the Reformation. In June 1519, Luther was forced to admit that he believed the Bible to be the only true Christian authority, thus denying the doctrine of papal infallibility, one of the cornerstones of the Catholic faith. Luther and his followers, who initially had only wanted to reform abuses within the Church, now openly split with Rome. The following year Leo X declared Luther a heretic and issued the bull *Exsurge Domine* to condemn his ideas and ban all Protestant literature. Luther publicly burned the bull in Wittenberg in December. The reform movement was growing rapidly north of the Alps – but in Leo X's Rome there was little recognition of the seriousness of the situation.

Meanwhile, a powerful new figure had entered the political stage. On 12 January 1519, Emperor Maximilian I died and was succeeded by his nineteen-year-old grandson Charles V, who had already inherited the Duchy of Burgundy from his father and the Kingdom of Spain from his other grandfather, Ferdinand I. Thanks to his unique inheritance, Charles V was now head of an immense empire – Spain, the Low Countries, the German states and Naples, as well as Spanish territories across the Atlantic – and his bitter rivalry with Francis I would transform the political map of Europe. The two men could not have been more different. Francis I was strong, and fond of hunting, jousting, banquets and the pleasures of life. Charles V, with his drooping Habsburg jaw, was no horseman, but rather an austere, devout and single-mindedly devoted governor of his realm.

In May 1521, Leo X abandoned his alliance with France to sign a treaty with Charles V, the terms of which had been secretly negotiated by Cardinal Giulio. Accusing Francis I of violating the borders of the Papal States, Leo X assembled his army to drive the French out of Italy, appointing Guicciardini as commissary-general to the papal armies and Giovanni delle Bande Nere to take charge of the cavalry. That October, the pope went to his villa at Magliana to enjoy some hunting and to convalesce from a minor illness. He was still there on Sunday 24 November when news arrived that his troops had ousted the French from Milan, whereupon the pope returned to Rome the following day to be greeted by cheering crowds. The next morning, however, he was not well and had to leave an audience abruptly when he began to shake uncontrollably. On Wednesday he felt better, though weak, and his doctors diagnosed a fever, but nothing serious. They were wrong. He was suffering from a bad attack of malaria, probably contracted while he was hunting in the swamps near Magliana. Two days later, on 29 November, he fainted, and the following day the fever worsened dramatically. By midnight on 1 December 1521, the pope was dead, just ten days short of his forty-sixth birthday.

Leo X's unexpected death was a disaster for the Medici, who had expected his pontificate to last several more decades. With both Giuliano and Lorenzo also gone, and the next generation still young, the family's position in Florence itself was under threat. But they still had influence in Rome. Cardinal Giulio, together with his cousins and friends in the College of Cardinals, now needed to use all their energies to engineer the election of a pope who would be favourable to the Medici cause.

13

AGE OF IRON

Pope Clement VII

1521–1530

Giulio (43), Cardinal de' Medici, Pope Clement VII

    Alessandro (10), *his illegitimate son*

    Ippolito (11), *the illegitimate son of his cousin, Giuliano*

    Caterina (2), *daughter of his cousin, Lorenzo*

Lucrezia (51), *his cousin,* m. Jacopo Salviati

    Cardinal Giovanni Salviati (32), *their son*

    Maria (22), *their daughter (see below)*

    Cardinal Innocenzo Cibò (30), *son of his cousin, Maddalena*

    Clarice (28), *daughter of his cousin, Piero,* m. Filippo Strozzi

Giovanni delle Bande Nere (23), *his cousin,* m. Maria Salviati

    Cosimo (2), *their son*

Thanks to the skill with which he had negotiated the alliance between Leo X and Charles V, Cardinal Giulio de' Medici was the Emperor's favoured papal candidate and widely tipped as a front-runner in the upcoming election. However, the conclave, which opened on 27 December 1521, was not only deeply divided between the French and Imperial factions, but also by the enmity between the Medici and the Soderini clans. Cardinal Francesco Soderini was determined to do everything possible to block the election of another Medici pope.

It was soon evident that Giulio could not acquire enough votes for his own election; but he might be able to scupper the chances of his enemies. With the conclave in deadlock behind the closed doors of the Vatican, on 9 January he addressed his colleagues: 'I see that it is impossible for us to elect a pope from among our number; I have put forward three or four names, but they have been rejected, and I cannot accept the candidates proposed by the other side.'[1] He then suggested the unusual step of considering candidates who were not present in the conclave. 'They must be of good character,' he insisted; and when asked to name one, he named Cardinal Adrian Dedel of Utrecht, 'who is a venerable man, aged sixty-three, and much respected for his piety.' This compromise candidate, who lived in Spain and had been Charles V's tutor, was duly elected that day as Pope Adrian VI.

It was not until late August 1521 that the new pope's galley docked at Ostia, and Adrian VI finally arrived in Rome. Right from the start it was evident that the pontificate of this devout churchman would be very different to that of his predecessor. One of his first acts was to make a stinging attack on the extravagance of the papal court and to urge the cardinals to moderate their luxurious lifestyles. He set up a commission to examine the venal offices introduced by Leo X, a move that caused widespread panic in Rome among those who feared they were about to lose their jobs and perks.

Although Adrian VI confirmed Giulio's position as vice-chancellor, many were surprised to see that he showed no special favour to the man who had engineered his election. Moreover, Giulio's cousin and friend Filippo Strozzi lost his post as papal banker when Adrian VI transferred the account to the Fuggers, Charles V's German financiers. However, the pope did take Giulio's side in his conflict with Cardinal Soderini, notably after Giulio's agents intercepted a French courier travelling to Rome with letters that implicated several of Soderini's nephews in a

French-backed conspiracy to expel the Medici from Florence. Soderini was arrested and imprisoned in Castel Sant'Angelo; Francis I reacted by refusing to pay his ecclesiastical dues and threatening to start a schism by electing another pope.

Cardinal Giulio did not have to wait too long for another chance to gain the papal tiara. By April 1523, Adrian VI was threatening both Francis I and Charles V with excommunication unless they agreed a truce in their rivalry and joined his crusade against the growing menace of the Turks in the eastern Mediterranean. Even Charles V, who had also expected favours from Adrian VI, had misgivings about the zeal of his old tutor, and when the pope's health began to decline that summer, the Emperor instructed his ambassador in Rome to ensure that Giulio would be elected as the papal successor. In August, Adrian VI's intermittent fever turned serious after he contracted a chill; he died on 14 September.

The second conclave in three years opened on 1 October 1523, and it remained in deadlock for more than six weeks, split along exactly the same lines as it had been in 1521, with neither Cardinal Giulio nor his French counterpart able to secure the necessary two-thirds majority. In the end, the election was decided by a quarrel in the French camp. Cardinal Pompeo Colonna, a Roman by birth, 'impetuous and proud by nature' and hitherto 'most hostile' to Cardinal Giulio, as Guicciardini explained, 'lost his temper with the cardinals in his party because they would not elect Cardinal Jacobazzi, who was one of their faction and also a Roman'.[2] That night, 'acting on impulse, he went to Cardinal de' Medici and offered him his support and Medici, in the utmost secrecy, promised to make Colonna his vice-chancellor and recorded this promise in a document written in his own hand'. It was a very tempting offer, enough to persuade Colonna to defect from the French camp along with several of his Italian colleagues. The following morning, 19 November, Giulio was duly elected as Clement VII – the second Medici pontiff.

The new pope was forty-five years old and in excellent health, a man of moderate habits, who enjoyed listening to music during his frugal meals. A famous patron of writers and musicians, Clement VII continued Leo X's projects at St Peter's, the Vatican and the sumptuous Villa Madama, as well as the Medici projects in Florence. He was a hard worker, lacking the hedonistic streak of his cousin – he did not hunt, nor did he enjoy the bawdy humour of buffoons. And, despite the divisions in the conclave, he was a popular choice: one diplomat reported that 'he distributed more favours on the first day of his pontificate than Adrian VI did in his entire life'.[3]

One of the first to benefit was Cardinal Colonna, who was given the post of vice-chancellor that he had been promised. Others included Cardinal Niccolò Ridolfi, the son of Leo X's sister Contessina, who was appointed to the Archbishopric of Florence, Clement VII's old see. Filippo Strozzi was reinstated as papal banker, and he moved into a palace by the Vatican for easy access to the papal apartments. He would prove a key figure in the new regime. There was also a job for Clement VII's cousin Giovanni delle Bande Nere, who, thanks to the intervention of his wife Maria Salviati, took up service in the papal army.

For the Medici, a second pope in the family was a huge triumph, another chance to establish themselves among Europe's ruling elite. But there were very few male members left among the descendants of Old Cosimo, and the dynastic future of this branch rested precariously on the two illegitimate boys: the pope's cousin Ippolito, and the pope's son Alessandro. On the other side of the family there was another young boy, Cosimo, the son of Giovanni delle Bande Nere and Maria Salviati, whose marriage had united the two branches of the family; and, of course, Giovanni himself.

As for Florence, early in 1524 Clement VII appointed Cardinal Silvio Passerini to govern the city. He took up residence at the Palazzo Medici with Ippolito as the family representative in the city. Although Ippolito was allowed to hold public office, the fourteen-year-old was too young to lead the regime, which was run by Passerini acting on orders from Rome. Alessandro – who was presented in public as the illegitimate son of Lorenzo, Duke of Urbino, though many suspected the truth of his parentage – moved into the villa at Poggio a Caiano, with his 'half-sister', the legitimate daughter of Lorenzo and Madeleine de la Tour d'Auvergne.

The business of governing Florence was, though, the least of Clement VII's worries. As pope, he faced a formidable list of problems. Thanks to Leo X's wanton extravagance, the papal treasury was empty.

Sebastiano del Piombo, *Clement VII*, 1526 (Naples, Gallerie Nazionali di Capodimonte).

After Raphael, *The Donation of Constantine*, early 1520s (Vatican Palace, Stanza di Costantino). The papal claim to secular power in Italy was based on a document, forged in the eighth century, according to which Constantine transferred the Papal States to Pope Sylvester I following the Emperor's miraculous recovery from leprosy by baptism.

The Turks were menacing not only the eastern Mediterranean but also the Empire: having captured the island of Rhodes and expelled the Knights of St John, in August 1526 they destroyed the armies of Louis II of Hungary at the Battle of Moháçz and captured his capital, Buda. The Protestant reform movement was spreading rapidly north of the Alps, depriving Clement VII of yet more income. By 1526 the rulers of both Prussia and Saxony had converted to the new religion, and Martin Luther had published not only his translation of the Bible, an act forbidden under Church law, but also his order for Protestant services, which dismissed the Eucharist and the miracle of transubstantiation – the focal point of the Catholic mass – in favour of a sermon and a discourse on the Bible. Above all in the formidable problems faced by the pope, Charles V and Francis I were on the brink of war, their huge armies preparing to fight for control of northern Italy.

Clement VII may have shown ample political skill during Leo X's pontificate; but he was unprepared for the maelstrom of the looming Habsburg–Valois conflict. In the interests of the papacy, he needed to remain neutral. However, Clement VII's priority was the Medici, and to safeguard the future of his family in Florence he needed to find himself on the winning side – a tricky call.

In March 1524, Clement VII sent Nikolaus von Schönberg, a Dominican friar who was Archbishop of Capua, to France, Spain and England to try and negotiate a peace: he returned empty-handed. Schönberg went to Spain again in early September, while another legate travelled to the French court, but these efforts were also unsuccessful. That same month, Francis I invaded Italy, and Charles V followed suit. As the two foreign forces lined up on the Lombard plain, Clement VII still hoped that a peaceful solution could be found. But when news arrived in Rome on 28 October that the French had taken Milan, he changed his mind and began secret talks with Francis I. Prominent among his demands were French protection for the Medici in Florence and the betrothal of the five-year-old Caterina to the king's eldest son.

Clement VII and Francis I announced their alliance on 5 January 1525, and their armies launched two simultaneous attacks on Charles V. A detachment of 10,000 troops went south to take Naples, while the rest of the army concentrated on the Imperial-held fortress at Pavia, just south of Milan. Giovanni delle Bande Nere joined the siege of Pavia with his 2,000 soldiers and 200 cavalry; but on 20 February he was badly wounded by gunshot, in his right leg, during a skirmish under the walls.

He was fortunate not to have been fighting four days later, when the Imperial troops, heavily armed with portable arquebuses, slaughtered Francis I's army. Contemporary accounts of the Battle of Pavia suggest that more than 12,000 Frenchmen were killed or captured, with negligible losses on the Imperial side.[4] There was a hideous sight in Venice that April: 'many dead bodies have come by sea into the Lido perhaps a hundred or more thrown up by the sea, they were naked and some were wounded,' it was reported; 'they had been carried down the Po from the battlefield at Pavia [and] the corpses that were found were buried'.[5] It was a disaster not only for Francis I, who was taken prisoner and sent to Spain, but also for Clement VII. He had picked the losing side. With a powerful Imperial army positioned just north of the Apennines, the survival of the Medici in Florence was under serious threat. The pope was forced to agree terms with Charles V, who demanded an immediate payment of 25,000 ducats and an alliance *against* France. In return, the treaty that Clement VII now signed with Charles de Lannoy, Charles V's viceroy in Naples, on 1 April promised Imperial protection for the Medici in Florence. However, the price of this protection was 100,000 ducats, to be raised by taxing the Florentines. A week later, Filippo Strozzi reported that the city's treasury was almost dry.[6]

Nor was this alliance destined to last. It is hardly surprising that Clement VII's critics thought him weak and indecisive. In March 1526, Francis I was released from captivity in Spain, having renounced his claims to Naples and Milan; but it was soon evident that the king had no intention of keeping his word. In Rome, his envoys persuaded Clement VII to break his agreement with Charles V, and in May this second Medici pope signed the League of Cognac with France, Venice, Florence and Milan against the Empire. Charles V responded by attempting to split the league, and hatched a dubious plan with his ally, Cardinal Colonna, to force the pope to leave it. In June, he wrote to his ambassador in Rome: 'if you are unsuccessful in gaining Clement, speak secretly to Cardinal Colonna, so that he may set in hand, as if of his own initiative, the matter recommended by his agents and give him secretly every support'.[7] On 20 September, the Colonna family launched a raid on Rome, looting the Vatican and forcing Clement VII to take refuge in Castel Sant'Angelo. The pope found it difficult to raise the sum they demanded to stop the fighting and had to hand over his wealthy relatives, Filippo Strozzi and Cardinal Giovanni Salviati, as hostages. That November, he was able to enact some revenge when he deprived Colonna not only of the post of vice-chancellor but also of his red hat.

Meanwhile in northern Italy, the situation had become increasingly ominous after Milan surrendered to the Imperial armies under the command of Charles of Bourbon in July. That autumn, Bourbon's troops were reinforced by 9,000 soldiers from Naples, led by the Spanish viceroy, Charles de Lannoy, and by another 12,000 men who crossed the Alps from Germany under the command of Georg von Frundsberg. On 25 November, during a skirmish at Governolo in Mantuan territory, Giovanni delle Bande Nere was wounded again, hit by an arquebus ball, and this time his right leg had to be amputated. A witness reported his bravery on hearing the surgeon call for ten men to hold him down: 'not even twenty could hold me,' he was reported to say, with a smile.[8] But the operation was not a success and he died five days later, probably of gangrene.*

Clement VII's continuing efforts to negotiate peace met with no response. He also worried about Florence, where the cost of the war was draining the economy – over the past six months, the city had sent 270,000 ducats to the papal armies.[9] To add to his fears about the impending crisis in northern Italy and the growing unpopularity of the Medici regime in Florence, he was assailed by his weeping cousin Clarice, begging him to do something about her husband Filippo Strozzi, held hostage in Naples. 'The poor pope is embattled on every side, just like a ship buffeted by winds in a stormy sea,' reported the Mantuan ambassador on 10 January.[10] His position worsened in early February 1527, when he found he had been betrayed by an ally, Napoleone Orsini, who had conspired with the Imperial commander Lannoy and the Colonna family – traditionally the rivals of the Orsini – to have the pope murdered. And two weeks later, Bourbon and Frundsberg left Piacenza with 20,000 troops to march south towards Florence and Rome. On 29 March, the pope made a final attempt to stave off disaster by offering peace terms to the Imperial commanders. Lannoy and Frundsberg agreed; but their men mutinied, and, tempted by stories of the fabulous riches to be found in Rome, they joined up with Bourbon and advanced on the city. Clement VII appealed to his army for help, but it was too late.

In Rome, the morning of 6 May 1527 was unusually foggy. Bourbon was fortunate in being able to get through the city's defences with ease, but he died in the first assault. His troops, however, swarmed into the city, where they caused carnage on an appalling scale. Palaces, houses, shops and churches were systematically looted and set on fire. Women were raped, all the patients in the Ospedale Santo Spirito were mur-

---

*   In a macabre postscript, his body was exhumed in 2012; it confirmed that his leg had been amputated below the knee.

dered, the rich were ransomed and those who could not pay were killed, leaving the streets strewn with corpses. Many of the soldiers were German Protestants, and they ridiculed the Catholic Church and its manifestations, smashing crucifixes and precious relics, parading through the streets dressed in cardinals' red robes, and using the Sistine Chapel as a stable. Clement VII took refuge from the terror in Castel Sant'Angelo, along with some 3,000 courtiers, servants, women and children. When the papal army, under the command of Francesco Maria I della Rovere, belatedly arrived at the gates of Rome on 22 May, they took one look at the state of the city and decided against an attempt to rescue the pope.

News of the catastrophe reached Florence on 11 May – and was greeted with jubilation. The city had been all but beggared by Clement VII, who had taken a total of 651,460 florins out of the Florentine coffers over the previous year to fund his disastrous campaigns.[11] On 16 May, the city voted to expel the Medici and restore the republic, electing Niccolò Capponi as the new gonfalonier. The next day, the unpopular papal governor, Cardinal Passerini, left with his wards Ippolito and Alessandro, while little Caterina was placed in the safety of a monastery. Maria Salviati, widow of Giovanni delle Bande Nere, and her eight-year-old son Cosimo were put under house arrest at the family villa at Trebbio, but managed to escape, thanks to the help of a guard who had served under her husband.

On 6 June 1527, Clement VII agreed terms with the Imperial troops, who took possession of Castel Sant'Angelo the next day. He was to pay a ransom of 400,000 ducats and to surrender the papal fortresses at Ostia, Civitavecchia and Civita Castellana, and the cities of Parma, Piacenza and Modena to the Emperor. He was also to hand over seven hostages and remain a prisoner in the castle until the first 150,000 ducats had been paid. He raised this sum by setting up a furnace on the castle roof and melting down his gilded tiaras and chalices, as well as the great bronze angel from the top of the fortress.

The pope was finally released in early December, and he left for Orvieto with a small group of cardinals and a large escort of Imperial troops. He was a broken man. The papacy was bankrupt and he was living in a small, dilapidated episcopal palace with neither jewels nor vestments. His position as spiritual leader of Christendom was diminishing rapidly: that year, Protestantism had become the official religion in Sweden, Denmark, Lüneburg and Saxony. Worst of all, his policies had led to the collapse of the Medici regime in Florence and his family's exile – again – from the city.

Despite his pitiful position, Clement VII was still head of the Church, and Orvieto was soon thronging with petitioners. There were envoys from Francis I, urging him to declare war on Charles V, and ambassadors from Henry VIII of England, asking for the king's divorce from Catherine of Aragon – with envoys from Spain insisting that the pope refuse Henry's request, as Catherine was Charles V's aunt. Above all, he was urged to return to Rome, which he refused, reluctant to be any closer to the French and Imperial armies now fighting for control of Naples.

In July 1528, a severe outbreak of typhus decimated the soldiers in the French camp outside Naples, and by the end of August more than half of them were dead. The French began a retreat on 28 August, but the following day disaster struck when, at the Battle of Aversa, they were massacred by the Imperial army under Philibert, Prince of Orange. The war for southern Italy was over.

Clement VII finally returned to Rome on 6 October 1528, to find a scene of utter devastation: only 20 per cent of the houses were occupied, churches had been stripped of their treasures, and the economy was in ruins. At the end of the month, he sent a personal letter to Charles V: 'We must rejoice at coming safely to shore after such a terrible shipwreck, even though we have lost everything,' adding that 'before our eyes lies a miserable and mutilated corpse, and nothing can alleviate our sadness… but the prospect of peace… which is dependent on your restraint and agreement.'[12]

Early in January 1529, Clement VII held a consistory at the Vatican despite suffering from a heavy cold, which worsened overnight to become a serious fever. Two days later, convinced he was dying, he summoned his cousin Ippolito to his bedroom, where he created the eighteen-year-old a cardinal. Ippolito accepted this honour with great reluctance: as the figurehead of Cardinal Passerini's regime, he had assumed that his future lay as ruler of Florence – when the Medici returned – and that his cousin Alessandro, a year younger, would have

Titian, *Equestrian portrait of Charles V*, 1547 (Madrid, Prado).

the Church career. But surely Ippolito had heard the rumours that Alessandro was Clement VII's son and would inevitably be the favourite. Although the doctors predicted the worst for the pope, he recovered. By the end of the month he was well enough to appoint legates to Naples to negotiate the return of the fortresses of Ostia and Civitavecchia and the release of the hostages. He also began secret talks in Florence with Gonfalonier Capponi, though when this was discovered Capponi was instantly sacked and replaced by a rabid anti-Medicean.

Meanwhile, Charles V, having ousted the French from Naples in the previous August, consolidated his Italian victory with a resounding defeat over Francis I at the Battle of Landriano, near Milan, on 21 June 1529. The Emperor was now the undisputed master of the peninsula – and Clement VII was entirely dependent on his goodwill. On 29 June, the two rulers signed the Treaty of Barcelona, and this time the alliance would hold. Clement VII had learned a chilling lesson of *Realpolitik*. The two rulers agreed on common action against the Protestants and the Turks, who were now threatening Vienna, the capital of Charles V's brother Ferdinand of Austria. The pope also promised to crown Charles as Holy Roman Emperor.* In return, the Emperor promised military support to restore the Medici to Florence, sealing the alliance with the betrothal of his illegitimate daughter Margaret of Austria to Clement's son Alessandro.

On 17 August 1529, Clement VII and Philibert of Orange signed the contract for the conquest of Florence. It was an expensive project for the impoverished pope. He was to source the heavy artillery, supply 5,500 troops and pay 280,000 ducats for the venture: 80,000 ducats up-front, another 50,000 ducats once the city had been taken, and the final instalment of 150,000 ducats to be raised by taxes once Florence was again under the Medici yoke. That month, he borrowed 15,000 ducats from his banker, Filippo Strozzi, giving him twenty-six venal offices as security.[13]

Charles V left Spain on 28 July to sail to Italy for his Imperial coronation, arriving in Genoa a fortnight later. Both Cardinal Ippolito and Alessandro were there to welcome him, and it was observed that he received the cousins very warmly. He was less well disposed towards

---

* This was to prove the last ever papal coronation of an Emperor.

the ambassadors sent by Florence, who hoped to persuade him to break his alliance with the pope. Initially, he refused to see them; but they were finally given an audience in late August. 'The Emperor received them coldly and some of his courtiers, in the hearing of the envoys, said that Florence was to be taken by force,' it was reported. [14] But the envoys had a tempting offer for Charles V: 'the ambassadors have promised His Majesty 400,000 ducats if they can keep their liberty' from the Medici.

Already, however, Philibert of Orange was marching north from Rome with 10,000 Imperial troops and surrounding the heavily fortified city of Perugia, which capitulated on 10 September. Four days later, they crossed the Florentine frontier: Cortona quickly surrendered, followed by Arezzo. In Florence, despite the guards placed at the gates, hundreds of wealthy families fled the city. Charles V, who had left Genoa for Piacenza, held a council meeting at which, against the advice of his generals, he gave orders for Orange to slow his advance. Perhaps he was tempted by the generous offer of cash made by the Florentine ambassadors; more likely, he hoped that Florence – like Perugia, Cortona and Arezzo – might be cowed and surrender without a fight. There is no evidence that Charles V was planning to break his alliance with Clement VII. When the Florentines sent envoys to the Imperial camp to negotiate with Orange, he refused to discuss the issue without authorization from the pope. The *Signoria* also sent envoys to Rome to deal directly with Clement VII, but Orange arrested the men and would not let them continue their journey without papal permission. In late September, Clement VII sent his trusted adviser, Schönberg, as legate to act on his behalf at the negotiations at Orange's camp, which was now at Figline, some 15 miles south-east of Florence. Schönberg was under strict orders to refuse to sign any deal that did not include the restoration of the Medici. Clement VII also insisted on tax-free status for the Medici, an amnesty for all his supporters, a resident governor to enforce his policies, the payment of compensation and the return of all the Medici palaces. As he must have known, these demands were totally unacceptable to the Florentines, who were equally implacable: 'Florence in ashes,' one of the envoys declared, 'rather than under the Medici.' [15]

On 7 October 1529, Clement VII left Rome to travel to Bologna for the Imperial coronation, taking the less comfortable route through the Tiber Valley and the Romagna in order to avoid Tuscany. He was given a magnificent reception when he entered Bologna on 24 October, carried on his throne through streets hung with the Medici coat-of-arms; on the same day, outside the walls of Florence, Orange and his 11,000 soldiers set up camp.

Two weeks later, Charles V arrived in Bologna, which had been redecorated with even greater magnificence. He made his formal entry into the city with his future Medici son-in-law Alessandro, who was given the honour of riding with the courtiers of the Imperial train. The Emperor was received by Clement VII in his full pontifical regalia at the steps of San Petronio, where Charles dismounted, knelt before the pope and kissed his foot. The Imperial and papal courts remained in residence in Bologna for the next five months. Host to this glittering assembly of princes, cardinals, ambassadors, prelates, humanists, musicians, poets and artists, the city was briefly the political and cultural capital of Europe. The banquets, balls, hunting parties, mock battles and jousts with which these potentates were entertained were a stark contrast to the privations being suffered by the Florentines under siege by the Emperor's armies, some 60 miles to the south.

Charles V and Clement VII were lodged in adjacent apartments in Bologna's town hall, the Palazzo Pubblico. The two men had much to discuss, not least the future of Milan and other states in northern Italy – now that the area was under Imperial control – as well as the threats posed by the Protestants and the Turks, and, of course, Florence. Talking face to face, their policy differences emerged with more clarity.

Charles V wanted to settle the issue of Florence as quickly as possible to free up his forces for the task of defending the eastern borders of the Empire against the Turks. The situation became clearer when Orange himself arrived in Bologna on 11 November, with depressing news. Thanks to the foresight of the *Signoria*, which had ordered the destruction of all buildings and crops within a one-mile radius of Florence, there was no food available for the Imperial troops. Moreover, Orange had only enough men to control the southern perimeter of the city walls. The artillery and the soldiers promised by the pope had not yet arrived, nor was there enough cash to pay his men, who were growing increasingly mutinous. Without more money and more troops, Orange insisted, the siege would inevitably fail. Charles V now attempted to negotiate a compromise with Clement VII. One sugges-

tion, that the Imperial troops should be allowed to ransack Florence to make up for their lack of wages, appalled the pope. The Emperor then suggested that the Medici could be given a different duchy: a portion of Milan could be made over to Alessandro to give the family its own personal fiefdom. Clement VII, however, was adamant – it was Florence he wanted, and the city had to be forced to capitulate.

In the end, to safeguard his alliance with Clement VII, Charles V yielded and the two men agreed to satisfy Orange's demands. The pope promised to provide 70,000 ducats a month to pay the Imperial troops. Despite his severe financial problems, he managed to raise 100,000 ducats during October for the war effort; and by the end of the month, Siena had agreed to supply the huge quantities of ordnance needed by Orange – some 2,000–3,000 pounds of gunpowder each day.[16] All the cardinals' mules in Bologna were requisitioned to transport more pieces of artillery across the snow-bound Apennines, and Orange's army was reinforced in late December 1529, when 8,000 Imperial troops and 4,000 papal soldiers marched south. These additions raised the size of the besieging army to 30,000 men, large enough to secure Florence's northern flank and encircle the city. Clement VII also arranged for two famous military architects to be sent to assist Orange: Antonio da Sangallo the Younger and Baldassare Peruzzi. In early January 1530, Peruzzi drew up a plan of Florence's fortifications, which still survives in the archives, and he seems to have made a clandestine visit into the city itself to spy out the city's defences.[17] The architects proved their worth on 20 January, when Orange's artillery launched a successful attack that destroyed a large section of the fortifications, enabling him to move his troops closer to the walls. Clement VII's goal was at last in sight.

In Bologna, the spectacular celebrations for the Imperial coronation took place in San Petronio on 24 February – Charles V's birthday and the anniversary of his victory over Francis I at the Battle of Pavia. Once again, Clement VII's son Alessandro was given a prominent place in the Emperor's retinue, while Cardinal Ippolito had to be content with his position in the papal procession. Also in Bologna for the event was their ten-year-old cousin Cosimo, with his mother Maria Salviati, who was using any opportunity that came her way to bring him to the attention of powerful political figures. Less welcome were the envoys

Giorgio Vasari, *Clement VII crowns Emperor Charles V in San Petronio, Bologna*, 1558–63 (Florence, Palazzo Vecchio).

sent by the Florentine *Signoria* to attend the ceremony. Their luggage was closely searched at the city gates, and Clement VII received them with obvious reluctance; Charles V refused to receive them at all, on hearing that they had nothing new to offer.

Two days after the coronation, Orange made a second visit to Bologna, to complain again about the lack of money, men and supplies, and about Alfonso d'Avalos, Marquis of Vasto, who was in command of the troops besieging the city's northern flank. With Clement VII running out of financial options – he was persuaded not to sell a batch of cardinal's hats to provide cash – Charles V agreed to take over responsibility for Avalos's troops, while the pope would continue to fund Orange. They also agreed to save money by cutting the use of artillery and concentrating instead on strengthening the blockade in an attempt to starve Florence into submission.

The new tactics soon took effect. By the middle of April almost 200 Florentines were dying each day from hunger, despite some supplies from Pisa getting through via the fortified town of Empoli. However, Clement VII, who had now returned to Rome, was increasingly anxious about the slow progress of the siege. He found the daily reports from Florence confusing, and to placate his paymaster, Orange sent him a cork model of Florence, so that the Pope could more easily understand what was happening.[18] Clement VII fussed and worried all spring, and became even more perturbed in May 1530 when he heard that plague had broken out in the Imperial camp. Then, at the end of May, the welcome news arrived that Orange had finally taken Empoli, cutting Florence off from the outside world. It was now just a matter of time. However, the costs were escalating dramatically: by July, Clement VII had spent more than 700,000 ducats on the venture, far more than the sum of 280,000 ducats envisaged in his original contract with Orange.

And still Florence continued to hold out against the Imperial forces, all through June and July 1530. Finally, on 5 August Clement VII received the dramatic news that Orange had defeated the Florentine army at the Battle of Gavinana – despite losing his own life in the fighting. The city had no option but to capitulate.

Clement VII had managed to restore the Medici family to Florence, but at a terrible price. His campaign of death and destruction, which eventually cost more than 1 million florins, had reduced the city's population by as much as 50 per cent. Even his supporters were appalled by the lack of scruples he had shown towards his fellow countrymen in pursuing his family's interests. Moreover, the Medici may have been restored but they now headed what was effectively a puppet regime. It was the Emperor who was the ultimate power in Florence.

14

IMPERIAL POODLES

Pope Clement VII, Ippolito,
Alessandro and Cosimo

1530–1543

THE TWO BRANCHES OF THE MEDICI FAMILY IN 1531

Descendants of Cosimo, son of Giovanni di Bicci:

Pope Clement VII (54)

Alessandro (20), *his illegitimate son,*
betrothed to Margaret of Austria, *daughter of Charles V*

Cardinal Ippolito (21), *illegitimate son of his cousin, Giuliano*

Caterina (12), *daughter of his cousin, Lorenzo*

Cardinal Innocenzo Cibò (40), *son of his cousin, Maddalena*

Cardinal Niccolò Ridolfi (30), *son of his cousin, Contessina*

Cardinal Giovanni Salviati (41), *son of his cousin, Lucrezia*

Maria Salviati (32), *daughter of his cousin, Lucrezia (see below)*

Filippo Strozzi (42), w*idower of his cousin, Clarice*

Descendants of Lorenzo, son of Giovanni di Bicci:

Lorenzino (17), *son of Pierfrancesco di Lorenzo*

Cosimo (12), *son of Giovanni delle Bande Nere and Maria Salviati*

On 6 July 1531, eleven months after their surrender, Florentines gathered in the piazza in front of the Palazzo della Signoria. They were there to hear Charles V's ambassador read an Imperial decree outlining the shape of their new government. Its head was to be Alessandro de' Medici. 'Florence, like all other states, would be better governed,' intoned the ambassador, 'by one single person rather than by many.'[1] They heard, with horror, that the proud *Signoria* had been abolished, to be replaced by a senate of Medici supporters, elected for life.

It had taken several months for Charles V and Clement VII to agree on how best to formalize Alessandro's position. The pope, brought up in the household of his uncle Lorenzo the Magnificent, had imbibed the mantra of upholding the family's traditional role as 'first citizens' of the republic; but the Emperor, royal to the core, had no misgivings about the exercise of absolute power. They settled on a compromise. In a masterly piece of diplomatic evasion, Alessandro's title would not be 'Duke', as he had hoped, but 'Governor of the Republic of Florence and Head of the Government in Perpetuity'. Florence remained a republic, but in name only; and the real power in the city was the Emperor himself. The envoy warned the crowds that any violation of the decree would be seen as an act of rebellion against Charles V and would result in the city being absorbed into the Empire – as would also happen if Alessandro were to die without an heir.

Charles V exercised his control over Florence through two men: Cardinal Innocenzo Cibò, cousin to Clement VII, and Alessandro Vitelli, the commander of the Imperial garrison now stationed in the city. Unsurprisingly, Vitelli, who had played a key role in forcing the surrender of Florence in 1530, was not a popular choice. The most visible expression of the new regime was the new Fortezza da Basso, a pentagonal stronghold on the northern edge of the city, built by Alessandro, on the orders of Charles V, to house Vitelli and his soldiers. And the Emperor insisted that the fortress had to be finished before Clement VII's son could marry his daughter. The project was urgent, so that 'the workers laboured on feast days as well as weekdays and even on Easter Day' to build a structure that proved massive in both size and unpopularity.[2] To Bernardo Segni, writing his history of Florence a few years later, 'it placed a yoke over the necks of the Florentines of a kind never before experienced, a fortress through which they lost all hope of ever living in freedom'.[3]

Alessandro disliked his cumbersome Florentine title and badgered his father for a noble tag. In February 1532, one of his agents told him that 'the pope is completely against making you duke and absolute lord of the city'; however, in April Clement VII relented and agreed to name him 'Duke of the Republic, as they call the Doge in Venice'.[4]

Alessandro paid little attention to the legal terminology, for whatever words were deemed politic by his father to maintain the illusion that Florence was still a republic, he had no doubt that he was the absolute ruler of the city. To prove his point, he minted his own coinage, replacing the republican emblems embossed on the old florin – St John the Baptist, the city's patron saint, and the Guelf lily – 'with the head of Duke Alessandro on one side and saints Cosmas and Damian on the other'.[5] He silenced the great bell of the Palazzo della Signoria and confiscated all weapons, even those placed as votive offerings in the shrine at Santissima Annunziata. The Florentines, too, began to drop their old republican ways in favour of courtly behaviour. Diarist Agostino Lapini noted that 'coaches began to be used in Florence that had never been seen before'.[6] Another chronicler noted that men 'began to wear beards' and donned fancier doublets, 'slashed in many places so that the silk lining can be seen'.[7]

The new duke commissioned two portraits from his court artist, Giorgio Vasari, one of himself and one of Lorenzo the Magnificent. Vasari's fulsome praise of the latter showed how the Medici myth had begun to grow: 'I wanted to portray all the great qualities that adorned his life,' he explained to Alessandro, 'his outstanding leadership, not just in his eloquence but in everything, especially his judgement, which has provided a light for his descendants and this great city.'[8] As for the portrait of Alessandro, it was telling evidence of the progress the Medici had made in the four decades since Lorenzo's death. Dressed in armour and holding the baton of command, the duke was depicted as a dynastic prince, with no need whatsoever of the republican toga. Vasari explained the imagery he had included in the painting: a circular chair to symbolize the duke's perpetual power; three bound figures to represent his people, 'with neither arms nor legs, but guided by his wishes'; a red cloth 'to show the blood shed by those who had challenged the

Giorgio Vasari, *Lorenzo the Magnificent*, 1534 (Florence, Uffizi).

greatness of the house of Medici'; ruined buildings to represent the 1530 siege; and a 'dry branch of laurel sending out shoots', which represented 'the house of Medici, once dead but now in the person of Duke Alessandro able to produce offshoots for ever'.[9]

Duke Alessandro's regime was despotic, though he made sure of his popularity with the poorer classes by walking around the streets, stopping in shops and taking the time to listen to their complaints in person. Francesco Guicciardini was one of Alessandro's closest aides, and evidently he was a pragmatist, believing that 'the duty of good citizens, when their country falls into the hands of a tyrant, is to gain influence with him and to persuade him to do good, not evil'.[10] Others disagreed though, and the duke's unpopularity with the city's leading families, even with those who had supported the restoration of the Medici, increased when he brought in new men from the countryside to staff his administration. The situation was not helped by his serial seduction of their wives and daughters, including those who had become nuns. Alessandro's more permanent mistress, Taddea Malaspina, a young widow related to Cardinal Cibò, gave birth to two illegitimate children: a son, Giulio, in 1533, and two years later a daughter, Giulia, both named after Alessandro's father. Significantly, Clement VII gave instructions to Cibò that Giulio was to be Alessandro's heir.

Duke Alessandro's opponents gathered in Rome – at the palace of his cousin, Cardinal Ippolito. Lively and hedonistic, he presided over one of the grandest courts in the city, famous for its banquets, hunting parties and cultural entertainments as well as for the beauty of his mistress, Giulia Gonzaga – a young widow who would narrowly escape the Turkish sultan's harem.* Among the exiles and refugees welcomed by Cardinal Ippolito were the Florentine republicans who had been expelled in 1530 as well as his cousins Cardinal Salviati and Cardinal Ridolfi. Filippo Strozzi joined them in 1533, having fled Florence after earning the enmity of Duke Alessandro, who felt threatened by the banker's immense wealth and influence. Strozzi's financial resources were a welcome boost to Ippolito's campaign to replace his cousin as ruler of Florence. The plotters made plans to get rid of Alessandro – including a fanciful project to place a casket of gunpowder in the

---

* In August 1534, the Turkish pirate Khair ad-Din Barbarossa, who was spending the summer raiding the Italian coast in search of boys for the sultan's armies and girls for his harem, failed in his kidnap attempt on Giulia Gonzaga.

bedroom of one of the duke's mistresses.[11]

Clement VII, aware of the rivalry, did what he could to mediate between the two cousins; but he had no intention of allowing Cardinal Ippolito to displace his son. He refused to allow Ippolito to give up his red hat, though he did do much to enhance his career, appointing him to the lucrative post of vice-chancellor in 1532. He also appointed Ippolito as legate to Vienna, after alarming reports reached Rome that Sultan Suleiman was advancing on Hungary with an army of 150,000 men and was planning to send ships carrying 40,000 soldiers to Italy. Under pressure from Charles V, the pope offered 50,000 ducats to the Emperor's brother, Ferdinando of Austria, for his campaign against the Turks; and Ippolito left for Vienna in July 1532 with a large armed guard to protect the money chests.[12] He commemorated this journey, and his desire for a secular career, in a stunning portrait of himself by the Venetian painter Titian, in which Ippolito was shown wearing Hungarian costume, complete with scimitar and a very gaudy peacock-feather hat. He arrived at the Imperial court on 12 August, just days after the Turks had been defeated on the borders of Austria and had retreated to Belgrade.

In an attempt to balance the Medici's dependence on Charles V, Clement VII arranged the marriage of his fourteen-year-old cousin Caterina to Henri, Duke of Orléans, the second son of Francis I. Catherine de' Medici, as she was henceforth known, was escorted to Marseilles by her uncle, Filippo Strozzi. The banker also loaned the pope 130,000 ducats for Catherine's dowry, receiving papal jewels, taxes in the Papal States and Church income from Spain as security.[13] In September 1533, the pope left Rome with Cardinal Ippolito for Livorno, where they boarded a French royal galley to sail to Marseilles for the marriage, which was attended also by Cosimo and his mother Maria Salviati (who was determined not to miss this chance of promoting her son's interests). Clement VII would never know that the death of the Dauphin three years later, after an energetic game of tennis, would make Henri heir to the French throne – with the pope's little cousin the future Queen of France.

In February 1534, Clement VII began what would be his last artistic

Giorgio Vasari, *Duke Alessandro de' Medici*, 1534 (Florence, Uffizi).

Michelangelo, *The Last Judgement*, commissioned 1534 (Vatican Palace, Sistine Chapel).

project, the fresco of the *Last Judgement* in the Sistine Chapel: 'the Pope has directed Michelangelo to paint in the Chapel and that the Resurrection, for which the model has already been made, will be done above the altar,' reported the Spanish ambassador.[14] But that summer, the pope, whose health had been poor for some time, fell seriously ill with stomach troubles. Cardinal Ippolito was worried enough to promise that he would abandon his secular ambitions. As the Mantuan envoy reported in July, 'he has been cured of his fantasy to resign his cardinal's hat and will pursue his ecclesiastical career and be a good son as he has always been, although he has not yet started preparations to take religious orders'.[15] Ippolito had managed to extract more funds from the papal coffers in return: according to the envoy, 'His Holiness has paid all his debts, which are very large, and is giving him an allowance of 100 ducats a month'. Clement VII's condition continued to worsen, with sickness and high fever. He received the last rites on 24 August but astonished his doctors by recovering. However, on 21 September he had a relapse – and died four days later. In his will, the rival cousins were the beneficiaries: he left Florence to Alessandro and the rest of his possessions to Cardinal Ippolito.

Clement VII's successor was the sixty-six-year-old Cardinal Alessandro Farnese, elected as Paul III with the support of Cardinal Ippolito. However, the new pope refused to honour Clement VII's debts to Filippo Strozzi, which amounted to 80,000 ducats, a move that left the banker in serious financial trouble.[16] Paul III announced that Church reform would be his priority; but more privately, he intended to advance the fortunes of his own family.

Relations between Duke Alessandro and Cardinal Ippolito now deteriorated. Indeed, Strozzi was lucky to escape a botched attempt at murder by Alessandro's hitmen in Rome, though he lost his daughter in mysterious circumstances in Florence. Ippolito was convinced that he himself was another of his cousin's intended victims, and he sent envoys to Spain to convince Charles V that Alessandro was a despot – which was true – and ought to be deposed. He urged the Emperor to annul the betrothal between Alessandro and Margaret of Austria and to appoint him in Alessandro's stead as Duke of Florence, claiming to have the support of the Strozzi, Salviati, Rucellai, Pazzi and Ridolfi families, as well as that of other leading Florentines. The Emperor agreed to hear to the case but made no promises. One of Ippolito's courtiers, Paolo Giovio, predicting disaster, wished the cousins would make peace, 'otherwise the pheasant and the peacock will both lose their tails'.[17]

With Charles V intending to listen to both sides of the argument in September 1535, Cardinal Ippolito left Rome in late July for Naples, to await the arrival of the Emperor. Earlier that month, Charles V had captured La Goletta and Tunis from the Turks. With his lantern jaw and hunched back, Charles V was an unlikely military hero, but he could boast the success of his navy, which had inflicted a heavy blow on the Turkish admiral, Barbarossa. Travelling with Ippolito to congratulate the Emperor, and to plead their case against Duke Alessandro, were Filippo Strozzi, Cardinal Salviati, Cardinal Ridolfi and several other Florentine exiles. Unfortunately Ippolito never reached Naples, for on 10 August he died suddenly of fever *en route*, at Itri, in the arms (it seems) of Giulia Gonzaga. He was just twenty-five years old, and inevitably there were rumours of poison, though it is more likely to have been malaria. Strozzi and the other exiles continued on to Naples. A later arrival in the city was Duke Alessandro himself, who had left Florence in early December, shortly after the Imperial commander Vitelli had moved his troops into the completed Fortezza da Basso.

Charles V spent the traditional Christmas and New Year holiday at the royal court in Naples in early January 1536 held a formal audience to hear the accusations against his future son-in-law. The exiles accused Alessandro of breaking the terms of his agreement with the Emperor by his tyrannical behaviour – among the examples they cited was his arbitrary decision to replace the republican emblems on the Florentine florin with the Medici saints and *palle*. But their case was countered at every turn by the silver-tongued Francesco Guicciardini, acting as Alessandro's lawyer. The Emperor gave his judgement in favour of the duke; but he did annul the sentences of those who had been banished from Florence in 1530. Strozzi and the rest of the exiles left Naples, but, fearful of the duke's reprisals, they did not go home.

Duke Alessandro's marriage to the fourteen-year-old Margaret of Austria finally took place on 26 February 1536 in Naples, amid splendid celebrations attended by Charles V and the cream of the Italian nobility. There were banquets, masquerades and musical entertainments, with the Emperor himself participating in a joust and dancing at a masked ball. On 11 March, Alessandro left for Florence to prepare for

Titian, *Cardinal Ippolito de' Medici*, c.1533 (Florence, Palazzo Pitti).

Charles V's state visit, on his way north from Naples. In Alessandro's large entourage, which included over a thousand soldiers, were his two cousins Lorenzino and Cosimo. They would provide the end of one chapter of the Medici story, and the start of another.

Charles V made his ceremonial entry into Florence on 29 April. 'Enter, Caesar, into your most devoted city, which has never before seen a greater nor a worthier prince,' read the splendid Latin inscription emblazoned above the gate.[18] Watching, as the huge cavalcade of courtiers and troops rode through the streets, the Florentines were cruelly reminded that it was this same army that, less than six years before, had forced them to surrender their liberty. Significantly, the cavalcade did not end, as had been customary, at the Palazzo della Signoria, but at the ducal residence, the Palazzo Medici.

Duke Alessandro had commissioned a series of triumphal arches along the processional route to extol his father-in-law's achievements. The designer of the arch at San Felice, where Charles V was hailed as Conqueror of Africa, was Vasari, who had been found early that morning by the duke 'half-dead with exhaustion', as Vasari told a friend, 'asleep on a bundle of branches'.[19] He had had, by his own admission, 'an extraordinary month and no sleep for the last five nights' while preparing for the visit, and the duke, 'in the presence of all his men, told me: your work, my Giorgio, is the greatest, most beautiful, best interpreted and most quickly finished of that of all the other masters'. It was praise indeed. Duke Alessandro rewarded Vasari with a gift of 300 florins, on top of the 400 florins named in the contract – and the artist used the bonus to marry off one of his sisters and to enable another to enter a convent.[20]

The new Duchess of Florence made her ceremonial entry into Florence six weeks later, on 15 June. One of the entertainments planned by Duke Alessandro was a play, written by his cousin Lorenzino. Although Lorenzino was the legitimate heir of the other branch of the Medici family, he had been ignored by Clement VII and had resented the success of his bastard cousins. However, instead of joining the exiles at Cardinal Ippolito's palace in Rome, he had remained in Florence, playing the part of loyal courtier – while in reality waiting for an opportunity to murder the duke. And now the play presented an opportunity. He arranged for the scenery to be erected in such a way that it would collapse onto the audience. Unluckily for Lorenzino, though, the painter working on the project informed Vasari, who, 'seeing what a terrible disaster could result and that it was in fact an attempt to murder three hundred persons, said that he would inform the duke'.[21] Lorenzino had no option but to cover his tracks and pretend it had all been a technical fault.

Lorenzino's attempts to assassinate his cousin finally met with success on 6 January 1537. In the end, it was Duke Alessandro's lust for a married woman (who was proving difficult to seduce) that set the scene for his downfall. Lorenzino staged a rendezvous between the pair, offering up his own bedroom in the Casa Vecchia as a venue. Alessandro arrived in eager anticipation; however, it was not the beauty he desired who came through the door but Lorenzino himself, with a companion, who held the duke down while Lorenzino stabbed him to death. Then, after locking the room, Lorenzino fled the city, riding to Venice to join Strozzi and the other exiles.

The murdered body of Duke Alessandro was discovered the next day, Sunday 7 January, by Cardinal Cibò, who arranged for the corpse to be smuggled out of the Casa Vecchia wrapped in a carpet and discreetly deposited in San Lorenzo. In the eyes of some, the assassin's actions transformed him from Lorenzino ('Little Lawrence') into Lorenzaccio ('Bad Lawrence'). 'Duke Alessandro, my lord on this earth, killed like a wild beast by the cruelty and envy of his cousin,' wailed Vasari; 'how many swords he had, how many weapons, how many salaried soldiers, how many fortresses, but he had nothing against one single sword and two wicked traitors.'[22] But few in Florence shared Vasari's grief.

Cardinal Cibò was well aware of the constitutional implications of the murder. As Alessandro had no legitimate son, Charles V was now technically head of the Florentine state. There remained, though, Alessandro's illegitimate son Giulio, whom the late Clement VII had declared to be Alessandro's heir. Using his position as the Emperor's official representative in Florence, Cibò intended to follow Clement VII's wishes and have the four-year-old Giulio installed as duke, with himself acting as regent. However, he was in no position to enforce this claim. Vitelli, the garrison commander who might have helped him

Agnolo Bronzino, *Duke Cosimo I*, 1543–4 (Florence, Uffizi).

was some 70 miles away at his home in Città di Castello. By the time that Vitelli and his troops rode into Florence on the Monday afternoon, it was too late.

That morning, 8 January 1537, Francesco Guicciardini and other leading Florentines seized the initiative and proposed another Medici, the seventeen-year-old Cosimo, as Alessandro's successor; there was no question of trying to restore the republic, which would incur the wrath of Charles V. Remarkably, the city was relatively calm when Vitelli and his soldiers returned, and both Cibò and Vitelli were obliged to back Guicciardini's decisive action. Two days later, the Senate voted unanimously to give Cosimo the title 'Head and Leader of the City', pending Imperial confirmation. Within hours of the vote, just to remind Cosimo who actually held power in Florence, Vitelli and his soldiers ransacked the Palazzo Medici, removing all cash, silver plate, jewels and other valuables, and took Alessandro's young widow, Margaret of Austria, to the safety of the Fortezza da Basso.

There was much in favour of Cosimo. His genealogical claim was incontrovertible. Both his father, Giovanni delle Bande Nere, and his mother, Maria Salviati, were great-great-grandchildren of Giovanni di Bicci, founder of the Medici bank. Cosimo was also young and inexperienced, qualities which Cibò and Vitelli on the Imperial side, and prominent Florentines on the other, all expected to be able to exploit in their favour. They were to be disappointed. Well built, strong and sporty, this son of a military hero and a professional soldier in his own right would prove to be very much his own man.

Cosimo's first priority was to extinguish the threat posed by Filippo Strozzi and the exiles, who were making plans with Francis I for a military campaign against him. Soon after coming to power, he issued a decree pardoning any exile who chose to return to Florence; but few did. On 31 July 1537, with their enemies gathering in the hills north of Pistoia, Cosimo and Vitelli launched a surprise attack and defeated them at the Battle of Montemurlo. Strozzi was among the prisoners. The historian Bernardo Segni gave a moving account of the sad parade of captives that passed through the streets on 1 August: 'the prisoners were put on poor, weak horses for more security and greater derision,' he wrote, and 'in the late afternoon in the scourge of the heat, they were brought into Florence'.[23] 'But there was no celebration' among the crowds 'watching such noble and illustrious citizens in a state of such misery and ridicule, especially Filippo who had been the most successful private citizen in Italy until this day.' Fifteen of the captives were executed, the rest imprisoned, including Strozzi, who was consigned to a cell in the Fortezza da Basso.

Meanwhile, Charles V prevaricated about confirming Cosimo's position. His ambassador, the Count of Cifuentes, had spent a month in the city early in the summer of 1537 and, although he had agreed to recognize Cosimo as ruler, he remained evasive about his title. The following year, Cosimo sent envoys to Nice – where Pope Paul III, Charles V and Francis I were holding a summit – with instructions to persuade the Emperor to reduce the Imperial garrison in Florence and allow Vitelli to be replaced with one of Cosimo's own men. Reportedly satisfied with Cosimo's achievements so far, the Emperor complied with both requests. Cosimo also seized the opportunity to dismiss Cardinal Cibò after discovering that he had started rumours that Cosimo was paying an apothecary to poison Giulio, the young son of Duke Alessandro. Charles V finally confirmed Cosimo's title as Duke of Florence in September 1538. Three months later, in his cell in the Fortezza da Basso, Filippo Strozzi committed suicide, in imitation of Marcus Porcius Cato, the Roman republican who preferred death to life under Julius Caesar.

With possession of a dukedom, the Medici were transformed into a hereditary dynasty – and one in need of heirs. Two days after coming to power in January 1537, Cosimo had sent an envoy to Charles V asking permission to marry Duke Alessandro's widow, Margaret of Austria; but this plan fell through when the Emperor agreed to her marriage to Paul III's grandson, Ottavio Farnese. The pope offered his grand-daughter Vittoria Farnese instead, but Cosimo refused the offer. Using his Imperial connections, he negotiated instead his betrothal to Eleonora of Toledo, the daughter of Pedro de Toledo, second son of the Duke of Alba and Charles V's viceroy in Naples. The couple were married by proxy in Naples, and Eleonora made her ceremonial entry into Florence on 29 June 1537. At the Palazzo Medici, the bride and groom were greeted by the sight of the coats-of-arms of their two families in the embrace of the double-headed Imperial eagle, a fitting reminder of their true position. Inside, there were tableaux of Medici history, with scenes all designed to glorify the Medici: Leo X's magnificent entry into Florence, Giovanni delle Bande Nere's military exploits, Clement VII's coronation of Charles V, and so on. There was no mention of their fame as bankers.

On his succession, Cosimo had moved into the Palazzo Medici, but in May 1540, in a highly symbolic move recorded by the diarist Lapini, 'it has been confirmed that the illustrious Duke Cosimo is to live in the palace where the *Signoria* once resided'.[24] The Palazzo della Signoria, the seat of the Florentine republic since its inception in 1293, was now renamed the Palazzo Ducale, and the large square in front became the Piazza Ducale. Also living in the palace was Cosimo's mother, Maria Salviati, who had the care of his illegitimate daughter Bia, born around 1535, and Alessandro's two illegitimate children, Giulio and Giulia. It was an early sign of Duke Cosimo's political acuity: by putting these last two under ducal protection, he lessened the chance of their becoming the focus of opposition to his rule. There were soon additions to the nursery. On 3 April 1540, nine months and four days after her arrival in Florence, Eleonora gave birth to a daughter, Maria. A son, Francesco, was born in March 1541, followed by Isabella (September 1542) and Giovanni (September 1543), and more children were to follow. One visitor to the nursery reported that the children 'live in great style', and 'their rooms have gilded leather hangings and all of them, legitimate and bastards alike, are under the care of Signora Maria'.[25]

Maria Salviati, who died on 12 December 1543 at the age of forty-four, had done much to shape her son's character. At home, Duke Cosimo was a modest family man. 'He does not live like a prince in the elegant grandeur used by other princes or dukes,' noted the Venetian ambassador, 'but always eats with his wife and children at a moderate and plain table.'[26] He also made an effort to be accessible to his subjects, for 'when he left the palace to hear mass or to go about the city, he rode a small bay horse so that people who wanted to speak to him could do so with ease'.[27] On formal occasions, however, Cosimo I adopted from Eleonora the strict etiquette of the Spanish court, often seeming to appear haughty and aloof. In September 1541, he was in Lucca, where Charles V was holding a summit with Paul III, and was very annoyed to find the Duke of Ferrara given the honour of riding into the city on Charles V's right, while Cosimo had to be content with being on the left; he was very touchy about rank. The issue of precedence was key in the courtly aristocratic society of sixteenth-century Europe, and this incident sparked off a rivalry between the two dukes and their respective houses – the Este, whose noble title dated back to the eleventh century, and the parvenu Medici.

The new duke set about establishing his authority in Florence with dogged perseverance, imposing strict measures to maintain public order. He issued a decree forbidding the Florentines from carrying weapons and set up an efficient network of spies in the city to report on potential threats to his regime, though his respect for the rule of law made him less unpopular than his despotic predecessor. Cosimo was also determined to restore Florence's reputation as a city of culture. In 1542, he founded the Accademia Fiorentina to encourage men of letters to promote the Tuscan language and Medici historiography – and the academy also enabled him to keep an eye on what these potential subversives were writing.

Cosimo I was operating in a world much changed since the death of Clement VII. Along with him, a new generation of rulers had taken over many of the Italian states: Ercole II d'Este in Ferrara (1534), Guidobaldo I della Rovere in Urbino (1538), Francesco Gonzaga in Mantua (1540) – and in 1540 Charles V secretly invested his son Philip as Duke of Milan, though the duchy continued to be governed by an Imperial viceroy. The Habsburg–Valois rivalry had not abated, but, thanks in part to the political skills of Pope Paul III, its focus had shifted from Italy to northern Europe. More worrying for Italian rulers was the growing power of the Turkish Ottoman Empire and its increasingly domination of the Mediterranean. Charles V's victory at Tunis had proved short-lived, for in 1537 the Turks had seized Corfu and other Venetian islands in the eastern Mediterranean, and in the following year Barbarossa had inflicted a savage defeat on the joint Imperial, Venetian and papal fleet off Greece, at the Battle of Prevesa.

Above all, though, there had been dramatic changes in Rome, where Paul III's measures to reform the Church had begun to eradicate the secular splendour of the Medici popes. Paul III gave red hats to

Agnolo Bronzino, *Portrait of Eleonora of Toledo with her son*, 1545 (Florence, Uffizi).

prominent theologians and approved new religious orders, including the Jesuits, all dedicated to reform of the Church. He had continued Clement VII's commission for Michelangelo's fresco of the *Last Judgement* in the Sistine Chapel; but it was unveiled in 1541 to mixed reactions. To some, it was a work of artistic genius, but most were disgusted by the naked figure of Christ and condemned it as an inaccurate – even heretical – depiction of the event. Paul III had also finally bowed to pressure to reform abuses in the Church. The report of his commission, *Consilium de emendanda ecclesia*, called for far-reaching changes to the ways in which the Church ran its affairs, and Paul III announced a council to implement its recommendations.

At the same time, Protestantism was continuing its relentless advance across northern Europe and now posed a serious threat to Charles V's authority in Germany. Paul III made repeated attempts to find a solution to the religious differences in the Empire, but the mood in Rome – where the new generation of hard-line churchmen saw Protestantism as a heresy that had to be eradicated – had become increasingly intransigent. Efforts to reconcile Catholics and Protestants ceased after 1541. The following year, Paul III established the Roman Inquisition as a central body to root out Protestant heresy in Italy, with the hardline Cardinal Gianpietro Carafa as its head. In Florence that year, two friars, the Augustinian Pietro Martire and the Capuchin Bernardino Ochino, fled abroad before they could be arrested by the Inquisition. And finally, in 1543, after endless delays because of the rivalry between Charles V and Francis I, Paul III's council for the reform of the Catholic Church finally opened in Trent.

In Florence, Cosimo I had been busy exploiting the political situation for his own ends. On 13 June 1543, Lapini recorded the dramatic news 'that Emperor Charles V has returned the fortresses to Cosimo I'.[28] The duke had astutely seen an opportunity in Charles V's desperate need for money to replenish the Imperial coffers, which had been depleted by the cost of financing wars against Francis I, the Turks and the Protestants. In return for the substantial sum of 200,000 florins, Cosimo was able to negotiate the return of the fortresses at Pisa and Livorno, and the withdrawal of the hated Imperial troops from Florence. On 7 July 1543, the jubilant Florentines watched as Cosimo I formally took possession of the Fortezza da Basso, that much-loathed symbol of foreign domination. The Imperial standard, with its double-headed eagle, was lowered from the ramparts, and the Florentine flag rose in its place.

Cosimo I had inherited a state that was destitute, dilapidated and disloyal. Since then, he had done much to stabilize the Medici regime in Florence. His wife, Eleonora of Toledo, had secured the immediate future of the dynasty with two sons, and more could be expected. The first years of his rule saw him impose his authority in Florence and free the city from Imperial control. His priority now was to improve the Florentine economy.

15

THE NEW AUGUSTUS

Cosimo I

1544–1559

THE MEDICI IN 1544

Duke Cosimo I (25)
Eleonora of Toledo (22), *his wife*

> Maria (4), *their daughter*

> Francesco (3), *their son*

> Isabella (2), *their daughter*

> Giovanni (1), *their son*

Giulio (11) and Giulia (9),
the illegitimate children of his cousin, Duke Alessandro

Catherine de' Medici (25) m. Henri, *his cousin*

'It is the duty of a just prince always to apply himself to the improve-ment of the businesses of his citizens' ran the text of one of the many decrees issued by Cosimo I in his efforts to reform the economy of his state.[1] He was aware, unlike many rulers of the period, that measures designed to enhance the welfare of his subjects would also directly benefit his own coffers. He approached the task with awesome efficiency, and it is difficult to overstate his appetite for hard work. According to the Venetian ambassador, he got up at dawn, 'two or three hours before daybreak in winter', and toiled away all morning before breaking for lunch, the main meal of the day, in the middle of the afternoon.[2] He diligently read the piles of papers that arrived daily from his diplomats, bureaucrats, petitioners, engineers, architects and artists – answering the correspondence in person. There were also the formal audiences for foreign ambassadors and meetings with his privy councillors to attend. He stuck to this punishing daily schedule wheth-er at home in the Palazzo Ducale or away from Florence on the many lengthy trips he made to all corners of Tuscany, supervising his projects with minute attention to detail.

The scope of Cosimo I's reforms was immense. He reorganized the state bureaucracy, the treasury and tax system, improved roads and waterways, removed trade barriers between the different cities of the state, and curbed the restrictive practices of the guilds. He built a for-tified city at Portoferrario – which he renamed Cosmopoli – drained the Maremma swamps, built a new harbour at Livorno, and improved the port facilities at Pisa, where he based his new fleet. He appointed Giovanni Battista Belluzzi as his military architect and put him in charge of securing the state borders with a string of imposing fortress-es. Belluzzi would go on to use this experience to write an informative treatise on defence. In Florence, Cosimo ordered repairs to the fortifi-cations damaged during the siege of 1529–30, constructed aqueducts to improve the water supply, and spent 70,000 florins on rebuilding the bridge of Ponte Santa Trinita after it collapsed in 1557 when the Arno burst its banks and flooded the city.[3]

Most importantly, Cosimo encouraged new industries: porcelain works and coral-cutting shops in Florence, sugar refining at Pisa, glass-making at Prato, paper factories in Pescia, the mining of precious met-als at Pietrasanta, and more. He also stimulated the textile industry to enable Florentine merchants to sell luxurious silks, velvets and taffetas on the world market. In short, after decades of factional violence and civic strife, his subjects could concentrate on what they were good at: making money. 'The soul of the Florentine,' as one contemporary wittily remarked, 'is cash.'[4]

Although Florence's leading families had lost their active roles in politics, Cosimo I ensured their loyalty by granting them control over the state bureaucracy, which he radically reorganized and enlarged to provide a centralized body through which he could efficiently administer his state. The power of this bureaucracy was amply visible in the great palace he built next to the Palazzo Ducale to house its thirteen departments, each in a separate section of the building behind the uniform classical facade. The Uffizi (literally, 'Offices') was the first purpose-built office-block in Europe, and it cost a massive 400,000 florins. Prominent outside was a life-size statue commissioned by Cosimo – of himself – flanked appropriately by allegories of Severe and Just Government. He also turned his attention to Florence's charitable institutions. At the Ospedale degli Innocenti, the city orphanage, for example, he organized proper funding, allocating it a portion of every criminal fine imposed by the courts, and he required the head of the orphanage to live in the building and to eat all his meals with the staff.

Above all, Cosimo I transformed Florence into a splendid setting for the display of his ducal prestige, providing work for hundreds of

The Uffizi, Florence, begun in 1560.

builders, masons, sculptors, painters and labourers in the process. As his court artist Giorgio Vasari sycophantically explained, the duke, 'who is most excellent in everything', was a patron of the arts on a princely scale: 'he enjoys not only building palaces, cities, fortresses, harbours, loggias, squares, gardens, fountains, villas and the like, which are beautiful, magnificent and most useful to his subjects but, as a Catholic prince, he also he especially enjoys building and improving the temples and holy churches of God, in the tradition of the great King Solomon'.[5] Among his religious projects were a new octagonal choir for the Duomo and frescoes in San Lorenzo, where he also built a tomb for his father. He planned a grandiose chapel for the tombs of himself and his descendants too, though in the event this project was not begun until after his death.

Cosimo was insatiably greedy for social status. His ambition was to establish the Medici as Italy's premier house, whatever the cost – and thanks to his reform of the Tuscan economy he could afford to pay the bribes necessary for the privilege of upgrading his ducal status. It was his bad luck that Pope Paul III was unwilling to oblige. So, until a more accommodating pontiff could be elected, he concentrated his energies on the creation of an image to prove that the Medici were the equals of kings and emperors.

His first task in this project was to acquire the essential trappings of royal power. Cosimo I spared no expense in the embellishment of the ducal residences: the Palazzo Ducale, the Palazzo Pitti, his suburban villa on the south bank of the Arno, and the Villa Medici at Castello, a few miles north of the city. He erected two fountains – supplied with water from the new aqueducts – in the piazza in front of the Palazzo Ducale, and he ornamented its loggia with statues, including Cellini's elegant bronze *Perseus and Medusa*. Inside, he converted the old government halls into rooms of princely grandeur. He remodelled the chamber of the Great Council of the republic into a superb reception hall and built apartments for himself and Eleonora, all richly ornamented with gilded ceilings, grand staircases, inlaid marble fireplaces and the costly tapestries that were one of the hallmarks of wealth in sixteenth-century Europe. Both Charles V and Francis I had their own tapestry workshops to make these expensive hangings, and in 1545 Cosimo I opened his own *atelier*, poaching Flemish weavers from the court of his rivals, the Este dukes of Ferrara.

Benvenuto Cellini, *Perseus and Medusa*, 1545–54 (Florence, Loggia dei Lanzi).

Another accessory of princely prestige was a collection of rarities, and Cosimo I spent liberally on his acquiring his own. One of his prized items was billed as a unicorn's horn, 5 feet long, a curiosity for which he paid a German dealer 10,000 *scudi*.[6] Vasari recorded that the collection in Cosimo I's study included 'a large number of antique marble and bronze statues, little modern paintings, superb miniatures and an immense collection of gold, silver and bronze medals'.[7] The duke ordered his agent in the Levant 'to buy as many antique medals as you can, in gold, silver, copper or other metals, whether Ancient Roman or Greek or Egyptian', and to 'look out for Greek books which are rare here, also buy seeds of herbs and plants, especially those that are rare'.[8] His agent in Venice sent him nine antique heads, bought from a contact in Athens for 600 *scudi*, 'which truly seems to me to be a good price'.[9] When a group of Etruscan bronzes, including the famous *Chimera*, were found near Arezzo in 1553, Cosimo added these to his collection and requested the men 'to continue the dig to see if any other good pieces can be found', cautioning them 'that care is to be taken so that nothing is broken or ruined'.[10]

Work on the Palazzo Pitti started after 1549, when Cosimo I and Eleonora bought this fifteenth-century palace, built by Old Cosimo's ally Luca Pitti. The duke and duchess remodelled it to create a splendid suburban villa, with copses for hunting thrushes and small game birds, and elaborate gardens laid out on the hill behind. The Boboli gardens, which were widely admired as some of the finest of the period, were laid out with groves of cypresses, holm oaks, and laurels and dwarf fruit trees.[11] Among the plants he ordered were saffron crocuses and 1,000 asparagus crowns. The gardens were ornamented with great fountains and magnificent *all'antica* statues, along with sculpted figures of the duchess's favourite dwarves, fishponds, grottoes and even an open-air theatre. He created another superb garden at the villa at Castello, which he had inherited from his father, filled with fountains and grottoes, as well as a series of statues proclaiming the virtues and merits of both Cosimo I and Florence: Wisdom, Nobility, Valour, Liberality, the Arts, Sciences, Peace and Law.

Like other Renaissance rulers Cosimo I cultivated his public image with care. It was no coincidence that he chose to ornament his official seal with the figure of Hercules, the hero once used by the Florentine republic to boast the greatness of the city. One of the historians at the duke's Accademia Fiorentina – though 'propagandist' might be a better title – developed the myth of Cosimo I as the new Hercules. He argued that Hercules had been the founder of the Etruscan civilization, and he made fanciful parallels between the hero's twelve deeds and the twelve Etruscan cities that were now Cosimo I's dominion. The duke also exploited his links with Roman Emperor Augustus, who had also succeeded to power one January after the assassination of a relation, and who, like Cosimo, had taken on the task of easing the path of his dominion from a republic to a hereditary principality. Both Hercules and Augustus provided themes for Cosimo's portraits and commemorative medals as well as for the decoration of his palaces and villas. There were statues of the deeds of Hercules in the great hall of the Palazzo Ducale while Augustus's emblem of the Goat (Capricorn in the Zodiac) could be seen spouting water in the fountain of Hercules and

Etruscan statuette of the Chimaera, fifth century BC
(Florence, Museo Archeologico Nazionale).

Antaeus at Castello and among the stalactites ornamenting Eleonora's grotto at Palazzo Pitti. Cosimo even commissioned a life-size marble statue of himself as Augustus, clad in Roman imperial armour.

Above all, Cosimo I was obsessed with creating a lineage for the parvenu Medici dynasty, a vital element in his campaign for dynastic supremacy. Vasari recorded that Bronzino 'painted several small pictures on tin, all the same size, of all the famous men of the house of Medici, beginning with Giovanni di Bicci and the line of Old Cosimo down to the Queen of France and the other line descending from Lorenzo, Old Cosimo's brother, down to the duke and his sons'; he thought that these portraits were 'all natural, animated and most true to life'.[12] In the Palazzo Ducale, Vasari decorated the duke's private apartments (the so-called Apartment of Leo X) with scenes from the lives of six Medici heroes: Old Cosimo, Lorenzo the Magnificent, Leo X, Clement VII, Giovanni delle Bande Nere and Cosimo I himself. Ancestor cycles were the *sine qua non* of dynastic rule in sixteenth-century Europe: they gave patrons the opportunity to boast the age and renown of their houses through the titles and fiefs won on the battlefield by their forbears. Cosimo's ancestors were, of course, better known for their banking skills than for military exploits – though one historian of the Accademia Fiorentina obligingly invented a Medici reputed to have led the Florentine armies to victory against the Goths at the beginning of the fifth century. The room dedicated to his father, Giovanni delle Bande Nere, bristled with violent scenes of battle, but otherwise there was little evidence of military prowess. The plump figure of Leo X appeared on horseback, viewing the carnage of the Battle of Ravenna, while Clement VII's capture of Florence is depicted in a bird's-eye view of the city under siege by the Imperial armies. More bizarre was the apocryphal scene of Lorenzo the Magnificent, dressed in *all'antica* armour and mounted on a grey charger, directing 'his' troops in the capture of Sarzana. Devising an illustrious lineage for the older Medici was hard work – banking fortunes and republican government were hardly the pursuits of princes, so Vasari's panels mainly promoted them as wise statesmen and discerning patrons of the arts.

Under Cosimo I's direction, the Medici myth was being steadily codified by the historians of the Accademia Fiorentina, which he had so generously endowed for their benefit. One of the most important texts to emerge was Vasari's *Lives of the Painters, Sculptors and Architects*,

Vincenzo Danti, *Cosimo I as Emperor Augustus*, c.1570 (Florence, Bargello).

dedicated to the duke, which firmly established the Medici as hero-patrons of the arts on a scale that far outstripped their actual contribution. Though the author had little need to embroider the scale of Old Cosimo's *oeuvre*, he did embellish it with fictitious stories that emphasized the banker's ability to recognize artistic talent. Lorenzo the Magnificent's role as a patron needed more assistance, and among the myths Vasari invented to boost his hero's role was the school set up in his gardens where promising artists, notably Leonardo and Michelangelo, were trained in the art of antique sculpture under his sponsorship.

Above all, Vasari's text established the supremacy of Tuscan art and the notion that it was the Medici themselves who had been responsible for the Renaissance. In his dedicatory letter to the duke, he promised, in suitably loquacious prose, to tell him about all those artists:

> … who first revitalized the arts, then improved and adorned them step by step until finally they reached that level of beauty and majesty that they possess today; and because almost all of them were Tuscans, and mostly Florentines, many of whom were helped and encouraged in their works by your illustrious ancestors, it is possible to say that in your state, indeed in your most blessed house, the arts have been reborn thanks to the generosity of your ancestors.[13]

Most importantly for the future of the Medici dynasty, Cosimo I's marriage was proving exceptionally fruitful. Eleonora gave birth to eleven children, eight of whom survived into adulthood: Maria (born 1540), Francesco (1541), Isabella (1542), Giovanni (1543), Lucrezia (1545), Garzia (1547), Ferdinando (1549)* and Pietro (1554), the last named after his maternal grandfather. There was no lack of sons to inherit the title. Also in the nursery in the Palazzo Ducale was their cousin Dianora, the daughter of Eleonora's much-loved brother Don Garzia de Toledo, whose wife had died shortly after Dianora's birth in 1553. The ducal couple had ambitious plans for their family, and this was evident in the scholarly education that both the boys and girls received, under the

---

* The babies who died were: an earlier Pietro (born 1546), who died aged ten months; Antonio (born 1548); Anna (born 1553), who died aged five months.

watchful eye of Cosimo's own former tutor, Pierfrancesco Riccio. They learned Latin and Spanish, and they studied the works of the philosophers and historians of Ancient Rome; they also had music lessons, learning to play several instruments, and acquired equestrian skills under a riding instructor.

Above all, Cosimo I craved to be recognized as Italy's premier noble. His campaign to achieve this eminence received a setback in 1545, when he heard that his ambassador to Francis I had been placed below that of Duke Ercole d'Este. His dreams were heavily dependent on the favour of foreign rulers, so he set about wooing these men with characteristic diligence. He paid Charles V 200,000 *scudi* for the small state of Piombino, as well as acquiring from the Emperor the island of Elba, with its rich mineral deposits. He sent lavish presents to ingratiate himself with both the French and the Imperial courts, including Bronzino's *Lamentation* to Charles V's chief minister, Nicholas Granvelle, and the same artist's *Allegory of Venus and Cupid* to Francis I.†
The rewards soon came. In 1546, Charles V made Cosimo a Knight of the Golden Fleece, the prestigious chivalric order founded in 1430 by Philip II, Duke of Burgundy. The Emperor had granted this coveted honour to many Imperial and Spanish nobles, as well as to the kings of Scotland, Denmark, Poland, Portugal and France; but he had granted it to just six other Italians, all of whom were commanders in the Imperial army. Cosimo I ensured that this celebrated little gilded fleece, dangling from its golden collar, shone prominently in many of his portraits.

Vital for Cosimo's ambitions was the co-operation of the papacy, which, initially at least, proved hard to obtain. Although he was careful to distance himself from the Habsburg–Valois rivalry, which continued to divide Europe, the duke was perceived as an Imperial ally by Paul III, who wanted the backing of both Charles V and Francis I for his council on Church reform, which had opened at Trent. Nor did the situation improve when Francis I died in 1547 and was succeeded by his son, Henri II. Although the succession meant that Cosimo's cousin Catherine de' Medici was now Queen of France, the new king continued his father's policy of implacable opposition to the Emperor.

By the time Paul III himself died two years later, Cosimo I had

---

† The *Allegory of Venus and Cupid* is now in the National Gallery, London.

taken steps to secure the election of a more amenable papal successor. The conclave, which opened on 29 November 1549, was still in session at the end of the year, and it was not until 8 February 1550 that Cosimo's allies in the Vatican finally engineered the election of their candidate as Julius III. The new pope rewarded Cosimo I with the present of a statue of Mercury to add to his growing collection of antique sculpture; and his pontificate soon provided the Medici duke with an opportunity for political gain.

In 1551, war broke out in northern Italy between Julius III, Charles V and Henri II, putting Church reform on hold when the fighting forced the closure of the Council of Trent. The following summer, with the French in the ascendancy, the Sienese took advantage of Charles V's weakness to expel the garrison of Imperial troops – which the Emperor had installed to guarantee their loyalty – and turned to Henri II for help in securing their independence. When Cosimo I was asked by Charles V to use the Florentine army to retake Siena, he reacted with extreme caution, unwilling to be drawn directly into the Habsburg–Valois conflict. Cosimo offered minimal resistance when a large French army – led by Piero Strozzi, the son of his old enemy – advanced into Tuscany; and that October, he received Cardinal Ippolito d'Este, Henri II's new governor of Siena, with all appearances of warmth, assuring him that he had no intention of fighting the French for possession of the city. Behind this pro-French stance, however, Cosimo I was secretly negotiating terms with Charles V; and prominent among his demands was the title to Siena. Cosimo's political skills were growing.

It took the Emperor and the duke some time to work out the military, financial and political details of their alliance. Cosimo I agreed to appoint Giangiacomo Medici, Marquis of Marignano and one of Charles V's captains, as commander of his army. (Marignano was not a relation of Cosimo but, confusingly, from a Milanese family of the same name). Finally, on 24 January 1554, the Florentine troops marched south to engage the French. Five days later, Piero Strozzi took the Florentine fortress of Foiano, but this victory was overturned on 2 August when Marignano inflicted a savage defeat over the French at the Battle of Marciano – a triumph commemorated by Cosimo I in a magnificent octagonal church dedicated to the Virgin of Victory. Early that evening in Florence, 'three horsemen arrived, one after the other, with garlands on their heads and olive branches in their hands,' wrote an excited Lapini, 'bringing the most wonderful news of the complete rout of Piero Strozzi's men'.[14] Strozzi himself had been wounded; more than 4,000 soldiers were dead, and some 2,000 men were prisoners. Cosimo I's armies now moved south to lay siege to Siena itself, which finally surrendered eight months later, thanks in large part to the duke's military architect Belluzzi, whose knowledge of the complicated method of supplying water to this hilltop city enabled the Florentines to starve it into submission

By the time of Siena's surrender, yet another conclave was under way in Rome, where Julius III had died in March 1555. It was split, inevitably, by French and Imperial rivalries. This time, Cosimo devised a cunning plan: he informed the cardinals that his agents had 'intercepted' a letter containing the shocking news that Piero Strozzi was about to march on Rome with the French army to force the election of the French candidate, Cardinal Ippolito d'Este. The letter was undoubtedly a forgery, but it successfully ruined Este's chances. Above all, it was evidence of how adept the duke had become in the devious tactics necessary to survive and prosper in the world of sixteenth-century politics. Unfortunately for Cosimo I, things did not go according to plan. Pope Marcellus II, an ailing Church reformist elected on 9 April, began by announcing drastic cuts in his household and expenditure, and by urging Henri II and Charles V to start peace talks. Before the month was out he had suffered a fatal stroke. The second conclave of the year, lasting just eight days, brought unwelcome news for Cosimo I and Charles V when the cardinals chose the hardline reformist Cardinal Gianpietro Carafa. The new pope, Paul IV, was a difficult character, stubborn and dictatorial, with a ferocious temper. Worse, he came from an old Neapolitan family and detested the Spanish.

The enmity between pope and Emperor was exacerbated that September when Charles V finally agreed to the Peace of Augsburg, which formally recognized the co-existence of Protestantism with Catholicism in the German states. A furious pope accused the Emperor of heresy. Tensions heightened in the summer of 1556 as the pope assembled an army of French troops in Rome. On 4 September, Charles V's viceroy in Naples, the Duke of Alba, crossed into the Papal States to seize Ostia and other key border fortresses – though he refrained from marching on Rome. Days later, far away in Spain, Charles V abdicated, worn out by years of unremitting hard work, and retired to the monastery of Yuste (Estremadura), where he died two years later.

Charles V had already split his empire, transferring power in Spain, Milan, Naples, the Netherlands and the Americas to his son Philip II, while his brother now succeeded him as Emperor Ferdinand I. The pope refused to recognize either ruler. Philip II continued the fight against Paul IV, acquiring the support of several Italian princes, notably Cosimo I, with whom he signed an alliance in May 1557. Cosimo's price was the king's confirmation of his title of Duke of Florence and Siena, a significant step up the ladder of his ambition.

That summer, when Alba and his Spanish troops advanced on Rome, Paul IV was forced to capitulate. The pope henceforth devoted his energies to Church reform. As head of the Inquisition under Paul III, he had proved his dedication to eradicating abuses in the Church; but he refused to reconvene the Council of Trent, preferring the ruthless methods of the Inquisition to the subtler skills of mediation and negotiation. He gave Michele Ghislieri, his successor as Inquisitor-General, draconian powers to arrest not only anyone suspected of Protestant sympathies, but also anyone accused of blasphemy, homosexuality and pimping, as well as actors and buffoons, and even those who failed to observe the Church's ban on eating meat on a Friday. In September 1557, Paul IV issued his first *Index librorum prohibitorum* (*Index of Forbidden Books*), which led to the burning of many humanist texts across Italy.

The Medici duke was careful to comply with orders: Ghislieri himself reported that 'although Florence is poorly provided with inquisitors, the duke is most zealous in giving us every help'.[15] In private, however, Cosimo I began to make plans for the election of a more favourable successor to the papal throne. He identified Cardinal Giovanni Medici, the brother of his army commander, as a man with whom he could do business; more precisely, he viewed him as someone who might be persuaded to make him King of Tuscany in the event of Cosimo obtaining the papal tiara for him.

By this time, Cosimo I had made plans for his three daughters to marry into the Italian aristocratic elite. Maria, the eldest, was betrothed to

Alfonso d'Este, eldest son of the Duke of Ferrara, an attempt by Cosimo to heal the breach between the two families over precedence. But Maria died in 1557, before the marriage had taken place, and it was decided that Alfonso should marry the youngest Medici daughter Lucrezia instead. Isabella had been betrothed to Paolo Giordano Orsini, Lord of Bracciano, when she was just ten years old. Cosimo had also arranged the betrothal of Duke Alessandro's illegitimate daughter Giulia to a Neapolitan noble, and then, after her first husband died, married her to a distant cousin, Bernardetto de' Medici.

These unions were celebrated in Florence in magnificent style. Typically, given his ambitions, Cosimo I lost no opportunity to display his princely prestige in the rituals of court life. The San Giovanni festivities in 1549, for instance, had included an enactment of the battle between David and Goliath, as well as a procession of floats carrying allegorical triumphs of the Ancient Roman heroes Julius Caesar, Pompey, Trajan and, of course, Augustus.[16] A few years later he added another innovation to the feast, staging a chariot race in the piazza at Santa Maria Novella, which was transformed into an Ancient Roman circus for the occasion. The race would become a standard feature of San Giovanni.

The marriages of Isabella, aged fifteen, and Lucrezia, two years younger, took place during the San Giovanni festivities in June 1558. The weather, unfortunately, was dismal. Agostino Lapini recorded in his diary that 'from the first day of May up to the afternoon of Sunday 19 July it rained; it lasted for two months and nineteen days and everyone was terrified because it was clear that little grain would be harvested, or other crops'.[17] Despite the rain, there was plenty of fun. Alfonso d'Este arrived in Florence on 19 June and was welcomed with displays of fireworks. There were games of *calcio* – a type of football, without rules, played between teams of twenty-seven youths – in the piazza at Santa Croce on 29 June and another at Santa Maria Novella on 2 July, with the players dressed in splendid silver and gold outfits. On 3 July, Alfonso and Lucrezia attended a nuptial mass in the Palazzo Ducale, and the groom left Florence for France three days later, leaving his young bride behind. Isabella too remained in Florence while Orsini, a mercenary soldier by trade, was away fighting, and she took up residence in the Palazzo Medici.

The following year, 1559, was a watershed in Cosimo I's reign – and in the history of Europe. On 3 April, Philip II and Henri II signed the Treaty of Cateau-Cambrésis, bringing the long and violent decades of enmity between their fathers to an end. The reconciliation of these great powers was cemented in a double marriage: Philip II wed Elisabeth of Valois, the daughter of the French king and Cosimo's cousin, Catherine de' Medici; and the Duke of Savoy, an Imperial ally, married Margaret of Valois, Henri II's sister.

Tragically, during the wedding celebrations in France that July, Henri II died after being pierced in the eye by a lance while jousting. He was succeeded by his sickly fifteen-year-old son Francis II, with Catherine de' Medici acting as regent. These circumstances meant that Cosimo I now had an ally behind the French throne. Moreover, a month later the hated Pope Paul IV died, and Cosimo could put into action his plans for the election of Cardinal Medici, arranging for one of his agents to be among the courtiers attending the cardinals in the Vatican. The conclave, which opened on 5 September, remained split between French and Imperial factions, but this time there were further complications. Catherine de' Medici's candidate was Cardinal Ippolito d'Este, the uncle of Cosimo's new son-in-law Alfonso; and on 3 October, with the conclave still in session, Ercole II d'Este died, making Alfonso the new Duke of Ferrara.

Cosimo I immediately turned the situation to his advantage. He sent troops to Ferrara to secure the succession, while Alfonso II returned home from France; and then Cosimo went in person to meet his son-in-law, who landed at Livorno on 14 November 1559. Undoubtedly, the business of the conclave, still in session, was high on their agenda. Cosimo I had written to both Catherine de' Medici and Cardinal d'Este in an effort to persuade the French faction to support Cardinal Medici. But it was not until the middle of December, after more than four months of haggling, that Catherine de' Medici accepted that Este would never acquire the necessary two-thirds majority and agreed to compromise. She now instructed the French cardinals to vote for Cosimo I's man. Cardinal Medici was elected as Pope Pius IV on Christmas Day.

Cosimo I had achieved much over the previous fifteen years. His reforms had reversed the decline of the Tuscan economy, his administration had brought stability to the duchy, and Florence itself was beginning to take on the appearance of a ducal capital. Thanks to his canny diplomatic skills, his indefatigable energy – and a degree of good fortune – he had established good relations with Philip II of Spain, Emperor Ferdinand I and his cousin the French regent, Catherine de' Medici; and he had his own candidate on the throne of St Peter. Cosimo I intended to exploit this favourable position to advance the Medici cause.

16

GRAND DUKE

Cosimo I
1560–1574

Duke Cosimo I (41)
Eleonora of Toledo (38), *his wife*

> *Their seven children:*
> Francesco (19)
> Isabella (18) m. Paolo Giordano Orsini
> Giovanni (17)
> Lucrezia (15) m. Duke Alfonso d'Este
> Garzia (13)
> Ferdinando (11)
> Pietro (6)

Catherine de' Medici (41), *his cousin, Queen of France*

Dianora (7), *his niece*

Giulio (28), illegitimate son of Duke Alessandro

Giulia (25), *Giulio's sister,* m. Bernardetto de' Medici

Bernardo Salviati (52), *his uncle*

Cosimo I's hope that Pius IV would favour his dream of making the Medici the premier dynasty in Italy received a boost just weeks after the papal election. In a consistory in the Vatican, on 31 January 1560, the new pope created three cardinals, giving red hats to two of his own nephews (one of whom, Carlo Borromeo, would eventually achieve sainthood), while the third went to Cosimo's teenage son Giovanni. And that was not all. The pope transferred to Giovanni the titular church of Santa Maria in Domnica, in Rome, so that the new cardinal could have the title that had once belonged to Leo X; and then he appointed him as Archbishop of Pisa.

At the end of March, Cardinal Giovanni left for Rome, where, once the arcane ceremonies associated with his new dignity had been completed, he was able to indulge his passion for antiquities with visits to the great sculpture collections in the city. He bought his own pieces, as he wrote enthusiastically to Cosimo in May: 'I have found many beautiful things of the sort that would please Your Excellency.'[1] Evidently, he shared his father's tastes. When he left Rome in the middle of June, his major-domo had to pack up no fewer than thirteen chests of antiquities, including bronze heads, a porphyry table and 'a marble statue of a small boy', which the cardinal had bought as a present for his mother.[2]

When Cardinal Giovanni returned to Rome in the autumn, he came in the company of his parents, who were making a state visit for talks with Pius IV – talks that, the duke hoped, would secure a royal title. They were given a splendid reception at the gate of Santa Maria del Popolo, where Cardinal Ippolito d'Este greeted them formally before escorting them through the city. It was 'a huge cavalcade among which were the courtiers of seven cardinals with pontifical mules and hats in the customary manner, led by eighty pack mules and followed by numerous Florentines living in Rome, with their servants dressed in various liveries and all the ambassadors resident in the city,' the papal master-of-ceremonies recorded.[3] Cosimo I must have been disappointed, though, that his talks with the pope were only a partial success. Pius IV favoured him with lavish presents, including an antique statue of *Hercules and Antaeus* and a giant granite column that had recently been unearthed in the ruins of the Baths of Caracalla. He also agreed to Cosimo's request to grant Paolo Giordano Orsini the title of Duke of Bracciano, giving his daughter Isabella the same rank as her sister

THE FAMILY MEDICI

Lucrezia, Duchess of Ferrara. Furthermore, the pope promised to give a red hat to the duke's uncle, Bernardo Salviati. But there the favours ended – Pius IV was evasive on the subject of the royal title that Cosimo so passionately desired.

During his stay in Rome, the duke fell ill with a fever in late November 1560: Cardinal d'Este reported that he had 'taken a medicine which was very effective, though this evening his stomach became turbulent again and he has some pain'.[4] Cosimo recovered in time for Christmas, but Lucrezia's health then began to fail. In April 1561, the duke's daughter died of tuberculosis shortly before her sixteenth birthday. Cosimo held her obsequies in San Lorenzo, ordering all shops to close as a mark of respect. And illness continued to dog the family. That autumn, eldest son Francesco returned from Rome with a high fever, after lobbying on his father's behalf at the papal court; Cosimo was worried enough to cut short his own business trip to Livorno. (Fortunately, Francesco recovered, and the following May Cosimo sent him to Madrid, in the hope of persuading Philip II to agree to his plan of betrothing his heir to the king's widowed sister, Joanna of Portugal.) Then, the high-spirited Isabella had a miscarriage after falling off her horse, and spent several months regaining her health.

Worse was to come that autumn, as real tragedy struck the Medici. In October 1562, Cosimo and Eleonora went hunting at the ducal castle of Rosignano, near Livorno, where they were joined by their sons, Cardinal Giovanni and Garzia, who had been hunting in the Maremma swamps further south. On 20 November, Cardinal Giovanni died suddenly, aged just nineteen – followed on 12 December by the death of fifteen-year-old Garzia. The unexpectedness of this calamity quickly gave rise to colourful rumours. It was widely believed that Garzia had stabbed Giovanni with a dagger during an argument, and that when Garzia had confessed his crime to his father, Cosimo had murdered his younger son in anger. It was a fanciful if lurid tale, and one which Cosimo I was at pains to scotch in a letter to Francesco in Spain, insisting that both boys had died of malaria, caught in the Maremma swamps.* And finally, to cap this series of tragedies, five days after Garzia's death Eleonora died of tuberculosis at the age of forty.

In the space of less than two years, the family had been ravaged,

---

* The diagnosis was recently confirmed by modern paleopathologists. Gáldy, p. 160.

and Cosimo I was devastated by the loss of his wife, two sons and his daughter. He had been very fond of Eleonora, and he now donated her clothes as alms to San Lorenzo – a generous present, for the expensive silk and velvet dresses could be recycled as vestments. Of the eleven children she had borne him, only four now remained alive: Francesco, now twenty-one, Isabella (twenty), Ferdinando (thirteen) and Pietro (eight). Less than two months after Cardinal Giovanni's death, Pius IV gave Ferdinando a red hat, an action reflecting Cosimo I's political clout. The teenager took his late brother's place at the papal court as well as Giovanni's titular church of Santa Maria in Domnica. With Francesco in Spain, Cosimo I relied heavily on Isabella, who now took charge of her youngest brother Pietro and their cousin Dianora, who were still learning their lessons in the Palazzo Ducale. (Six years later, these two children would be married to each other, with Don Garzia de Toledo putting up a dowry of 40,000 ducats for Dianora and Cosimo I settling a large estate on his son.) When Francesco returned from Madrid nine months later, 'he went straight to Poggio a Caiano to see his father and on Monday 20 September in the evening he entered Florence together with his father, without any sort of celebration, except for some artillery and all this was done for the love of the duchess, his mother, and his brothers who were dead'.[5]

The grieving Cosimo sought refuge from his pain by immersing himself in his projects for economic reform and cultural renovation, which he commemorated in a series of twelve medals, an appropriately Herculean number to record his own labours in bringing peace and prosperity to Tuscany. One medal represented Justice, symbolized by the giant column given by Pius IV which the duke had erected in the piazza at Florence's Santa Trinita. Another medal recorded the foundation of his own chivalric order, which he dedicated to Pope Stephen I, whose feast day, 2 August, marked the military victories at Montemurlo (1 August 1537) and Marciano (2 August 1554).

Chivalric orders were one of these courtly accessories that denoted royal power in sixteenth-century Europe and Cosimo's new order should be seen in the ocntext of the duke's campaign to promote the prestige of the Medici dynasty. At a more practical level, his Knights

The Column of Justice in Florence's Piazza Santa Trinita. An antique column excavated in the Baths of Caracalla in Rome, it was given to Cosimo I by Pope Pius IV in 1600; on top is a porphyry statue of Justice (1581).

of St Stephen were pledged to fight the Turks in the Mediterranean. One of their earliest victories came in 1565, when, fighting with Philip II's navy, they helped to lift the Turkish blockade of Malta, which had been under siege for five months. And the order had a political context in Cosimo I's efforts to bring peace to Tuscany. The duke shrewdly based his knights not in Florence but at Pisa, a choice designed to improve relations with the city, which had a long history of rivalry with Florence. He also conspicuously embellished Pisa with the grand church of Santo Stefano for the Knights, and with the Palazzo dei Cavalieri as their headquarters.

Underlining the importance Cosimo placed on the arts, in 1563 he founded the Accademia del Disegno, an association for architects, painters and sculptors, which he constituted along the lines of the Accademia Fiorentina. He took a close interest in all his artistic projects. In March that year, Vasari, busy painting the ceiling of the great hall in the Palazzo Ducale with a cycle on the history of Florence, sent Cosimo a design for the scene of the duke planning the conquest of Siena. Cosimo I dismissed it with characteristic vigour: 'Those advisers that you have included in the scene,' he informed the painter, 'are not necessary, because it was us alone who did the planning, but if you like you could include a figure of Silence and some other virtues in their place.'[6]

Cosimo even made his own modest contributions to the history of the decorative arts, developing a method of tempering chisels to make them strong enough to carve porphyry. He also discovered a quarry of multicoloured marbles at Seravezza in the mountains north of Pisa, and he used the stone to ornament the floors, fireplaces and tables in the Palazzo Ducale. His passion for coloured marbles sparked off the development of the Florentine craft of *pietre dure*, inlaid work using semi-precious stones. Immensely expensive, this was an excellent method of displaying ducal wealth. Vasari recorded a table he designed for Francesco, who shared his father's luxurious tastes, which was made using pieces of alabaster, jasper, cornelian, lapis lazuli and agate, at the cost of more than 20,000 florins.[7]

By the early 1560s, three decades of unremitting hard work in the service of his country had taken their toll on Cosimo I's astonishing reserves of energy and determination. In 1564, he ostensibly handed over the day-to-day administration of the duchy to Francesco, though

Giovanni Antonio de' Rossi, *Cosimo I and his family*, onyx cameo portrait, *c.*1560 (Florence, Museo degli Argenti).

he reserved the title 'duke' for himself. His retirement, however, was largely nominal. He kept a close eye on Francesco, complaining frequently of his son's shortcomings. A dour, shy man, Francesco was far less interested in the business of government than his father would have wished. Cosimo still continued to exercise tight control over his artistic projects, and most importantly over the direction of foreign policy. Above all, he continued to hope that Pius IV might eventually be persuaded to grant him a royal title – and he did all that he could to ingratiate himself with the pope.

Pius IV's most urgent priority was Church reform and, with the Habsburg–Valois wars finally over, he had reconvened the Council of Trent in January 1562. Attended by cardinals, bishops, the religious orders and lay ambassadors from across Europe, this council was a landmark in the history of religion. Its decrees redefined the basis of the Catholic faith, notably those dogmas rejected by Protestants, such as transubstantiation and papal infallibility; and in November 1564 Pius IV issued the bull *Professo fidei* to enforce its decisions. Cosimo I took care to show his support. The following year, he began work to transform the interiors of two important Florentine churches, Santa Croce and Santa Maria Novella, in conformity with the new regulations, dismantling the carved medieval rood screens to give the congregation a clear view of the Eucharist on the altar, where the 'miracle' of transubstantiation took place.

Cosimo I was also looking for a bride for Francesco. His ambitions to marry his heir to Joanna of Portugal had fallen through after Philip II refused his consent, and the duke must have been disappointed that the parvena Medici were not seen as being of sufficient rank to attract a Spanish princess. However, Emperor Maximilian II, who had succeeded his father Ferdinand I in 1564, was more amenable. Cosimo was perhaps also fortunate that the Emperor had several sisters in need of husbands and was prepared to compromise on social status – the duke's former son-in-law Alfonso II d'Este was also negotiating for one to be his own bride. Francesco himself contributed to the diplomatic overtures on his behalf, sending a bronze Mercury, sculpted by Giambologna, to Maximilian II as a sweetener. Privately, about this time, he also embarked on what would be a long love affair, with Bianca Cappello, the daughter of a Venetian patrician.

The overtures were successful. The betrothal of Francesco and

Bartolomeo Ammannati, *Fountain of Neptune*, 1563–75 (Florence, Piazza della Signoria).

Joanna of Austria was announced on 21 March 1565, 'and that day all the shops were closed and there were fireworks in the evening and great celebrations,' reported Lapini.[8] In mid-December, the bride arrived at Poggio a Caiano, where she was graciously received by Cosimo I, 'who gave her a most beautiful necklace hung with large pearls and lovely diamonds and rubies and other precious gems that was worth several thousands of *scudi*'. The necklace was indeed superb: according to the inventory of the ducal wardrobe, it contained 27 diamonds, 105 rubies and 3,435 pearls.[9]

With the help of his daughter Isabella, Cosimo I had planned extravagant festivities to celebrate this prestigious marriage. Joanna of Austria made her official entry into Florence on 16 December 1565. The Neptune fountain in the piazza, in front of the ducal palace, had been completed just days before, and the city was lavishly decorated with triumphal arches and other ephemera glorifying the Habsburg–Medici union. After the noisy cavalcade through the streets, the bride was escorted into the Palazzo Ducale, up the magnificent marble staircases and into the great hall for the wedding feast. Vasari and his assistants had just finished painting the ceiling with the scenes of Florentine history, from the city's foundation by Augustus up to Cosimo I's capture of Siena, with the image of the *Apotheosis of Cosimo I* at the centre. The programme for the decoration had been devised by the historians of the Accademia Fiorentina who invented several Medici heroes to play their part in this great cycle of battles. Vasari had relished the challenge, describing how 'on that ceiling I had the opportunity to do almost everything that man could imagine, every type of pose, faces, vestments, clothes, helmets, shields, cap badges, horses, harness, caparisons and artillery, ships, storms, rain, snow and so many other things that I cannot remember them all'.[10] The celebrations continued over the Christmas and New Year holiday and into Carnival. On 17 February 1566, there was a mock battle in the piazza at Santa Maria Novella, followed four days later by a spectacular entertainment, a series of twenty-one triumphs 'called the Genealogy of the Gods, who had come from heaven to earth to honour the said marriage; it was done at night with five hundred actors and thousands of torches and was most beautiful'.[11]

During the wedding celebrations, Cosimo's attentions were drawn to Rome, where, on 9 December 1565, Pius IV had died from the complications of gout. The conclave to elect his successor had opened ten days later. As before, Cosimo I had surreptitiously installed his own agent among the conclavists to advance his interests – and he had his son, Cardinal Ferdinando, in the Vatican to help influence the voting. In early January 1566, rumours that their candidate, Cardinal Giovanni Ricci, had been elected turned out to be false. The deadlock inside the Vatican was finally broken, abruptly, on 7 January, when it was announced that the cardinals had made a very unexpected choice. The new pope was Cardinal Michele Ghislieri, the ex-Inquisitor-General, who chose to be called Pius V. This son of a Piedmontese shepherd had joined the Dominican order as a youth, and he would continue to wear his coarse black habit under his fine white pontifical robes. Strict and ascetic, he took the spiritual view on all issues and imposed Christian morality on his flock. Among the more repressive measures of his pontificate was expelling the Jews from the Papal States – though he failed to convince the cardinals to agree to his plans to punish adultery with death or to outlaw prostitutes.

For Cosimo I the new pope offered a second opportunity to achieve his ambition for a royal title, Cosimo I was doubly determined to gain favour with Pius V, and he was quick to adapt to the new regime at the Vatican. In July 1566, a prominent Florentine cleric, Pietro Carnesecchi, was charged with heresy by the Inquisition, and the duke dutifully handed him over to Rome. As a former loyal servant of both Leo X and Clement VII, Carnesecchi deserved better treatment from the Medici; but at an *auto-da-fé* in Rome, in September the following year, he was found guilty of heresy and condemned to be beheaded in public and then burned. Cosimo I also began to enforce Pius V's anti-Semitic policies in Florence: Lapini recorded that 'Jews have been ordered to wear a yellow O on their hats'.[12] The duke was also assiduous in introducing the pope's standardized form of the Latin mass (the Tridentine mass), from 1570, and other Counter-Reformation measures to Florentine churches; and he appointed a priest – his cousin Alessandro – to represent his interests at the papal court. In 1569, in another gesture towards the Counter-Reformation, the Archbishop of Florence presided over a novel addition to the Maundy Thursday celebrations, one that was inspired by Church reformers like Cardinal Borromeo: 'he washed the feet of twelve poor men, and this was the first time that poor men's feet had been washed, because in the old days it was done to the canons of the cathedral and not the poor... each of the men was given a coin, a loaf of bread, a white hat with a garland of olives and a white coat'.[13]

Cosimo I's efforts to curry favour with Pius V finally bore fruit. At the end of 1569, news arrived that the pope had agreed to grant the duke royal status, with the title 'Grand Duke of Tuscany' – a title that would give him precedence over all the other duchies in Italy. On 13 December, Lapini recorded that a service of thanksgiving was held in the Duomo 'to mark the great happiness for our duke, who has been given a royal crown above his coat-of-arms by Pope Pius V'.[14] Cosimo, who had to be carried to the church in a litter because of a gouty foot, had earned this favour, continued Lapini, 'notably because the duke has always been a defender of the holy Catholic Church and a great supporter of justice'. In February 1570, the new grand duke left for

Overleaf: Giorgio Vasari, *The Apotheosis of Cosimo I*, 1563–5 (Florence, Palazzo Vecchio, Salone del Cinquecento).

BELLVM SEN·SVMMA
DENTIA MEN·XIIII
·D·PROVI
FINITVR

PRINCIPE

CONSTITVTA

CIVITATE

AVCTO

SPQF OPT

ETRVRIA

PACATA

IMPERIO

Rome, where he was crowned by Pius V on 5 March, in the Sistine Chapel. It was a very proud moment. Henceforth, Cosimo I would bow only to popes, emperors and kings. And the Medici had achieved a new stature on the world stage.

Cosimo I returned from Rome keen to demonstrate his gratitude to the pope. Pius V had insisted that the widowed grand duke should regularize his relationship with his mistress Camilla Martelli, by whom he now had two children: Giovanni, born in 1567, and Virginia, a year younger. The couple married a month after his coronation, but, despite being wife of the grand duke, Camilla did not receive a courtesy title. The relationship was frowned on by both of Cosimo's sons, Francesco and Cardinal Ferdinando, though their sister Isabella loyally supported her father. And all three offspring pursued their *own* clandestine relationships: Isabella had recently begun an affair with her husband's cousin Troilo Orsini; Francesco's relationship with Bianca Cappello continued unabated, despite his marriage to Joanna of Austria; and Cardinal Ferdinando would soon begin a celebrated romance with Clelia Farnese, the beautiful daughter of Cardinal Alessandro Farnese, his rival at the papal court.

Grand Duke Cosimo I also continued to champion Pius V's policies on Church reform, including restrictions on Jews. Work began in Florence on a ghetto for the Jewish population, on the site 'where the public prostitutes and the very poor had been for a long time,' Lapini commented, 'and it is closed every evening, earlier or later depending on the season, and opened again early in the morning'.[15] In addition, Cosimo founded a religious confraternity dedicated to the Blood of Jesus at San Lorenzo, in response to Pius V's encouragement for new confraternities dedicated to doctrines explicitly rejected by the Protestants – such as the miraculous nature of the Eucharist. These associations soon became important in the religious and social lives of their members, who paraded their relics in processions on feast days, raised money to do good works, and gathered regularly for club dinners.

The increasingly pious atmosphere of Counter-Reformation Florence was evident in the Duomo, where Lapini witnessed the defrocking of a country priest, on Pius V's orders, in September 1570. 'First they removed the chalice from his hands and then they took off his chasuble,' he recorded, 'then, one after the other, his alb, surplice and cassock, leaving the scoundrel in just his shirt and hose.'[16] The priest's crime was vile enough, though: he had confessed to murdering a farm labourer and taking his wife 'by whom he had had several children'. Lapini noted the archbishop's display of reluctance to take such action against an anointed priest: 'He wore only a surplice over his rochet and no other vestments in order to show that he was doing this unwillingly,' the diarist explained, 'but it was necessary to obey the pope who had ordered him to do this.'

Cosimo ensured, too, that he supported the pope's foreign policy. When Pius V signed an alliance with Philip II and Venice against the Turks in May 1571, the grand duke celebrated the event with a solemn mass in the cathedral and a procession of the clergy through the streets of the city. The Turks had become a real menace in the Mediterranean, especially after their conquest of the Venetian island of Cyprus the previous autumn; but in October 1571, the allied navies won a resounding victory at the Battle of Lepanto. The Christian fleet, led by Philip II's brother, Don John of Austria, lost just 15 of their 300 ships and captured 117 Turkish vessels. Among those fighting in the battle were Isabella's husband, Paolo Giordano Orsini, and Dianora's father, Don Garzia, as well as a contingent of Cosimo I's Knights of St Stephen. When news of the triumph arrived in Florence, the grand duke ordered the shops to close and the bells to ring; in the evening there was a display of fireworks, 'as is the custom for great celebrations'.[17]

Cosimo I also offered help to his cousin, Catherine de' Medici, who was struggling to maintain control of France for her young son, Charles IX. The kingdom's premier families, already political rivals, had lined up on either side of the religious divide – the Bourbons with the Protestants and the powerful Guise clan with the Catholics – and the country had been engulfed in civil war since 1562. Cosimo I kept the Florentines up to date with regular masses and other festivities to celebrate Catherine de' Medici's Catholic victories. He also gave his cousin more practical assistance, sending troops and large sums of cash to help her efforts to bring peace to the kingdom. In 1572, in yet another attempt to reconcile Catholic and Protestant subjects, Catherine betrothed her daughter, Marguerite of Valois, to the Protestant Henri of Navarre. The wedding took place in Paris on 18 August, but the celebrations turned violent six days later, when thousands of Protestants were murdered by Catholic mobs rampaging through the streets of the city. Lapini recorded the details of the St Bartholomew's Day massacre; the mass of the Holy Spirit was held in Florence's Duomo on 14 September 'as a sign of the great joy at the death of these Protestants', followed by the customary firework displays.[18]

Meanwhile, Cosimo I had worries about his own dynasty. His son's marriage to Joanna of Austria might have brought the prestige of an Imperial alliance; but his daughter-in-law had so far failed to give Francesco a son (it was widely believed then that the mother was responsible for the sex of her offspring). Francesco evidently continued to do his duty in the marital bed, despite the charms of his mistress. His wife had given birth to her first child, Eleonora, in 1567, fifteen months after the wedding. The birth of their first daughter was celebrated in somewhat muted style: 'the shops stayed open that day' but 'they placed four vats of wine outside the Palazzo Ducale, holding about sixty barrels, and anyone who wanted could have some,' reported Lapini, 'and that evening there were fireworks'.[19] The following year brought a second daughter, Romola, who survived for just twelve days; a third, Anna, arrived at the end of 1569. After a fourth daughter, Isabella (born 1571), who lived for less than a year, a fifth, Lucrezia, was born fourteen months later.

Joanna's misery at not producing a male heir must have been compounded by the arrival of other baby boys in the family. Both Isabella and Dianora produced sons. Isabella gave birth to Virginio in 1572, an heir to the Duchy of Bracciano. Although she had not broken off her affair with her husband's cousin, it seems that the boy was conceived while Paolo Giordano was at home, recuperating after the victory at Lepanto. The following year, Pietro and Dianora had a boy, named Cosimino. Now, Joanna of Austria resorted to desperate measures. In April 1573, she travelled across the Apennines to Loreto, where she offered prayers at the shrine of the Virgin, in the hope of conceiving the son that her husband, and her father-in-law, so urgently wanted.

Cosimo's health, however, had begun to fail, after a series of strokes that left him unable to talk or write. In August 1573, Lapini noted that 'the grand duke has begun to bathe in water brought from Bagno di San Filippo', referring to the hot thermal springs, rich in sulphur, south of Siena.[20] They did not provide a cure. Cosimo I died in the Palazzo Pitti on 21 April 1574, at the age of fifty-four. His widow Camilla, reluctant to remain at the court of the new grand duke, chose to enter the convent of Santa Monica.

The thirty-seven years of Cosimo I's reign had been astonishingly beneficial for Tuscany. Florence, which had been impoverished when he came to power in 1537, could now claim to be the capital of a large and prosperous state. Moreover, Cosimo's campaign to place Florence at the zenith of European culture was an audacious story of political spin, with a level of success that modern politicians might envy. Above all, thanks to his unswerving determination and canny political skills, the Medici had levered themselves into becoming the leading dynasty in Italy and members of the European ruling elite.

17

ADULTERY

Francesco I and Cardinal Ferdinando

1574–1587

Grand Duke Francesco (33)
Joanna of Austria (27), *his wife*

> *Their daughters*
> Eleonora (7), Anna (5) and Lucrezia (2),

Bianca Cappello (26), *his mistress*

Isabella (32), *his sister,*
m. Paolo Giordano Orsini, *Duke of Bracciano*

> Virginio (2), *their son*

Cardinal Ferdinando (25), *his brother*

Pietro (20), *his brother*
m. Dianora Garzia di Toledo (21), *his cousin*

> Cosimino (1), *their son*

Giovanni (7), *his half-brother*

Virginia (6), *his half-sister*

Alessandro (39), *his cousin, Archbishop of Florence*

Catherine de' Medici (55), *his cousin, Queen Mother of France*

If the crowds that gathered to watch Cosimo I's funeral cortège pass, on its route from the Palazzo Ducale to San Lorenzo, did not show much grief, they were certainly astounded at the unprecedented grandeur of the event. Just over a century had passed since his namesake, Old Cosimo, had been buried in a simple ceremony at the same church; but tastes had changed, and so had the status of the Medici.

Cosimo I's successor as Grand Duke of Tuscany was determined to use his father's funeral to demonstrate that the family now belonged to the cream of European nobility. He chose to model the ceremony on the opulent obsequies staged by King Philip II in Brussels in 1558 after the death of his own father, Charles V. It was a very conceited choice – the Medici dynasty, for all its pretensions to majesty, was hardly on a par with the ancient lineages of Spain and the Holy Roman Empire.

The pompous procession began with trumpeters, their instruments muffled with black cloth, followed by a hundred wax torches, six riderless horses draped with black caparisons and black plumes nodding on their heads, and Cosimo's catafalque, with his treasured collar of the Golden Fleece carried on a velvet cushion by one of his courtiers. Finally came the new grand duke himself, dressed in a long black hooded gown, as copied by his tailors from illustrations of the outfit Philip II had worn in Brussels.

For the occasion, San Lorenzo was transformed into a veritable Temple of Death, its facade covered entirely in black cloth, against which hung the grand-ducal arms and a depiction of the collar of the Golden Fleece. The interior of the church was also draped in black cloth – the suppliers of this material must have had a profitable month, so too the craftsmen involved in the project. Hanging on the black curtains screening the side chapels were images celebrating the achievements of Cosimo I's reign, extolling his virtues as unifier of Tuscany, as bringer of peace and prosperity, as palace-builder, and so on. Along the walls stood skeletons in mourning, a fashion much in vogue in Counter-Reformation Italy and one of the few details not to have been inspired by Charles V's obsequies. In the middle of this macabre setting shone the gilded catafalque, crowned by a pyramid on which burned thousands of candles imported from Venice.

Despite the showiness of Cosimo's funeral, Francesco I emerged reluctantly onto the grand-ducal stage, showing no relish for his new responsibilities. Unlike his father, he was not interested in politics nor in the economic health of Tuscany, and he chose to leave his government in the hands of bureaucrats while blindly following Philip II's lead on international issues. He cut peepholes in the walls of his audience rooms so that he could watch official meetings without having to attend them. And he kept his subjects at arm's length, asking his architect, Bernardo Buontalenti, to design a door (the Porta delle Suppliche) in the side wall of the Uffizi, through which they were to post their petitions.

Shy and moody, Francesco I devoted his time instead to his artistic and scientific interests. He spent liberally on enlarging the family collection of antiquities, happy to pay, for example, 50 *scudi* for a medal of Emperor Commodus even though he acknowledged 'it does seem somewhat overpriced'.[1] Above all, he was obsessed with scientific research. He built laboratories at the Casino Mediceo near San Marco, where he studied the effects of fire and poisons, investigated the secrets of perpetual motion, and experimented with reproducing Chinese porcelain.

His unusual interests, and his character, were amply evident on the walls of the room in the Palazzo Ducale where he kept his collections. This small but ornately decorated study contained a series of expensive bronze statues and elaborate painted panels celebrating the four elements – earth, air, fire and water – and the mythological, historical and technological relationships between art and nature. He had himself portrayed in a scene, *The Alchemist's Laboratory*, not as a grand duke but as the alchemist himself, dressed in workman's overalls and wholly absorbed in stirring a pan of green liquid boiling on a small brazier, happy in his seclusion.

The secretive existence and diffident nature of the grand duke inevitably gave rise to rumours of all sorts of vices and debaucheries. True, it was public knowledge that he preferred the company of Bianca Cappello to that of his wife, and he installed his mistress in a grand palace on the site of the gardens where Machiavelli had once discussed republican ideals with his friends. Francesco I nevertheless did his duty in the Palazzo Ducale, where Joanna of Austria produced five children in the first seven years of their marriage – though it was her misfortune

Jan van der Straet, *The Alchemist*, 1570–2 (Florence, Palazzo Vecchio, Studiolo of Francesco I).

that they were all girls. She had yet another daughter, Maria, the year after her father-in-law's death, and her misery increased when Bianca had a son, Antonio, soon afterwards. Humiliated by her husband's callous behaviour, Joanna tried unsuccessfully to persuade her brother, Maximilian II, to allow her to return home. For his part, the Emperor refused to pay her dowry – on the contrary, it was Francesco I who had to pay for the privilege of his wife's Imperial rank by sending large sums of money to finance Maximilian II's campaigns against the Turks. It might have been some comfort to the grand duchess that her unenviable position made her popular with the Florentines – who disliked the manner in which the grand duke flaunted his mistress – and with her brother-in-law Cardinal Ferdinando, who disliked Bianca and urged Francesco I to be more discreet.

Cardinal Ferdinando had become a powerful figure in Rome since receiving his red hat at the age of thirteen. When Pius V had died in 1572, he exploited his influence to engineer the election of Cardinal Ugo Boncompagni as Gregory XIII, though his role in the conclave was not quite as pivotal as he boasted to his brother. Among the new pope's favours to the Medici was the appointment of the grand duke's cousin Alessandro as Archbishop of Florence and then as a cardinal. Less popular in Florence was Gregory XIII's decision to reform the Julian Calendar, which had been established by Julius Caesar – but with a small error that had multiplied over the centuries. The Gregorian Calendar came into effect in Catholic Europe on 4 October 1582, with the result that ten days were 'lost', for the next day was dated 15 October. For some, there were unfortunate consequences. As the diarist Lapini recorded, 'on 1 November, because the past month of October had only twenty-one days, missing a third of those it should have had, all the salaried staff at the ducal court were paid a third less than usual… as were the magistrates, the soldiers and everyone else'.[2]

The grand duke and the cardinal were not close; and their relationship was aggravated by the fact that, until Joanna of Austria produced a son, it was Ferdinando who was Francesco I's heir. With this situation in mind, Ferdinando declined to take his final priestly vows. Francesco I disapproved of his brother's extravagant expenditure, which far exceeded his large income, the bulk of which, 80,000 *scudi*, was paid out of the grand-ducal coffers according to the terms of Cosimo I's will.[3] And when Ferdinando asked his brother to help the mother of a certain

Florentine goldsmith, who had been left destitute after her son was sentenced to three years in the galleys for theft, the grand duke's response was harsh. 'The case of Bernardino the jeweller was so dreadful that it deserves no favour whatsoever,' he replied, brusquely, 'and I hope you will excuse me if I do not satisfy your request.'[4] But Cardinal Ferdinando was nevertheless a useful intermediary at the papal court, and his lavish expenditure included the cost of favours to their allies in Rome. In 1576, for example, Francesco I sent his brother a chest 'containing crystal glass made in my kilns and I want you to send ten pieces to Bishop Cicala, which I promised him'.[5]

The two brothers also had very different political priorities. Francesco I's alliance with Philip II had brought Ferdinando the coveted position of Cardinal-Protector of Spain, in charge of Philip's interests at the papal court. However, the cardinal needed a wider network of allies to enhance his standing in Rome. Ferdinando was a political animal, skilled in the devious arts of diplomacy, and he used his talents to cultivate relations with the rulers of Italy's other princely courts and, more controversially, with France. Catherine de' Medici and Henri III, the third of her sons to inherit the French throne, were pursuing a very different policy to that of Philip II regarding the religious wars raging in northern Europe. While Philip II was using his army to force his Protestant subjects in the Netherlands to return to the Catholic faith, Catherine de' Medici and Henri III hoped to reconcile the two religions. Much to the dismay of both the pope and Philip II, Catherine negotiated the Edict of Beaulieu in 1576 to allow freedom of worship in most of France – and the cardinal had to defend his cousin's position to the pope, insisting that she was a good Catholic but needed to make peace with the Protestants to ensure the survival of her son's realm.

In the overtly pious atmosphere of Counter-Reformation Rome, Cardinal Ferdinando was careful to display his devotion in public. During the Jubilee year of 1575, for example, he played a prominent role in welcoming pilgrims to the city, serving them in person along with several other nobles, including his brother-in-law, Paolo Giordano Orsini. In private, however, he was more interested in displaying his princely status. He lived in great style at the Palazzo di Firenze in central Rome, and was famous for his sumptuous hospitality and gambling parties (for which he was censured by Gregory XIII), as well as for hunting expeditions at La Magliana, which had once belonged to Leo X. His passion for the chase alarmed some of his more high-minded colleagues, who warned Francesco I that 'the cardinal is not attending to state matters but is continually hunting'.[6] Ferdinando's most ambitious project in Rome was the Villa Medici, which he began building on the Pincian hill in 1576. One of the grandest residences in the city, it was set in beautiful gardens ornamented with his superb collection of antique sculpture, one of the few tastes he shared with his brother.

It was rumoured, too, that Cardinal Ferdinando had a beautiful mistress: Clelia, the daughter of his rival at the papal court, Cardinal Alessandro Farnese. One Roman satirist lampooned the pair, describing how 'the doctor [*medico*] rides the Farnese mule'.[7] Ferdinando might have been able to laugh off this jibe – and he was certainly more discreet in these matters than Francesco I – but more shameful to the Medici family was that the scandalmongers had got hold of a much more damaging piece of gossip. By 1574, the adulterous affairs of the brothers' sister Isabella and sister-in-law Dianora had become headline news in Rome.

Sixteenth-century princesses of the rank of Isabella and Dianora were expected to behave with decorum – and certainly not to be observed on the streets of Florence late at night carousing with several young men in a coach, as Isabella had been in her youth. She had been married to Paolo Giordano Orsini at the age of sixteen, but, with her husband often absent on military campaigns, she lived in Florence rather than on the Orsini estates at Bracciano. Lively, clever, extravagant and a gifted musician, she presided over the Medici court after the death of her mother with vivacious energy; and she began her affair with Troilo Orsini, her husband's cousin, not long after her wedding. She signed her letters to her lover 'your slave forever' and made little effort to be discreet.[8]

Isabella was close to Dianora, sharing the same cultural interests and a taste for dangerous liaisons; for Dianora was dallying with Bernardino Antinori, a courtier and Knight of St Stephen, as an antidote to her unhappy marriage to Isabella's younger brother Pietro. It

seems the reluctant husband had had to be forced to bed his bride, though the couple managed to produce a young son, Cosimino.

While Cosimo I had been alive, he turned a blind eye to the indiscretions of both princesses, of whom he was extremely fond. But now, Cardinal Ferdinando was worried enough to urge his brother to take steps to put a stop to what had become a stain on the family honour; and Francesco would prove less tolerant than his father, now that the affairs had become an international scandal. The grand duke attempted to separate Dianora and Antinori by arresting his sister-in-law's lover on a charge of brawling and imprisoning him on the island of Elba. However, Antinori bombarded Dianora with reams of poetry from his cell, musing on whether 'there has ever been anyone in the world who had a body so graceful and lovely' and 'what powerful and benevolent star adorned you with such glorious gifts'.[9]

In the summer of 1576, Francesco I decided on more drastic action: he had the unfortunate Antinori killed. A few days later, on 10 July, Dianora herself was strangled at the Medici villa at Cafaggiolo. 'Having danced until eleven o'clock, she had gone to bed and was surprised by Lord Pietro with a dog leash at her throat,' the Ferrarese ambassador reported.[10] 'The poor lady put up a very strong defence,' he continued, and two of Pietro's fingers were badly bitten in the fight as 'the bed was all convulsed'. The most damning piece of evidence that this was a premeditated murder was that her corpse 'was placed in a coffin prepared for this event'.

Evidence suggesting that Francesco I himself was complicit in this crime came in a letter the next morning, in which Pietro succinctly informed his brother that 'last night at three o'clock an accident happened to my wife and she died, so Your Highness can be at peace'.[11] The grand duke let it be known that Dianora had died of a heart attack, but informed Philip II that 'Lord Pietro, our brother, had killed her himself because of the treachery she had committed in behaviour inappropriate for a lady'.[12] However, the truth was known in Florence. 'It is said by everyone that she was murdered,' recorded Lapini, who lamented the death of a woman who was 'beautiful, gracious, courteous and pretty' with 'two eyes that were as beautiful as stars.'[13] A few days later, Cosimino, now three years old, also died in suspicious circumstances – it is hard to believe that this was coincidental. As for Pietro, the following year he took up residence at the Spanish court, at

Pieter Paul Rubens, *Joanna of Austria*, 1621 (Paris, Louvre).

the invitation of Philip II, and was to remain there for the rest of his life.

On 16 July 1576, just six days after Dianora's murder, Isabella died unexpectedly; and it soon emerged that she too had been strangled by her husband. Once again, it seems that the crime had the tacit approval of the grand duke, who put it out that his sister had died of an epileptic seizure – but then proceeded to remove her portraits from the family collection. The Ferrarese ambassador sent his master a lurid account of how Isabella had been asphyxiated by Paolo Giordano Orsini and how her corpse was placed in a coffin, which, like that of Dianora, had been prepared in advance. The envoy recorded that when the coffin reached Florence it was 'forced open for anyone who wished to see... her eyes bulging open' before her burial in San Lorenzo, under cover of darkness.[14] Isabella's lover, Troilo Orsini, escaped to France and the protection of Catherine de' Medici, but Francesco I's henchmen tracked him down: he was murdered in Paris the following year.

Family honour had been assuaged and Francesco I, chillingly, showed little remorse for his part in the crimes. But their notoriety would adversely affect Medici prospects in later years.

In May 1577, ten months after the murders of the two princesses, Joanna of Austria finally gave birth to a boy, her seventh child. Lapini observed 'great happiness' at the Palazzo Ducale, for 'that morning a large quantity of coins were thrown from the windows' and 'they put sixteen vats of wine out on the steps... so that whoever wanted wine could fill their barrels, buckets or other vessels, which was a great sight, and there were fireworks for two nights running'.[15] Francesco I ensured that the San Giovanni celebrations that year were particularly splendid. On the eve of the feast, a procession of wagons made its way through the streets carrying a series of religious triumphs, including a tableau staged by the Company of St George with an immense mechanical dragon belching great quantities of fire from its mouth and tail.[16]

The long-suffering Joanna of Austria was soon pregnant again; but Francesco I's hopes for a second heir were dashed when she died during childbirth, in April 1578, 'with the baby, which was thought to be a boy, still inside her and also dead; and the midwife tried to pull it out by tugging at an arm which had come out but the arm broke and, before cutting it off, this little arm was baptized'.[17] 'The night she died, and for the whole of the following week,' Lapini continued, 'it was very cold with frost and ice', which killed the grapevines and the fruit ripening on the trees, 'and it seemed to everyone that the heavens were showing their grief at the death of Duchess Joanna, whom everyone thought was almost a saint.'

Just one month later, Francesco I married Bianca Cappello. Initially, the union was kept secret – the indecent haste with which it had taken place would certainly have shocked the Florentines – and it was not until the following year, 1579, that the grand duke announced his plans for a public celebration. That September, watched by her father and a large retinue of Venetian patricians, Bianca was crowned Grand Duchess of Tuscany, an event celebrated by several days of entertainments, banquets, dances, masques, jousts and a mock fight in the courtyard of the Palazzo Pitti. Cardinal Ferdinando, who had long disliked his brother's mistress, was appalled that a commoner had been elevated to the rank of grand duchess – his father, after all, had not honoured his second wife in this way – and he was well aware that, at the age of thirty-four, Bianca was still capable of bearing a legitimate son. Philip II was more pragmatic, accepting a loan of 900,000 ducats from Francesco I in return for royal recognition of the marriage; he publicly confirmed his support by investing the grand duke as a member of the coveted Order of the Golden Fleece.

One visitor to Florence in 1580 was the French essayist Michel de Montaigne, who was able to form his own impressions of the new grand duchess. He noted in his travel diary that Bianca was 'beautiful by Italian standards, with a likeable and arrogant face, large bust and breasts the way they like them' and 'certainly clever enough to have bewitched this prince to keep him devoted to her for a long time'.[18] He was in Florence again the following June for the Feast of San Giovanni, where with the crowds in the stands, he watched the chariot race in Piazza Santa Maria Novella. Despite his distaste for affairs of state, Francesco I evidently enjoyed the more ceremonial aspects of grand-ducal rule, and presided over this event from his private box, in the company of the grand duchess. The piazza had been transformed into a Roman-style circus with pyramids at each end to mark the course. In the race itself, the grand duke's team led until the last lap, when the Strozzi team started to make up ground – and won, as the crowds roared their approval. Medici honour was restored the next day, when Cardinal Ferdinando's horse won the *palio*: the rivalry between the Medici and the Strozzi, which had coloured the history of Florence since the fourteenth century, had been reduced to a sporting competition.

Montaigne also took the opportunity to visit the sumptuous gardens at the Pratolino villa, which Francesco I was building for Bianca. There he saw Giambologna's half-finished statue *The Apennines*, a giant half-man/half-mountain encrusted with falling rocks and dripping with water. He was particularly impressed by the ingenious way in which water was used to play 'music and harmony', to cause 'the movement of several statues and doors', with 'several animals that plunge in

Justus Utens, *Villa Medici at Pratolino*, late sixteenth century (Florence, Museo di Fienze com'era).

to drink, and things like that'.[19] Most entertaining was the grotto with 'seats that squirt water on your buttocks'; moreover, 'if you flee from the grotto and climb the castle stair... a thousand jets of water come out of every other step of the stairs, right up to the top of the house, and give you a soaking'. The fame of these grottoes and fountains spread across Europe. Wilhelm V, Duke of Bavaria, wrote to Francesco I asking for materials for such fashionable garden features, and the grand duke was happy to comply: 'I am sending Your Excellency some chests filled with those grotto and fountain ornaments that you wanted... if you need more let me know and I will try to find them, but I will need a bit of time.'[20]

Given his interests in science and the arts, it is unsurprising that Francesco I encouraged advances in these fields. He was grateful to one

physicist who had sent him a treatise, thinking it showed 'the clarity and value of your intelligence', though he apologized for not having had time to read it properly 'since at the moment I am in the country and fully occupied at the present enjoying my hunting and bird sports'.[21] He continued his father's policy of promoting Florence as the zenith of Italian culture, and in 1583 he founded a new institution, the Accademia della Crusca, to address the task of purifying the Italian language. The name was a witty choice, alluding to the process of separating the chaff (*crusca*) from the perfect grain, and zealous academicians did just that, replacing all foreign – that is, non-Tuscan – words and phrases with the vocabulary used by Dante, Petrarch, Boccaccio and other writers of the region.*

In March 1581, Francesco I wrote to Cardinal Ferdinando with news of his latest artistic project at the Uffizi: 'I have started to convert the first part of the corridor above the magistrates' offices into a gallery and I plan to put many statues there, large and small,' he explained, 'and I want you to send me two mule-loads of marbles and stones, which I have listed in the enclosed note… as soon as possible.'[22] The focus of Francesco I's gallery – which would become the world-famous Uffizi art collection – was the Tribuna, an octagonal room where he housed his pictures, jewels, statuettes and other valuables and curios. Its centrepiece was a casket decorated with eight miniature amethyst panels showing gilded scenes displaying the events of his reign; and it was an indication of the importance he attached to connoisseurship that all but two of the scenes commemorated him as a patron of the arts.

Keen to build his collection of exotica, in 1583 Francesco I wrote to Filippo Sassetti, a Florentine merchant planning an adventurous trip: 'we understand that you are going to the Indies from where we would like to have seeds, plants and other extravagant and unusual things'.[23] After an eight-month voyage from Lisbon to Cochin (Kochi), on the south-west coast of India, Sassetti informed the grand duke of his safe arrival, despite some 'terrible storms off the Cape of Good Hope'.[24] Most of the letter was concerned with the plants – he was very taken with pineapple, 'the tastiest fruit there is'; and he enclosed a list of items he was sending home, including a bezoar stone, a 'por-

---

* The remarkable success of this campaign is still evident today in the widespread belief that the best Italian is spoken in Tuscany.

Giambologna, *Appennino*, 1579 (Pratolino, Villa Demidoff).

Workshop of Alessandro Allori, *Bianca Cappello*, c.1580 (Tokyo Fuji Art Museum).

cupine stone' that was 'something quite rare', an unusual type of coconut, and a silk coat from Bengal, embroidered with pearls and rubies. Sassetti also despatched several chests to Cardinal Ferdinando containing rolls of Chinese silks and Indian cottons, along with swords, hangings, coins from the Indian kingdoms and a sandalwood bed, 'which is most fragrant'.[25]

Francesco I received more exotic goods in March 1585 when four young Japanese princes arrived in Florence, on their way to Rome in the company of several Jesuits. The diarist Lapini was astonished that it had taken them two years to sail from Japan to Lisbon. After disembarking at Livorno, they met the grand duke in Pisa and presented gifts that must have appealed to his love of curiosities:

> … an inkwell made of a shiny, black, highly scented wood, and a piece of this wood, two pieces of paper made of the bark of a tree on one of which was written in their own language, the most holy names of God and the Virgin Mary; two other pieces of paper made of bamboo that were so delicate that it was difficult to imagine how they could be written on; a silk cocoon the size of a man's head; an outfit of their tradition; [and] two or three stones that shaved like our razors.[26]

In a tragic postscript to the catalogue of Medici deaths during the reign of Francesco I, his son and heir Filippo died in 1582, aged just four. Lapini recorded the gruesome details of the autopsy at San Lorenzo: 'His body was taken to the old sacristy where all the doctors who had treated him were assembled,' whereupon 'they sawed off the top of his head taking a piece like a dish, and under the first layer, above the brain, they found almost a glassful of water, which they all agreed must have been the cause of his death.'[27]

The boy's demise brought the issue of succession back onto the agenda, as Cardinal Ferdinando was once again the heir-apparent. Their brother Pietro was unwilling to marry again, but there was the contentious matter of Antonio, Francesco's illegitimate son by Bianca. Ferdinando now took steps to secure his own position, persuading Philip II to refuse recognition of Antonio as Francesco I's legitimate heir. Bianca, however, did not give up hope of producing a legitimate son, reputedly resorting to witchcraft to achieve her aim. When Francesco I told Ferdinando in 1586 that she was pregnant, the cardinal's spies at the Florentine court were able to reassure him that his sister-in-law was suffering from a stomach disorder.

In Rome, Cardinal Ferdinando was expanding his political network. Gregory XIII died on 10 April 1585, and two days later the cardinal wrote to Francesco I asking for funds to help oil the negotiations in the forthcoming conclave: 'eight or ten thousand *scudi* used well and wisely,' he advised, would enable them 'to do something our way'; but his high-minded brother refused.[28] Ferdinando was also annoyed to find that Philip II had decided not to entrust him with the leadership of the Spanish faction in the conclave, a role which, as Cardinal-Protector of Spain, should have been his by right. Despite these setbacks, he remained optimistic that he had secured enough friends in the College of Cardinals to sway the decision. Rejecting the candidates recommended by his brother and the Spanish king, he put his energies behind a relatively unknown figure, Cardinal Felice Peretti. Ferdinando's candidate was duly elected as Pope Sixtus V – and the Medici cardinal would later get his reward.

Cardinal Ferdinando had also began negotiations for marriages designed to strengthen Medici ties with two of Italy's leading princely courts. In April 1584, Francesco I's eldest daughter Eleonora, aged seventeen, married Vincenzo Gonzaga, heir to the Duke of Mantua; the couple were grandchildren of Emperor Ferdinand I, and thus first cousins. The dowry had been agreed at 300,000 *scudi*, a third of which would remain in Florence until the birth of Eleonora's first son. Francesco I staged lavish celebrations for the wedding, with bullfights, buffalo races, masked balls, a game of *calcio* (in which the groom played for the red team against the golds) and a hunt in the grand-ducal park, which Vincenzo 'very much enjoyed having killed a great number of wild beasts of every sort'.[29]

When the festivities were over, Cardinal Ferdinando escorted his niece to Mantua in person. Two years later, Lapini reported the happy news that Eleonora had given birth to a son, and thus 'on 12 May Grand Duke Francesco sent 100,000 *scudi* to the Prince of Mantua, the husband of his eldest daughter, as it is the custom to send the remainder of the promised dowry when the first male child is born'.[30]

Cardinal Ferdinando forged another useful alliance, with the Duke of Ferrara. He had been negotiating with Cardinal Luigi d'Este for the betrothal of his half-sister, Virginia, to Cesare d'Este, the illegitimate cousin of Alfonso II and currently heir to the Duchy of Ferrara. The wedding celebrations in Florence, in February 1586, were timed to coincide with the last week of Carnival. For this matrimonial occasion, the entertainments included a ball at the Palazzo Pitti and the customary games of *calcio*, in which the groom again took part, as well as jousts and masques. Francesco I also spent 25,000 *scudi* on staging a play, *The Faithful Friend* by Giovanni de' Bardi, with scenery designed by his architect Buontalenti and 'stupendous' music and singing by Alessandro Striggio. It was not quite an opera but it marked an important stage in the development of the genre.[31]

In 1587, Eleonora did become Duchess of Mantua after the death of Vincenzo's father, Duke Guglielmo Gonzaga. That same year, Tuscany too faced a succession crisis. While Cardinal Ferdinando was staying with his brother at Poggio a Caiano, Francesco I died very suddenly, on 19 October, his death followed just a day later – as his corpse was on its way to Florence – by that of his wife Bianca. It seems that they had both succumbed to malaria. Although Cardinal Ferdinando ordered an official autopsy on his brother's body, he did nothing to quell the rumours that Bianca had been involved in her husband's death and that she had subsequently committed suicide. Moreover, he refused to accord Bianca the honour of a grand-ducal funeral: while he buried his brother in San Lorenzo with Joanna of Austria, he had Bianca put into a commoner's grave; he also drew up documents questioning her son Antonio's paternity and enacted a *damnatio memoriae* on the grand duchess, erasing her coat-of-arms in all public places and restoring those of Joanna.

Francesco I's thirteen-year reign had done much to enhance the Medici reputation for connoisseurship of the arts; but in truth, it had done little else. The Medici themselves were in dire dynastic trouble: of the six sons Duchess Eleonora had produced for Cosimo I, only Cardinal Ferdinando and Pietro were still alive, and both were childless. The new grand duke would need papal permission to renounce his red hat in order to marry, a favour he knew Sixtus V would be reluctant to grant. Moreover, he was thirty-six years old and had doubts about his ability to sire the children that would give the Medici a future. He had much to do.

18

CARDINAL
TO
GRAND DUKE

Ferdinando I

1587–1609

Grand Duke Cardinal Ferdinando I (38)

Pietro (33), *his brother*

Giovanni (20), *his half-brother*

Virginia (19) *his half-sister,* m. Cesare d'Este

His nephews and nieces:

> Eleonora (21),
> m. Vincenzo Gonzaga, *Duke of Mantua*
>
> Virginio Orsini (15), *son of his sister,* Isabella
>
> Maria (12), *daughter of his brother,* Francesco

His cousins:

Cardinal Alessandro (52), Archbishop of Florence

Catherine de' Medici (68), *Queen Mother of France*

When Francesco I's brother changed his roomy clerical skirts for the tight doublet and hose of the secular world, one of his subjects likened his portly form to a barrel of anchovies; but the mirth soon died down when it became clear that the new Grand Duke Ferdinando I would be a ruler in the mould of his father, Cosimo I.[1]

Implicitly critical of his brother's lack of leadership, he informed the Ferrarese ambassador of his belief that ruling princes 'should apply themselves to the governing of their states because this is what God has called upon them to do'.[2] Relaxed and sociable where Francesco had been moody and aloof, Ferdinando revelled in his new prestige. He would make a concerted effort to improve the Tuscan economy and he would spend conspicuously on public statements of Medici authority. He was a shrewd political operator, his years in Rome having trained him well in the black arts of diplomacy. As grand duke he would instruct his ambassadors to use bribes liberally, and advised them not to target chief ministers, who 'are not so easy to corrupt', but instead approach 'the men working under them', whom, he felt, could be 'won over'.[3] Dropping his brother's policy of single-minded support for Spain, he also went on to cultivate relations with the Holy Roman Empire and above all with France, while his power-base in Rome, led by his cousin Cardinal Alessandro, continued to give him influence at the papal court.

Ferdinando I made his first public appearance in Florence on 4 November 1587, when he left the Palazzo Ducale for the first time since the death of his brother to visit the miraculous image of the Virgin at Santissima Annunziata. Lapini reported that 'around ten o'clock in the morning the Grand Duke Cardinal Ferdinando went out to thank the Blessed Virgin of the Annunciation and to hear mass, dressed in his cardinal's robes of purple cloth, as were the decorations of his coach, with his red biretta on his head'.[4] He was given a rapturous reception when he appeared at the palace door, as 'everyone began shouting: *Palle! Palle!* Hurrah! Hurrah!' But the cumbersome title by which the diarist correctly addressed him would have to change, and he needed Sixtus V's permission to resign the cardinalate so as to marry. He had already chosen his bride: Christine of Lorraine, the granddaughter of his cousin Catherine de' Medici. The pope, angry that Ferdinando was making preparations for the wedding while still a Prince of the Church, granted the request with some reluctance. And so, on 30 November 1587, the Feast of St Andrew, Lapini could report that 'our grand duke removed his cardinal's robes and put on his sword and the other accoutrements of a grand duke'.[5]

Ferdinando I's choice of bride was a political move, designed to cement his ties with France and to display his support for Catherine de' Medici and her son, King Henri III. France was again in turmoil, as the so-called War of the Three Henrys – involving also the Protestant Henri of Navarre and the Catholic Henri, Duke of Guise – threatened to break up the kingdom. Initially, Henri III had supported his brother-in-law Henri of Navarre, whom he had named as his heir; but the king had recently changed his allegiance and joined the Catholics, led by Guise, and had named a new heir, Cardinal Charles de Bourbon. Ferdinando I's betrothal to Christine of Lorraine reflected the new political situation: his bride was not only Catherine's granddaughter but she was also first cousin to Henri of Guise.

Catherine de' Medici put her signature to the betrothal on 8 December 1587, at the royal palace at Blois, where she celebrated the event with a ball; but a week later she fell seriously ill with a lung infection. She was convalescing in bed when Henri III discovered that their new allies, Henri of Guise and Cardinal Bourbon, were plotting regicide. On 23 December, the king informed her that he had ordered Guise's assassination and the arrest of the cardinal, and that he intended to name Henri of Navarre as his heir again. None of this helped improve Catherine's health: her condition worsened dramatically, and she died from pleurisy on 5 January 1588.

Ferdinando I held obsequies for his late cousin at San Lorenzo. Three weeks later, on 25 February, his marriage took place by proxy at Blois. His bride, sixteen years his junior, brought him a dowry of 700,000 florins as well as costly tapestries and other lavish presents from Catherine de' Medici.

In the weeks that followed, the Medici family gathered in Florence to welcome the new grand duchess. Ferdinando I's niece Eleonora arrived on 17 April, with her husband Vincenzo, Duke of Mantua, followed a few days later by his half-sister Virginia and Cesare d'Este, heir to the Duke of Ferrara. Christine of Lorraine made her formal entry

Orazio Scarabelli, *Naumachia at Palazzo Pitti*, 1588
(Florence, Uffizi, Gabinetto dei Disegni).

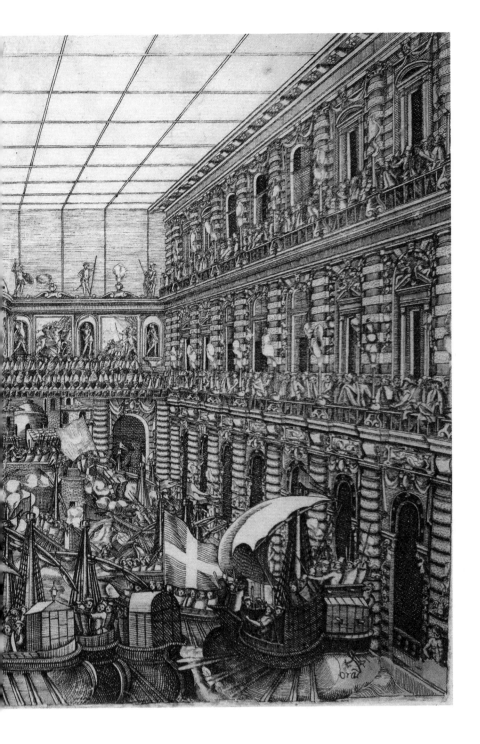

into the city on 30 April, through streets ornamented with arches, statues and decorations that displayed the dynastic achievements of the nouveau Medici alongside those of the ancient House of Lorraine. Lapini thought it 'a stupendous event', done 'with such pomp and ceremony, of livery, of lords, knights and gentlemen' – he, for one, was certainly impressed by the efforts to show that the Medici court was as sophisticated as its royal rivals.[6]

Over the next few days, guests were lavishly entertained with banquets, balls and jousts, and by a number of *intermezzi* – musical entertainments involving huge casts of singers, actors, dancers and musicians. The performance of the drama *La Pellegrina* ('The Female Pilgrim') was particularly impressive; in one scene, all the gods and goddesses appeared seated on 'clouds', descending from Olympus with the aid of pulleys and winches as they sang the praise of the bridal couple. There was a *naumachia*, or mock sea battle, in the courtyard of the Palazzo Pitti, which was flooded for the occasion, and the guests watched with delight as twenty ships, manned by Christian sailors, successfully attacked a Turkish castle. Ferdinando I also put on public events for the entertainment of Florentines, including a game of *calcio* in the piazza at Santa Croce, with the teams in liveries of turquoise and scarlet satin, and ample food and drink: 'in the middle of the piazza were four tables piled high with various delicious sweetmeats including sugared pistachio cakes and other things and… great quantities of precious wines, all white, in silver flasks'.[7] There was a hunt in the piazza a few days later, but the lions, bears and bulls proved reluctant to fight, much to the disappointment of the crowds who had gathered to watch the spectacle.

That summer, while Ferdinando I and his court were enjoying the pleasures of life at the grand-ducal villas to escape the torrid heat of the Florentine summer, shocking news arrived from France that Henri III had been assassinated by a Catholic fanatic on 2 August. Christine of Lorraine was distraught at the death of her uncle. 'The grand duke takes her out hunting or fishing every day to console her,' reported one courtier; Ferdinando also made her a present of the villa at Petraia, 'and yesterday she went to take possession of it, accompanied by the grand duke and all the princes and princesses of the blood, and there was a most wonderful banquet laid out.'[8] Much better news reached Ferdinando's ears in the autumn, when he was informed that his wife was pregnant; the joy increased on 12 May 1590 when she gave birth to a son and ducal heir: Cosimo. 'The church bells rang almost all night and there was much rejoicing, despite the rain,' recorded Lapini. [9] Two days later, the proud father attended mass at the Duomo, where 'seventy or more prisoners passed through the middle of the choir, with garlands of olive branches on their heads': they had been released from prison 'by order of the grand duke', in addition to which 'alms were distributed at the Palazzo Pitti and there were three days of holidays and three evenings of fireworks in the usual places'.

The former cardinal was assiduous in performing his religious duties, which did much to enhance Ferdinando I's standing in Rome. A week before Cosimo's birth, Lapini noted his public appearance with the grand duchess, 'who was in the last month of her pregnancy, and they gave bread to the poor living by the walls of Florence... as they had done during Holy Week in April... when they gave at least one *giulio* to every poor household'.[10] Ferdinando introduced several Roman practices to Florence. To commemorate the birth of Cosimo, he introduced the papal ritual of an annual distribution of dowries, handing out elegant little satin purses containing 40 ducats to poor girls in San Lorenzo.[11] He also instructed the Lenten preachers to urge the Florentines to improve their morals: in 1588, for example, preachers 'censured the inns in our city', blaming them 'for the ruin of young men and girls' and proposing 'that it would be a good thing to close them'; and 'everyone said that this was the grand duke's wish'.[12]

The following year, Ferdinando I celebrated the Feast of the Immaculate Conception of the Virgin, on 8 December, by holding a Forty-Hours Devotion in the Duomo. This was a ritual of continuous prayer that had had been developed by Cardinal Borromeo in the aftermath of the Council of Trent. While a cardinal in Rome, Ferdinando had set up a printing press as part of the Counter-Reformation mission to convert heretics and non-believers; now he was grand duke, he obtained permission from the pope to produce the Bible 'in the Syriac, Chaldean, Arabic, Persian and Ethiopian languages, so that they can be sent to these regions, to those people who want it so they can be catechized'.[13] In a more decorative contribution to papal policy, he commissioned a gilded armillary sphere, a model of the planets in their orbits around the earth, based on the theory of the Greek astronomer Ptolemy, whose writings had recently been challenged by scientists like

Copernicus but which were still upheld by the Catholic Church.

Above all, Ferdinando I was active in the fight to protect Christian Europe from the Turks. When an Ottoman army invaded Hungary in 1593, he contributed funds to the Imperial campaign and dispatched Florentine troops, under the command of his half-brother Don Giovanni – who had already seen action fighting with Philip II's armies against the Protestants in the Netherlands – to join the forces assembled by the pope. The Turks were extending their empire across the Middle East to threaten the Shah of Persia, who sent envoys to Europe in the hope of assistance from Florence, Venice and Rome. On the advice of the pope, Ferdinando I could only offer moral support to the shah's envoys. Their arrival, however, caused quite a stir. Not only did they refuse to remove their turbans on greeting the grand duke, but they took off their shoes and insisted on eating their meals – which were cooked by their own chefs – while seated on the floor.

The grand duke's chivalric order, founded by his father, was directly involved in defending the Mediterranean from the Turkish menace. These Knights of St Stephen won an important victory in 1607 at the Algerian port of Bona, where they took 1,500 prisoners, and the following year they attacked a convoy of Turkish ships off Rhodes capturing 9 vessels, 700 slaves and booty worth some 2 million ducats. The importance that Ferdinando I attached to the actions of the Knights was evident in portraits of him, many of which showed him dressed in the robes of the order's grand master. It was evident, too, in Santo Stefano, in Pisa, where he commissioned a painting of his father being invested as the first grand master: it hung alongside the banners of captured Turkish ships, which festooned the church. The crusading theme was prominent in the temporary decorations erected for the entry of Christine of Lorraine, whose ancestors included Duke Godfrey of Lorraine, leader of the First Crusade in the eleventh century. The grand duchess commissioned a cycle of paintings of Duke Godfrey for her villa at Petraia, while Ferdinando I decorated an entire room in the Palazzo Pitti with scenes of the Knights' battles against the Turks, having himself portrayed – in Roman armour – receiving the captured prisoners after the Battle of Bona.

To conquer the Turkish threat Ferdinando I strengthened Tuscany's coastal defences and commissioned a new harbour fortress at Livorno. This was designed by the clever and cultured Don Giovanni, whose successful career as a soldier in the Netherlands and Hungary had given him practical knowledge of fortifications. An amateur designer, who worked closely with court architects, he was also involved with designing Livorno's Duomo, the centrepiece of Ferdinando's new town.* Although work on the harbour had been begun by Cosimo I, it was under Ferdinando that this modest fishing village was transformed into an international port, fully equipped with modern warehouses and linked to Florence by a canal. He encouraged trade, by avoiding imposing levies on ships using the wharves, and stimulated the growth of this new town by waiving taxes on all new residents, including Jews, for fifteen years.[14] By the time Ferdinando persuaded the pope to grant civic status to Livorno, in 1606, the city was the third-largest in Tuscany. The Grand Duke commemorated his achievement with a massive marble statue of himself dressed in the robes of the Knights of St Stephen.

Trade was a priority for Ferdinando I, who encouraged the export of Florentine goods across Europe and the Middle East, though his plans to set up a trade mission in Brazil were not successful. His efforts to improve the economy were much praised by an English schoolmaster, Sir Roger Dallington, whose extensive survey of the duchy (1596) revealed much about the economic and social habits of the grand duke's subjects. He noted their frugal use of all parts of the vine: eating the grapes, making wine from the juice, bundling up the prunings to sell for kindling, feeding the leaves to both oxen and their compost heaps, and selling the pips as pigeon-feed. The schoolmaster was particularly impressed with Ferdinando I's plans to expand the silk industry by planting mulberry trees in 'such plenty along the banks of the Arno, and about the ditches of towns and other public places' so as to provide leaves to feed the silkworms.[15] Ferdinando I also encouraged the production of the Florentine craft of *pietre dure*, started by his father, and in 1588 expanded the factory (the Opificio di Pietre Dure) at the Casino Mediceo so that it could train a body of craftsmen to produce works on a commercial scale. This style of artwork and furniture, with its ornamental inlays of semi-precious stones, would prove a profitable business for the luxury end of the economy.

---

* Don Giovanni was also a member of the grand-ducal privy council and entrusted with prestigious diplomatic missions to Rome and Spain. In 1598, for example, he was sent to Madrid to offer Ferdinando I's condolences to Philip III on the death of his father, Philip II, and to congratulate the new king on his accession.

Jacques Bylivelt, *Piazza della Signoria*, pietre dure plaque, 1599
(Florence, Museo degli Argenti).

However, behind the magnificent facade of the grand-ducal court there was growing evidence of an economic slump, one that was affecting all Europe and which brought rising prices and a fall in real incomes, at all levels of society. In Tuscany, the earnings of tenant farmers had dropped so much that many preferred to rely on charity in the streets of Florence rather than pursue the thankless task of labouring in the fields.[16] Nevertheless, thanks to Ferdinando I's policies, Florence suffered less than elsewhere. He was assiduous in offering aid during natural disasters, as when, for example, in the autumn of 1589 the Arno flooded, causing extensive damage; the grand duke, at Poggio a Caiano at the time, hurried back to his stricken city, taking a boat to Prato to avoid the flooded roads. He then 'visited all the monasteries, promising them help and assistance, and gave orders for bread to be delivered, not just once but for the following fifteen or sixteen days... and helped many poor people, giving them bread and one *scudo* to each household'.[17] He also 'issued a decree ordering everyone to clean up their houses and empty the cellars and anyone who threw anything into the Arno would be fined 25 *scudi*'.

After a poor harvest the following year, Ferdinando I issued a proclamation banning bakers from making fancy cakes, 'because of fear of famine'.[18] With grain stocks dangerously low, on 6 February 1591 Lapini reported that 'today, Wednesday, they started, in God's name, to give bread to the poor, of whom there were a good number, because of the terrible famine, that no one... can recall a worse one... and they are giving out this bread in various places on Mondays, Wednesdays and Fridays'.[19] The grand duke did much to care for his stricken subjects. In March, 'they began to send the poor to the Ospedale San Onofrio, and when they arrived they were washed in hot water to remove the filth and then shaved, and reclad in ticking, and they stayed inside and were given food in the morning and evening'.[20] On 22 April he was obliged to issue another proclamation to control what the bakers could use to make bread, which 'is to be mixed with bran and siftings of bran with up to a quarter of white flour, but no more... and any baker who breaks the rule will be fined... and all the bread he has baked will be given to the poor'.[21] He also instructed his agents in Poland to buy wheat, which was then shipped from Danzig to Livorno: on 1 May 'seventy carts of wheat arrived in Florence through the Porta San Frediano', with another two hundred carts arriving three weeks later.[22]

Despite Ferdinando's efforts to show concern for his subjects, the court itself was becoming increasingly remote from the lives of ordinary people. He granted special privileges to courtiers to enable them to transform their old mercantile residences into stately palaces; and the courtiers, descendants of the city's old republican families, were now graded by complex rules of etiquette adopted from the royal courts of Europe. An English visitor was struck by their excessively genteel table manners: 'They touch no meat with the hand but with a fork of silver or other metal, each man being served with his fork and spoon, and glass to drink, and as they serve small pieces of flesh (not whole joints as with us), so these pieces are cut into small bits, to be taken up with the fork.'[23] Ferdinando I also codified the dress of those serving as government officials, reviving the use of the *lucco*, the traditional long and sleeveless Florentine coat. Lapini described how the officials were 'to wear a red silk cloth *lucco* with hose of the same colour and slippers or shoes of black velvet; in winter they could wear a *lucco* of woollen cloth of the same colour with a lining; the lieutenants must wear a cape over their left shoulder of purple silk' and 'the senators must always wear a *lucco* made of black woollen or silk cloth lined with red or purple silk'.[24]

Inside the Palazzo Ducale, the Medici dynasty was recovering from the fragile state in which it had been left at the end of Francesco I's rule. Christine of Lorraine produced a regular stream of children for her husband, each birth celebrated with the usual fireworks and noisy celebrations as well as free wine at the Palazzo Ducale. After Cosimo, who was born in May 1590, came Eleonora (November 1591); Caterina (May 1593), named in memory of her redoubtable French grandmother; Francesco (May 1594); Carlo (March 1596); Filippino (1598); Lorenzo (1599); Maria Maddalena (June 1600); and finally, her ninth child, Claudia in June 1604. Although little Filippino died at the age of just four, the others – four girls and four boys – all survived into adulthood. She ensured that the children received a wide education and she chided them if they did not work hard at their studies. One of Cosimo's tutors was Galileo Galilei, who had been appointed by Ferdinando I to the Chair of Mathematics at Pisa University, while the young prince also received instruction in cavalry skills from one of the Knights of St Stephen. All the grand-ducal children had lessons in mathematics, architecture and drawing alongside the conventional curriculum of religious instruction, classical history and literature, foreign languages and music – and they were encouraged to debate political issues at the dinner table.

Ferdinando I's own involvement in European politics had taken a dramatic turn when, with the encouragement of Christine of Lorraine, he became embroiled in the religious wars sweeping France after the assassination of the childless Henri III in 1588. Although the designated heir, Henri of Navarre, was supported by many Catholics as King Henry IV, including by Christine's relations, a Protestant monarch was anathema to the hardline Catholic League, who declared their candidate, Cardinal Bourbon, as Charles X. Moreover, the League had the powerful backing of both Sixtus V, who had issued a decree declaring Henri IV's succession invalid, and Philip II, who made plans to invade France in support of the League.

In a move that was surprisingly bold for an ex-cardinal, Ferdinando I took up the cause of the Protestant king, sending more than 1 million florins to aid Henri IV's war effort. And at one point he dispatched Don Giovanni with eight ships and a thousand soldiers to the French fortress of Château d'If, off Marseilles, which his half-brother successfully defended against the forces of the Catholic League. Inevitably, Ferdinando I's decision infuriated both the pope and the Spanish king, but it would bring considerable benefits for the Medici family.

In March 1590, Henri IV defeated the Catholic army at the Battle of Ivry and laid siege to Paris. Two months later, Cardinal Bourbon died, whereupon Philip II claimed the French throne for his daughter Isabella: she was the granddaughter of Henri II and Catherine de' Medici. With the Spanish army forcing Henry IV to retreat from Paris, the war was threatening to escalate into a wider European conflict. Then, at the end of August, Sixtus V suddenly died. Philip II engineered the election of Urban VII, who survived a mere two weeks before his own demise. Philip II took advantage of the power vacuum in Rome to invade Brittany, sending his son-in-law, the Duke of Savoy, into Provence, while his agents in the Vatican engineered the election of another pro-Spanish pope. Within weeks, Gregory XIV had excommunicated Henri IV, ordered all French cardinals to support the Catholic League and started making plans to send an army to France to assist the Spanish forces.

Meanwhile, Ferdinando I was intent on preventing the success of papal policy, working hard on the diplomatic circuit to increase support for Henri IV. In February 1591, Cardinal Charles of Lorraine, the grand duchess's elder brother, arrived in Florence on his way south to Rome to receive his red hat from Gregory XIV, and Ferdinando encouraged his brother-in-law to promote Henri IV's cause among his colleagues at the papal court. That October Gregory XIV died, less than a year after his election; and the fourth pope in two years, Innocent

IX, also elected with Spanish support, lasted just two months in office. Ferdinando I's twenty-two-year reign would see seven popes, and the instability such papal attrition created at the heart of the Catholic Church gave the grand duke the opportunity to canvass in Henri IV's favour.

In early January 1592, the cardinals went back into the Vatican, where anger at the way the Spanish had been able to manipulate the previous three conclaves ensured the election of a more independently minded candidate. This time the new pope was a Florentine, Ippolito Aldobrandini, who chose the name Clement VIII in honour of the city's last pontiff. The news of his election was greeted by three days of festivities in Florence; but initially Ferdinando I was less sanguine, because the new pope had been a prominent anti-Medicean in his youth and had also shown himself to be fiercely opposed to Henri IV.

In the end, it was the promise of support from the moderates among both Catholics and Protestants in France that persuaded Henri IV to change tactics. Towards the end of 1592, he made the dramatic – and pragmatic – announcement that he wanted to renounce his Protestant faith. He asked Ferdinando I to use his influence in Rome to persuade Clement VIII to accept this momentous decision. The grand duke urged the pope to receive Henri IV's ambassadors, but the pope (after threats from Philip II) refused to see them; however, in a canny diplomatic move Clement VIII let it be known that their secretaries would be welcome at the Vatican. In April 1593, Henri wrote to Ferdinando, pledging his word that he was ready to adopt the Catholic faith, but the pope remained sceptical of what looked like a political manoeuvre. Nevertheless, on 25 July 1593, surrounded by the tombs of his predecessors at St-Denis, Henri IV formally became a Roman Catholic – as he is famously supposed to have said, 'Paris is worth a mass'. He was crowned at Chartres the following February, before making his formal entry into his capital on 22 March 1594.

The grand duke continued his diplomatic campaign at the papal court, where Clement VIII had begun to consider lifting Henri IV's sentence of excommunication, though many of his cardinals continued to doubt the sincerity of the king's conversion. Ferdinando I's cousin, Cardinal Alessandro, shrewdly advised the pope not to discuss the issue in consistory but rather to approach each of the cardinals separately. Finally, on 17 September 1594, in the splendour of St Peter's, Clement

VIII formally absolved Henri IV and declared him to be the 'Most Christian King of France and Navarre'. The following April, Cardinal Alessandro was appointed as legate to France to negotiate the peace treaty between Henri IV and the Catholic League.

In order to ensure the success of these negotiations, Ferdinando I needed to prioritize the maintenance of good relations with Clement VIII, even when papal policy came into conflict with family interests. In 1597, Alfonso II d'Este, Duke of Ferrara, died. With no sons of his own, he had named as his heir his illegitimate cousin Cesare, husband of Ferdinando I's half-sister Virginia. Unfortunately, Ferrara was a papal fief, and Clement VIII refused to recognize the succession, making it clear that he intended to seize the duchy by force. The grand duke was in a difficult position, but he chose not to intervene to help his brother-in-law when, on 12 January 1598, papal troops captured Ferrara. Cesare and Virginia were compelled to leave the duchy that had been governed by the Este family for more than 300 years. Cesare had to make do with his title of Duke of Modena, an Imperial fief, and on 30 January he made his formal entry into what was now his new capital.

Meanwhile in France, in his efforts to bring peace to that kingdom, Cardinal Alessandro pragmatically agreed to the Edict of Nantes signed by Henri IV on 13 April 1598, which granted toleration to Protestants and ended almost four decades of religious wars. The cardinal and Ferdinando I persuaded a reluctant Clement VIII that allowing heretics the freedom to worship was the only way that Henri IV could impose his authority in his realm. Cardinal Alessandro also presided over peace talks between Henri IV and Philip II, after the Spanish king had been forced to the negotiating table by a bankrupt treasury, and it was largely thanks to his efforts that the two monarchs finally signed a treaty at Vervins, on 2 May.

In 1599, with Henri IV securely in power in France, Ferdinando I embarked on the ambitious finale of his international project: a royal marriage for the Medici. Although his own daughters Eleonora and Caterina were too young, the grand duke proposed that Henri IV should marry his niece Maria, the youngest daughter of his late brother Francesco I and Joanna of Austria. There were, though, several difficulties in the way, not least the fact that Henri IV already had a wife – Marguerite of Valois, the daughter of Henri II and Catherine de'

Medici. But Ferdinando I could count on papal support for annulling this union, as Clement VIII was keen to consolidate the king's new Catholic faith with a wife from a family that had always been loyal to Rome. Ferdinando could also tempt Henri IV with an immense dowry of 700,000 *scudi*, some of which would be used to repay the massive financial debt that the king owed to the grand duke. On 17 December 1599, Clement VIII duly annulled Henri IV's first marriage; and four months later, just four days after her twenty-fourth birthday, Maria was betrothed to Henri IV.

For much of the summer of 1600, Ferdinando I was busy with preparations for the wedding, determined to spend whatever was necessary on a display appropriate for this regal match. On 5 October, Maria's coach arrived at the Duomo, its façade ornamented for the occasion with huge paintings recounting the histories of Florence and France. Dressed in a white and gold gown, embroidered with '1,500 diamonds, 600 rubies and an enormous quantity of pearls', the bride was attended by her ten-year-old nephew Cosimo, her sister Eleonora (Duchess of Mantua) and her cousin Flavia Peretti (Duchess of Bracciano, the wife of Virginio Orsini, Ferdinando's nephew).[25] The nuptial mass was celebrated by the papal legate, a mark of the importance that Clement VIII attached to the union.

After the ceremony, the guests retired to the Palazzo Ducale, where Ferdinando I hosted a magnificent banquet for the new queen in the great hall. The bridal table was set under a canopy made of cloth-of-gold and 'the sideboards were laden with linen, dishes and bowls made of crystal, lapis-lazuli, amethyst, heliotrope, agate, sardonyx and other precious stones, and many statues of silver'.[26] The menu, cooked by Ferdinando's head chef with the assistance of three Frenchmen, consisted of fifty-four dishes designed to amuse the eyes as well as satisfy the stomach: veal pies in the form of unicorns and dragons; castles made of salami; pies filled with live birds; and, most sensationally, turkeys dressed to look like hydras, the multi-headed monsters of classical mythology. The following night, 6 October, there was a performance of Jacopo Peri's *Euridice*, a musical spectacular of *intermezzi*, based on a libretto by Ottavio Rinuccini. It was the first staging of a drama told completely in musical form – and the Florentines would claim it, not uncontroversially, as the first opera. On 17 October, Maria – or Marie de' Medici, as she would henceforth be known – left for

Agnolo Bronzino, *Marie de' Medici as a Girl*, 1551 (Florence, Uffizi).

Marseilles, accompanied by a fleet of Tuscan galleys commanded by Don Giovanni, and celebrated her marriage again, this time with Henri IV, in Lyons Cathedral on 17 December. And ten months later, news arrived that Marie de' Medici had given birth to an heir to the French throne, Louis, on 27 September 1601.

When Pope Clement VIII died in March 1605, Ferdinando I was able to use his influence in the conclave to ensure the election of Cardinal Alessandro on 1 April. Once again, a Medici occupied the Vatican. The new pope chose the name 'Leo XI' in honour of the first member of the family to sit on the throne of St Peter's; but this third Medici pontificate was to prove very short-lived. Leo XI fell ill shortly after his coronation and died before the end of the month. The second conclave that year ended on 16 May, when Camillo Borghese was elected and became Paul V.

Ferdinando I now sought to balance his ties to France with an Imperial alliance. In 1607 he opened negotiations with Archduke Charles of Austria, the brother of the Emperor, for the betrothal of his son Cosimo to the archduke's daughter Maria Magdalena. The marriage took place by proxy at Graz on 14 September 1608, and the bride left Austria a week later for the long journey south. Once again, in Florence the grand-ducal artists, musicians and cooks all displayed their talents, as they welcomed the nineteen-year-old Maria Magdalena. She made her entry into the city on 18 October and was crowned by Ferdinando I in a magnificent ceremony at the Porta al Prato. That evening, there was a banquet in the great hall of the Palazzo Ducale, where the tables were decorated with forty huge sugar sculptures and napkins ingeniously folded to resemble various animals. Several days of celebrations followed – a *calcio* match, the annual distribution of dowries to poor girls, theatrical entertainments, a procession of the Knights of St Stephen, an equestrian ballet, and more besides. The highlight of the festivities was a performance of *Jason and the Golden Fleece*, which took place on the Arno with a fleet of gilded gondolas dramatically capturing their prize from an elegant temple built on an artificial island in the middle of the river.

Giambologna, *Equestrian monument of Ferdinando I*, 1608
(Florence, Piazza della Santissima Annunziata).

In addition to these lavish but ephemeral celebrations, Ferdinando I also spent liberally on more permanent projects designed to transform Florence into a setting of Medici splendour. According to a list of his annual expenditure, the grand duke's outlay included 200,000 *scudi* on his castles and fortifications, 36,000 *scudi* in salaries to his courtiers, 12,000 *scudi* for his wardrobe expenses, 15,000 *scudi* on his stables, and 1,000 *scudi* for the upkeep of his lions and other wild animals. 'He spends more than 12,000 *scudi* on ornamenting buildings, and commissions various projects from different craftsmen, particularly works in marble, casting bronze statues and other like things, which are highly esteemed by foreign visitors, and his Highness sends gifts to different places which earn him great praise and reputation.'[27] For example, on 4 October 1608, just ten days before Maria Magdalena's entry, Giambologna's imposing bronze equestrian statue of the grand duke was unveiled in the Piazza Santissima Annunziata, made from melted-down cannons captured from the Turks at the Battle of Bona. Among his lavish presents were costly portraits of Henri IV and Clement VIII composed of inlaid semi-precious stones, produced in his *pietre dure* factory at the Casino Mediceo, and which were sent to France and Rome (around 1600). Neither did he stint on the family villas, laying out splendid gardens at Petraia and starting work on La Ferdinanda, a hunting lodge at Artimino, in the hills south of Poggio a Caiano.

With the Medici regime securely established, it was no longer necessary to rely on the family's fifteenth-century achievements. Instead, Ferdinando I promoted his father as the founder of the dynasty, placing statues and busts of Cosimo I on buildings across the city and decorating the great hall of his palace with scenes of Cosimo's life, culminating in his coronation as grand duke. Ferdinando also commissioned a great bronze equestrian statue of his father, which was unveiled in the Piazza Ducale in 1595 and judged by Lapini to be 'beautiful and marvellous'. In 1604, Ferdinando began work on his most ambitious project, the Cappella dei Principi (Chapel of the Princes) at San Lorenzo, the third Medici chapel at the family church and another project designed by his half-brother Don Giovanni. It was intended to contain the tombs of himself and his successors. An inordinately grandiose statement of Medici dynastic prestige, this family mausoleum was clad in marble and semi-precious stones and ornamented with inlaid *pietre dure* coats-of-arms of all the major cities of Tuscany. Yet, as a visible symbol of the what the future would hold in store, it remained – and remains – unfinished.

Ferdinando I died on 3 February 1609 at the age of fifty-eight. In his will, he requested that the huge sum usually spent on grand-ducal funerals was to be donated instead to the fund he had set up for the distribution of dowries. He had done much to stabilize the Medici regime. While decades of warfare had drained the coffers of both France and Spain, thanks to Ferdinando I's economic policies Tuscany was comparatively prosperous. He had continued to enhance the reputation of the Medici as famous patrons of the arts. Above all, though the future of the dynasty had been uncertain when he had succeeded as grand duke, he left four sons. And he had used his diplomatic talents to give the Medici real prestige: his own choice of wife ensured that his successor as grand duke could claim royal ancestry as the great-grandson of Henri II of France; and the new grand duchess was niece of the Emperor, while Ferdinando's own niece was now Queen of France.

19

THE UNLUCKY PRINCE

Cosimo II, Christine of Lorraine and

Maria Magdalena of Austria

1609–1628

Grand Duke Cosimo II (19)
Maria Magdalena of Austria (20), *his wife*

    Maria Cristina (0), *their daughter*

Christine of Lorraine (44), *his widowed mother*

Don Giovanni (42), *his uncle, half-brother of his father*

His seven siblings
Eleonora (18)
Caterina (16)
Francesco (15)
Carlo (14)
Lorenzo (10)
Maria Maddalena (9)
Claudia (5)

Marie de' Medici (34), *his cousin*

    Three of their children
    Louis (8)
    Elisabeth (7)
    Gaston (1)

Grand Duke Cosimo II inherited a peaceful, stable and prosperous state as well as a level of international prestige that was the envy of other Italian dynasties. Three months short of his nineteenth birthday at his succession, he was an amiable character and a keen huntsman, with the Medici taste for culture. He ensured that Florence's fame as a centre of excellence in music, theatre, literature and the visual arts continued to flourish – and three years later, in 1612, the Accademia della Crusca published the first edition of its famous dictionary of the Tuscan language. Cosimo II was also fascinated by the innovations taking place in the sciences. One of his first acts was to appoint his old tutor, Galileo, as Philosopher and Mathematician-in-Chief at the grand-ducal court. Yet, though he was young, Cosimo's health was not good, for he was in the early stages of tuberculosis, and he would rely heavily on the political acumen of his mother, Christine of Lorraine. She encouraged her son to continue Ferdinando I's policies of promoting economic growth, of fighting the Turks and of maintaining good relations with France, the Empire and Spain.

There was another strong-willed woman in Cosimo II's life – his wife Maria Magdalena of Austria, whose position at court became increasingly prominent as she gave birth to a succession of sons. On 14 July 1610, less than a year after the arrival of her first child Maria Cristina, she produced an heir, whom the grand-ducal couple named Ferdinando after Cosimo's father. A third child arrived in June 1611, another son, who was named Gian Carlo after her father Archduke Charles, followed by Margherita (May 1612); Mattias (May 1613); Francesco (October 1614), named after Cosimo II's brother, who died that year at the age of twenty; Anna (July 1616), and finally Leopoldo (November 1617): a total of five sons and three daughters in just nine years of marriage.

One of Cosimo II's first duties was to find husbands for his sisters. The youngest, Claudia, had been betrothed to Federigo Ubaldo della Rovere, heir to Duke Francesco Maria II of Urbino, shortly before Ferdinando I's death. Both the bride and groom were small children, and they would not actually marry until 1621. Maria Maddalena, who was severely disabled, would never marry; but the other two, Eleonora and Caterina, with their royal connections and large dowries, were tempting prizes. And Cosimo II had ambitious plans for them: Duke Carlo Emanuele of Savoy, a widower, and Henry, Prince of Wales, the eighteen-year-old heir to the Protestant King James I of England (James VI of Scotland). Early in 1612, Cosimo reached an agreement with James for the betrothal of Caterina and Henry, insisting that in return for her handsome dowry Caterina and her court must be able to continue to worship as Catholics. Cosimo sent his uncle, Don Giovanni, to Rome to obtain papal approval; but Paul V remained unconvinced by the argument that this union would improve the chances of England returning to the Catholic fold and refused his consent, threatening Cosimo II with severe sanctions if he insisted on pursuing the project. As it turned out, the project fell through for a quite different reason in November 1612, when the Prince of Wales died of typhoid.

Cosimo II's plans for Eleonora also ran into difficulties. The protracted marriage negotiations finally broke down in 1615, after Duke Carlo Emanuele insisted that Eleonora's dowry should include several territories belonging to the Duke of Mantua and to France, which would then be added to the Duchy of Savoy. It was a ludicrous demand, and Cosimo II withdrew. He then offered Eleonora as a bride to Philip III of Spain, another widower, who had succeeded to the throne of Spain in 1598. Cosimo was still awaiting a decision from Madrid when Eleonora herself died in 1617.

Caterina, meanwhile, had been betrothed to Ferdinando I, Duke of Mantua. This was not the royal match for which Cosimo had hoped, but it was prestigious nonetheless. The negotiations were complicated by Duke Ferdinando's secret marriage to one of his mother's ladies-in-waiting – which he swore had never happened. Christine of Lorraine insisted that the mistress be locked up in a convent before her daughter's marriage could take place.

Ferdinando I's goal of ensuring that the Medici had close ties with all the major European powers was proving something of a headache for his son. In France, in May 1610, the year after Cosimo II's accession, Henri IV was assassinated by a Catholic fanatic, leaving Marie de' Medici acting as regent for her young son Louis XIII. The Florentine court went into mourning, and Cosimo's artists started work painting the twenty-six scenes of Henri IV's triumphs and the series of gigantic skeletons that were to decorate San Lorenzo for the lavish obsequies held in September. Henri IV's death shattered the fragile peace between Bourbon France and the Habsburg powers of Spain and the Empire, and it was not until 1612, with the grand-ducal ambassadors playing their part in the negotiations, that the two sides finally agreed a treaty. Then, much to the relief of Cosimo II, Philip III and Marie de' Medici cemented their alliance with two betrothals: Louis XIII was to marry Philip's daughter, Anne of Austria, while the French king's sister Elisabeth was to marry Infante Philip, heir to the Spanish throne.

Cosimo II's relations with France became increasingly complicated after 1617, when the fifteen-year-old Louis XIII, frustrated by Marie de' Medici's refusal to allow him to make his own decisions, seized power. The young king then imprisoned his mother in the royal château at Blois, sacked her chief minister and ordered the assassination of Concino Concini, a Florentine who had been part of her court since her marriage. Placed in a difficult situation, Cosimo II agreed to Louis XIII's request to confiscate Concini's Tuscan estates; but he continued, in secret, to pay the allowance his father had given to the dowager queen and instructed his ambassadors to do all they could to mediate in the bitter dispute between mother and son.

After two years of house-arrest at Blois, the intrepid Marie de' Medici, now forty-four years old, managed a daring night-time escape by climbing out of a first-floor window of the château, carrying just her jewel box.* Though Louis XIII and his mother were formally reconciled a month after the escape, it took some time for friendly relations to be restored.

By this time, the political situation in Europe had worsened dramatically with the outbreak of the Thirty Years' War in 1618, following the murder of two Catholic ministers of the King of Bohemia – Cosimo II's brother-in-law, Ferdinand – who were thrown out of a window of his castle on 23 May by a Protestant mob: the event known as the Defenestration of Prague. Once again, the Empire was divided by the rival religions, and although the fighting was largely confined to central Europe, most of the continent's rulers were involved. Cosimo II himself was drawn into the conflict in 1619, when Maria Magdalena of

---

* She later included this event in the famous cycle of scenes from her life which she commissioned from Pieter Paul Rubens to decorate the Palais de Luxembourg, her residence in Paris, which she had modelled on the Palazzo Pitti.

Pieter Paul Rubens, *The Return of Marie de' Medici to her son, Louis XIII*,
1622–5 (Paris, Louvre).

Austria's brother succeeded as Emperor Ferdinand II. Under pressure from his wife, the grand duke was now obliged to send funds to Vienna for the recruitment of a regiment.

Cosimo II also had problems in his relations with Rome, where the death of his cousin, Cardinal Alessandro, shortly after his election as Leo XI in 1605, had left the Medici without a representative at the papal court. The new pope, Paul V, did not rectify this situation until 1615, when he gave a red hat to Cosimo II's younger brother Carlo: with an income of 70,000 *scudi* a year from the grand-ducal coffers, this new Prince of the Church would become an influential figure in Rome. Meanwhile, Cosimo II's decision to aid his brother-in-law, the Emperor, was unpopular with Paul V, who had ordered the Italian princes to maintain a neutral stance towards the war north of the Alps.

Another issue incurring papal disapproval was Cosimo II's patronage of Galileo, especially after the scientist's work came to the attention of the Inquisition. An ardent supporter of Galileo, Cosimo ordered his ambassadors in Rome, Madrid, Paris, Prague and London to send the astronomer any information he requested regarding scientific developments in these capital cities. Cosimo also hosted regular meetings with Galileo and other learned men to debate scientific issues – including the contentious theory, advanced in 1543 by the Polish astronomer Nicolaus Copernicus, that the sun was the centre of the universe. The idea that the earth was not the focus of God's universe appalled conservatives in the Catholic Church. In 1610, Galileo published his *Siderius nuncius* (*The Starry Messenger*), which he dedicated to Cosimo II. In it, he announced his discovery of four satellites of Jupiter, which he had found using his own adaptation of the recently invented telescope, and which he had named 'the Medici stars' in honour of Cosimo II and his brothers. His observations, that it was not just the earth around which celestial bodies orbited, lent significant support to Copernicus's ideas. By the end of 1613, the debate over 'heliocentrism' had become very heated in Florence, where several preachers sniffed heresy and vociferously denounced the theory in their Advent sermons.

The issue was debated at the grand-ducal dining-table that December, when the guests included the Professor of Mathematics at Pisa University, a pupil of Galileo. As he related to Galileo, 'last Thursday I dined at their Highnesses' table... and the grand duke asked me... whether I had a telescope and I answered that I had and gave an account of my observation of the Medicean planets the preceding night'.[1] Another guest, the professor continued, had told Christine of Lorraine that he did not believe in these 'celestial novelties', arguing that it was impossible for the earth to move around the sun 'for the reason that Holy Scripture was manifestly contrary to it'. After dinner, Christine of Lorraine, torn between admiration for Galileo's genius and her own deeply held religious beliefs, invited the professor to join her in her private apartments: 'I entered Her Highness's apartments where the grand duke and duchess were present,' he continued, 'and, after a few inquiries as to my condition in life, she began to argue against me with the help of the Holy Scripture; and I, after making a proper protest, began a theological exposition in such a masterly way that you would have been delighted to hear me.'

While Cosimo II and Maria Magdalena were persuaded by the professor's words, Christine of Lorraine remained unconvinced. Galileo wrote to her, setting out his reasons for believing that heliocentrism was compatible with Church doctrine, and then published an expanded version of the correspondence, *Letter to the Grand Duchess*, in 1615. Paul V condemned Galileo's views as heresy, and, although the astronomer was not called before the Inquisition at this stage, he was ordered to abstain from teaching his beliefs. While Christine of Lorraine and other pious Catholics followed the Church line, the topic continued to be debated among the learned Florentines at Cosimo's court.

Under Cosimo II, that court became increasingly grandiose. He kept his artists, musicians and dramatists, even his cooks, busy producing the elaborate ephemera that accompanied the plays, operas, lavish banquets, tournaments and hunting parties he held to entertain his court. Florence was acquiring its own aristocracy as the grand duke handed out noble titles to the city's old mercantile families, investing them as dukes and marquises in grand ceremonies in the Palazzo Pitti. In 1616, he announced a competition for the enlargement of the palace. The winner, Giulio Parigi, extended the facade by six bays to create a magnificently grand sight – and the Palazzo Pitti now replaced the Palazzo Ducale as the official grand-ducal residence. Cosimo II also began work on a sumptuous new suburban villa (later, Poggio Imperiale) in the hills just south of Florence and expanded the Medici art collection with works imported from across Europe. In 1620, he appointed Justus Sustermans as his court painter. The artist moved from Antwerp

Overleaf: Jan van der Straet, *Jousting in Piazza Santa Croce*, 1561–2 (Florence, Palazzo Vecchio, apartments of Eleonora of Toledo).

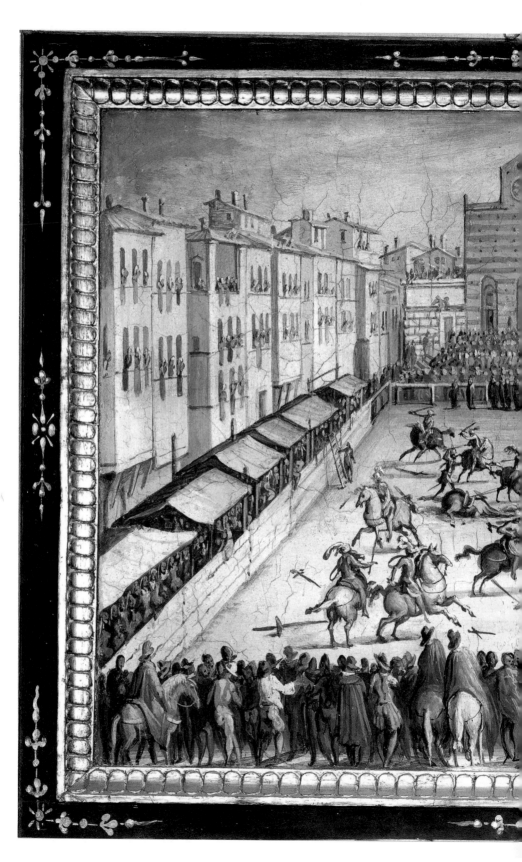

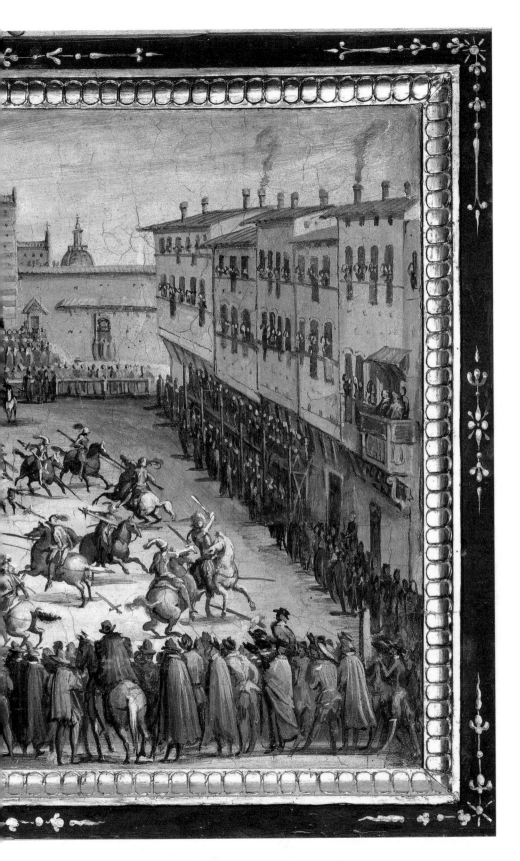

to Florence, where he spent the rest of his life producing quantities of Medici portraits.

Cosimo II spent liberally in Livorno, too, which was fast becoming an important international port. By 1620, the city's population had reached 10,000, double the size it had been when Cosimo came to power. He built an extension to the harbour walls to improve security and commissioned the sculptor Pietro Tacca to add four bronze statues of chained African slaves to the base of the statue of Ferdinando I, erected by his father, which overlooked the wharves. Cosimo II encouraged immigration by offering concessions to foreign merchants and a safe haven for Jews, Muslims, Protestants and others suffering religious persecution in their own countries. In 1611 he took in 3,000 Muslims who had been expelled from Spain by Philip III – though he soon regretted his generosity after several violent incidents, and they were deported to Africa. He also built a new residential quarter in Livorno for the Knights of St Stephen, who continued their successful attacks

Garden façade of the Palazzo Pitti, Florence, begun 1560.

on Turkish pirates in the Mediterranean. More successful in his actions against the Turks than in his forays into the politics of mainland Europe, the grand duke was careful to instruct his ambassadors to trumpet these achievements abroad.

Livorno may have been flourishing, but the economy in the rest of Tuscany was becoming less prosperous. Thanks to decades of war and a succession of poor harvests, much of Europe was suffering an economic decline. Florence was particularly hard hit as her high quality silk and wool textile industries were unable to compete with cheaper foreign manufacturers in northern countries, notably Holland and England. Cosimo II did take measures to stem the decline in agriculture: he set up a commission to find ways of increasing production; he also began work on a new grain market in Florence and built a canal to facilitate the transport of crops from the farmlands of southern Tuscany. Unfortunately, his generous grants of estates to his new dukes and marquises meant that much of the land that had once been farmed now lay fallow, to provide for hunting parks and other aristocratic pleasures. In the city, poverty was beginning to become a serious problem. When a severe typhus epidemic broke out in 1620, adding to the miseries of the economic depression, Cosimo II ordered an inspection of the living conditions of the poor; his officials reported cellars filled with rotting waste and rubbish, and wells contaminated by sewage.

Cosimo II's own health problems were not improving. His tuberculosis was exacerbated by stomach troubles, and he spent much of the time in bed, leaving his government increasingly in the hands of his privy council and members of his family, not least his uncle, Don Giovanni, and the two women in his life, his mother and wife. Around 1617, desperate for a cure, he commissioned an extravagant *pietre dure* plaque ornamented with gold, jasper, lapis-lazuli and more than 250 diamonds, showing him kneeling in prayer at the altar of the recently canonized St Carlo Borromeo. He intended to send this ex-voto image to the saint's chapel in Milan Cathedral once his prayers were answered and he was restored to health.

That restoration never came. Cosimo II died before the plaque was finished, succumbing to the tuberculosis on 28 February 1621, at the age of just thirty. Later that year, his brother Cardinal Carlo, who had inherited the Casino Mediceo near San Marco according to the terms of Cosimo's will, commissioned a huge cycle of forty-five frescoes of Medici history to decorate five rooms of the palace, one each dedicated to Cosimo I, Francesco I and Ferdinando I, and two to the short life of his brother. The artists celebrated Cosimo II's achievements against the Turks in one room and his enlightened patronage of the arts and sciences in the other, in scenes depicting Cosimo II paying homage to allegorical figures of Music, Poetry, Sculpture and Painting as well as Astronomy – the last holding Galileo's telescope to the sky, to show the grand duke the Medici stars.

Cosimo's son and heir, Ferdinando II, was only ten years old at his father's death. Anticipating this situation, Cosimo had appointed his mother and wife to act as regents until the new grand duke came of age. The two women celebrated their role in a group portrait, painted by Sustermans, showing Florentine senators paying homage to their new young ruler, flanked by the stern figures of his mother and grandmother, both dressed in black with widow's caps on their heads. These formidable women would have a decisive impact on the future of the Medici family, and it was unfortunate – to say the least – that, in the context of the Thirty Years' War, they were on opposing sides of the political divide. Christine of Lorraine, who had played an important role in nurturing the foreign policy of both her husband and son, was an ally of France; while Cosimo's widow Maria Magdalena, being the sister of Emperor Ferdinand II, had the greater political clout. One of Maria Magdalena's first acts was to take over the new grand-ducal villa under construction behind the Palazzo Pitti and to rename it Poggio Imperiale; she also decorated it with paintings commemorating her powerful Imperial Habsburg ancestors, including Maximilian I and Charles V, while the life of her Medici husband was relegated to small scenes in the ceiling.

The regents may have differed on the direction of foreign policy, but they were united in their devotion to the Catholic Church. Maria Magdalena, in particular, was an avid collector of relics, which she housed in a chapel built for the purpose in the Palazzo Pitti. Although they were not the religious bigots of popular legend, both women were staunch supporters of the Counter-Reformation, and they injected a new level of piety into the Medici regime. While Cosimo II and his predecessors had chosen their advisers on merit, the regents appointed ecclesiastics to administrative and judicial positions – even their court dramatists and musicians started composing operas on religious subjects. In Rome, an increasingly confident Catholic Church was spreading reform. Paul V had died a month before Cosimo II's death, and his successor, Gregory XV, who was the first Jesuit-trained pope, set up a congregation (*Propaganda Fide*) to oversee missionary work in Europe and the Far East; he also canonized many of the heroes of the Counter-Reformation, notably the prominent Jesuits Ignatius Loyola and Francis Xavier.

Gregory XV's successor, Urban VIII, was elected in 1623 with the support of Cardinal Carlo, and he continued to promote Church reform. His edicts banning beggars in Rome, along with 'dishonest women, their protectors and pimps', were echoed in Florence, where, under the regents, prostitutes were forbidden from visiting churches on feast days, on pain of a 10 *scudi* fine for the first offence and 25 *scudi* for further infringements.[2] The regents also increased the powers of the Inquisition at Santa Croce and encouraged religious orders to move to the city: out of a population of 66,056 inhabitants counted in a census of 1622, there were 916 friars and 4,001 nuns.[3] All clergy and members of religious orders were exempt from taxation, so as their numbers grew they added considerably to Florence's financial woes, burdening the rest of the increasingly impoverished population.

The economic slump that had started at the beginning of the century continued to worsen, exacerbated by poor harvests and famine. Florence's regents did little to halt the decline, prioritising the spiritual health of their subjects over the economic health of the duchy, and, as unemployment rose, so did the quantities of beggars on the streets. While some believed that it was their Christian duty to give alms to the poor, many others demonized the beggars, using the timeless argument that they were to blame for their condition. Following the lead of the pope, the regents decided that forcible confinement of beggars was necessary to maintain civic order and to dissuade others from leaving their low-paid jobs to seek charity on the streets. They were also ruthless in punishing those who resorted to criminality to survive: one man's unduly harsh death-sentence for petty theft was commuted following intercession with the regents by his friends – but he was still doomed to a life-sentence on the galleys.

In spite of the growing poverty around them on the streets, the regents continued to live in style at the Palazzo Pitti, spending extravagantly on the trappings of power that they believed befitted their royal lineage. In a telling sign of her priorities, Maria Magdalena, advising her son Mattias on how to behave while making a trip away from court, told him to choose the company of 'people who are known for the nobility of their blood', as well as to obey the Jesuits who accompanied him, avoid playing cards, and be assiduous in his religious observances.[4] Christine of Lorraine sent her disabled daughter, Maria Maddalena, to the convent of the Crocetta where, as she was unable to climb staircases, special ramps were installed in her rooms, as well as a grate through which she could watch the nuns saying mass – she was later joined by her niece, Maria Cristina, Ferdinando II's eldest sister, who also seems to have been disabled.

While the widow and mother of Cosimo II exercised power, Ferdinando and his siblings continued their education in the Palazzo Pitti under the watchful eye of the regents, who placed much emphasis on their religious instruction and insisted that they spoke both French and German as well as study Latin, history, geography, mathematics and astrology. According to the tutor employed to teach the last two subjects – a priest who had been one of Galileo's pupils – Ferdinando displayed a particular talent for the sciences. After his fourteenth birthday on 14 July 1624, the regents grudgingly permitted the shy grand duke to sit in on meetings of government committees; but they refused him access to the regency council, the real seat of power.

The two women were also making plans to control the teenager's future, notably in the choice of a wife. But here politics intervened, for they found it impossible to agree on a suitable bride for Ferdinando II. As the Thirty Years' War raged, Christine of Lorraine was stoutly opposed to a Habsburg princess, while Maria Magdalena of Austria was equally determined that her son should not be married into the royal house of France. In the end, they compromised by betrothing the grand duke to his first cousin Vittoria della Rovere, the baby child of Federigo della Rovere and Claudia, the youngest daughter of Christine of Lorraine. Vittoria was a far cry from the royal brides chosen for

Ferdinando's predecessors; but in June 1623 she had become the heiress to the Duchy of Urbino after the death of her father, and the regents anticipated that this small state would become part of Tuscany when Duke Francesco Maria II della Rovere, a man in his seventies, eventually died.

The betrothal was announced in September 1623, and the eighteen-month-old Vittoria returned to Florence with her mother, to be educated under the care of her grandmother. Unfortunately, the regents had seriously underestimated the political guile of Pope Urban VIII. In April the following year, he persuaded Francesco Maria II to sign a treaty leaving Urbino, which was a papal fief, to the Church on his death. Despite engineering Urban VIII's election a year earlier, all Cardinal Carlo could secure for the Medici family was the magnificent collection of tapestries, jewels and paintings assembled by dukes of Urbino over the previous two centuries.

When it came to choosing another marriage partner – this time a second husband for Vittoria's mother Claudia – Maria Magdalena won the battle with Christine of Lorraine. In 1625, the twenty-two-year-old widow was betrothed to Leopold V, Archduke of Austria, who was Maria Magdalena's brother. The groom arrived in Florence on 5 January 1526 for the wedding, which had been timed to coincide with Carnival, and it was celebrated with the usual Medici pomp in festivities that included balls, banquets, hunts and theatrical and musical entertainments, as well as the usual Carnival parties. When Claudia left for Innsbruck with her husband, she left Vittoria behind, and Christine of Lorraine sent the four-year-old to join her disabled aunt and cousin at the convent of the Crocetta for her education.* Maria Magdalena's rising star was also evident when she quashed a plan proposed by her mother-in-law and Marie de' Medici to betroth one of Ferdinando II's sisters, Margherita or Anna, to Gaston, Duke of Orléans, the younger brother of Louis XIII and heir presumptive to the French throne.

There was less fuss about the choice of a husband for Maria Magdalena's daughters. In 1628, the sixteen-year-old Margherita was betrothed to Odoardo Farnese, Duke of Parma. The marriage took place in Florence on 9 December, and the court hosted several weeks of festivities. There was a high-brow opera, *Flora*, extolling the glories

---

* It was the customary that a wife did not take the children of her first marriage to the home of her second husband.

of Florence in the language of classical mythology, and more light-hearted entertainment at Villa Poggio Imperiale, where the guests watched dancers dressed as peasants capering around the grounds. There was also a dramatic mock battle in the form of an elaborately choreographed equestrian ballet, *The Challenge of Ismen*, in the gardens of the Palazzo Pitti.

By the time this latest Medici wedding took place, Ferdinando II had reached his majority. In February 1628, the regents sent him and his brother Gian Carlo on a tour of European courts, and the teenagers visited Urban VIII in Rome, before going on to Ferrara and Venice, and then Prague, where they were affectionately received by their uncle, Emperor Ferdinand II. During his travels, in July Ferdinando celebrated his eighteenth birthday – and in August 1628, on his return from Prague, he formally took over the reins of power from his mother and grandmother.

His father's short reign had bequeathed Ferdinando II a state that, at least initially, was largely prosperous and tranquil; but Cosimo II's choice of regents had been disastrous, for their policy of prioritizing the Church at the expense of the economy marked the start of Florence's financial decline. Furthermore, their decision to marry Ferdinando to his cousin Vittoria della Rovere would have far-reaching implications for the Medici dynasty. Under Christine of Lorraine and Maria Magdalena, the Medici began their descent from splendour into decadence. And the luck that had accompanied the family's meteoric rise to power in the previous century would now vanish.

20

SCIENCE AND RELIGION

Ferdinando II

1628–1670

Grand Duke Ferdinando II (18)

Christine of Lorraine (63), *his grandmother*

Maria Magdalena of Austria (39), *his mother*

His siblings:
Maria Cristina (19), *in a convent*
Gian Carlo (17)
Margherita (16), *Duchess of Parma*
Mattias (15)
Francesco (14)
Anna (12)
Leopoldo (11)

His uncles and aunts:
Cardinal Carlo (33)
Lorenzo (29)
Maria Maddalena (28), *in a convent*
Claudia (24), *Archduchess of Austria*
Ferdinand II (50), *Emperor*

His cousins:
Vittoria della Rovere (6), *his fiancée*
Marie de' Medici (53), *Queen Mother of France*

> Louis XIII, *King of France (26), her son*
> Gaston, *Duke of Orléans (20), her son*

Ferdinando II was good-natured and highly intelligent, but he came of age at a difficult time. For most of his reign, Europe would be torn apart by war: between Catholics and Protestants in the Empire, between Spain and its rebellious subjects in the Netherlands, and above all between the rival powers of Bourbon France and Habsburg Spain. Unfortunately, Ferdinando lacked the strength of character to exploit this complex political situation, and he found it hard to assert his own personality in the privy council, where his redoubtable mother and grandmother still held sway. Although he took his duties as ruler seriously, he much preferred scientific experiment to family argument, and he was a keen amateur scientist.

By Medici standards, he was also a frugal man. According to the English diarist, John Evelyn, who was in Florence in 1644, he put his own surplus wine up for sale at the door of the Palazzo Pitti, a habit that did much to bolster his popularity in a city where poverty was growing at an alarming rate. By now, cloth production in Florence, once one of the richest cities in Europe, had declined dramatically. In 1575 the city's factories were producing 33,000 pieces a year, but by the middle of the seventeenth century the figure had fallen to 6,000, thanks largely to the restrictive practices of the guilds that left the industry unable to compete with cheaper goods manufactured in England and Holland. Although reluctant to take on the formidable task of reforming the guilds, Ferdinando II did take measures to help the poor. He asked his ministers to report on living conditions in Florence, and they warned him that there were 'many houses where, because of misery, there is not even the comfort of a bed, people sleeping on a little uncovered and filthy straw, and some others have foul and stinking straw mattresses'.[1] Among other measures he took, he set up a fund to help the unemployed, to which he donated 3,000 *scudi* a month, and he loaned 40,000 *scudi* to the Silk Guild on condition that it provide work for 800 people.[2]

Money was so scarce that it was hard to find work even as a servant in the palaces of the nobility. As many as 2,500 Florentines, some 4 per cent of the population, were in the hospitals catering for paupers, abandoned children or the sick: this was almost twice the proportion as that in Venice.[3] Foreign visitors were shocked at the size of the crowds begging for alms at church doors and to see the numbers of women forced to earn a living on the street. Worried about the threat of civic violence, Ferdinando II erected marble plaques across the city to remind his subjects of the laws banning unruly behaviour. 'Every person is prohibited from gambling of any sort, making a noise or uproar or urinating within forty yards of the church of San Silvestro under pain of a fine of two *scudi*,' read one notices, 'and prostitutes and dishonest women of any sort are prohibited to stand or live within sixty-six yards of the said church under pain of 25 *scudi*.'[4]

Ferdinando's sense of duty came to the fore in the autumn of 1630, when Florence was hit by an outbreak of bubonic plague that raged for six months and killed more than 7,000 people, some 10 per cent of the inhabitants. He took personal charge of the emergency, imposing a quarantine on the city, and ordering all shops and businesses to close and all citizens to remain inside their houses for forty days (the *quarantenaria*). Church doors were locked, and priests were directed to say mass on the deserted streets to comfort those listening behind their shuttered windows. The grand duke organized teams to remove corpses and to fumigate the houses of plague victims; and he turned the magnificent gilded rooms of his fortresses and villas into hospital wards, paying salaries to those doctors who were prepared to care for the sick. While the rich fled to their country estates, Ferdinando insisted on remaining in his stricken capital, where, despite the danger, 'he went out into the city every day on foot', according to Gian Carlo.[5] Among those who died was the Archbishop of Florence, who had also remained behind with his flock.

Regrettably for the Medici, Ferdinando II was less decisive in protecting the interests of his family. He acquiesced with hardly a murmur in April 1631 when Urban VIII annexed the Duchy of Urbino after the death of Duke Francesco Maria II, Ferdinando's prospective father-in-law. With both Christine of Lorraine and Maria Magdalena piously obedient to papal policy, Ferdinando backed away from this chance to add the duchy's revenues of 300,000 *scudi* a year to his own depleted coffers.[6] He was equally weak in his dealings with his uncle, Emperor Ferdinand II. While fighting the French in northern Italy, the Imperial army brutally sacked the city of Mantua, and Ferdinando II meekly paid the 500,000 ducats demanded by the Emperor for the campaign, fearful that Florence would otherwise suffer the same fate. Despite his intention of remaining neutral in the Habsburg–Bourbon conflict, Ferdinando submitted to his mother's desire to establish two of his four

Titian, *Venus of Urbino*, 1538 (Florence, Uffizi); just one of the many Renaissance masterpieces that came to Florence as part of the dowry of Vittoria della Rovere.

brothers at the Imperial court. In 1631, Mattias and Francesco left for Vienna along with Maria Magdalena – but the boys' mother died of a fever on the journey north. Both Mattias and Francesco would serve in the Imperial army fighting the Thirty Years' War, and four years later Francesco was dead too, from plague, at the Siege of Ratisbon.

It was not entirely Ferdinando II's fault that his influence at the major courts of Europe was on the wane. The death of Maria Magdalena coincided with unexpected events in France, where Louis XIII and his devious chief minister, Cardinal Richelieu, exiled the king's mother Marie de' Medici and declared many of Christine of Lorraine's relations to be rebels for joining a revolt against Louis. Just how far the Medici star had fallen was evident when Ferdinando's plans to marry his brother Gian Carlo to Anna Carafa, the daughter of a Neapolitan aristocrat, were scotched by Philip IV of Spain, who insisted on marrying the girl to a relative of his own chief minister, the Duke of Olivares. Gian Carlo was appointed Admiral of the Spanish fleet in recompense, but he resigned the post after a visit to Madrid, where he felt he had not received the honours due to his rank. He was not the only Medici to be touchy about his status, a telling sign of the family's declining fortunes. When Urban VIII issued a decree requiring all cardinals, regardless of their secular position, to use the title 'Eminence', Cardinal Carlo was outraged and refused to surrender his title of 'Highness', the proud mark of his membership of Europe's aristocratic elite.

Ferdinando II had his own quarrel with Urban VIII, over Galileo, who was living in Florence under the grand duke's protection. The scientist had survived the plague, fortified by the concoctions of his daughter, Sister Maria Celeste, who sent him a pot of 'very efficacious' medicine made from 'dried figs, walnuts, rue and salt mixed with honey' and advised him to eat a spoonful of it every morning.[7] An ardent admirer of Galileo, Ferdinando II had appointed him to his privy council and opened a school at Orsanmichele to enable poor pupils to be educated in Galilean mathematics. But trouble erupted in 1632, when Galileo published the *Dialogue*, his treatise on the solar system. The Inquisition ordered its confiscation – and Ferdinando was furious. On 24 August, his secretary wrote to Francesco Niccolini, the Florentine ambassador in Rome, demanding an explanation from Urban VIII: 'I have orders to inform your Excellency of His Highness's great surprise that a book, placed by the author himself in the hands of the supreme authority in Rome... in which everything... was amended, added or removed at their will... and which was finally licensed both here and there... should now become an object of suspicion.'[8] The official reason given was that it did not conform *exactly* to the original manuscript; but, as one Florentine in Rome suspected, 'this is the pretext; the real fact is that the Jesuits are working most valiantly in an underhand way to get the work banned'.[9] That autumn, the Inquisition summoned Galileo to Rome.

Against the advice of his grandmother, Ferdinando II stoutly refused to comply with the request and ordered Niccolini to make his views clear to Urban VIII. But the pragmatic ambassador advised caution in dealing with the stubborn pope, because 'making a great ado will only exasperate him and spoil everything'.[10] Early in 1633,

Ferdinando was forced to cave in to the demands of the Inquisition and agreed to send the scientist to Rome for trial. All he could do was make a very public statement of his support for Galileo, who left Florence on 20 January in a grand-ducal litter and was accommodated in Rome as a guest of Ambassador Niccolini at the embassy, the Villa Medici. Ever frugal, though, the grand duke refused to pay more than a month's living expenses for Galileo, so Niccolini had to pay for his guest out of his own pocket. On 22 June 1633, the Inquisition found Galileo guilty of heresy, forced him to recant his heliocentric beliefs and placed all his works on the Index of Forbidden Books. He was sentenced to life imprisonment.

The following day, Urban VIII commuted Galileo's sentence to house arrest at the Villa Medici, a much more salubrious spot than the dungeons of the Inquisition. Finally, in December 1633, after much lobbying on the part of Ferdinando II, the pope allowed Galileo to serve his sentence at his villa in Arcetri, just outside Florence, where, increasingly blind, he remained for the rest of his life, frequently visited by the grand duke. Some years later, in 1641, the English scientist Robert Boyle – another fan of Galileo – was in Florence and was shocked to meet churchmen who considered the astronomer's blindness as just punishment for his heretical beliefs. (Boyle also recorded the unpleasant experience of being 'somewhat rudely pressed by the preposterous courtship of two friars whose lust makes no distinction of sexes'.)[11] When Galileo died in January 1642, Ferdinando II's plans for a grand funeral for his hero were vetoed by the Inquisition.

Thanks to Ferdinando II's determined support for the famous astronomer, Florence still retained its reputation as a centre of intellectual excellence. Among the projects promoted by the grand duke was the publication of *Dell'arcano del mare* written by the English explorer, Sir Robert Dudley. Charting the coastlines of both the Atlantic and Pacific oceans, it was the first maritime atlas to appear in print, though this magnificent volume was not designed to be of use to a sea-captain but rather to provide Ferdinando II with gifts to impress foreign dignitaries. The grand duke also promoted the first edition of Galileo's printed collected works, a project in which Ferdinando's youngest brother Leopoldo played a leading role. Leopoldo, easily the cleverest of the brothers and an amateur scientist like Ferdinando, was also a member of the Accademia della Crusca, contributing important work

Giovanni Battista Foggini, *Cardinal Leopoldo de' Medici*, 1670 (Florence, Uffizi).

to the third edition of its dictionary. Famous across Europe for its championing of the Tuscan language, this Florentine institution inspired Cardinal Richelieu to set up the Académie Française in 1635.

Although the developing disciplines of science were in vogue at courts across seventeenth-century Europe, it is a little-known fact that the first scientific academy was founded in Florence, in 1657, thus pre-dating both the Royal Society in London (1662) and the Académie des Sciences in Paris (1663). Set up by Ferdinando II and Leopoldo, the Accademia del Cimento – literally 'Academy of Experiment' – was designed to develop the heritage of their hero, Galileo. Despite being keen to overturn the ban on his teachings, the brothers were wary of risking confrontation with the Church authorities and instead concentrated on his advances in physics – the nature of the vacuum, the effect of changing temperatures on fluids and metals, and so on – rather than his controversial astronomical theories. Ferdinando and Leopoldo took an active role in the academy's work, providing rooms in the Palazzo Pitti for laboratories and hosting its meetings, which took place wherever the court happened to be – in Florence or at one of the Medici villas, at Pisa (where the family celebrated the Christmas and New Year holiday), or Livorno (where they spent Lent), with its plentiful fish market.

The motto of the Accademia del Cimento was 'test and test again' (*provando e riprovando*). One of its experiments was to test the widespread belief that insects were generated spontaneously, so the academicians filled their laboratories in the Palazzo Pitti with lumps of decaying flesh, some covered and others open to the air.[12] The answer was the same every time: the flesh exposed to the air developed maggots, which turned into common flies, but none appeared on the covered specimens. So, the Cimenteans concluded, insects were like animals, birds and fish, born from eggs of the same species.

Despite his reputation for frugality, Ferdinando II continued to celebrate the rituals of court life with banquets, dances, music, dramas, jousts and other entertainments. A visitor to the Palazzo Pitti was full of praise for an amphitheatre in the Boboli gardens, shaded with laurels, which he thought was 'capable of two thousand men, who may

Giovanni da San Giovanni, *The Muses expelled from Parnassus*, 1635 (Florence, Palazzo Pitti).

all fit here with ease and behold the sports of cavalry which are often exhibited upon this fair green spot of ground by the nobility: the great duke and the court beholding all this from the windows of the palace while the rest of the nobility and ladies are seated conveniently in the amphitheatre under the trees'.[13] There were grand celebrations for the wedding of Ferdinando's sister Anna and Archduke Ferdinand of Austria in 1646. The couple were first cousins, and there was a large age gap – the groom was eighteen, while the bride was just short of her thirtieth birthday. Nevertheless, Anna gave birth to a daughter, Claudia, after seven years of marriage. Deaths too provided ceremonial opportunities: Ferdinando II held splendid obsequies in San Lorenzo for both his uncle, Emperor Ferdinand II, who died in 1637, and for his cousin, Emperor Ferdinand III, who died twenty years later. (The new Emperor Leopold I would later be betrothed to the baby Claudia.) This last ceremony lasted for three hours and was, according to an Englishman in the congregation, accompanied 'by the best voices and other music in Italy'.[14]

Giovanni da San Giovanni, *Lorenzo the Magnificent welcoming the Muses to Florence*, 1635 (Florence, Palazzo Pitti).

In other ways, the Medici enthusiastically contributed to the cultural life of Florence. Cardinal Carlo acquired a large collection of contemporary art and was the patron of several dramatic societies, as well as a keen huntsman and breeder of racehorses. Gian Carlo, a playboy who, after the failure of his marriage plans, devoted himself to a life of pleasure, was also a patron of theatrical societies and a collector of paintings, notably still-lives, landscapes and family portraits. Leopoldo, who gave his drama society its own theatre in the Palazzo Medici, wrote poetry and collected coins, stamps, prints and paintings; his collection of artists' self-portraits later formed the basis of the renowned display in the Uffizi corridor. More serious-minded than Gian Carlo or Ferdinando, Leopoldo amassed a famous library to which he allowed scholars free access: according to the grand-ducal librarian, it was one of the best in Florence, 'the largest in size, the most universal in variety and the most illustrious for the quality of the books he owns'.[15]

Ferdinando II embellished the Palazzo Pitti with two projects commemorating the Medici dynasty, though not ancestor cycles in the narrative style so beloved by earlier generations of the family. He commissioned Pietro da Cortona to decorate his apartments in the palace with the magnificent soaring Baroque ceilings which the painter had perfected in works for patrons in Rome, notably Urban VIII. The rooms, named after the gods Venus, Jupiter, Mars, Apollo and Saturn, each showed a deity participating in the Medici story. The cycle culminated in the throne room, where Jupiter could be seen giving the crown of immortality to the first grand duke, Cosimo I.

The second project was a fresco cycle celebrating the life of Lorenzo the Magnificent in a series of allegories that offered mythological proof for the Medici myth: of how the culture of the classical world was destroyed by barbarians, colourfully depicted as vicious satyrs and harpies, forcing the Muses to leave Parnassus; and of how they were led to the safety of Florence, where they were welcomed by Lorenzo and allowed to flourish in peace until his death. More conventional was the cycle commissioned by Ferdinando II's uncle, Lorenzo, for his villa La Petraia, to extol the golden age of Medici power from Leo X to Cosimo II. This turned out to be the last of the thirty or so cycles of family history commissioned over a period of about a hundred years.

Although it was no longer a priority for the Medici to prove the glories of their past, their future remained a problem. Ferdinando II's fiancée, Vittoria della Rovere, was emerging from childhood under the watchful protection of the nuns of the Crocetta in 1634 when Christine of Lorraine – now approaching her seventieth birthday – began to worry that the betrothal arranged between her grandchildren might be broken off after her death. Very likely, this was Ferdinando's intention, for he certainly had little affection for the pretty but vain and excessively pious Vittoria, now twelve years old. However, he agreed to placate his grandmother. On 2 August, the marriage was celebrated in private, though the bride was too young to consummate the union. The formal wedding took place three years later, in August 1637, when the highlight of the celebrations was a splendid performance of *The Marriages of the Gods* staged by Gian Carlo. A friend of Galileo judged it 'marvellous' on account of 'the melodious music, the beautiful scenery, the inventive machinery and the costumes'.[16] The comedy celebrated the Olympian marriages of Jupiter and Juno, Vulcan and Venus, Neptune and Amphitrite, and Pluto and Proserpina – none of which could be described as exemplars of domestic bliss, and would turn out to be a prophetic choice of theme. At least when Christine of Lorraine died the following December she was happy in the knowledge that her grandchildren were irrevocably joined.

By the summer of 1639, Vittoria, now aged seventeen, was five months pregnant when Florence was hit by an outbreak of smallpox. She caught the disease but fortunately recovered (her level of scarring is unknown) to give birth, on 20 December, to her son Cosimo. Sadly the baby died the next day and his corpse was put on display at the Palazzo Pitti, a tiny crown set on his head. In May 1641, Vittoria had another child, a daughter, who also did not survive long. On this occasion, the mother's labour lasted nineteen hours, but thanks to her iron constitution Vittoria recovered. As Leopoldo put it to Mattias, 'she has weathered a powerful hurricane'.[17] Finally, on 14 August 1642 and after five years of marriage, Vittoria gave birth to a healthy son, who was also named 'Cosimo'. Having now done his dynastic duty and sired an heir, Ferdinando II chose to live apart from his wife, while she devoted her energies to educating her son as a pious Catholic prince.

Justus Sustermans, *Ferdinando II and Vittoria della Rovere,* 1660s
(London, National Gallery).

In the following year, 1643, Ferdinando II decided to launch his first military campaign. Its object was to help his brother-in-law Odoardo Farnese, Duke of Parma, retake the city-state of Castro, on the southern border of Tuscany, which had been seized by Urban VIII. Ferdinando, with his brothers Gian Carlo and Mattias, led the Florentine army to a resounding victory, though it was one in name only. The huge cost of the war emptied the grand-ducal coffers, further straining an already weak economy; and the debt was still unpaid when Farnese died three years later. Finally, in 1649 the victory was overturned in a savage fashion when Urban VIII's successor, Innocent X, razed the city to the ground. It was never rebuilt. The experience made Ferdinando even more determined to keep out of the wider European conflict still raging between France and the Habsburgs.

Prospects in Rome were sunnier. The election of Pope Innocent X in 1644 had been an opportunity for Cardinal Carlo to display the Medici talent for political manoeuvring in the conclave. Opting initially to support the French candidate, he swapped sides to back Spain and then played a significant role in the election of Cardinal Giambattista Pamphili. The new pope would reward Cardinal Carlo generously for his help. Relations between Tuscany and Rome, which had deteriorated in the aftermath of the trial of Galileo and the War of Castro, began to improve.

The first sign of Innocent X's good will came within weeks of the election when he named two new cardinals: his own nephew, and Cardinal Carlo's nephew, Gian Carlo. The latter was a surprising appointment, for this ex-Admiral of the Spanish navy was hardly suited to the clerical life. With a string of mistresses and an illegitimate son, he had a libidinous reputation which, as Harold Acton would later put it, 'would not have been out of place in the *Satyricon*', and his womanizing soon caused such a scandal at the papal court that he was forced to leave Rome.[18] He set up residence instead at the Medici villa of Castello, where he built superb gardens, named his flowers after his concubines and hosted famously debauched banquets. When he died of a stroke in January 1663 at the age of fifty-two, he left behind debts of more than 135,000 *scudi*, which Ferdinando II decided to repay by auctioning off his brother's valuable collection of art, books and furniture.

Meanwhile, Ferdinando II had more pressing family worries. His heir, Cosimo, had been a lively character and a keen sportsman as a child (aged eleven, he had shot a goose in mid-air with his musket); but he had grown into a gloomy, taciturn teenager firmly under the control of his dominating mother. Ferdinando's hopes that his son would share his interest in science had been trampled by Vittoria della Rovere, who insisted on an educational timetable focused on the extensive study of religious texts at a level more appropriate for a future priest than a grand duke. She commissioned court artist Justus Sustermans to paint a portrait of the Holy Family showing herself as the Virgin and Cosimo as her child. That there was no resemblance between the figure of Joseph and the grand duke demonstrated how this pious – some might say bigoted – woman did everything possible to distance her son from his father. Thanks to her, Cosimo had become fanatical in his strict observance of the faith – much in the manner of the Inquisition, which around this time began sending men onto the streets of Florence, every Friday morning, to sniff for meat cooking and so identify those transgressing the Church fast.

What particularly alarmed Ferdinando was his son's lack of interest in the opposite sex. Cosimo made little effort to hide his dislike of flirting with young girls, preferring instead the company of his priests. It was not a very positive augury for the future head of the Medici dynasty, so Ferdinando took two steps to rectify the situation. In August 1658, the year of Cosimo's sixteenth birthday, he opened negotiations with Gaston, Duke of Orléans (and second son of Marie de' Medici) with a view to marrying his chaste heir to the duke's pretty thirteen-year-old daughter, Marguerite-Louise. And, in a move that electrified the gossips at court, he resumed marital relations with his wife, after a gap of eighteen years. By this time, Ferdinando was now aged forty-eight and the grand duchess thirty-six. Despite Vittoria's age, in the summer of 1660 Florence was humming with the news that she was pregnant once again. On 12 November 1660, she gave birth to another son, who was named Francesco Maria.

Meanwhile, the plans to betroth Cosimo to Marguerite-Louise had run into problems. The princess, as spirited as she was pretty, did not want to drop her royal status to marry the heir of a minor Italian state. However, the death of Gaston of Orléans while the negotiations were underway made her a ward of her cousin, King Louis XIV; and Ferdinando II's ambassadors in Paris had the ear of Cardinal Mazarin, the king's chief minister. Despite her protests, Louis XIV ordered her to accept the proposal. It was a coup for the Medici, but one that was to have disastrous results.

The marriage was celebrated at the Louvre in April 1661, the reluctant Marguerite-Louise mollified by the lavish gift of a pearl necklace worth 60,000 *scudi* from her new husband and other jewels valued at 150,000 *scudi*. She left Paris a few weeks later, after a tearful farewell to her lover, Charles of Lorraine, travelling to Marseilles with a huge retinue that included more than forty ladies-in-waiting. She caused scandal the moment she stepped onto Tuscan soil. On disembarking at Livorno, where she was received by Ferdinando II's sister Margherita, Duchess of Parma, she refused to give her hand to her new aunt, on the grounds that the duchess was not of royal blood.

Marguerite-Louise made her formal entry into Florence on 20 June, wearing a white satin dress embroidered with pearls and precious gems, and riding in a carriage that cost 117,000 *scudi*. The wedding celebrations, which were masterminded by Cardinal Gian Carlo and Leopoldo, were some of the most splendid ever seen in Italy. The highlight was a performance of *Il mondo festeggiante* ('The World in Celebration'), a four-hour spectacular of music and drama that took place in the gardens of the Palazzo Pitti. An audience of 20,000 guests watched Cosimo and his knights, dressed in magnificent armour and riding richly caparisoned horses, perform a choreographed battle followed by an elegant ballet. The gods then descended from Olympus, with the aid of ingenious mechanical contraptions, to congratulate the bridal couple. In private, though, there was much less to celebrate. Cosimo did his marital duties with obvious distaste, performing without passion and very infrequently; astonishingly, he insisted on his doctor's presence in the bedroom. Not surprisingly, his very attractive, vivacious bride was soon turned off by her boorish husband.

Accustomed to Louis XIV's glittering court at Versailles, Marguerite-Louise and her courtiers enlivened the provincial tedium of the Palazzo Pitti with French frivolities. She was passionate about ballets, often taking part in them herself, much to the displeasure of Cosimo, who disapproved of dancing and disliked music, unless it was religious. To keep his court in order, Ferdinando II curtailed the fun, sending his daughter-in-law's companions back to France. And, with Marguerite-Louise now refusing to perform her connubial role, he was forced to ask Louis XIV to order she allow Cosimo back into her bed – as well as to stipulate that she should conform to Tuscan etiquette and not insist on her royal status. Ferdinando II was particularly vexed by the war that had developed between his wife and daughter-in-law. The two women loathed each other: the royal princess could not tolerate giving precedence to a member of a very minor dynasty, while Vittoria considered Marguerite-Louise's love of dancing, music and picnics in the fresh air as inappropriate behaviour for a future grand duchess. Cosimo, who had been dominated by his mother since birth, inevitably took Vittoria's side.

It was not until August 1663, more than two years after her arrival in Florence, that Marguerite-Louise finally gave birth to a child, a son named Ferdinando. The birth of an heir was a great relief to Ferdinando II, but Marguerite-Louise's subsequent refusal to resume marital relations with Cosimo marked the start of his daughter-in-law's very public rebellion against the Medici – which soon became headline news across Europe. The Venetian ambassador reported on how 'she says she has married beneath her, which offends the sensitivities of [the Medici] and cares nothing for the discomfort of her father-in-law, who wishes her to lead a quieter life, nor for the anger of her husband… and wants to go back to France'.[19] But she needed Louis XIV's permission to return home and this the king would not grant: he ordered his ambassador, the Duke of Créqui, who was in Italy in May 1664 negotiating peace between France and Pope Alexander VII, to notify Marguerite-Louise accordingly.

Ferdinando II resorted to coercion. He turned down Marguerite-Louise's request to be allowed to live apart from her husband and instead locked her into her apartments in the Palazzo Pitti; but she refused to eat anything that had not been cooked by her own French chefs. In the autumn of 1664, in an effort to improve the situation, Ferdinando II sent Cosimo on an extended tour of northern Italy, where the pious prince spent his time visiting religious shrines; and when the court left Florence for the hunting season, Ferdinando sent his daughter-in-law first to the villa at Lappeggi and then to Poggio a Caiano, with an armed guard to prevent her escape. He even persuaded the pope to order her, on pain of excommunication, to obey her husband, but she stubbornly refused. The following month, little Ferdinando, now eighteen months old, was taken away from her.

A year of boredom ensued, under house arrest at Poggio a Caiano – and then Marguerite-Louise suddenly announced her intention of returning to her husband. By Christmas 1665 she was back at court. Initially, at least, relations between Cosimo and his wife appeared cordial. She was observed enjoying herself at a banquet in the Palazzo Pitti to celebrate Twelfth Night, and by the end of 1666 Florence was buzzing with the news that pretty Marguerite-Louise – a still popular figure among ordinary Florentines – was again pregnant. She, however, was much less delighted by her pregnancy than her in-laws. She tried to induce a miscarriage by energetic riding expeditions and – after Ferdinando II took away her horses – by fasting and taking long, brisk walks; but all to no avail. She even survived an attack of fever, which killed hundreds of people in Florence in the summer of 1667. Despite everything, on 11 August she successfully gave birth to a daughter, Anna Maria Luisa. Then, as she had done after the birth of Ferdinando, she refused to resume marital relations with her husband.

Despite the difficulties attending his son's marriage, Ferdinando II took the risky decision to arrange Church careers for the other remaining males in the family, including his only other son, Francesco Maria. In 1667 he started to hunt for benefices for the seven-year-old boy. That year, his brother Mattias died from the complications of gout – it is unclear why this career soldier never married – and the studious Leopoldo was given a red hat to replace Cardinal Carlo, who had recently died, at the age of seventy-one. The new cardinal's motto was 'always upright, always the same'. Unlike his reprobate brother Gian Carlo, he would prove a conscientious Prince of the Church.

In an effort to improve relations between Cosimo and Marguerite-Louise, and to broaden his son's rather limited horizons, Ferdinando II sent him on a foreign tour in October 1667, first to visit his Habsburg relations in Austria, and then on to Augsburg, Brussels and Amsterdam – the bill for the trip coming to 25,000 *scudi*.[20] The wilful Marguerite-Louise still refused to see her husband when he returned the following May, so Ferdinando sent him away again. This time, Cosimo travelled to Spain and Portugal with a large retinue that included his confessor, his doctor and several interpreters. In January 1669, he set sail for England, reaching Plymouth on 22 March, but only after storms had forced his galleys onto the Irish coast. He travelled to London by coach and visited Cambridge, before leaving for Rotterdam during the summer, and then carrying on to Paris, where he stayed for six weeks. Cosimo was received with honour by Louis XIV, whose luxurious palace at Versailles much impressed the provincial Tuscan prince. Ferdinando II was relieved to see that Cosimo received a much warmer reception from Marguerite-Louise when he returned to Florence in February 1670.

Grand Duke Ferdinando II died just three months later, on 26 May 1670, suffering from dropsy. After a grandiose funeral at San Lorenzo, attended by 1,500 monks and friars and the Knights of St Stephen, he was buried in the church's Medici family vault, the Cappella dei Principi. He had been grand duke for almost fifty years – a long reign. Unfortunately, it had been one that had seen the Tuscan economy decline sharply and the Medici lose some of their lustre. Nevertheless, he had secured a royal marriage for one son and a Church career for the other, and, with the help of his brothers, had done much to enhance the reputation of the Medici as cultured patrons of the arts and sciences. How would the new grand duke build on this legacy?

21

VANITY

Cosimo III

1670–1723

Grand Duke Cosimo III (28)
Marguerite-Louise d'Orléans (25), *his wife*

  Ferdinando (7), *their son*

  Anna Maria Luisa (3), *their daughter*

Vittoria della Rovere (48), *his mother*

Francesco Maria (10), *his brother*

Cardinal Leopoldo (53), *his uncle*

Cosimo III is not one of history's most edifying characters. Vain, conceited, unimaginative and a religious bigot, he lacked any shred of political ability. Initially, he strove to maintain a neutral stance in the war between Emperor Leopold I and King Louis XIV that broke out soon after his accession; but he proved incapable of dealing with the new balance of power that would develop between France, Spain and the Empire. He was no more capable of dealing with his wilful wife, and, abandoning his father's frugal habits, he would spend lavishly on a court that was notorious for its pomp, bleeding the Tuscan economy dry to maintain the illusion of wealth and status. Europe's superpowers, convinced that Cosimo's extravagance proved his coffers were indeed filled with gold, exploited the gullible grand duke to finance their wars. And in stark contrast to his father, Cosimo III lacked interest in the arts and sciences, ensuring that Florence was soon a cultural backwater in a continent elsewhere brimming with innovation. His long reign would prove a catastrophe for the Medici.

One of Cosimo III's first acts was to give his mother Vittoria a leading role in his regime, a decision that brought disastrous consequences for his marriage. His reunion with Marguerite-Louise after his return from his travels in 1670 resulted in the birth of a second son a year later – a boy they named Gian Gastone in honour of his maternal grandfather Gaston, Duke of Orléans. But now relations between the grand-ducal couple broke down completely: she accused him of being a mother's boy – which he was – while he found her behaviour exasperating. Vittoria della Rovere took her son's side in every argument and vindictively refused her daughter-in-law a seat in the privy council. Marguerite-Louise continued to petition Louis XIV to allow her to return to France, despite the stern refusals that had greeted her previous requests. Early in 1672, she announced that she had a lump in her breast and asked the king to send her a French doctor, who diagnosed a nervous complaint and recommended a trip to a French spa; but Cosimo III, seeing the ruse for what it was, refused to let her go.

That December, Marguerite-Louise was at Poggio a Caiano when she wrote to her husband that: 'I have made a resolution, which will come as no surprise when you consider your malicious behaviour towards me over the last twelve years, that I cannot live with you any longer, I make you as unhappy as you make me; I ask you therefore to agree to a separation.'[1] She added: 'I will stay here to wait for a reply from the king'. The grand duke allowed her to remain at Poggio a Caiano but insisted on the ignominy of house arrest: she was to be accompanied by soldiers when she went out and locked into her rooms every evening; and no one could visit her without Cosimo's permission. Marguerite-Louise remained a prisoner at the villa for the next two and a half years, deprived of all contact with her young children, who were put into the care of Vittoria della Rovere. Finally, Louis XIV gave way, giving her permission to go the convent of Montmartre – and Cosimo III agreed to the formal separation. In June 1675, shortly before she left, she asked if she could see her children once more, a favour which her mean-spirited husband granted with some reluctance, ordering his chief minister to inform her that they 'will be at Castello to say their goodbyes to you as the grand duke has ordered' and to warn her 'not to cry or upset them'.[2]

Left in the charge of their grandmother, the children – Ferdinando, Anna Maria Luisa and Gian Gastone – were forbidden to communicate with their mother and subjected to the same narrow, religious curriculum she had imposed on Cosimo III, though her determination to train them for lives of piety, rectitude and obedience would not prove so successful. Nor would the measures work for Vittoria's own youngest son Francesco Maria, also in the schoolroom at the Palazzo Pitti. Just three years older than Ferdinando, and by all accounts a jolly, clever child who worked hard at his studies, Francesco Maria was destined for a career in the Church. At the age of fifteen he was given the lucrative benefice of the abbey of Monreale, worth 22,000 *scudi* a year, and after the death of Cardinal Leopoldo he inherited his uncle's scholarly collection of books. He would, it was hoped, soon be named as his uncle's successor in the College of Cardinals.

Cosimo III's own, excessive piety was very public in Florence, where he visited 'five or six churches every day'.[3] According to an English visitor, Cosimo 'had a machine in his own apartments, whereon were fixed little images in silver of every saint in the calendar... before which he continually performed his offices'. His religious advisers ensured that his regime was run on theological rather than political lines, with the legal system under the control of the ecclesiastical authorities and the economy directed in the interests of the Church. Cosimo III and his mother favoured the Jesuits and the strict new religious orders. They established colleges throughout Tuscany for the training of priests and missionaries and – in another break with his father's legacy – banned the teaching of Galilean physics. They also turned a blind eye to priestly indiscretions, and unsurprisingly there was much anger in Florence at 'the friars who are allowed to exercise their depravities with impunity though the women they seduce are punished'.[4]

By contrast, Cosimo III attempted to reform the morals of his lay subjects in a heavy-handed manner, enforcing his edicts with an army of informers whose arbitrary denunciations terrorized the Florentines. All citizens were ordered to kneel down, wherever they were, every Friday afternoon when they heard the tolling of the great bell of the Duomo and to recite 'three paternosters and three Ave Marias in memory of the three hours that our Lord Jesus Christ remained alive on the hard trunk of the Cross for our redemption'.[5] A state lottery proved hugely popular until Cosimo III's priests warned him that the ticket-holders were committing the sin of gambling; so he ordered that every Saturday be devoted to the glory of the Virgin, closing theatres that day and banning parties as well as dancing and busking, from dawn to midnight.

Following Rome's lead, Cosimo also implemented anti-Semitic policies, which banned all contact between Jews and Christians, with the latter now forbidden to enter Jewish houses or shops, or to work as servants or wetnurses in Jewish households. Jews visiting Christian prostitutes were fined 300 *scudi*, as were the prostitutes themselves – though the Jewish client was liable for the fine if the woman was unable to pay. In 1685, 'wishing to remedy the damage and unfairness done to artisans by allowing the Jews to practise their trades in this city', Cosimo prohibited Jews from selling any sort of cloth, foreign or locally produced, as well as all items of haberdashery such as gold thread, buttons, braid or ribbons.[6]

The grand duke's prohibitions did not end there. Carnival, the traditional season of feasting and fun, was 'so meagre and wretched that there was more laughter at times of plague,' according to one Florentine.[7] Cosimo III had extended the Lenten ban on meat to include eggs and dairy products, and had ordered church bells to ring out fifteen minutes before midnight on Shrove Tuesday to warn party-goers that the fast was about to begin. Young people were banned from dancing on feast days and 'all innkeepers are forbidden... to serve prostitutes, even for a short time, or give them food and drink... under pain of a fine of 100 *scudi* or, if they cannot pay, three lashes of the rope, and the prostitutes are to be publicly whipped'.[8] The custom of holding parties for young men and girls to meet (and flirt) was deemed 'a great incentive to commit rapes, abortions and infanticides, and to cause brawls and other scandals' – one can almost hear Vittoria's voice here – and parents were ordered to stop the practice.[9] Girls had to be 'dressed in plain outfits without silver or embroidery', brides were allowed to wear clothes made of rich textiles for just two years, and widows were always to dress in black, 'without any sort of trinkets'.[10]

The notable exception to these harsh edicts was, of course, Cosimo III himself. He boasted his rank by dressing in the elaborate lacy cravats and curly wigs of European royalty, and, on one occasion when ordering his secretary to find hair for a new wig, he insisted that it be cut from 'a young girl' so that it would be 'finer and more delicate'.[11] He spent lavishly on the rituals of court life, holding a magnificent funeral for his mother, when she died at the age of seventy-two: her courtiers wept openly, but the Florentines, who blamed Vittoria delle Rovere for much of their misery, showed little sadness. He celebrated extravagantly when Leopold I's armies finally forced the Turks to abandon their siege of Vienna in 1683 – a campaign to which Cosimo had been obliged to contribute substantial financial resources. In a mock battle at the church of Ognissanti, a 'castle' filled with fireworks was attacked by 'Turkish' soldiers, the loud bangs and fire from exploding crackers making it look and sound like a real battle. He also staged a funeral at Santissima Annunziata for the souls of all the Christians who had died at Vienna, arriving at the church, with his court, in a procession of forty carriages. That evening at San Lorenzo, statues of Turks were slowly burnt in a stupendous machine, consumed by a figure of Faith armed with chalice and sword.

Another drain on the grand-ducal purse was Marguerite-Louise. If Cosimo III thought that his marital travails would end following their separation, he was much mistaken. To his embarrassment, she was enjoying herself very publicly at Versailles. Cosimo's ambassador sent reports of gambling, midnight swims, and of an affair with one of her grooms. Incensed by her scandalous behaviour – an affront to his dignity – the grand duke informed Louis XIV of his displeasure. A furious Marguerite-Louise responded in a vitriolic letter in January 1680, in which she accused Cosimo of 'doing all you can to turn the king against me,' adding that 'not an hour nor a day goes by when I do not wish you dead… what I dislike most is that we shall both go to Hell and then I will have the torture of seeing you even there'.[12] She promised to be 'as extravagant as possible just to annoy you' and, true to her words, piled up debts, forcing Louis XIV to ask Cosimo III to raise her allowance or return her dowry to satisfy her creditors. When Cosimo refused, the king accused him of avarice. After much negotiation, Cosimo agreed, in his own words, 'to drink the bitter chalice' – and settled another 10,000 *scudi* a year on his extravagant, estranged wife.[13]

Cosimo III's need for money – to satisfy the demands of Louis XIV, Leopold I and, above all, of his own vanity – soon beggared the ailing Florentine economy. His religious policies were enormously costly, not least the handsome pensions he gave to all Protestants, Muslims and Jews who converted to Catholicism. They also led to a huge increase in the numbers of churchmen in Florence – by 1680 they numbered some 10,000, a sixth of the total population – adding yet more untaxable mouths to the rising tide of the unemployed. When textile workers rioted in front of the Palazzo Pitti, demanding either work or bread, Cosimo was forced to pay them himself to avoid a civil war. His punitive taxes stifled commercial activity, one visitor observing that 'the people of Florence are very highly taxed; there is an imposition laid upon everything they either wear or eat'.[14] The economy degenerated further through Cosimo's sale of monopolies in all areas of production, including the manufacture of different types of hats and tobacco, for example, and all aspects of the printing trade. He also raised money by savagely cutting all official salaries, forcing bureaucrats to steal from public funds to supplement their meagre wages. The city was awash with corruption, as priests grew fat and beggars starved.

No twig himself, following the humiliating departure of his wife Cosimo had consoled himself at the dining-table, refusing – it was said – to eat any capon that weighed less than 7 kilograms. He grew very

Venus de' Medici, antique marble statue probably dating from the first century BC (Florence, Uffizi, Tribuna).

large and in 1681 fell seriously ill. His condition was supposed to be a secret, so he was furious to learn that Marguerite-Louise was making plans to return to Tuscany in the event of his death to act as regent for her son. Those responsible for the leaks, he discovered, were Ferdinando's maths teachers, who were regularly in touch with the grand duchess; Cosimo vindictively sentenced them to twenty years in prison.

Although his resentment of Marguerite-Louise did not abate, Cosimo III did recover his health, after his doctors advised a strict vegetarian diet with plenty of exercise – a regime he adopted with the same obsessive zeal as he undertook his religious observances. He was often at his villa at Ambrogiana, where he had built a convent for the Alcantarinis, an austere Spanish order of barefoot friars who allowed neither meat nor wine on their table.

Cosimo's obsessions did not entirely exclude other interests. He was fond of gardening, and he developed a passion for fruit trees, sending agents to the Indies and the Americas to hunt for rare plants. Although intolerant of Galileo's ideas, he encouraged some scientific research in fields acceptable to the Church authorities and gave generous grants to antiquarians and men of letters. He appointed Paolo Falconieri, a close friend of Cardinal Leopoldo, to take charge of the Medici art galleries at the Uffizi; and he obtained papal permission to the magnificent collection of antiquities assembled in Rome by his great-grandfather, Ferdinando I. These classical statues went on display at the Uffizi alongside the famous Titians and Raphaels that had been his mother's dowry. Otherwise, Cosimo III did not display the Medici taste for patronage of the arts.

Such a taste was, though, inherited by his son Ferdinando, a keen connoisseur of art who began amassing his own collection. The grand-ducal heir was also a gifted musician, who sang well and played several instruments, including the harpsichord. He would develop a life-long love of Venetian art and music, carrying on a long correspondence with Alessandro Scarlatti, who wrote several operas for him.

Ferdinando was a thorn in Cosimo III's pious flesh. He detested his father, treated him with contempt and mocked the army of priests that filled the Palazzo Pitti. The grand duke autocratically refused Ferdinando any role in state affairs and made futile attempts to reform his son's increasingly extravagant behaviour. When asked to make economies, Ferdinando refused, so Cosimo III suggested selling family heirlooms. 'I will never agree to disposing of our most precious treasures,' Ferdinando stubbornly replied, believing 'there must be a thousand other ways of dealing with this.'[15] He must have reminded Cosimo III uncomfortably of Marguerite-Louise, whose good looks he had inherited.

Most alarming to the grand duke was the friendship between Ferdinando and his slightly older uncle, Francesco Maria. The two princes enjoyed music and hunting as well as more dissolute pleasures at the Medici villas, returning to Florence only when Cosimo III was absent. They were very popular figures in the city, in contrast to the grand duke himself, who was thoroughly disliked. In 1686, Francesco Maria was made a cardinal by Pope Innocent XI and then appointed to the prestigious post of Cardinal-Protector of Spain and the Empire; but he made little effort to change his lifestyle. At his villa at Lappeggi, a short carriage-ride south of Florence, his guests enjoyed idle pastimes in the stunning gardens as well as indulging in cross-dressing banquets (where women dressed as men served the male diners dressed as women). To end the gargantuan meals, cups of the fashionable chocolate, imported from Spain at vast expense, were drunk.

Even before Francesco Maria acquired his red hat, Cosimo III had started trawling the courts of Europe for a dutiful, pious bride for Ferdinando. His first choice had been Maria Isabella, the daughter of King Pedro II of Portugal; but the king had insisted that Ferdinando renounce his claim to the grand duchy, so that, should Gian Gastone fail to produce an heir, it would then become part of the Portuguese empire. Understandably, these conditions were too harsh for Cosimo and in 1587 he settled on Violante, the fourteen-year-old daughter of the Duke of Bavaria. Taking steps to mould the character of his prospective daughter-in-law, Cosimo had his secretary ask the head of the Augustinian Order to find her a Jesuit confessor, 'to direct the princess's conscience, a holy and discreet man, who can cultivate and feed those seeds of piety… and be capable of making her spirit pliable and undemanding'.[16]

Niccolò Cassana, *Grand Prince Ferdinando*, 1687 (Florence, Uffizi, Vasari Corridor).

To Cosimo's fury, Ferdinando refused to consider marriage unless he was allowed to visit Venice, that renowned centre of Italian music and vice. Forced into a corner, the grand duke reluctantly agreed, but he wrote out a pompous set of instructions for his son stipulating that 'the prince is… to abstain from entertainments that might damage his soul… or be improper to his rank… he must not fraternize in an unseemly manner with musicians or actors… or become involved in conversations, even less in parties, with prostitutes, but restrict himself to noble and innocent pleasures'.[17] Ferdinando responded by returning to the dreary court in Florence with a *castrato* named Cecchino, with whom he was infatuated, to continue his life of dissipation.

Ferdinando and Violante were eventually married by proxy in November 1688, in Munich, and on 9 January 1689 the bride made her formal entry into Florence. Shy, young and eager to please, she fell in love with her husband at first sight, though her feelings were not reciprocated. One observer judged that 'she could not boast of beauty or prettiness, but her graceful manners, refinement and goodness instantly gave her the approval and affection of the Florentines'.[18] At the Porta San Gallo, the grand-ducal family watched an immense procession of soldiers and churchmen parading past their box, which had been covered with panes of glass to keep out the bitter cold. The extravagant festivities continued with a spectacular performance of *Il Greco in Troia* ('The Greek at Troy'), complete with a huge mechanical Trojan Horse, in the Pergola theatre, which Ferdinando had transformed with the aid of stage designers from Venice. On 22 February, Shrove Tuesday, there was a joust between two teams: the 'Turks', led by Ferdinando, wore green satin embroidered with pearls and gems, and the 'Europeans', headed by Gian Gastone, appeared in a red French-style outfit.

Cosimo III spent prodigiously on the wedding in an attempt to show that his court was the equal of Vienna or Versailles; and there would soon be more expenses to satisfy his vanity. In 1690, he was furious to learn that Vittorio Amadeo, Duke of Savoy, had been rewarded with the title 'Royal Highness' after signing a treaty with Emperor Leopold I and Charles II of Spain. Cosimo III wrote immediately to the Emperor asserting that, as a grand duke and the premier nobleman in Italy, he should have the same honour. Leopold I ignored the request but did propose an Imperial alliance by offering his brother-in-law, Prince Johann Wilhelm, the Elector Palatine, as a suitable husband for the grand duke's twenty-three-year-old daughter Anna Maria Luisa. She had recently been rejected as a bride by the widowed Charles II – not least because of the infamous reputation of her mother – and now Cosimo III agreed to the Imperial offer, on the condition that he himself was made a 'Royal Highness'. Leopold granted Cosimo the title in February 1691, and the marriage took place in April, whereupon Anna Maria Luisa left Florence to take up residence in Düsseldorf.

On the face of it, the metamorphosis of the Medici from republican bankers to royal highnesses was an astonishing feat; but it was an empty and costly victory. Much to his dismay, Cosimo III's new tag was not recognized by either Louis XIV or Charles II, and it took a lot of money and hard work in Rome, on the part of Cardinal Francesco Maria, to persuade Innocent XII to receive his ambassadors with the honour due to royalty. And, in return for the Imperial favour, Leopold I made relentless demands for money, insisting on annual dues of 500,000 *scudi* in order for Cosimo to secure his feudatory rights. The grand duke was forced to increase the taxes on 'his most beloved subjects'. In June 1692, he imposed a levy on coachmen, on maids and on wigs, as well as on horses – mules, asses, nags and racehorses all had to be registered, and the state spies ensured that nothing was missed. His Royal Highness was an object of derision across Italy.

Moreover, Cosimo III's new ties with the Empire caused problems in his relations with Louis XIV, who tried to buy his loyalty by offering a French princess as a bride for Gian Gastone. Cosimo III refused the offer, partly out of fear that his second son would become a hostage to force his support of France; but the real reason was that he could not afford to pay the allowance Gian Gastone would need in order to live at the French court in a manner befitting a Medici prince. But Gian Gastone did need a bride. After four years of marriage, Ferdinando's wife still had no child – possibly Violante was barren, but it is known that Ferdinando contracted syphilis on one of his trips to Venice, where he enjoyed not only opera but the company of courtesans. Increasingly worried about the succession, Cosimo III ordered special masses to be said in all Florentine churches to encourage Violante to conceive. And when the credulous grand duke was persuaded by a priest that God would grant Ferdinando an heir if he erected a certain column – the sexual innuendo was not lost on the Florentines – he gave the priest

Andrea del Sarto, *Madonna of the Harpies*, 1517 (Florence, Uffizi). Prince Ferdinando acquired many sixteenth-century altarpieces, including this one, from churches in Florence during the 1690s.

permission to collect alms for the purpose. The priest pocketed the money, using it to build himself a house.

Up to this point, Cosimo III had tended to ignore Gian Gastone, an amiable character who spent his time studying antiquities and rare plants in the privacy of his rooms in the Palazzo Pitti. But the future of the dynasty now depended on this shy young man, and Cosimo asked his daughter, Electress Anna Maria Luisa, to find a bride for her brother. There were two provisos: she had to be rich, and she had to be capable of bearing children. On this occasion Cosimo was less bothered about rank. The Electress did find someone, her husband's sister-in-law, confusingly another Anna Maria. She was the daughter of the Duke of Saxe-Lauenburg; she was also a wealthy widow with lands in Bohemia and a daughter from her first marriage. Indeed, she ticked all of Cosimo III's boxes, and moreover he assumed the match would make Gian Gastone an Imperial prince. The grand duke paid his dues to Leopold I that year, 1695, without question; but Ferdinando laughed at his father's vanity, publicly opposing the marriage on the grounds that it would increase Tuscany's reliance on the Empire and threaten links with France.

Unfortunately for Cosimo III, Anna Maria also opposed the marriage. She did not want to marry into a minor ruling house, and neither were her Bohemian subjects keen on the match. Eventually, the Electress succeeded in persuading her sister-in-law of the good character and handsome looks of her brother, and the betrothal took place in March 1697. Cosimo III, desperate to have his hands on the dowry, made no objections to the bride's demands that her husband reside in Bohemia, nor even to Leopold I's refusal to make Gian Gastone an Imperial prince. And, autocratic as ever, Cosimo assumed that his docile son would submit meekly to his authority; but it would not be long before Gian Gastone would become as stubbornly opposed to his father as Ferdinando already was.

In September 1697, after two months at the court at Düsseldorf, the newly married couple moved to Anna Maria's castle at Reichstadt.* Unfortunately, all was not well. As Gian Gastone later informed his father, 'nineteen days after the giving of the marriage ring, if not before, my princess began to give me a taste of her shrewish nature, sulking

---

* Reichstadt is now Zákupy in the Czech Republic.

and shouting at me because I did not want to leave Düsseldorf' and 'there were endless sulks, tears and tantrums'.[19] Fond of hunting, and it seems overly attached to her horses, Anna Maria loved rural life; but for Gian Gastone, who was used to the urban luxury of the Medici court, it was too quiet. He lasted just six months in Reichstadt before leaving for Versailles, where he was presented at court by Marguerite-Louise and was a great success with Louis XIV. Cosimo III, obsessed with the succession and anxious about Ferdinando's failing health, ordered Gian Gastone to return to Anna Maria – she had informed Cosimo that it was her husband's fault that she was not pregnant. After a year at Versailles, Gian Gastone did go back to Bohemia, offering a compromise to his wife: he would spend the summer in Reichstadt if they could winter at the Imperial court in Prague. Anna Maria refused, and so did Cosimo III, who insisted that Gian Gastone remain with his wife. The young husband obeyed, but, as he explained to his father, having 'done everything in my power to adapt myself to her' he still found her 'domineering and arrogant' and 'not a dish to be eaten twelve months of the year'.[20]

Beyond the Medici's dynastic and marital worries, the political map of Europe was about to change in dramatic ways – and to throw Cosimo III's lack of diplomatic talent in the spotlight. In 1700, Charles II of Spain, now seriously ill and childless, named Louis XIV's grandson Philip of Anjou as his heir, in a move opposed by Leopold I, who claimed the Spanish throne for his second son, Archduke Charles of Austria. In May, Cosimo travelled to Rome to discuss the issue with Innocent XII, who counselled him to remain neutral. Charles II died on 1 November 1700, and the War of the Spanish Succession broke out three months later. In April 1701, Philip of Anjou made his state entry into Madrid. After centuries of enmity, France and Spain were now united under Bourbon rulers, allies against the Habsburg Empire. The situation was bound to be tricky for Cosimo III. When Louis XIV bribed Cardinal Francesco Maria to renounce his protectorship of the Empire and instead become Cardinal-Protector of France and Spain, Cosimo caved in. Ignoring the pope's sage advice, he agreed to recognize Anjou as King Philip V of Spain. The new king did not, however, reciprocate the gesture and recognize Cosimo III's title of Royal Highness.

Cosimo III's lack of standing with Philip V was amply evident in 1702 when the king arrived in Naples, *en route* for northern Italy, where the French had launched a campaign against the Imperial army. Determined to show his support for his Bourbon ally, the grand duke offered his galleys for the king's journey; he also sent Cardinal Francesco Maria to Naples to act as escort. On 8 June, the royal party arrived at Livorno, where Cosimo had planned a magnificent reception, with huge crowds at the harbour and guns roaring salutes as the grand-ducal family waited on the quay to greet the king. It was an embarrassing moment. Philip V curtly refused to leave his galley, so Cosimo III, Ferdinando and Violante of Bavaria were obliged to go on board. The grand duke was further insulted when, after a perfunctory exchange of greetings, the king asked to be left alone for a private conversation with Violante, who was his maternal aunt.

Moreover, and much to Cosimo III's dismay, it soon became clear that the War of the Spanish Succession was not going well for the Bourbons. Leopold I had acquired three powerful allies – England, Holland and Portugal – and in early 1703 he sent Archduke Charles to Lisbon, from where, with the support of an Anglo-Dutch fleet, he invaded Spain. Cosimo III ineptly attempted to become neutral in the conflict, with disastrous consequences. He infuriated Louis XIV by allowing the English to use the port of Livorno; he infuriated the English by refusing to allow the Protestant priests on the ships to set foot in Tuscany; and he infuriated Leopold I by refusing to recognize Archduke Charles as King Charles III of Spain.

Then, the war turned decisively in favour of the Emperor. In August 1704, Prince Eugene of Savoy and John Churchill, Duke of Marlborough, defeated the French at the Battle of Blenheim and the English seized Gibraltar from Spain; they captured Barcelona the following year. In May 1706, Marlborough defeated the French at Ramillies, taking the Spanish Netherlands, and in September Prince Eugene defeated Louis XIV at the Battle of Turin, forcing the French to retire from Italy. Cosimo III was now at the mercy of the new Emperor Josef I – who had succeeded his father Leopold in 1705 – and faced with the double threat of an overland invasion by the Imperial army and a seaborne attack by the English. The Emperor's price for peace was a massive payment of 600,000 ducats, the provision of winter quarters for three Imperial regiments and Cosimo's recognition of Charles III as rightful King of Spain. Cosimo capitulated, although his ambassadors did manage to negotiate a reduction in the sum of money demanded by the Emperor.

Meanwhile, Gian Gastone, unable to stand life in Reichstadt with Anna Maria, had moved to Prague where he developed a taste for the low life, spending his time drinking in taverns, gambling and general debauchery. When he sold his wife's jewellery to finance his licentious lifestyle, she took him to court and refused to cohabit with him until the jewels were returned. Ferdinando urged his father to allow Gian Gastone to come home, but Cosimo III, still obsessed with the succession, insisted that his son could only return if he brought his wife with him. Anna Maria, however, had heard the lurid reports of the violent deaths a century earlier of the Medici brides Isabella and Dianora. Encouraged by her Capuchin confessor, she stubbornly refused to consider moving to Florence. But neither was Gian Gastone keen on the plan. After two months in Reichstadt, he escaped again, this time to enjoy the low life in Hamburg. Cosimo III ordered his son to Vienna, where it was hoped that the Emperor might be able to reconcile the couple; but this time the recalcitrant princess refused to obey her sovereign and remained entirely indifferent to the plea that by failing to conceive she would cause the extinction of the Medici dynasty.

Gian Gastone returned to Florence in June 1705, without his wife but with the promise that she would follow him in two years' time. And in 1707 he duly left for Reichstadt in order to escort Anna Maria to Florence. It can hardly have been a surprise when she reneged on her promise. Once again, neither the Emperor nor Cosimo III were able to make her change her mind; she even refused to submit to Pope Clement XI, who declared she was endangering her soul by refusing to obey her husband. Perhaps another wife was the answer? Cosimo III asked the pope to grant an annulment, and Clement XI sent the Archbishop of Prague to Reichstadt; but Anna Maria won the sympathy of the archbishop, telling him of her terror of being murdered like the Medici brides. Her tearful and contrite manner so touched him that he advised the pope to refuse Cosimo's request for an annulment.

In truth, neither of Cosimo III's sons was in a condition to sire a son, even if their barren marriages could be annulled. Ferdinando, ill with syphilis and tuberculosis, and often unconscious, had started to have epileptic fits; and Gian Gastone rarely emerged from his drunken stupor. In desperation, Cosimo turned to his brother, Cardinal Francesco Maria. This corpulent prelate, aged forty-eight, had several illegitimate children – proof enough of his virility, even if his loose living had begun to tell on his health. Reluctantly, he agreed to give up his influential position at the papal court to become a Medici stud – and Cosimo III began to search for a bride for him that would be acceptable to both Vienna and Paris.

In June 1709, Cosimo announced the betrothal of Francesco Maria and Eleonora Luisa Gonzaga, the twenty-three-year-old daughter of Vincenzo Gonzaga, Duke of Guastalla; and six days later, the groom resigned his cardinal's hat. Francesco Maria was delighted with his pretty young bride. His own charms, however, had faded with age. Eleonora was revolted by her husband's obesity and unhealthy, yellow complexion. Initially, she refused to consummate the marriage, terrified of the diseases he might pass on to her. There was still no sign of a child twelve months later, when a notice appeared beside the Palazzo Pitti that read: 'To Let This Year When the Medici Leave'.[21]

When Francesco Maria died of dropsy in February 1711, it was evident to all that the Medici dynasty had no future. What now bothered Cosimo III was the future of Tuscany.

Cosimo III was naive in supposing that the future of Tuscany rested in his own hands. Aware that Josef I was making plans to take over the grand duchy, he had sent envoys to the 1710 peace conference at Geertruidenberg, which was negotiating an end to the War of the Spanish Succession, with orders to obtain agreement for his daughter, Electress Anna Maria Luisa, to succeed her brother and subsequently for Florence to revert to a republic after her death. Both requests were robustly turned down – the Medici no longer had any clout on the international stage. The situation worsened when Josef I died in 1711 without a son. His successor was his brother, Charles III of Spain, who now took the title of Emperor Charles VI, leaving the Bourbon claimant Philip V as undisputed ruler of Spain. The following year, Cosimo III was appalled to learn that Anna Maria Luisa was to be passed over as Gian Gastone's heir by his awful daughter-in-law, Anna Maria. And worse, that the Emperor himself was to inherit Tuscany after her death.

In October 1713, Ferdinando finally died, having been bedridden for several years, leaving Gian Gastone, now aged forty-two, as the heir presumptive. A month later, Cosimo III issued an edict naming Electress Anna Maria Luisa as the next in line to the grand-ducal throne – but this desperate move was soon countered by Charles VI, who announced the following spring that Florence, according to documents 'found' by his ministers, had been an Imperial fief since the days of Charlemagne and that therefore it was his right to decide the succession. Technically, Florence was not an Imperial fief, though Siena was. Louis XIV now entered the bargaining, promising support for Anna Maria Luisa's succession on condition that Cosimo name a pro-French prince as her own heir. And the situation became even more complex in September 1714, when Philip V of Spain was betrothed to Elisabetta Farnese, the great-granddaughter of Cosimo III's aunt, Margherita. This was a union that, if fruitful, would add a Spanish claimant to the grand duchy.

Cosimo III was still procrastinating in late 1715 when the treaties ending the War of the Spanish Succession were finally signed, and when, early the next year, Elisabetta Farnese gave birth to a son, Don Carlos. With France and Spain both now making plans to secure Tuscany for Don Carlos, Cosimo III decided to re-open negotiations with the Emperor – but he had little with which to bargain. The future of Tuscany after the Medici had become an international issue, and one which the Medici themselves were seemingly powerless to influence. For his part, Cosimo stubbornly persisted in instructing his ambassadors in Vienna, Madrid and Paris to assert the rights of Anna Maria Luisa to inherit; but they were completely ignored.

Inside the walls of their magnificent Palazzo Pitti, the Medici limped on. Gian Gastone was virtually a recluse now, his new title 'grand prince' and the substantial increase in his allowance making little difference to his lifestyle, which revolved around alcohol. His sister-in-law Violante of Bavaria spent much of her time at Lappeggi, which she had inherited from the debauched Francesco Maria and turned into a court famous for its musicians and poets. And in 1716, Electress Anna Maria Luisa, now a wealthy widow after the death of her husband, returned to Florence, where she was soon able to manipulate her devoted father, encouraging him in his futile attempts to name her as Gian Gastone's heir.

Meanwhile, Cosimo III's health had begun to fail. In 1722, at the advanced age of eighty, he handed over his public duties to his second son, who managed to emerge from his drunken seclusion to play an active role in Florentine affairs for the first time in his life – even if he was often so inebriated that he fell off his horse. Behind the scenes though, Cosimo, with the help of his daughter, kept his hand firmly on the political and diplomatic tiller. In September 1723, when at his dining-table, he was attacked by a shivering fit that lasted for two hours. He ordered the inmates of all the convents and monasteries in the grand duchy to pray for his recovery. After enduring twelve days of agonizing treatment by his surgeon, who used a syringe to extract urine through his penis, Cosimo recovered the use of his bladder; but it was evident that he did not have long to live.

Cosimo III lasted another month before dying on 31 October 1723. His corpse was put on public display at the Palazzo Pitti in advance of his funeral at San Lorenzo, which was heralded by church bells across the city, tolling for more than five hours. He was buried in magnificent pomp with his ancestors in the Cappella dei Principi.

Characterized by political ineptitude, religious zeal and gross vanity, Cosimo's reign – the longest of all the Medici dukes – had been a disaster. He left a state burdened with debt and riddled with corruption, having reduced Tuscany to penury with the harsh taxes to finance his extravagant tastes. For the Medici, his reign had been a catastrophe. On his accession, the family had been respected at the major courts of Europe; they were so no longer. He had totally alienated his sons by his autocratic behaviour, by denying them any involvement in state affairs, and by forcing them into unhappy, barren marriages for political gain that never materialized. Thanks to his pride and arrogance, the Medici dynasty was all but over.

22

EXTINCTION

Gian Gastone

1723–1737

THE GRAND DUCAL FAMILY IN 1723

Grand Duke Gian Gastone (52)

Anna Maria Luisa (56), *his sister*

Violante of Bavaria (48), *his sister-in-law*

Grand Duke Gian Gastone celebrated his accession, at the age of fifty-two, in very quiet fashion, refusing to stage the grand coronation ceremony as his predecessors had done. One of his first acts was to cancel the edict imposing another 5 per-cent tax on his subjects, which his father had signed just before dying; another was to exclude his sister, Anna Maria Luisa, from politics.

Violante of Bavaria, by contrast, was to play a prominent role in the new regime, helping her often incapable brother-in-law by presiding over public audiences. Gian Gastone may have been a drunkard, but he was a kind, gentle personality with none of his father's religious bigotry or extravagant tastes. He sacked Cosimo III's army of theologians, monks and friars, disbanded the network of spies that had terrorized Florence, separated the government from domination by the Church and abolished the life pensions his father had paid to all those who had converted to Catholicism. He eased the tax burden on his poorer subjects, cut the price of wheat and reduced the unpopular levies Cosimo III had imposed on coachmen, maids, wigs and horses. He also issued a law making persecution of the Jews a punishable offence. Most welcome was the cancellation of the edicts banning gambling, parties, flirting and the other pleasures of life. Despite the tax cuts, Gian Gastone spent a mere fraction of the budget his father had devoted to grandiose ceremonial, and he was soon able to reduce the public debt by half.

These initiatives aside, the new grand duke showed no interest in the day-to-day management of his state, which he left entirely in the hands of his advisers. Instead, he abandoned himself to a life of pleasure and rarely left his apartments in the Palazzo Pitti. Further afield too, Gian Gastone was largely unconcerned about the unseemly scramble taking place in the corridors of power in Vienna, Madrid and Paris over the future of Tuscany, generally refusing to give audiences to foreign ambassadors unless absolutely necessary. The alliance between the Bourbon monarchies of Spain and France broke down early in his reign, when Louis XV reneged on his betrothal to the Spanish infanta and married a Polish princess instead. Philip V of Spain soon signed an alliance with Emperor Charles VI, who agreed to recognize the king's son Don Carlos as Gian Gastone's heir, a plan inevitably opposed by France and its allies. Gian Gastone himself simply ignored the issue, though he did agree to annul his father's edict of 1713 that named Anna

Maria Luisa as his heir. He was aware that his opinions counted for little internationally, but he did cherish hopes that Tuscany might revert to one of Violante's nephews, the sons of her brother, the Duke of Bavaria.

Violante took up residence in the Palazzo Pitti, where she tried to encourage Gian Gastone to moderate his dissolute lifestyle and take more interest in political affairs. Despite her efforts, the grand duke refused to read his state papers. Nor did his daily court rituals conform to standard etiquette: he held his official *levée* at noon, dined in the late afternoon and supped after midnight, eating and drinking to excess. He rarely bothered to get dressed, and spent much of his time in bed, lying on soiled sheets in a filthy nightshirt – there is even a portrait of him receiving visitors under the elaborate silk canopy of his four-poster. He was up all night, drinking, smoking, singing, laughing and joking with his hordes of 'courtiers' – a lively crowd of young men and women, chosen by his major-domo for their good looks rather than noble birth, and many of them picked up off the streets. Gian Gastone could not afford to pay their wages though, and in 1731 they were so hungry that they started fighting with the owners of food stalls in the market. Indeed the 'courtiers' were such a menace that Anna Maria Luisa arranged for guards to be stationed outside her apartment in the Palazzo Pitti.

On one occasion, Gian Gastone cancelled his official *levée* and rumours flew around Europe that he had had a stroke and was on the point of death – in fact, he had fallen over drunk in his apartments and twisted his ankle. In order to scotch the rumours, his ministers forced him to receive the envoys of the foreign powers squabbling over the future of Tuscany, so that they could see that he was still alive. With only two candles lighting the room, the diplomats might not have noticed the filthy state of his bedding; but the stench must have been unbearable.

Gian Gastone's reign, which had begun so auspiciously, was soon mired in corruption as the debauchery in the Palazzo Pitti spread out like a disease into Florence, where moral standards began to collapse, even among the religious orders. The seats in the Pergola theatre were filled with monks and friars for the matinee performances during Carnival in 1727; they had to be back in their convents by sunset, and wore masks with their habits so they could not be identified. Florence,

Overleaf: School of Marcuola, *Cosimo Riccardi visits Grand Duke Gian Gastone,* 1735 (Florence, Museo degli Argenti).

'where many people of both sexes and all ages… prefer to go begging even though they are capable of working', was filled with vagrants, especially small children sent out onto the streets by their parents for an early education in petty crime.[1] In an attempt to control the problem, Gian Gastone's ministers issued an edict giving foreign beggars eight days to leave Tuscany, otherwise boys over fifteen years of age would be sent to the galleys, while girls and women were to be publicly whipped.

In June 1729, on the advice of his ministers, Gian Gastone reluctantly agreed to attend the festivities for San Giovanni. A cavalcade of carriages ferried Gian Gastone, Anna Maria Luisa, Violante of Bavaria, the diplomatic corps and government ministers from the Palazzo Pitti to the church of Ognissanti, where the horse-race was to start. Unfortunately, the grand duke was already extremely drunk, and the crowds on the streets were appalled to see him vomiting out of his carriage window. Unable to stand, he had to be carried to a local bathhouse, where he was washed before going home in a replacement carriage. It would be the last time that the grand duke was officially seen in public – he did not leave the Palazzo Pitti for a year, and then only to visit the public baths at San Sperandino, a noted brothel. He made another unseemly appearance in May 1731, when Violante of Bavaria died of dropsy. She had requested a small private funeral at the convent of Santa Teresa, but the crowds that gathered in front of the Palazzo Pitti to say farewell to their much-loved princess were so large that the cortège was unable to move. Gian Gastone, stricken with grief, lost his temper and opened his bedroom window, screaming at them to disperse in a very undignified manner.

Abroad, the alliance between Empire and Spain had started to unravel. In November 1729, Philip V signed a treaty with France, Holland and Great Britain, ensuring military assistance to enforce the Tuscan succession of Don Carlos. Emperor Charles VI responded by marching his troops into northern Italy and promising Gian Gastone Imperial protection to stop Tuscany becoming part of the Spanish empire. The stand-off worsened in July 1730, when the pro-Spanish Cardinal Lorenzo Corsini was elected as Clement XII – a pope who was also a Florentine. His election was celebrated with six days of festivities in the city, though Gian Gastone did not take part.

It was a year before a peace was signed in Vienna, and this time all the major European powers – the Empire, Spain, France, Britain and Holland – agreed to recognize Don Carlos as Gian Gastone's heir. The grand duke was not in a position to do anything but acquiesce, so he instructed his ambassadors to negotiate terms, while also reputedly asserting that 'at the age of sixty-one I will father a beautiful son with no trouble at all'.[2]

In October 1731, thirty-two Spanish warships, sixteen English vessels and six thousand Spanish troops arrived at Livorno, followed in late December by Don Carlos himself, who was welcomed by huge crowds and noisy gun salutes from the fortresses. A few weeks short of his sixteenth birthday, he was good-looking and well mannered, and he visibly enjoyed the banquets and hunting parties held in his honour. Unfortunately, within days of his arrival, he caught smallpox. Gian Gastone ordered the treasured Florentine relic of St Zenobius to be put on display in the Duomo for three days to pray for the youth's recovery. He also cancelled the Carnival festivities with which Don Carlos was to have been welcomed to Florence.

Don Carlos recovered to make his entry into the city on 9 March, and there to be greeted with joy by the large crowds who were tiring of the drunken antics of their grand duke and his anarchic 'courtiers'. At the Palazzo Pitti, the Spaniard was received by the grand-ducal household and escorted to the guest apartments, where he was met by Anna Maria Luisa. According to the official account, 'after they had conferred a while', Don Carlos and Anna Maria Luisa 'went to the apartments of the Most Serene Grand Duke, who was obliged to stay in bed because of some inconvenience to his health, but was very impatient to see and embrace the Most Serene Infante'.[3] Gian Gastone's ministers had removed the rowdy 'courtiers', forbidden him to drink anything but water for twenty-four hours, and informed Don Carlos that the grand duke was bed-bound because of a 'weakness of a knee'. Gian Gastone seemed delighted with his new heir, showering him with presents, and Don Carlos remained in Florence for seven months. He sat in the grand-ducal throne at the San Giovanni ceremonies to receive the tributes from the cities of Tuscany; and he was lavishly entertained with banquets, balls, hunting and fishing expeditions, and opera and theatre, before finally leaving in October.

In 1733, just when the issue of Gian Gastone's heir seemed to have been finally settled, events conspired to put it back onto the agenda when a Polish succession crisis, in which Emperor Charles VI and Louis XV supported opposing claimants, rendered the Vienna treaty of 1731 void. On 1 January 1734, Charles declared war on Louis, who, with the support of Spain, defeated the Imperial forces in Italy. Once again, the warring powers negotiated a series of peace treaties carving up the minor principalities of Europe – and in 1735 Don Carlos, who had distinguished himself in the fighting, was rewarded with a grander prize than Tuscany: the title of King of Naples and Sicily. Gian Gastone had lost his heir. Instead, the new heir to the grand duchy was to be Francis, the former Duke of Lorraine who, by a curious thread of fate, was the grandson of Charles of Lorraine, one-time lover of Gian Gastone's mother Marguerite-Louise. Gian Gastone's ambassadors did manage one minor victory by persuading Charles VI to guarantee Tuscany's independence after his death. Francis of Lorraine was also the Emperor's heir – because he was married to Charles VI's daughter Maria Theresa – but he was not to be permitted to keep both titles when he ascended to the Imperial throne. Instead of being absorbed into the Empire, Tuscany was to be settled on another member of the Imperial family.

Before the European powers had the opportunity to change their minds again, Gian Gastone's health began to fail. Suffering from gout and kidney stones, and ravaged from his years of dissolute living and inebriation, he was ill enough in early 1737 for his chief minister and his sister to insist on expelling the army of 'courtiers' from the Palazzo Pitti. The Florentines, superstitious as ever, took a terrible thunderstorm and violent earthquake on 9 June as a sign of troubles to come. By the end of the month, Gian Gastone was unable to eat. He still had enough strength of mind to refuse Anna Maria Luisa permission to enter his bedroom, until, a few days later, the two were reconciled.

On 9 July 1737, at midday, Gian Gastone died. It was 200 years to the day since the first grand duke, Cosimo I, had begun his reign. All afternoon, the bells tolled across the city to mark the end of this remarkable dynasty.

EPILOGUE

REVIVAL

The death of Grand Duke Gian Gastone in 1737 was not quite the end of the Medici story. Although his sister, Anna Maria Luisa, could not – despite her father's machinations – inherit the grand-ducal throne, she was the sole heir to the magnificent collection of paintings, sculptures, books, jewels and other valuables amassed by the family over the centuries. When she died in 1743, she bequeathed this priceless accumulation to the new grand duke, Francis of Lorraine, on the condition that none of it should ever leave Florence. The Medici may have beggared the city by their greed, but this bequest did much to reverse its economic stagnation. By the end of the eighteenth century, Florence was one of the high spots of the Grand Tour that was considered *de rigeur* for a young European aristocrat's education. Above all, the Medici myth went on to become a central pillar of the city's reputation as the cultural capital of Europe, visited by the millions to see what Baedeker's guide described around 1900 as 'an amazing profusion of treasures of art, such as no other locality possesses'.

The Medici dynasty may have been brought to extinction, but their presence in Florence today is all-pervasive. The Palazzo della Signoria (now Palazzo Vecchio), built to celebrate the foundation of the republic and converted by Cosimo I into his ducal residence, bears witness to the success of the family's campaign to achieve ultimate power. Inside, Vasari's frescoes celebrate the glorious history of the family, while the quantities of letters, account-books, inventories and other documents preserved in the Florentine archives testify to the less than glorious methods by which they seized and exercised that power. Both the Uffizi, where Cosimo I housed his administration, and the Palazzo Pitti are filled with artistic treasures acquired by the Medici – Lorenzo the Magnificent's priceless collection of sardonyx and amethyst vases, the antique statues bought in Rome by Cardinal Ferdinando, the paintings by Titian and Raphael that formed the dowry of Vittoria della Rovere, and hundreds of family portraits. Duke Alessandro's hated fortress, the Fortezza da Basso, is now an exhibition centre, hosting trade fairs. In the science museum (Museo Galileo), Galileo's telescopes, and one of his fingers, sit beside the scientific instruments and books acquired by Ferdinando II and his brother, Cardinal Leopoldo. The Medici villa at Poggio a Caiano, with its innovative facade commissioned by Lorenzo the Magnificent, also contains the rooms where the unhappy French princess, Marguerite-Louise, was imprisoned by her husband Cosimo III. The grottoes and fountains that ornamented the superb villa that Francesco I built for his mistress, Bianca Cappello, at Pratolino have long gone; but the family villa at nearby Cafaggiolo, where his brother Piero strangled his pretty wife Dianora, still survives. So too does the villa at Lappeggi, where Cardinal Francesco Maria hosted his chocolate-fuelled orgies, and where Violante of Bavaria held her literary salons.

Above all, it is the family mausoleum at San Lorenzo, the Cappella dei Principi, that is the most eloquent statement of the Medici rise and fall. Begun by Ferdinando I in 1604, the chapel was still unfinished when his great-great-grandson Gian Gastone died in 1737. Designed on a majestic scale, it was intended to rival the burial chambers of the royal houses of Europe in grandeur. Its interior is lined with exorbitantly expensive semi-precious stones and ornamented with *pietre dure* panels, decorated with pearls and lapis-lazuli; but most of the niches, intended to contain gilt bronze statues of the grand dukes, are empty. This grandiose display of dynastic pride proved over-ambitious. Nonetheless, it is an eloquent testimony to the remarkable Medici family, to its astonishing achievements and its dismal decline.

Johann Zoffany, *The Tribuna of the Uffizi*, 1772–7 (Windsor, Royal Collection).
Overleaf: Florence, Cappella dei Principi, begun 1604 but never finished.

Partial Genealogy of the Medici family

The dates in italic are last known references
† indicates illegitimate children

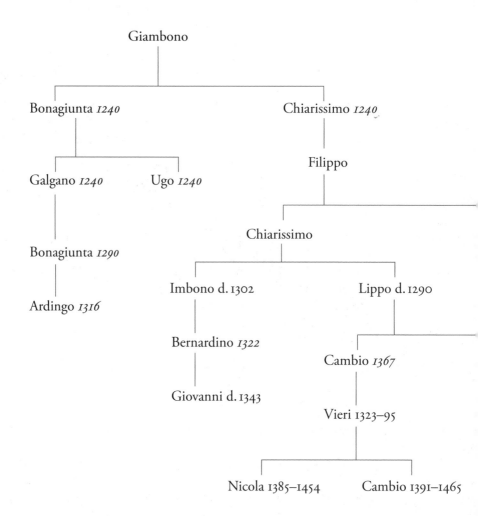

Giambono

Bonagiunta *1240*

Chiarissimo *1240*

Galgano *1240*   Ugo *1240*

Filippo

Bonagiunta *1290*

Chiarissimo

Ardingo *1316*

Imbono d. 1302

Lippo d. 1290

Bernardino *1322*

Cambio *1367*

Giovanni d. 1343

Vieri 1323–95

Nicola 1385–1454   Cambio 1391–1465

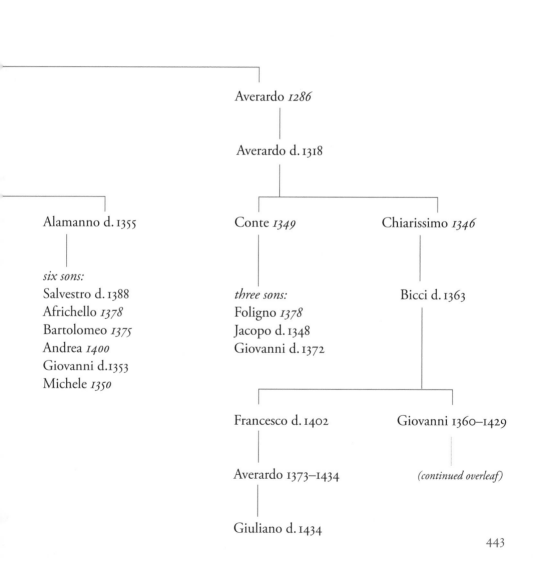

Averardo *1286*

Averardo d. 1318

Alamanno d. 1355

six sons:
Salvestro d. 1388
Africhello *1378*
Bartolomeo *1375*
Andrea *1400*
Giovanni d.1353
Michele *1350*

Conte *1349*

three sons:
Foligno *1378*
Jacopo d. 1348
Giovanni d. 1372

Chiarissimo *1346*

Bicci d. 1363

Francesco d. 1402

Averardo 1373–1434

Giuliano d. 1434

Giovanni 1360–1429

(continued overleaf)

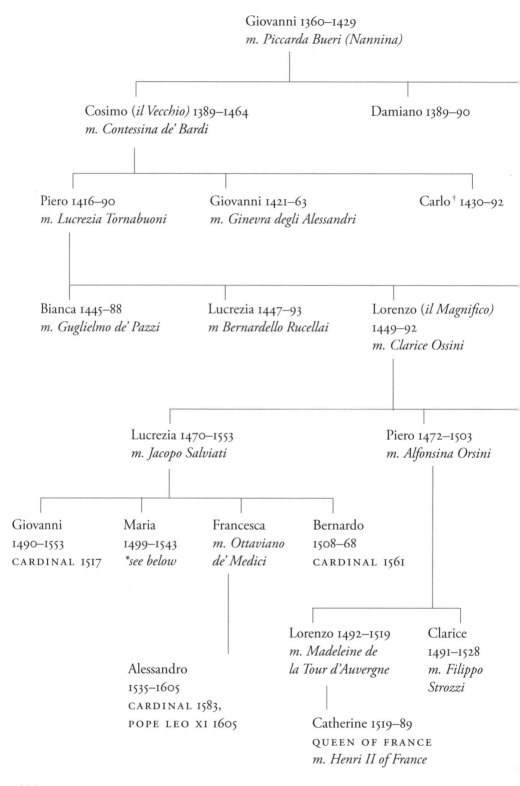

Giovanni 1360–1429
m. Piccarda Bueri (Nannina)

Cosimo (*il Vecchio*) 1389–1464
m. Contessina de' Bardi

Damiano 1389–90

Piero 1416–90
m. Lucrezia Tornabuoni

Giovanni 1421–63
m. Ginevra degli Alessandri

Carlo † 1430–92

Bianca 1445–88
m. Guglielmo de' Pazzi

Lucrezia 1447–93
m Bernardello Rucellai

Lorenzo (*il Magnifico*)
1449–92
m. Clarice Ossini

Lucrezia 1470–1553
m. Jacopo Salviati

Piero 1472–1503
m. Alfonsina Orsini

Giovanni
1490–1553
CARDINAL 1517

Maria
1499–1543
*see below

Francesca
m. Ottaviano
de' Medici

Bernardo
1508–68
CARDINAL 1561

Lorenzo 1492–1519
m. Madeleine de
la Tour d'Auvergne

Clarice
1491–1528
m. Filippo
Strozzi

Alessandro
1535–1605
CARDINAL 1583,
POPE LEO XI 1605

Catherine 1519–89
QUEEN OF FRANCE
m. Henri II of France

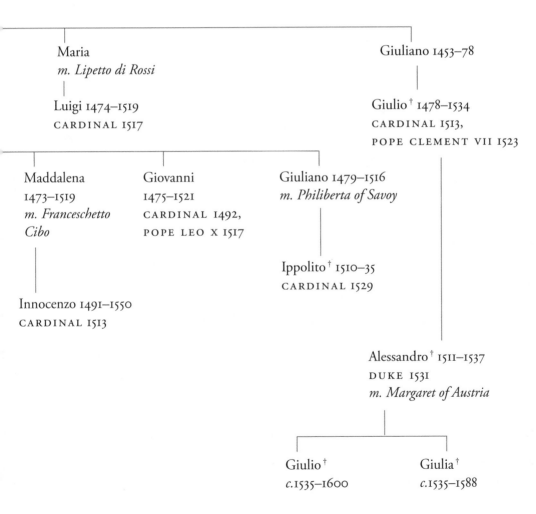

Lorenzo 1395–1440
m. Ginevra Cavalcanti

(continued overleaf)

Maria
m. Lipetto di Rossi

Luigi 1474–1519
CARDINAL 1517

Giuliano 1453–78

Giulio † 1478–1534
CARDINAL 1513,
POPE CLEMENT VII 1523

Maddalena
1473–1519
*m. Franceschetto
Cibo*

Giovanni
1475–1521
CARDINAL 1492,
POPE LEO X 1517

Giuliano 1479–1516
m. Philiberta of Savoy

Innocenzo 1491–1550
CARDINAL 1513

Ippolito † 1510–35
CARDINAL 1529

Alessandro † 1511–1537
DUKE 1531
m. Margaret of Austria

Giulio †
*c.*1535–1600

Giulia †
*c.*1535–1588

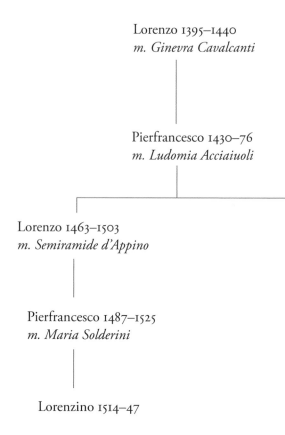

Lorenzo 1395–1440
m. Ginevra Cavalcanti

Pierfrancesco 1430–76
m. Ludomia Acciaiuoli

Lorenzo 1463–1503
m. Semiramide d'Appino

Pierfrancesco 1487–1525
m. Maria Solderini

Lorenzino 1514–47

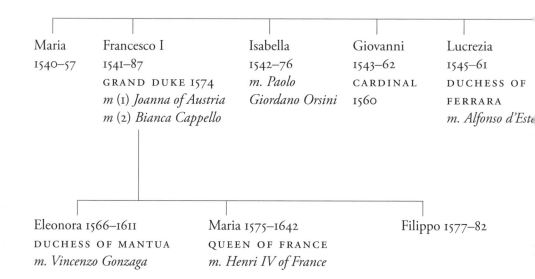

Maria	Francesco I	Isabella	Giovanni	Lucrezia
1540–57	1541–87	1542–76	1543–62	1545–61
	GRAND DUKE 1574	*m. Paolo*	CARDINAL	DUCHESS OF
	m (1) *Joanna of Austria*	*Giordano Orsini*	1560	FERRARA
	m (2) *Bianca Cappello*			*m. Alfonso d'Este*

Eleonora 1566–1611
DUCHESS OF MANTUA
m. Vincenzo Gonzaga

Maria 1575–1642
QUEEN OF FRANCE
m. Henri IV of France

Filippo 1577–82

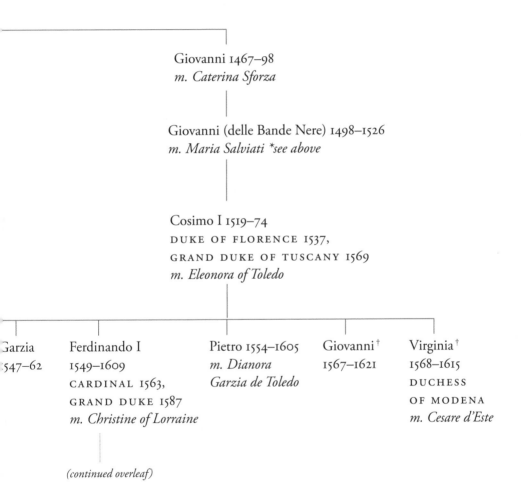

Giovanni 1467–98
m. Caterina Sforza

Giovanni (delle Bande Nere) 1498–1526
*m. Maria Salviati *see above*

Cosimo I 1519–74
DUKE OF FLORENCE 1537,
GRAND DUKE OF TUSCANY 1569
m. Eleonora of Toledo

Garzia
547–62

Ferdinando I
1549–1609
CARDINAL 1563,
GRAND DUKE 1587
m. Christine of Lorraine

Pietro 1554–1605
*m. Dianora
Garzia de Toledo*

Giovanni †
1567–1621

Virginia †
1568–1615
DUCHESS
OF MODENA
m. Cesare d'Este

(continued overleaf)

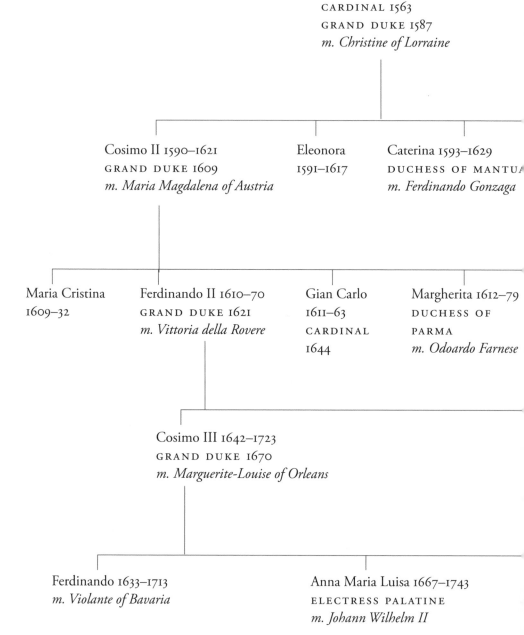

Ferdinando I 1545–1609
CARDINAL 1563
GRAND DUKE 1587
m. *Christine of Lorraine*

Cosimo II 1590–1621
GRAND DUKE 1609
m. *Maria Magdalena of Austria*

Eleonora
1591–1617

Caterina 1593–1629
DUCHESS OF MANTUA
m. *Ferdinando Gonzaga*

Maria Cristina
1609–32

Ferdinando II 1610–70
GRAND DUKE 1621
m. *Vittoria della Rovere*

Gian Carlo
1611–63
CARDINAL
1644

Margherita 1612–79
DUCHESS OF
PARMA
m. *Odoardo Farnese*

Cosimo III 1642–1723
GRAND DUKE 1670
m. *Marguerite-Louise of Orleans*

Ferdinando 1633–1713
m. *Violante of Bavaria*

Anna Maria Luisa 1667–1743
ELECTRESS PALATINE
m. *Johann Wilhelm II*

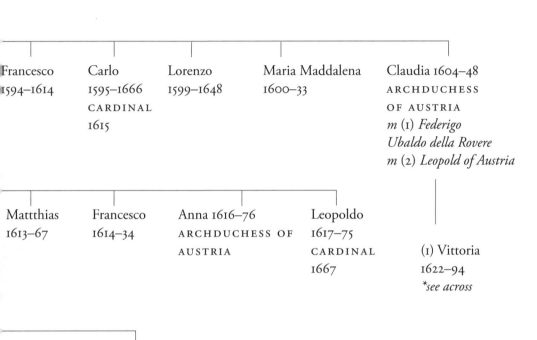

Francesco
1594–1614

Carlo
1595–1666
CARDINAL
1615

Lorenzo
1599–1648

Maria Maddalena
1600–33

Claudia 1604–48
ARCHDUCHESS
OF AUSTRIA
m (1) *Federigo
Ubaldo della Rovere*
m (2) *Leopold of Austria*

Mattthias
1613–67

Francesco
1614–34

Anna 1616–76
ARCHDUCHESS OF
AUSTRIA

Leopoldo
1617–75
CARDINAL
1667

(1) Vittoria
1622–94
see across

Francesco Maria 1660–1711
CARDINAL 1686 (res. 1709)
m. *Eleonora Gonzaga*

Gian Gastone 1671–1737
GRAND DUKE 1723
m. *Anna Maria of Saxe-Lauenburg*

The Italian Peninsula *c.*1500

HOLY ROMAN EMPIRE

Trento

Turin

Milan

Brescia

REPUBLIC OF VENICE

Pavia

Verona

DUCHY
OF
SAVOY

DUCHY OF MILAN

Venice

HUNGARY

Parma

REPUBLIC OF GENOA

Modena

Ferrara

Genoa

Bologna

Imola

Ravenna

OTTOMAN EMPIRE

Forlì

REPUBLIC
OF LUCCA

Florence

Urbino

Pisa

REPUBLIC OF
FLORENCE

Arezzo

Ancona

Ligurian Sea

Siena

Perugia

Adriatic Sea

Piombino

REPUBLIC
OF
SIENA

Assisi

CORSICA

Orvieto

Viterbo

PAPAL STATES

Ostia

Rome

KINGDOM OF NAPLES

Mediterranean Sea

Gaeta

Capua

Bari

Naples

SARDINIA

Amalfi

Brindisi

Ottranto

Tyrrhenian Sea

Palermo

Reggio

SICILY

Florence and Environs

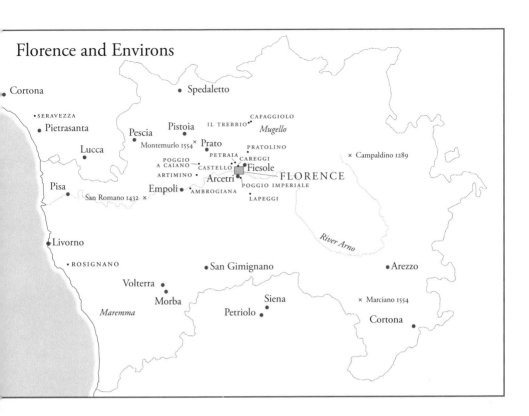

Cortona

Spedaletto

SERAVEZZA

Pietrasanta

Pistoia   IL TREBBIO   CAFAGGIOLO

Pescia   Mugello

Lucca   Montemurlo 1554 ✕   Prato   PRATOLINO

POGGIO   PETRAIA   CAREGGI   ✕ Campaldino 1289

A CAIANO   CASTELLO   Fiesole

Pisa   ARTIMINO   Arcetri   FLORENCE

San Romano 1432 ✕   Empoli   AMBROGIANA   POGGIO IMPERIALE

LAPEGGI

Livorno   River Arno

ROSIGNANO

San Gimignano   Arezzo

Volterra

Morba   Siena   ✕ Marciano 1554

Maremma   Petriolo   Cortona

Florence *c.*1500

1 Palazzo Medici

2 S. Lorenzo and Medici chapels

3 Biblioteca Laurenziana

4 S. Maria del Fiore, *Il Duomo*

5 Baptistery

6 S. Maria Novella

7 S. Croce and Pazzi chapel

8 Uffizi

9 Palazzo Vecchio (Signoria / Ducale)

10 Piazza Signoria (Ducale)

11 Ponte Vecchio

12 Palazzo Strozzi

13 S. Marco

14 Fortezza da Basso

15 Fortezza S. Miniato

16 Palazzo Pitti

17 Boboli Gardens

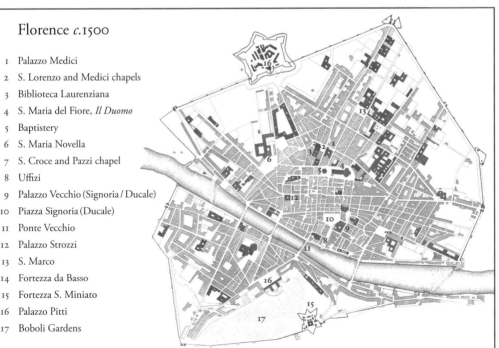

BIBLIOGRAPHY AND SOURCES

ACTON
Acton, Harold, *The Last Medici*, London: Macmillan, 1980

ACTON & CHENEY
Acton, Harold and Edward Cheney, *Florence. A Travellers' Companion*, London: Constable, 1986

ADAMS
Adams, Nicholas, 'Baldassare Peruzzi and the Siege of Florence: Archival Notes and Undated Drawings', *Art Bulletin*, 60 (1978), pp. 475–82

BAROCCHI & BERTELÀ
Barocchi, Paola, and Giovanna Gaeta Bertelà, *Collezionismo mediceo: Cosimo I, Francesco I, e il Cardinale Ferdinando. Documenti 1540–1587*, Modena: Franco Cosimo Panini, 1993

BERTI
Berti, Luciano, 'Profilo del Granducato, l'anno 1600', in *Rubens e Firenze*, edited by Mina Gregori, Florence: La Nuova Italia, 1983, pp. 1–17

BESCHI
Beschi, Luigi, 'Le sculture antiche di Lorenzo il Magnifico', in *Lorenzo il Magnifico e il suo mondo*, edited by G.C. Garfagnini, op. cit., pp. 291–317

BLACK
Black, Christopher F., *Italian Confraternities in the Sixteenth Century*, Cambridge and New York: Cambridge University Press, 1989

A. BROWN 1992
Brown, Alison, *The Medici in Florence: The Exercise and Language of Power*, Florence and Perth: Leo S. Olschki and University of Western Australia Press, 1992

A. BROWN 1994
—, 'Lorenzo and Public Opinion in Florence', in *Lorenzo il Magnifico e il suo mondo*, edited by G. C. Garfagnini, op. cit., pp. 61–85

J. BROWN
Brown, Judith C., 'Concepts of Political Economy: Cosimo I de' Medici in a Comparative European Context', in *Firenze e la Toscana dei Medici nell'Europa del'500*, 3 vols, Florence: Leo S. Olschki, 1983, Vol. I, pp. 279–93

BRUCKER 1957
Brucker, Gene, 'The Medici in the Fourteenth Century', *Speculum*, 32 (1957), pp. 1–26

BRUCKER 1962
—, *Florentine Politics and Society 1343–1378*,
Princeton, NJ: Princeton University Press, 1962

BRUCKER 1967
—, *Two Memoirs of Renaissance Florence*,
New York: Harper Torchbooks, 1967

BRUCKER 1968
—, 'The Ciompi Revolution', in *Florentine
Studies: Politics and Society in Renaissance
Florence*, edited by N. Rubinstein, London:
Faber & Faber, 1968, pp. 314–56

BRUCKER 1971
—, *The Society of Renaissance Florence*, New
York: Harper & Row, 1971

BRUCKER 1984
—, *Florence: The Golden Age 1138–1737*,
Berkeley, CA: University of California Press,
1984

BRUCKER 1994
—, 'The Economic Foundations of Laurentian
Florence', in *Lorenzo il Magnifico e il suo
mondo*, edited by G.C. Garfagnini, op. cit.,
pp. 3–15

BULLARD 1980
Bullard, Melissa Meriam, *Filippo Strozzi and
the Medici: Favor and Finance in Sixteenth-
Century Florence and Rome*, Cambridge and
New York: Cambridge University Press, 1980

BULLARD 1987
—, 'The Magnificent Lorenzo de' Medici:
Between Myth and History', in *Politics and
Culture in Early Modern Europe: Essays in
Honour of H. G. Koenigsberger*, edited by P.
Mack and M.C. Jacob, Cambridge and New
York: Cambridge University Press, 1987, pp.
25–58

BULLARD 1992
—, 'Lorenzo de' Medici: Anxiety, Image
Making, and Political Reality in the
Renaissance', in *Lorenzo de' Medici. Studi*,
edited by G.C. Garfagnini, Florence: Leo S.
Olschki, 1992, pp. 3–40

BULLARD 1994
—, 'In Pursuit of *Honore et Utile:* Lorenzo de'
Medici and Rome', in *Lorenzo il Magnifico e il
suo mondo*, ed. G.C. Garfagnini, op. cit., pp.
123–42

H. BUTTERS 1994
Butters, Humfrey, 'Lorenzo and Naples', in
Lorenzo il Magnifico e il suo mondo, edited by
G. C. Garfagnini, op. cit., pp. 143–51

H. BUTTERS 1996
—, 'Lorenzo and Machiavelli', in *Lorenzo the
Magnificent*, edited by Michael Mallett and
Nicholas Mann, op. cit., pp. 275–80

S. BUTTERS 2010
Butters, Suzanne B., 'Contrasting Priorities:
Ferdinando I de' Medici, Cardinal and Grand
Duke', in *The Possessions of a Cardinal: Politics,
Piety and Art 1450–1700*, edited by Mary
Hollingsworth and Carol M. Richardson,
University Park, PA: Pennsylvania State
University Press, 2010, pp. 185–225

CARL
Carl, Doris, 'La casa vecchia dei Medici e il suo
giardino', in *Il Palazzo Medici-Riccardi in
Firenze*, edited by G. Cherubini and G. Fanelli,
Florence: Giunti, 1990, pp. 38–43

CAVALCANTI
Cavalcanti, Giovanni, *Istorie Fiorentine*, 2 vols,
Florence: Tipografia all'Insegna di Dante,
1838–39

CHANEY
Chaney, Edward, *The Evolution of the Grand
Tour*, London and New York: Routledge, 1998

COCHRANE
Cochrane, Eric, *Florence in the Forgotten
Centuries 1527–1800*, Chicago and London:
University of Chicago Press, 1973

COFFIN
Coffin, David R., *The Villa in the Life of
Renaissance Rome*, Princeton, NJ: Princeton
University Press, 1979

COMPAGNI

Bornstein, Daniel E. (ed.), *Dino Compagni's Chronicle of Florence*, Philadelphia, PA: University of Pennsylvania Press, 1986

CONTI

Conti, Giuseppe, *Firenze: Dai Medici al Lorena*, Florence: R. Bemporad & Figlio, 1909

CUMMINGS

Cummings, Anthony M., *The Political Muse: Music for Medici Festivals 1512–1537*, Princeton, NJ: Princeton University Press, 1992

D'ACCONE 1994

D'Accone, Frank A., 'Lorenzo the Magnificent and Music', in *Lorenzo il Magnifico e il suo mondo*, edited by G.C. Garfagnini, op. cit., pp. 259–90

DANTE

Dante Alighieri, *The Divine Comedy*, 3 vols, Harmondsworth: Penguin, 1973

DBI

Dizionario Biografico degli Italiani (www.treccani.it/biografie)

DEI

Dei, Benedetto, *La Cronica*, Florence: Francesco Papafava, 1984

DOREN

Doren, Alfred, 'Das Aktenbuch für Ghibertis Matthäusstatue an Or San Michele zu Florenz', *Italienische Forschungen des Kunsthistorischen Institutes in Florenz*, 1 (1906), pp. 1–58

ELAM 1978

Elam, Caroline, 'Lorenzo de' Medici and the Urban Development of Renaissance Florence', *Art History*, 1 (1978), pp. 43–66

ELAM 1990

—, 'Il palazzo nel contesto della città: strategie urbanistiche dei Medici nel gonfalone del Leon d'Oro', in *Il Palazzo Medici-Riccardi in Firenze*, edited by G. Cherubini and G. Fanelli, Florence: Giunti, 1990, pp. 44–57

EVELYN

Evelyn, John, *The Diary of John Evelyn Esquire F.R.S*,

edited by William Bray, London and New York: George Newnes / Charles Scribner's, 1818

FANELLI

Fanelli, Giovanni, *Firenze*, Rome and Bari: Laterza 1981

FERRAJOLI

Ferrajoli, Alessandro, *Il ruolo della corte di Leone X* Rome: Bulzoni, 1984

FORTINI BROWN

Fortini Brown, Patricia, '*Laetentur coeli*: The Council of Florence and the Astronomical Fresco the Old Sacristy', *Journal of the Warburg and Courtauld Institutes*, 44 (1981), pp. 176–80

FUBINI

Fubini, Riccardo, 'In margine all'edizione delle 'Lettere' di Lorenzo de' Medici', in *Lorenzo de' Medici: Studi*, edited by G.C. Garfagnini, Florenc Leo S. Olschki, 1992, pp. 167–232

GÁLDY

Gáldy, Andrea, 'Lost in Antiquities. Cardinal Giovanni de' Medici (1543–1562)', in *The Possessior of a Cardinal: Politics, Piety and Art 1540–1700*, edi by Mary Hollingsworth and Carol. M. Richardsor University Park, PA: Pennsylvania State University Press, 2010, pp. 153–65

GALILEO

The Private Life of Galileo: Compiled Principally Fr His Correspondence and That of His Eldest Daughte Maria Celeste, Boston: Nicholas and Noyes, 1870

GALLUZZI

Galluzzi, Riguccio, *Istoria del Granducato di Tosca sotto il governo della Casa Medici*, 8 vols, Florence: Gaetano Cambiagi, 1781

GARFAGNINI

Garfagnini, Gian Carlo (ed.), *Lorenzo il Magnifica il suo mondo: Convegno internazionale di studi (Firenze, 9–13 giugno 1992)*, Florence: Leo S. Olsch 1994

GASTON

Gaston, Robert, 'Liturgy and Patronage in San Lorenza, Florence, 1350–1650', in *Patronage, Art, a Society in Renaissance Italy*, edited by F.W. Kent ar

Patricia Simons, Oxford: Clarendon Press, 1987, pp. 111–33

GAYE
Gaye, Giovanni, *Carteggio inedito d'artisti dei secoli 14–16*, 3 vols, Florence: G. Molini, 1839–40

GIULIANO
Giuliano, Antonio, 'Novità sul tesoro fi Lorenzo il Magnifico', in *Lorenzo il Magnifico e il suo mondo*, edited by G.C. Garfagnini, op. cit., pp. 319–22

GOLDTHWAITE
Goldthwaite, Richard A., *The Building of Renaissance Florence*, Baltimore, MD: Johns Hopkins University Press, 1980

GORI 1926
Gori, Pietro, *Le Feste Fiorentine attraverso i secoli: Le Feste per San Giovanni*, Florence: R. Bemporad & Figlio, 1926

GORI 1930
—, *Firenze Magnifica: Le feste fiorentine attraverso i secoli*, Florence: R. Bemporad & Figlio, 1930

GUARINI
Guarini, Elena Fassano, '"Rome, Workshop of all the Practices of the World": From the Letters of Cardinal Ferdinando de' Medici to Cosimo I and Francesco I', in *Court and Politics in Papal Rome 1492–1700*, edited by Gianvittorio Signorotto and Maria Antonietta Visceglia, Cambridge and New York: Cambridge University Press, 2002, pp. 53–77

GUASTI 1877
Guasti, Cesare, *Alessandra Macinghi negli Strozzi: Lettere di una gentildonna fiorentina*, Florence: G.C. Sansoni, 1877

GUASTI 1884
—, *Le Feste di S. Giovanni Batista in Firenze*, Florence: Giovanni Cirri, 1884

GUASTI 1887
—, *Santa Maria del Fiore: La costruzione della chiesa e del campanile*, Florence: M. Ricci, 1887

GUICCIARDINI FLORENCE
Guicciardini, Francesco, *Storie Fiorentine*, Bergamo: Biblioteca Universale Rizzoli, 1998

GUICCIARDINI ITALY
—, *Storia d'Italia*, 4 vols, Rome: Avanzini e Torraca, 1968

GUICCIARDINI RICORDI
—, *Maxims and Reflections (Ricordi)*, Philadelphia, PA: University of Pennsylvania Press, 1965

HALE 1968
Hale, J. R., 'The End of Florentine Liberty: The Fortezza da Basso', in *Florentine Studies: Politics and Society in Renaissance Florence*, edited by Nicolai Rubinstein, London: Faber & Faber, 1968, pp. 501–32

HALE 1977
—, *Florence and the Medici: The Pattern of Control*, London: Thames & Hudson, 1977

HASKELL & PENNY
Haskell, Francis and Nicholas Penny, *Taste and the Antique*, New Haven, CT and London: Yale University Press, 1980

HATFIELD 1970A
Hatfield, Rab, 'The Compagnia de' Magi', *Journal of the Warburg and Courtauld Institutes*, 33 (1970), pp. 107–61

HATFIELD 1970B
—, 'Some Unknown Descriptions of the Medici Palace in 1459', *Art Bulletin*, 52 (1970), pp. 232–49

HATFIELD 1976
—, *Botticelli's Uffizi Adoration: A Study in Pictorial Content*, Princeton, NJ: Princeton University Press, 1976

HERLIHY & KLAPISCH-ZUBER
Herlihy, David, and Christiane Klapisch-Zuber, *Tuscans and Their Families: A Study of the Catasto of 1427*, New Haven, CT and London: Yale University Press, 1985

HOFMANN
Hofmann, W. von, *Forschungen zur Geschichte der kurialen Behördern von Schisma bis zur Reformation*, Rome: Loescher, 1914

HOLLINGSWORTH 1984
Hollingsworth, Mary, 'The Architect in Fifteenth-Century Florence', *Art History*, 7 (1984), pp. 385–410

HOLLINGSWORTH 1994
—, *Patronage in Renaissance Italy: From 1400 to the Early Sixteenth Century*, London: John Murray, 1994

HOLLINGSWORTH 1996
—, *Patronage in Sixteenth-Century Italy*, London: John Murray, 1996

HOLLINGSWORTH 2008
—, 'A Cardinal in Rome: Ippolito d'Este in 1560', in *Art and Identity in Early Modern Rome*, edited by Jill Burke and Michael Bury, Aldershot: Ashgate, 2008, pp. 81–94

HOLMES
Holmes, George, 'How the Medici Became the Pope's Bankers', in *Florentine Studies: Politics and Society in Renaissance Florence*, edited by N. Rubinstein, London: Faber and Faber, 1968, pp. 357–380

HYMAN
Hyman, Isabelle, *Fifteenth-Century Florentine Studies*, New York: Garland 1977

ILARDI
Vincent Ilardi, 'The Banker-Statesman and the Condottiere-Prince: Cosimo de' Medici and Francesco Sforza (1450–1464)', in *Florence and Milan: Comparisons and Relations*, 2 vols, Florence: La Nuova Italia, 1989, Vol. 2, pp. 217–39

IMBERT
Imbert, Gaetano, *La vita Fiorentina nel Seicento*, Florence: R. Bemporad & figlio, 1906

D. KENT 1978
Kent, Dale, *The Rise of the Medici*, Oxford: Oxford University Press, 1978

D. KENT 2000
—, *Cosimo de' Medici and the Florentine Renaissance*, New Haven, CT and London: Yale University Press, 2000

D. AND F.W. KENT
Kent, D.V. and F.W. Kent, 'Two Comments of March 1445 on the Medici Palace', *Burlington Magazine*, 121 (1979), pp. 795–6

F.W. KENT 1981
Kent, F.W., 'The Making of a Renaissance Patron', in *Giovanni Rucellai ed il suo zibaldone II: A Florentine Patrician and His Palace*, London: Warburg Institute, 1981, pp. 9–95

F.W. KENT 1987
—, 'Palaces, Politics and Society in Fifteenth-Century Florence', *I Tatti Studies*, 2 (1987), pp. 41–70

F.W. KENT 2004
—, *Lorenzo de' Medici and the Art of Magnificence*, Baltimore, MD: Johns Hopkins University Press, 2004

KNECHT
Knecht, R.J., *Renaissance Warrior and Patron: The Reign of Francis I*, Cambridge and New York: Cambridge University Press, 1994

KOHL
Kohl, Benjamin G., 'Francesco Barbaro: On Wifely Duties', in *The Earthly Republic: Italian Humanists on Government and Society*, edited by Benjamin G. Kohl and Ronald G. Witt, Manchester: Manchester University Press, 1978, pp. 189–228

LANDUCCI
Landucci, Luca, *Diario Fiorentino dal 1450 al 1516*, Florence: Sansoni Editore, 1985

LANGDON
Langdon, Gabrielle, *Medici Women: Portraits of Power, Love, and Betrayal*, Toronto and Buffalo, NY: University of Toronto Press, 2006

LAPINI
Lapini, Agostino, *Diario Fiorentino*, Florence: G.C. Sansoni, 1900

LAZZARO
Lazzaro, Claudia, *The Italian Renaissance Garden*, New Haven, CT and London: Yale University Press, 1990

LEE
Lee, Egmont, *Sixtus IV and Men of Letters*, Rome: Storia e Letteratura, 1978

LE TEMS
Le Tems Revient: Il Tempo si rinuova: Feste e Spettacoli nella Firenze di Lorenzo il Magnifico, Milan: Silvana Editoriale, 1992

LOWE
Lowe, K.J.P., *Church and Politics in Renaissance Italy: The Life and Career of Cardinal Francesco Soderini (1453–1524)*, Cambridge and New York: Cambridge University Press, 1993

MACHIAVELLI
Machiavelli, Niccolò, *Tutte l'opere di Niccolò Machiavelli*, 3 vols, London: Tommaso Davies, 1772

MALLETT 1996
Mallett, Michael, 'Horse Racing and Politics in Lorenzo's Florence', in *Lorenzo the Magnificent*, edited by Michael Mallett and Nicholas Mann, op. cit., pp. 253–62

MALLETT & MANN
Mallett, Michael, and Nicholas Mann (eds), *Lorenzo the Magnificent: Culture and Politics*, London: Warburg Institute, 1996

MANETTI
Manetti, Antonio di Tuccio, *The Life of Brunelleschi*, University Park, PA: Pennsylvania State University Press, 1970

MARCHI
Marchi, Piero, 'Le feste fiorentine per le nozze di Maria de' Medici nell'anno 1600', in *Rubens e Firenze*, edited by Mina Gregori, Florence: La Nuova Italia, 1983, pp. 85–101

MARTINES 1963
Martines, Lauro, *The Social World of the Florentine Humanists 1390–1460*, London: Routledge and Kegan, 1963

MARTINES 1980
—, *Power and Imagination: City-States in Renaissance Italy*, London: Allen Lane, 1980

MARTINES 2003
—, *April Blood*, London: Jonathan Cape, 2003

MASI
Ricordanze di Bartolomeo Masi calderaio fiorentino dal 1478 al 1526, Florence: G.C. Sansoni, 1906

MITCHELL
Mitchell, Bonner, *The Majesty of State*, Florence: Leo S. Olschki, 1986

MOLHO
Molho, Anthony, *Florentine Public Finances in the Early Renaissance, 1400–1433*, Cambridge, MA: Harvard University Press, 1971

MONTAIGNE
Montaigne, Michel de, *The Complete Works*, London: Everyman's Library, 2003

NAJEMY
Najemy, John M., *A History of Florence 1200–1575*, Oxford: Blackwell, 2008

NEWBIGGIN 1994
Newbiggin, Nerida, 'Piety and Politics in the *Feste* of Lorenzo's Florence', in *Lorenzo il Magnifico e il suo mondo*, edited by G.C. Garfagnini, op. cit., pp. 17–41

NEWBIGGIN 1996
—, *Feste d'Oltrarno: Plays in Churches in Fifteenth-Century Florence*, Florence: Leo S. Olschki, 1996

PASTOR
Pastor, Ludwig von, *The History of the Popes From the Close of the Middle Ages*, 29 vols, London: Kegan Paul, Trench, Trübner, 1894–1951

PHILLIPS
Phillips, Mark, *The Memoir of Marco Parenti: A Life in Medici Florence*, Princeton, NJ: Princeton University Press, 1987

PICCOLOMINI

Piccolomini, Aeneas Silvius, *Secret Memoirs of a Renaissance Pope*, edited by F.A. Gragg and L.C. Gabel, London: Folio Society, 1988

PIGAFETTA

Pigafetta, Filippo, 'Firenze, che più bella di lei non vede 'l sole', in *Magnificenza alla Corte dei Medici*, Milan: Electa, 1997, pp. 433–7

POLIZZOTTO 1992

Polizzotto, Lorenzo, 'The Making of a Saint: The Canonization of St Antonino, 1516–1523', *Journal of Mediaeval and Renaissance Studies*, 22 (1992), pp. 353–83

PREYER 1981

Preyer, Brenda, 'The Rucellai Palace', in *Giovanni Rucellai ed il suo zibaldone II: A Florentine Patrician and His Palace*, London: Warburg Institute, 1981, pp. 155–225

PREYER 1990

—, 'L'architettura del Palazzo Mediceo', in *Il Palazzo Medici-Riccardi in Firenze*, edited by G. Cherubini and G. Fanelli, Florence: Giunti, 1990, pp. 58–75

PRICE

Price, Russell, 'Paolo Vettori', in *Cambridge Translations of Renaissance Philosophical Texts*, edited by Jill Kraye, 2 vols, Cambridge: Cambridge University Press, 1997, Vol. 2, pp. 238–46

REISS 1992

Reiss, Sheryl E., *Cardinal Giulio de' Medici as a Patron of Art 1513–1523*, Ann Arbor, MI: Garland, 1992

REISS 2001

—, 'Widow, Mother, Patron of Art: Alfonsina Orsini de' Medici', in *Beyond Isabella: Secular Women Patrons of Art in Renaissance Italy*, edited by Sheryl E. Reiss and David G. Wilkins, Kirksville, MO: Truman State University Press, 2001, pp. 125–57

ROOVER

Roover, Raymond de, *The Rise and Decline of the Medici Bank 1397–1494*, Washington, D.C.: Beard Books, 1999

ROSS

Ross, Janet, *Lives of the Early Medici as Told in Their Correspondence*, London: Chatto & Windus, 1910

ROTH

Roth, Cecil, *The Last Florentine Republic*, London: Methuen, 1925

RUBINSTEIN 1942

Rubinstein, Nicolai, 'The Beginnings of Political Thought in Florence', in *Studies in Italian History in the Middle Ages and the Renaissance*, edited by Giovanni Ciapelli, Rome: Edizioni di Storia e Letteratura, 2004, pp. 1–41

RUBINSTEIN 1966

—, *The Government of Florence Under the Medici 1434–1494*, Oxford: Oxford University Press, 1966

RUBINSTEIN 1968

—, 'Florentine Constitutionalism and Medici Ascendancy in the Fifteenth Century', in *Florentine Studies: Politics and Society in Renaissance Florence*, edited by N. Rubinstein, London: Faber & Faber, 1968, pp. 442–62

RUBINSTEIN 1977

—, 'Lorenzo de' Medici: The Formation of His Statecraft', in *Art and Politics in Renaissance Italy*, edited by George Holmes, Oxford and New York: Oxford University Press, 1993, pp. 113–36

RUBINSTEIN 1983

—, 'Dalla repubblica al principato', in *Firenze e la Toscana dei Medici nell'Europa del '500*, 3 vols, Florence: Leo S. Olschki, 1983, Vol. 1, pp. 159–76

RUBINSTEIN 1987
—, 'Classical Themes in the Decoration of the
Palazzo Vecchio in Florence', *Journal of the
Warburg and Courtauld Institutes*, 50 (1987),
pp. 29–43

RUCELLAI
Giovanni Rucellai ed il suo Zibaldone, edited by
Alessandro Perosa, London: Warburg Institute,
1981

SAALMAN & MATTOX
Saalman, Howard and Philip Mattox, 'The
First Medici Palace', *Journal of the Society of
Architectural Historians*, 44 (1985), pp. 329–345

SANUDO
Sanudo, Marin, *I diarii di Marino Sanuto*,
58 vols, Venice: F. Visentini, 1879–1903

SAVONAROLA
Selected Writings of Girolamo Savonarola, edited
by Anne Borelli and Maria Pastore Passaro,
New Haven, CT and London: Yale University
Press, 2006

SCOPRITORI
Scopritori e viaggiatori del Cinquecento, Milan
and Naples: Riccardo Ricciardi, 1996

SHAW
Shaw, Christine, *Julius II: The Warrior Pope*,
Oxford: Blackwell, 1996

SHEARMAN 1975A
Shearman, John, 'The Florentine *Entrata* of
Leo X, 1515', *Journal of the Warburg and
Courtauld Institutes*, 38 (1975), pp. 136–54

SHEARMAN 1975B
—, 'The Collections of the Younger Branch of
the Medici', *Burlington Magazine*, 117 (1975),
pp. 12–27

STORICI E POLITICI
Storici e politici fiorentini del Cinquecento,
edited by Angelo Baiocchi, Milan and Naples:
Riccardo Ricciardi, 1994

TOMAS
Tomas, Natalie R., *The Medici Women: Gender
and Power in Renaissance Florence*, Aldershot,
Hants: Ashgate, 2003

TREXLER 1978
Trexler, Richard C., *The Libro Cerimoniale of
the Florentine Republic*, Geneva: Librairie Droz,
1978

TREXLER 1980
—, *Public Life in Renaissance Florence*, Ithaca,
NY and London: Cornell University Press,
1980

VASARI
Milanesi, Gaetano (ed.), *Le opere di Giorgio
Vasari*, 8 vols, Florence: G.C. Sansoni, 1981

VESPASIANO
The Vespasiano Memoirs, translated by Williamo
George and Emily Waters, London: Routledge
& Sons, 1926

G. VILLANI
Villani, Giovanni, *Cronica*, Florence: Magheri,
1823

M. VILLANI
Villani, Matteo, *Cronica*, Florence: Magheri,
1825

WALLACE
Wallace, William, 'An Unpublished
Michelangelo Document', *Burlington
Magazine*, 129 (1987), pp. 181–4

WRIGHT 1994
Wright, Alison, 'The Myth of Hercules', in
Lorenzo il Magnifico e il suo mondo, edited by
G.C. Garfagnini, op. cit., pp. 323–39

ZAMBOTTI
Zambotti, Bernardino, *Diario ferrarese dal anno
1476 sino al 1504*, in *Rerum Italicarum
Scriptores*, New Series, Vol. 24, Part 7, Bologna:
Zanichelli, 1928

ZIMMERMAN
Zimmerman, T.C. Price, *Paolo Giovio: The
Historian and the Crisis of Sixteenth-Century
Italy*, Princeton NJ: Princeton University Press,
1995

NOTES

PROLOGUE:
A CITY UNDER SIEGE

1 Sanudo, Vol. 53, p. 516; on wage rates, see Goldthwaite (Appendix 3).

2 Roth, pp. 203–4.

3 Ibid., p. 174.

4 Gaye, Vol. 2, pp. 210–11 n. 158.

5 Ibid., p. 211 n. 158; Roth, p. 238.

6 Ibid., pp. 211–12 n. 158; Roth, p. 270.

7 Wallace.

8 Roth, pp. 291–2, n. 147.

9 Ibid., pp. 269, 287 n. 82.

10 Ibid., p. 305.

11 Ibid., p. 322 n. 35.

12 Ibid., p. 299.

1
MIGRANTS

1 Brucker 1957, p. 2.

2 Ibid. 1957, p. 3.

3 Rubinstein 1942, p. 20.

4 Brucker 1957, p. 4.

5 Ibid., p. 4.

6 G. Villani, bk. 10, 129.

7 Brucker 1957, p. 3.

8 Ibid., p. 4.

9 Ibid., pp. 23–5.

10 Ibid., p. 3.

11 Ibid., p. 3.

12 Ibid., p. 3.

13 Najemy, p. 112.

14 Compagni, p. 44.

15 Ibid., p. 70.

16 G. Villani, bk. 8, 70.

17 Dante, Vol. 1, pp. 175–6.

18 G. Villani, bk. 11, 67.

19 Ibid., 94.

20 Ibid., 91–4; Brucker 1984, pp. 88–9.

21 Ibid., 100.

22 Ibid., 114.

23 Najemy, p. 133.

24 Brucker 1957, pp. 5, 8.

25 Najemy, pp. 133–5.

26 G. Villani, bk. 12, 2.

27 Ibid., 17.

28 Ibid., 21; Najemy, pp. 137–9.

29 Ibid., 55; Najemy, pp. 132–5.

30 Brucker 1962, pp. 16–17.

31 G. Villani, bk. 12, 73.

32 Ibid., 91.

2
SURVIVORS

1 M. Villani, bk. 1, 57.

2 Brucker 1957, pp. 23–5; Brucker 1984, p. 43.

3 Brucker 1957, p. 6 n. 32; DBI, Vieri de' Medici.

4 DBI, Vieri de' Medici.

5 Brucker 1957, pp. 6–7.

6 Ibid., pp. 7–8.

7 Ibid., p. 13.

8 Ross, pp. 2–3.

9 Brucker 1957, p. 8.

10 Ross, p. 4.

11 Brucker 1957, pp. 8–9.

12 Ibid., p. 9; Najemy, p. 229.

13 Ibid., p. 11.

14 Ibid., p. 14.

15 Ibid., p. 154.

16 Ibid., p. 14.

17 Ibid., p. 9.

18 For the details of what follows, see Brucker 1957, pp. 5–6.

19 DBI, Vieri de' Medici.

20 On Vieri's bank, see Roover, pp. 35–7; Brucker 1957, pp. 6–7.

21 Guasti 1887, pp. 199–205.

22 Ross, pp. 2–3.

23 Brucker 1962, p. 218.

24 Ibid., pp. 248–9.

25 Ibid., pp. 271–2.

26 Ibid., pp. 293, 308.

27 Ibid., p. 317.

28 Brucker 1957, pp. 12–13; for the petition, see Brucker 1971, pp. 120–1.

29 Brucker 1962, pp. 327, 331.

30 Ibid., p. 363.

31 Ibid., pp. 364–5.

32 Ibid., p. 363.

33 Brucker 1957, p. 20.

34 Ibid., p. 6 & n. 30.

35 Roover, pp. 36, 417 n. 12; on Giovanni's early career, see Brucker 1957, pp. 21–2.

36 Roover, pp. 36–7.

37 DBI, Vieri de' Medici.

38 Machiavelli, Vol. I, p. 117; Brucker 1957, p. 22 n. 139.

39 DBI, Vieri de' Medici.

40 Brucker 1957, pp. 11–12; DBI, Vieri de' Medici.

41 Roover, pp. 48, 419 n. 66.

42 D. Kent 1978, p. 41; Brucker 1957, p. 22.

3

THE FORTUNE

1 Roover, pp. 36–8, 40.

2 Ibid., pp. 39–41.

3 Ibid., p. 41.

4 Ibid., p. 36.

5 Holmes, p. 363.

6 Roover, pp. 41–4.

7 Ibid., p. 52.

8 Martines 1963, pp. 353–65, tables 1–4.

9 Holmes, p. 363 & n. 3.

10 Ibid., pp. 367–9.

11 Ibid., pp. 371–2.

12 Roover, p. 48.

13 Trexler 1980, p. 2 n. 4.

14 Holmes, pp. 362–3.

15 Ibid., p. 375.

16 Doren; Hollingsworth 1994, pp. 27–9.

17 Kohl, pp. 193–4 & *passim*.

18 Saalman & Mattox, pp. 336–7; D. Kent 2000, p. 247.

19 D. Kent 2000, pp. 33–8, 77–81.

20 Ibid., p. 403 n. 4.

21 Roover, p. 48.

22 Ibid., p. 47, table 8.

23 Ibid., pp. 49–50.

24 Holmes, p. 380.

25 Saalman & Mattox, pp. 344–5.

26 D. Kent 2000, p. 181; Brucker 1971, p. 190 (Doc. 88).

27 D. Kent 1978, p. 41 n. 15.

28 Ibid., p. 41.

4

POLITICS

1 D. Kent 1978, p. 99.

2 Ibid., pp. 116–17.

3 Roover, pp. 383–6.

4 D. Kent 1978, pp. 55–7.

5 Cavalcanti, Vol. 1, pp. 74–90; D. Kent 1978, pp. 211–20.

6 D. Kent 1978, p. 101.

7 Najemy, p. 258.

8 Martines 1963, pp. 369–78, tables 5–8.

9 Cavalcanti, Vol. 1, pp. 261–3.

10 D. Kent 1978, pp. 223–4.

11 Ibid., p. 234 & n. 65.

12 Ibid., p. 277.

13 Ross, pp. 15–16.

14 D. Kent 1978, p. 278.

15 Cavalcanti, Vol. 2, p. 418.

16 D. Kent 1978, pp. 279–80.

17 Molho 1971, pp. 63, 157–8.

18 D. Kent 1978, p. 283.

19 Molho 1971, pp. 215–21; D. Kent 1978, pp. 284–8.

20 Carl.

21 Molho 1971, p. 181, table 11.

22 Roover, pp. 54–5.

23 Ross, p. 20.

24 Cavalcanti, Vol. 2, pp. 399–421, D. Kent 1978, *passim*.

25 Ross, pp. 21–3.

26 Cavalcanti, Vol. 1, p. 521.

27 Ross, p. 24.

28 D. Kent 1978, p. 306.

5

FOR HONOUR AND PROFIT

1 D. Kent 1978, pp. 319–21.

2 Ibid., p. 133 & n. 127.

3 Ibid., p. 308 n. 81, p. 323.

4 Ibid., p. 331.

5 Ibid.

6 Ross, p. 26; Najemy, p. 277.

7 Guicciardini *Florence*, p. 82.

8 D. Kent 2000, p. 37.

9 Piccolomini, p. 102.

10 Roover, pp. 47, 55, tables 8 & 11.

11 Ibid., pp. 317–21.

12 Ibid., pp. 59, 143.

13 Ibid., pp. 56, 59.

14 Ross, pp. 39–40.

15 Ibid., pp. 14–15; on the correct dating of the letter, see Roover, p. 450 n. 81.

16 Ibid., pp. 40–1.

17 Ibid., pp. 42–3.

18 Roover, p. 217; Fortini Brown.

19 D. Kent 2000, pp. 183–4.

20 Gaston, p. 122.

21 Trexler 1980, p. 423.

22 D. Kent 2000, p. 132.

23 Ibid., p. 172.

24 Roover, p. 69, table 17.

25 A. Brown 1992, pp. 76–7.

26 Ibid., pp. 75–77.

27 Tomas, p. 17.

28 Ross, p. 151.

29 D. Kent 2000, p. 220.

30 Ross, p. 50.

31 Machiavelli, Vol. 1, p. 217.

32 Ibid., p. 223.

33 Ross, pp. 50–1.

34 Ibid., p. 51.

35 Ibid., pp. 52–3.

36 Ibid., p. 56.

37 Bullard 1994, p. 124.

6

THE REPUBLICAN TOGA

1 Piccolomini, p. 101.

2 Ross, p. 58.

3 Wright 1994, p. 323 n. 1.

4 D. Kent 2000, p. 283.

5 Roover, p. 31, table 5.

6 Ibid., pp. 72–4.

7 D. Kent 2000, p. 16.

8 Ross, pp. 58–9.

9 Ibid., p. 60.

10 Ibid., p. 143.

11 Roover, pp. 26–7.

12 D. Kent 2000, pp. 291–2.

13 Roover, pp. 70–1, 268, 270.

14 Ross, p. 59.

15 On the division of the fortune, see A. Brown 1992, pp. 73, 77.

16 Ibid., p. 80.

17 Ibid., p. 80.

18 Cavalcanti, Vol. 2, p. 193.

19 Ibid., p. 210.

20 Ibid., p. 211.

21 Guicciardini *Florence*, p. 90.

22 A. Brown 1992, p. 82.

23 Ibid., p. 84.

24 Trexler 1978, p. 78.

25 Newbiggin 1994, p. 31 n. 45.

26 Trexler 1978, p. 77; Trexler 1980, p. 76 n. 152.

27 Piccolomini, p. 100.

28 Newbiggin 1994, p. 31 n. 45.

29 Hatfield 1970b, p. 232; D. Kent 2000, p. 300.

30 Trexler 1980, p. 426.

31 D'Accone 1994, pp. 269–70 & *passim*.

32 Preyer 1981, p. 215 (doc. 14); on the match, see F.W. Kent 1981, pp. 66–7.

33 D. Kent 2000, p. 244.

34 Roover, p. 85.

35 Ross, p. 63.

36 Ibid., p. 64.

37 Ibid., p. 65.

38 Ibid., pp. 69–70.

39 Ibid., pp. 70–1.

40 A. Brown 1992, p. 55.

41 Ross, pp. 74-6.

42 Phillips, p. 8.

43 Ibid., p. 14.

7

THE SUCCESSION CRISIS

1 Ilardi, p. 237 n. 67.

2 Roover, p. 359.

3 Guasti 1877, p. 350; see also Roover, pp. 359–60.

4 Roover, pp. 218–20, 451 n. 88.

5 D. Kent 2000, p. 183.

6 Rubinstein 1966, p. 136.

7 F.W. Kent 2004, p. 12.

8 Guasti 1877, pp. 381–4; see also Phillips, p. 109.

9 Ibid., pp. 413–15; see also Phillips, p. 125.

10 Phillips, p. 121.

11 Ross, pp. 88–92.

12 Ibid., pp. 93–5.

13 Ibid., pp. 94–5.

14 Phillips, p. 145.

15 F.W. Kent 1987, p. 62 n. 106.

16 Landucci, p. 5.

17 Brucker 1994, p. 9.

18 Ross, pp. 102–3.

19 Guicciardini *Florence*, p. 99.

20 Rubinstein 1968, p. 459 n. 8.

21 Rucellai, p. 31; Goldthwaite (Appendix 1).

22 F.W. Kent 1981, p. 69.

23 F W. Kent 1987, p. 64 n. 111.

24 A. Brown 1992, p. 86.

25 Ross, pp. 105–6.

26 Ibid., p. 117.

27 A. Brown 1992, pp. 87–9.

28 F.W. Kent 2004, p. 22.

29 Ross, pp. 108–10.

30 Ibid., p. 115; on the springs at Morba, see ibid., pp. 111–15.

31 Ibid., p. 115–16.

32 Ibid., pp. 117–18.

33 Ibid., p. 120.

34 Ibid., pp. 122–3.

35 Newbiggin 1994, p. 33 n. 49.

36 Ross, pp. 123–4.

37 Ibid., p. 125.

38 Ibid., pp. 129–34.

39 Ibid., p. 141.

40 Ibid., p. 137.

41 Ibid., pp. 138–40.

42 Ibid., pp. 140–1.

8

YOUTH AT THE HELM

1 Ross, p. 154; Rubinstein 1977, p. 117.

2 Guasti 1877, pp. 607–9; see also A. Brown 1992, pp. 89–90.

3 A. Brown 1992, pp. 90–1.

4 Dei, pp. 146–7.

5 Ibid., pp. 85–6.

6 F.W. Kent 1981, p. 67.

7 Roover, p. 362.

8 Rubinstein 1977, p. 125.

9 A. Brown 1992, pp. 91–2.

10 Ross, p. 152; A. Brown 1992, pp. 77–8.

11 Ross, pp. 159–61.

12 Trexler 1978, p. 85.

13 Machiavelli, Vol. 1, pp. 268–9.

14 Newbiggin 1996, pp. 132–4.

15 Ibid., p. 205.

16 Beschi, p. 301; see also Giuliano.

17 Pastor, Vol. 4, p. 212n.

18 Ross, pp. 163–4.

19 Ibid., pp. 167–8.

20 Ibid., pp. 168–71.

21 Ibid., p. 153.

22 Ibid., pp. 172–3.

23 F.W. Kent 1994, p. 44.

24 Ross, p. 155.

25 F.W. Kent 2004, p. 72.

26 Mallett 1996, pp. 257–8 & *passim*.

27 A. Brown 1992, pp. 93–4 & n. 82.

28 A. Brown 1994, p. 67.

29 Martines 2003, pp. 100–1.

30 Ibid., p. 122.

31 Landucci, p. 19.

32 Ross, pp. 192–3.

33 Ibid., pp. 198-9.

34 Rubinstein 1977, p. 128.

35 Ross, p. 206.

36 Landucci, p. 23.

37 Ross, pp. 203–5.

38 Ibid., pp. 207–8.

39 Roover, pp. 366, 483 n. 56.

40 Ross, pp. 210–11.

41 Ibid., pp. 209–10.

42 Ibid., pp. 212–13.

43 Ibid., pp. 213–14.

44 Landucci, p. 25.

45 Ibid., p. 30.

46 A. Brown 1994, p. 77.

47 Ross, pp. 219–20.

48 Ibid., p. 221.

49 Ibid., p. 228.

50 Ibid., pp. 229–30.

51 Ibid., pp. 231–2.

9

PRIDE

1 Guicciardini *Florence*, pp. 145–6.

2 Landucci, p. 33.

3 Rubinstein 1987, pp. 37–8.

4 F.W. Kent 1994, p. 59.

5 Bullard 1992, p. 16.

6 F.W. Kent 1994, p. 54.

7   A. Brown 1992, pp. 152–3 n. 6.

8   A. Brown 1994, p. 64 n. 12.

9   Ibid., p. 64 n. 10.

10 Ross, p. 155.

11 Ibid., pp. 254–5.

12 Mallett 1996, p. 261.

13 Ross, p. 155.

14 Ibid., pp. 258–60.

15 Ibid., pp. 260–5.

16 Ibid., pp. 272–3.

17 Bullard 1994, p. 126.

18 Ibid., pp. 141–2.

19 Ross, pp. 327–30.

20 Bullard 1994, p. 137 n. 54.

21 Ibid., pp. 135–6.

22 Ibid., p. 139.

23 Bullard 1992, p. 8; Bullard 1994, p. 133.

24 Hollingsworth 1984, p. 404.

25 Bullard 1992, p. 12.

26 Butters 1994, p. 144.

27 Reiss 2001, pp. 125–6.

28 Landucci, p. 55.

29 Ross, p. 298.

30 Ibid., pp. 310–11.

31 Ibid., pp. 301–2.

32 Ibid., pp. 303–4.

33 Ibid., p. 309.

34 Bullard 1987, p. 43.

35 Landucci, p. 52.

36 Manetti, pp. 102–6.

37 Vespasiano, pp. 220–1.

38 Shearman 1975b, p. 25.

39 Bullard 1992, p. 13 n. 33; F.W. Kent 2004, p. 146.

40 F.W. Kent 2004, p. 147.

41 Newbiggin 1994, p. 23.

42 A. Brown 1994, pp. 69–70.

43 Roover, p. 362.

44 A. Brown 1992, pp. 96–8.

45 Guicciardini *Florence*, p. 177.

46 A. Brown 1992, pp. 170–1.

47 Ibid., pp. 172–3.

48 Ibid., pp. 176–7.

49 A. Brown 1994, pp. 79–80.

50 Ross, pp. 326–7.

51 Ibid., p. 330.

52 Ibid., p. 331.

53 Ibid., p. 336.

54 Ibid., pp. 332–5.

55 Machiavelli, Vol. 1, p. 316.

56 Landucci, pp. 64–5.

57 A. Brown 1994, pp. 61 n. 2, 79 n. 65.

10
NEMESIS

1   Guicciardini *Florence*, pp. 189–90.

2   Zambotti, p. 231.

3   Guicciardini *Florence*, p. 191.

4   Ibid., p. 198.

5   Ibid., p. 193.

6   Landucci, p. 69.

7   Ibid., p. 73.

8   Ibid., pp. 73–5.

9   Ibid., p. 114.

10 Mitchell, p. 64.

11 Landucci, p. 86.

12 Tomas, pp. 108, 119 n. 22.

13 Savonarola, pp. 139–50.

14 Guicciardini *Florence*, pp. 185–6.

15 Pastor, Vol. 5, pp. 203–4.

16 Savonarola, p. 211.

17 Guicciardini *Florence*, p. 255.

18 Ibid., p. 252.

19 Ibid., p. 320.

20 Ibid., pp. 348–9.

21 Ibid., pp. 363–4.

22 Ibid., pp. 390–1.

23 Ibid., pp. 471–2.

11
EXILE

1   Shaw, p. 171.

2   Guicciardini *Florence*, p. 473.

3   Ibid., p. 473.

4   Ibid., p. 413.

5   Lowe 1993, pp. 69–70.

6   Masi, p. 66.

7   Landucci, p. 276.

8   Ibid., p. 283.

9   Ibid., p. 273.

10 Bullard 1980, p. 60.

11 Shearman 1975a, p. 154.

12 Pastor, Vol. 6, p. 369.

13 Ibid., pp. 369–71.

14 Masi, pp. 76–7.

15 Pastor, Vol. 6, p. 400.

16 Landucci, p. 319.

17 Ibid., pp. 322–4.

18 Ibid., p. 331.

12
AGE OF GOLD

1   Cummings, p. 183 n. 26.

2   Ibid., p. 183, n. 27.

3   Pastor, Vol. 7, pp. 18, 22.

4   Lowe, p. 93.

5   Pastor, Vol. 7, p. 25.

6   Guicciardini *Italy*, p. 1022.

7   Pastor, Vol. 8, p. 473 (doc. 9).

8   Ibid., p. 151.

9   Ferrajoli, pp. 204–5.

10 Pastor, Vol. 8, p. 156 n.

11 Reiss 1992, p. 222.

12 Tomas, p. 155 n. 79; Reiss 2001, pp. 144–5 n. 27.

13 Bullard 1980, p. 85.

14 Price, p. 239.

15 Pastor, Vol. 7, p. 80 n.

16 Najemy, p. 430.

17 Tomas, p. 156 n. 111.

18 Shearman 1975a, p. 154.

19 Landucci, pp. 345–7.

20 Tomas, p. 188 n. 51.

21 Reiss 2001, p. 150 n. 75.

22 Bullard 1980, p. 90 n. 95.

23 Reiss 2001, p. 151 n. 79.

24 Polizzotto 1992, p. 362 n. 35.

25 Landucci, pp. 352–9.

26 Pastor, Vol. 8, p. 162.

27 Ibid., Vol. 7, pp. 132, 140.

28 Landucci, p. 361.

29 Guicciardini *Italy*, p. 1177.

30 Gori 1930, p. 107.

31 Ibid., p. 110.

32 Bullard 1987, p. 37.

33 Butters 1996, p. 275.

34 Machiavelli, Vol. 1, p. 316.

35 Hofmann, Vol. 2, pp. 168–71; Pastor, Vol. 8, p. 96.

36 Hofmann, Vol. 2, pp. 168–71.

37 Pastor, Vol. 8, p. 98.

38 Ibid., pp. 176–7.

39 Ibid., Vol. 7, p. 6–7.

13

AGE OF IRON

1 Pastor, Vol. 9, p. 22.

2 Guicciardini *Italy*, p. 1523.

3 Pastor, Vol. 9, p. 244.

4 Knecht, p. 224.

5 Sanudo, Vol. 38, pp. 188–9.

6 Bullard 1980, p. 134.

7 Pastor, Vol. 9, p. 310.

8 Wikipedia, *Giovanni delle Bande Nere*.

9 Reiss 1992, p. 59.

10 Pastor, Vol. 9, p. 502 (doc. 44).

11 Bullard 1980, p. 131.

12 Pastor, Vol. 10, pp. 30–1.

13 Bullard 1980, p. 152.

14 Sanudo, Vol. 51, pp. 417–18, 461.

15 Roth, p. 174.

16 Adams, p. 476 nn. 13, 16.

17 Ibid., pp. 478–81.

18 Ibid., p. 482.

14

IMPERIAL POODLES

1 Rubinstein 1983, p. 168.

2 Landucci, p. 371.

3 Hale 1968, p. 504.

4 Rubinstein 1983, p. 172.

5 Landucci, p. 371.

6 Lapini, pp. 98–9.

7 Landucci, p. 371.

8 Vasari, Vol. 8, pp. 240–1 (doc. 5).

9 Ibid., pp. 241–2 (doc. 6).

10 Guicciardini *Ricordi*, p. 98.

11 Zimmerman, p. 139.

12 Ibid., p. 123.

13 Bullard 1980, pp. 158–9.

14 Pastor, Vol. 10, p. 363 n.1.

15 Ibid., p. 510 (doc. 36).

16 Bullard 1980, p. 166.

17 Zimmerman, p. 139.

18 Vasari, Vol. 8, p. 255.

19 Ibid., p. 254.

20 Ibid., Vol. 7, p. 659.

21 Ibid., Vol. 6, p. 440.

22 Ibid., Vol. 8, pp. 269–70.

23 *Storici e Politici*, p. 720.

24 Lapini, p. 103.

25 Langdon, p. 41.

26 Hale 1977, p. 138.

27 DBI, Cosimo I.

28 Lapini, p. 104.

15

THE NEW AUGUSTUS

1 J. Brown, p. 287.

2 DBI, Cosimo I.

3 Lapini, p. 155.

4 Zimmerman, p. 145.

5 Vasari, Vol. 7, pp. 709–10.

6 Barocchi & Bertelà, p. 36 (doc. 32).

7 Vasari, Vol. 7, p. 603.

8 Barocchi & Bertelà, p. 3 (doc. 1).

9 Ibid., p. 7 (doc. 5).

10 Gáldy, p. 162 n. 28.

11 Lazzaro, p. 200.

12 Vasari, Vol. 7, p. 603.

13 Ibid., Vol. 1, pp. 1–2.

14 Lapini, pp. 112–13.

15 Pastor, Vol. 14, p. 482 (doc. 54).

16 Gori 1926, pp. 230-1.

17 Lapini, p. 120.

16

GRAND DUKE

1 Gáldy, p. 162 n. 28.

2 Ibid., pp. 157–8.

3 Coffin, p. 150.

4 Hollingsworth 2008, p. 88.

5 Lapini, p. 134.

6 Vasari, Vol. 8, pp. 364–5.

7 Ibid., Vol. 7, p. 616.

8 Lapini, pp. 142–3.

9 Ibid., p. 148; Barocchi & Bertelà, pp. 17–19 (doc. 17).

10 Vasari, Vol. 7, p. 702.

11 Lapini, p. 151.

12 Ibid., p. 157.

13 Ibid., p. 163.

14 Ibid., p. 165.

15 Ibid., p. 171.

16 Ibid., pp. 169–70.

17 Ibid., p. 174.

18 Ibid., p. 177.

19 Ibid., p. 154.

20 Ibid., p. 180.

17

ADULTERY

1 Barocchi & Bertelà, pp. 158–9 (doc. 170 and n).

2 Lapini, p. 220.

3 Guarini, p. 62.

4 Barocchi & Bertelà, p. 99 (doc. 100 n).

5 Ibid., p. 115 (doc. 117).

6 Coffin, p. 224.

7 Gori 1930, p. 168.

8 Langdon, p. 148.

9 Ibid., pp. 205–8 (Appendix C).

10 Ibid., p. 178.

11 Ibid.

12 Ibid., p. 179.

13 Lapini, p. 192.

14 Langdon, p. 166.

15 Lapini, pp. 194–5.

16 Gori 1926, p. 127.

17 Lapini, pp. 197–8.

18 Montaigne, p. 1134.

19 Ibid., p. 1132.

20 Barocchi & Bertelà, p. 229 (doc. 249).

21 Ibid., pp. 228–9 (doc. 248).

22 Ibid., p. 190 (doc. 205).

23 Ibid., p. 235 (doc. 256n).

24 Scopritori, pp. 904–13.

25 Ibid., pp. 918–21.

26 Lapini, pp. 240–1.

27 Ibid., p. 215.

28 Guarini, p. 74.

29 Gori 1930, p. 270.

30 Lapini, p. 251.

31 Gori 1930, p. 264.

18

CARDINAL TO GRAND DUKE

1 Butters 2010, p. 185.

2 Ibid., p. 225 n. 255.

3 Hale 1977, p. 151.

4 Lapini, pp. 261–2.

5 Ibid., p. 279.

6 Ibid., p. 283.

7 Ibid., p. 284.

8 Butters 2010, p. 213 n. 38.

9 Lapini, pp. 299–300.

10 Ibid., p. 298.

11 Butters 2010, p. 203.

12 Lapini, p. 267.

13 Butters 2010, p. 215 n. 73.

14 Ibid., pp. 192–3.

15 Acton & Cheney, p. 301.

16 Cochrane, p. 113.

17 Lapini, p. 291.

18 Ibid., pp. 304–5.

19 Ibid., p. 310.

20 Ibid., p. 314.

21 Ibid., pp. 315–16.

22 Ibid., p. 316–17.

23 Acton & Cheney, p. 304.

24 Lapini, p. 272–4.

25 Marchi, p. 88.

26 Ibid., p. 90.

27 Berti, pp. 3–4.

19
THE UNLUCKY PRINCE

1 Galileo, pp. 81–3 n. 1.

2 Pastor, Vol. 29, p. 373 nn. 3–4.

3 Fanelli, p. 129.

4 DBI, Maria Maddalena d'Austria granduchessa di Toscana.

20
SCIENCE AND RELIGION

1 Black, pp. 156–7.

2 DBI, Ferdinando II de' Medici.

3 Black, p. 199.

4 Imbert, p. 298 n. 209.

5 DBI, Ferdinando II de' Medici.

6 Pastor, Vol. 28, p. 61.

7 Galileo, p. 184.

8 Ibid., p. 211.

9 Ibid., p. 217.

10 Ibid., p. 220.

11 Acton & Cheney, pp. 306–7.

12 Cochrane, pp. 249–50.

13 Acton & Cheney, p. 145.

14 Ibid., p. 208.

15 DBI, Leopoldo de' Medici.

16 Gori 1930, p. 208.

17 Acton, p. 26.

18 Ibid., p. 29.

19 Galluzzi VII, p. 297.

20 Cochrane, p. 261.

21
VANITY

1 Galluzzi, Vol. 8, pp. 20–1.

2 Conti, p. 21.

3 Acton & Cheney, p. 311.

4 Conti, p. 279.

5 Imbert, p. 182.

6 Conti, p. 360.

7 Ibid., p. 208.

8 Ibid., pp. 165–6.

9 Ibid., p. 269.

10 Ibid., p. 378.

11 Imbert, p. 271 n. 109.

12 Galluzzi, Vol. 8, pp. 94–7.

13 Ibid., p. 141.

14 Acton & Cheney, p. 311.

15 Galluzzi, Vol. 8, p. 157.

16 Conti, pp. 147–8.

17 Ibid., pp. 96–7.

18 Ibid., p. 176.

19 Galluzzi, Vol. 8, pp. 241–4.

20 Ibid.

21 Acton, p. 251.

22
EXTINCTION

1 Conti, p. 811.

2 Ibid., p. 849.

3 Ibid., p. 829.

IMAGE CREDITS

p.3 Pontormo, *Cosimo de' Medici the Elder*; Uffizi, Florence / Google Cultural Institute / Wikimedia Commons.

pp.20–21 The 'Carta della Catena'; Museo di Firenze com'era, Florence / Bridgeman Images.

p.25 Florentine florin of 1347, with a fleur-de-lis on one side and John the Baptist on the other; Wiki. Commons.

p.26 Baptistery, Florence; Shutterstock.

p.30 Palazzo della Signoria (Palazzo Vecchio); Shutterstock.

pp.32–33 Giotto, *St Francis Renounces His Worldly Goods* (Sta Croce, Florence) © Alinari Archives / Corbis via Getty Images.

p.38 *The Expulsion of the Duke of Athens* (Palazzo Vecchio, Florence); Web Gallery of Art / Wiki. Commons.

pp.40–1 Domenico di Michelino, memorial to Dante (Duomo, Florence); De Agostini via Getty Images.

p.45 Francesco Traini, *Triumph of Death* (Pisa, Camposanto); Peter Barritt / Alamy Stock Photo.

p.48 Andrea Orcagna, tabernacle; M. Ramírez / Alamy Stock Photo.

p.52 Andrea da Firenze, *The Church Triumphant*, Sta Maria Novella, Florence; Sailko / Wiki. Commons.

pp.56–7 Ambrosio Lorenzetti, *Allegory of Good Government*, Palazzo Pubblico, Siena; Google Cultural Institute / Wiki. Commons.

p.65 Fra Angelico, *Miracle of Saints Cosmas and Damian*; De Agostini / Getty Images.

p.71 Lorenzo Ghiberti, *St Matthew*, Orsanmichele, Florence; Bridgeman Images.

p.72 Interior courtyard of the Palazzo Davanzati; Atlantide Phototravel / Getty Images.

p.76 The Old Sacristy, San Lorenzo; Sailko / Wikimedia Commons.

p.81 Masolino da Panicale, *Healing of the Cripple and Raising of Tabitha* (Brancacci Chapel, Sta Maria del Carmine, Florence); Bridgeman Images.

p.84 Nave of the church of San Lorenzo, Florence; Stefan Bauer / Wiki. Commons.

p.87 Luca della Robbia, *Cantoria*; Sailko / Wiki. Commons.

p.89 Medal of Cosimo de' Medici; Sailko / Wiki. Commons.

pp.90–1 Paolo Uccello, *Battle of San Romano*; National Gallery, London / Wiki. Commons.

pp.92–3 Justus Utens, *Villa Medici at Cafaggiolo*; The Museums of Florence / Wiki. Commons.

p.101 Pazzi Chapel, Basilica of Santa Croce; Gryffindor / Wiki. Commons.

p.102 Bonifacio Bembo, *Francesco Sforza*; NMUIM / Alamy Stock Photo.

p.108 Fra Angelico, *San Marco altarpiece*; Museo di San Marco, Florence / Directmedia / Wiki. Commons.

p.118 Donatello, *David*; Museo Nazionale del Bargello, Florence / Rufus46 / Wiki. Commons.

p.120 Mino da Fiesole, *Giovanni de' Medici*; Vincenzo Fontana / Corbis Historical via Getty Images.

pp.124–5 Benozzo Gozzoli, *Journey of the Magi* (Cappella dei Magi, Palazzo Medici-Riccardi); Wiki. Commons.

p.129 The Palazzo Medici, Florence; Allan T. Kohl / Creative Commons.

p.135 Mino da Fiesole, *Piero de' Medici*; Museo Nazionale del Bargello, Florence / Bridgeman Images.

p.139 Luca della Robbia, *Labours of the Months*; Victoria & Albert Museum, London / Bridgeman Images.

p.143 Antonio Pollaiuolo, *Portrait of a Young Woman*; Museo Poldi-Pezzoli, Milan / De Agostini via Getty Images.

pp.146–7 Fra Filippo Lippi. *The Feast of Herod* (Prato, Duomo); Bridgeman Images.

p. 153 Andrea del Verrocchio, *Lorenzo de' Medici*; National Gallery of Art, Washington / Wiki. Commons.

pp.154–5 Sandro Botticelli, *Adoration of the Magi*; Uffizi, Florence / Directmedia / Wiki. Commons.

p.156 Santa Maria Novella, Florence; Shutterstock.

p.157 Domenico Ghirlandaio, *Confirmation of the Franciscan Rule* (Sta Trinita, Sassetti Chapel, Florence); Mondadori Portfolio / Hulton Fine Art Collection / Getty Images.

p.160 Tazza Farnese; Ana al'ain / Wiki. Commons.

p.167 Bertoldo di Giovanni, medal; Sailko / Wiki. Commons.

p.177 Filippino Lippi, Carafa Chapel; Urnes / Wiki. Commons.

pp.182–3 Sandro Botticelli, *Primavera*; Uffizi, Florence / Wiki. Commons.

p.184 Antique sardonyx vase; Museo degli Argenti, Florence / De Agostini via Getty Images.

p.185 Poggio a Caiano, Villa Medici; Shutterstock.

p.195 Donatello, *Judith and Holofernes* (Palazzo Vecchio, Florence); Wiki. Commons.

p.199 Sandro Botticelli, *Portrait of a Woman* (Palazzo Pitti, Florence); Hulton Fine Art Collection / Getty Images.

p.200 Andrea del Sarto, *Punishment of the Gamblers*; ART Collection / Alamy Stock Photo.

p.203 *Martyrdom of Savonarola*; Museo di San Marco, Florence / World History Archive / Alamy Stock Photo.

p.207 Michelangelo, *David*; Accademia, Florence / Jörg Bittner Unna / Wiki. Commons.

p.211 Raphael, Pope Julius II in a detail from *Mass at Bolsena* (Stanza della Segnatura, Vatican Palace); Directmedia / Wiki. Commons.

p.215 Tempietto; Angelo Homack / Corbis Historical via Getty Images.

pp.218–19 Michelangelo, Sistine Chapel ceiling (Vatican Palace); EmmePi Travel / Alamy Stock Photo.

p.229 Raphael, *Portrait of Pope Leo X with two Cardinals*; Uffizi, Florence / Google Cultural Institute / Wiki. Commons.

p.230 After Raphael, *Giuliano de' Medici*; Metropolitan Museum of Art, New York / Wiki. Commons.

p.234 Raphael, *Lorenzo de' Medici*; Private Collection / Bridgeman Images.

p.241 Michelangelo, staircase of the Biblioteca Laurenziana; Biblioteca Medicea-Laurenziana, Florence / Bridgeman Images.

p.243 Andrea del Sarto, *Tribute to Caesar* (Poggio a Caiano, Villa Medici); De Agostini / G. Roli / Bridgeman Images.

pp.244–5 Raphael, *Coronation of Charlemagne* (Stanza dell'Incendio, Vatican Palace); VCG Wilson / Corbis via Getty Images.

p.253 Sebastiano del Piombo, *Clement VII*; Gallerie Nazionali di Capodimonte, Naples / De Agostini via Getty Images.

p.254 After Raphael, *The Donation of Constantine* (Stanza di Costantino, Vatican Palace); © Stefano Baldini / Bridgeman Images.

p. 260 Titian, *Equestrian portrait of Charles V*; Prado, Madrid/Wikimedia Commons.

p.264 Giorgio Vasari, *Clement VII crowns Emperor Charles V* (Palazzo Vecchio, Florence); Heritage Images / Hulton Fine Art Collection / Getty Images.

p.272 Giorgio Vasari, *Lorenzo the Magnificent*; Uffizi, Florence / Bridgeman Images.

p.275 Giorgio Vasari, *Duke Alessandro de' Medici*; Uffizi, Florence / Heritage Image Partnership Ltd / Alamy Stock Photo.

p.276 Michelangelo, *The Last Judgement* (Sistine Chapel, Vatican Palace); Alonso de Mendoza / Wiki. Commons.

p.279 Titian, *Cardinal Ippolito de' Medici* (Palazzo Pitti, Florence); Bridgeman Images.

p.282 Agnolo Bronzino, *Duke Cosimo I*; Art Gallery of New South Wales, Sydney / Google Cultural Institute / Wiki. Commons.

p.287 Agnolo Bronzino, *Portrait of Eleonora of Toledo with her son*; Uffizi, Florence / Google Arts and Culture / Wiki. Commons.

p.293 The Uffizi, Florence; Shutterstock.

p.294 Benvenuto Cellini, *Perseus and Medusa* (Loggia dei Lanzi; Florence); De Agostini Picture Library / G. Berengo Gardin / Bridgeman Images.

p.297 Etruscan statuette of the Chimaera; Museo Archeologico Nazionale, Florence / Sailko / Wikimedia Commons.

p.299 Vincenzo Danti, *Cosimo I as Emperor Augustus*; Museo Nazionale del Bargello, Florence / Rufus46 / Wiki. Commons.

p.312 Column of Justice in Florence's Piazza Santa Trinita; EyeEm / Alamy Stock Photo.

p.315 Giovanni Antonio de' Rossi, *Cosimo I and his family*; Museo degli Argenti, Florence / De Agostini Picture Library via Getty Images.

p. 317 Bartolomeo Ammannati, *Fountain of Neptune* (Piazza della Signoria, Florence); Wikimedia Commons.

pp.320–1 Giorgio Vasari, *The Apotheosis of Cosimo I* (Palazzo Vecchio, Florence); Google Cultural Institute / Wiki. Commons.

p.330 Jan van der Straet, *The Alchemist* (Palazzo Vecchio, Florence); Granger Historical Picture Archive / Alamy Stock Photo.

p.334 Pieter Paul Rubens, *Joanna of Austria*; Louvre, Paris / De Agostini Editorial via Getty Images.

pp.338–339 Justus Utens, *Villa Medici at Pratolino*; The Museums of Florence / Wiki. Commons.

p.340 Giambologna, *Appennino* (Villa Demidoff, Pratolino); David Lyons / Alamy Stock Photo.

p.342 Workshop of Alessandro Allori, *Bianca Cappello*, *c.*1580; Tokyo Fuji Art Museum, Tokyo / Bridgeman Images.

pp.350–1 Orazio Scarabelli, *Naumachia at Palazzo Pitti*; Uffizi, Florence / Paul Fearn / Alamy Stock Photo.

p.356 Jacques Bylivelt, *Piazza della Signoria*; Museo degli Argenti, Florence / Bridgeman Images.

p.363 Agnolo Bronzino, *Marie de' Medici as a Girl*; Uffizi, Florence / Bridgeman Images.

p.365 Giambologna, *Equestrian monument of Ferdinando I* (Piazza della Santissima Annunziata, Florence); Christine Webb / Alamy Stock Photo.

p.373 Pieter Paul Rubens, *The Return of Marie de' Medici to her son*; Louvre, Paris / Bridgeman Images.

pp.376–7 Jan van der Straet, *Jousting in Piazza Santa Croce* (Palazzo Vecchio, Florence); Google Cultural Institute / Wiki. Commons.

p.378 Garden façade of the Palazzo Pitti; Stefan Bauer / Wiki. Commons.

p.390 Titian, *Venus of Urbino*; Uffizi, Florence / Google Cultural Institute / Wiki. Commons.

p.393 Giovanni Battista Foggini, *Cardinal Leopoldo de' Medici*; Uffizi, Florence / Bridgeman Images.

p.394 Giovanni da San Giovanni, *The Muses expelled from Parnassus* (Palazzo Pitti, Florence); De Agostini Editorial via Getty Images.

p.395 Giovanni da San Giovanni, *Lorenzo the Magnificent welcoming the Muses to Florence* (Palazzo Pitti, Florence); De Agostini Editorial via Getty Images.

p. 399 Justus Sustermans, *Ferdinando II and Vittoria della Rovere*; National Gallery, London / Wiki. Commons.

p.412 *Venus de' Medici*, antique marble statue; Uffizi, Florence / De Agostini Editorial via Getty Images.

p.416 Niccolò Cassana, *Grand Prince Ferdinando*; Uffizi, Florence / Art Collection 2 / Alamy Stock Photo.

p.419 Andrea del Sarto, *Madonna of the Harpies*; Uffizi, Florence / Web Gallery of Art / Wiki. Commons.

pp.432–3 School of Marcuola, *Cosimo Riccardi visits Grand Duke Gian Gastone*; Museo degli Argenti, Florence / DEA Picture Library via Getty Images.

p.439 Johann Zoffany, *The Tribuna of the Uffizi*; Royal Collection, Windsor / Google Cultural Institute / Wiki. Commons.

pp.440–1 Cappella dei Principi, Florence; isogood / Alamy Stock Photo.

ACKNOWLEDGEMENTS

I would like to thank Giles Bancroft, Jules Bancroft, Elisabeth de Bièvre, Suzy Butters, Sarah Carr-Gomm, Alexander de Chalus, Thekla Clark and the late John Clark, Lizzy Currie, Flora Dennis, Laura Fearon, Jonathan Foyle, Tabitha Goldstaub, Jane Gordon, Richard Gordon, Miles Goslett, Priscilla Goslett, Allen Grieco, Deborah Hofman, Mark Hofman, Ali Hollingsworth, Archie Hollingsworth, Chris Hollingsworth, Edward Hollingsworth, Richard Hollingsworth, Rosamund Hollingsworth, Joan Jaggard, Bill Kent, John Kenyon, Mel Kingsbury, Toby Kingsbury, the late Julian Kliemann, Sally Laurence Smyth, Rachel Lloyd, Lauro Martines, Alexander Masters, Ann Matchette, Christopher Newall, John Onians, Rui Paes, Nigel Playford, Tim Porter, Clare Reynolds, Nigel Reynolds, Carol Richardson, Clare Robertson, Nick Ross, Hugo Rowbotham, Graham Rust, Gabriel Salaman, William Salaman, Henry Saywell, Kirsty Saywell, Richard Schofield, Thomas Tuohy, Amy Turner, Jamie Turner, Alastair Vivian, Camilla Vivian, Hugh Vivian, Trenham Weatherhead.

It has been a pleasure to deal with the team at Head of Zeus, especially with my courteous editor, Richard Milbank. Above all, I owe a huge debt to my agent, Andrew Lownie, for his stubborn and steadfast faith in the book.

INDEX